Daniil Kharms

AGM STUDIES

AVANT-GARDE & MODERNISM

Daniil Kharms

Writing and the Event

BRANISLAV JAKOVLJEVIC

Northwestern

University Press

Evanston

Illinois

Northwestern University Press
www.nupress.northwestern.edu

Printed in the United States of America

10 9 8 7 6 5 4 3 2 1

Library of Congress Cataloging-in-Publication Data
Jakovljevic, Branislav.
Daniil Kharms : writing and the event / Branislav Jakovljevic.
p. cm. — (Avant-garde and modernism studies)
Includes bibliographical references and index.
ISBN 978-0-8101-2553-7 (cloth : alk. paper) —
ISBN 978-0-8101-2554-4 (pbk. : alk. paper)
1. Kharms, Daniil, 1905–1942—Criticism and interpretation. 2. Literature, Experimental—Soviet Union—History and criticism. 3. Events (Philosophy) I. Title. II. Series: Avant-garde and modernism studies.
PG3476.K472Z73 2009
891.7842—dc22

2009023501

♾ The paper used in this publication meets the minimum requirements of the American National Standard for Information Sciences—Permanence of Paper for Printed Library Materials, ANSI Z39.48-1992.

To Jasse

Contents

Illustrations

Preface and Acknowledgments

> To the objection "You wrote that erroneously," respond: "That's how it always looks when I write it."
>
> —Daniil Kharms, *Diaries*, 1937

If I were asked to find a single word that describes Daniil Kharms, it would be *sinthome*. There is a certain quality of *zaum* and sound poetry in this neologism of Lacan's that combines, among other things, "symptom" and *saint homme*. By this I don't mean to either pathologize or sanctify Kharms. *Sinthome* is, to me, the most concise way to describe this misfit who has no home in any of the cultural formations that he comes in touch with. He challenges his American readers differently from his Russian or Serbian ones. He is symptomatic only insofar as he makes visible various manifestations of repressed ideological violence. Likewise, to call him *sinthome* does not make him a martyr or a secular, or even religious, saint. There are few twentieth-century authors who deserve to be called "sinthomatic," if we take Lacan's following words as one definition of this coinage: "the more saints, the more laughter." I have to interrupt Lacan's thought in order to make a disclaimer: I don't want to fashion Kharms into a holy fool, either; he was a thoroughly modern poet and thinker, and to call him a *iurodivy* would be to thoroughly misinterpret him. Back to Lacan: "The more saints, the more laughter; that's my principle, to wit, the way out of capitalist discourse" (Lacan 1987, 20). And here, under the rubric of "capitalist discourse," we have to include all the variations of modern statehood, including the Stalinist one. Many an informed reader of Kharms will object to his sinthomatization as a blatant politicization of an author who vigorously insisted on his apolitical positions. I would like to ask them to think again: what does it mean to proclaim oneself apolitical in the face of a radical and violent politicization of every facet of human, and even nonhuman, life?

Kharms remains a *sinthome* after the crumbling of the Stalinist state for two reasons. The first is that, if we take his apolitical attitude as a demand for rethinking the political as such, then it is necessarily a demand for a rethinking of the Stalinist political, that is to say, of revolutionary, politics. That is something that has yet to be properly done. The second is his theory of the perfect gift, which has, unfortunately, only gained in subversiveness over the past fifty years. According to Kharms, a perfect gift is an object with no use and no meaning. It is a purely nondiscursive object, and, as such, it reminds us that, at the present moment, there is no discourse outside the capitalist one.

Kharms belonged to the first post-Revolutionary generation of artists and poets in the Soviet Union. He came of age as an author at the time of Stalinist purges in politics and culture and, uncompromising as he was, he published only two poems during his lifetime, both of them at the very outset of his career. He died in the first months of the Nazi invasion of the Soviet Union, and his works fell into oblivion, only to begin to re-emerge in samizdat in the late 1960s. Like many other Russian writers of the mid-twentieth century, he was published and performed abroad—in Poland, Germany, and Yugoslavia—before it was safe to publish his works in the Soviet Union. After 1989, in Russia his work gradually gained classic status. His complete works were published in Russian over a period of five years straddling the turn of the century (1997–2002), and every year seems to bring a new collection of his previously published works. With the first publication of the complete works of authors such as Kharms and his older friend Kazimir Malevich, it is clear that, both in Russia and abroad, we are only beginning to appreciate and understand the depth and richness of the Russian avant-garde of the second and third decades of the twentieth century, and that there is a lot of work yet to be done. I hope that my book is a modest contribution to this vast project.

The first translation of Kharms's works into English was George Gibian's, titled *Russia's Lost Literature of the Absurd: A Literary Discovery* (Kharms 1971). Between then and 2006 there was only one new translation of his works, Neil Cornwell's, titled *Incidences* (Kharms 1993). These days, we are witnessing a resurgence of translations of Kharms into English. In 2006, Northwestern University Press published an excellent anthology of Kharms and other authors from his circle, *OBERIU: An Anthology of Russian Absurdism,* under the knowledgeable editorship of Eugene Ostashevsky. The following year a true connoisseur's collection of his writings came out, *Today I Wrote Nothing,* translated and edited by Matvei Yankelevich (Kharms 2007). By now, Kharms is an author of *New Yorker* repute. My book has benefited enormously from Yankelevich's and Ostashevsky's translations, and I hope that it will make some contribution in the English-speaking world to the general understanding of this important writer.

My relationship with Kharms evolved over many years, in several countries and languages. I was introduced to him in high school through excellent translations of his works into Serbian and Croatian. Later, I started reading him in Russian and writing about him in English. I shared a great part of that journey first with my wife, Jasminka, and then with my children, Nikola and Maria. It is their love, warmth, and joy that give me confidence to do the work I am doing. There are no words to express my gratitude to them. I am endlessly thankful to my parents, Rados and Branislava. My warm and loving gratitude goes to Lidija and Dejan for their patience and encouragement.

There are many people without whose help, support, and expertise I would have never been able to finish this book. First of all, there is Matvei Yankelevich: it would be insufficient to say that Matvei helped me with translations of Kharms's texts. Time and again, he demonstrated to me that poetry is not about language but about an attitude of selflessness and commitment. Also, I am extremely grateful to Peggy Phelan for her warm friendship, her trust, her endless encouragement, and her invaluable lessons in the ethics of the work we are doing. Also, I am indebted to Mikhail Yampolsky: his directness, his passion, and his unique and deep understanding of Kharms challenged me to give my best in this work. Big thanks are in order to Eugene Ostashevsky for sharing with me many of his translations and insights. I would also like to thank Yelena Gluzman for reading this work in far-off places. My special thanks goes to Mariellen Stanford and Michael St. Clair for helping me make my writing actually sound English. Their careful reading and their suggestions vastly improved the manuscript. I am grateful to Valery Sazhin for interrupting his own work on editing Kharms's notebooks in order to let me read them, and to Mikhail Karasik and Gleb Ershov for telling me about Kharms's legacy among recent generations of St. Petersburg artists. And thank you to the staff of the Manuscript Division at the Saltikov-Schedrin Public Library in St. Petersburg, Russia, and to Stedelijk Museum Archives in Amsterdam, Holland.

Daniil Kharms

Kukuruzov emerges from the smoke.

Kukuruzov: Hey, people! Come! Right here a bloody reckoning takes place. I have been waiting for this moment for almost four years. The time has come! Trumpets, please! (Wipes his sweaty forehead with a handkerchief.) Yes, if there is an afterlife, then the question is: Does everyone deserve one?

—Daniil Kharms

Introduction: The Writer of Disaster

Papers

Who was Daniil Yuvachev Kharms? His contemporaries remember a striking figure who stood in stark contrast to the bleak social and cultural background of Leningrad of the late 1920s: a tall, thin, blond man with pipe in hand, always carefully dressed, sometimes in a Sherlock Holmes–like outfit. Yuvachev not only wrote poetry but created an entire poetic persona. At times, this persona reached such levels of complexity that it verged on becoming an entire poetic society. Yuvachev assumed various "poses," from Conan Doyle's legendary private eye (figure 1) to the obscure figure of the privatdozent at St. Petersburg University, his own fictional brother Ivan Ivanovich. From the very outset of his literary career, his adoption of these poses paralleled his assumption of a series of pseudonyms, the most prominent of which was "Kharms." It emerged in 1924, first in his notebooks and later in the signatures of his poems. It last appeared in the order of his final arrest on August 23, 1941.

"Daniil Kharms" was not Daniil Yuvachev's only pen name. He signed his works with such pseudonyms as "Charms" and "Chorms," and some of these pseudonymic personas, such as "Daniil Dandan" and "Daniil Shardam," have entire opuses ascribed to them. However, Kharms's literary associations extended beyond his own fictional writings. He was either a member or the primary organizer of an entire series of groups active in Leningrad's vibrant avant-garde scene of the late 1920s. The most renowned was certainly the OBERIU (Association for Real Art), which was eventually

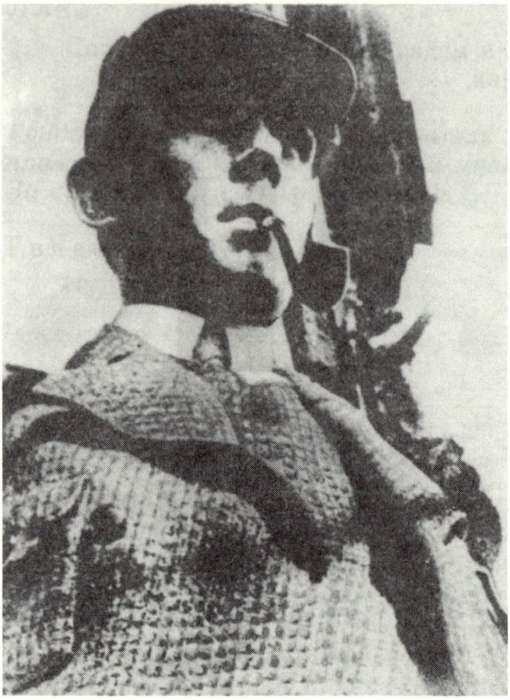

Figure I.

Daniil Kharms in the "pose" of Sherlock Holmes

recognized as the last Soviet avant-garde group of the pre–World War II era; the most cryptic was "Chinari," which was more a circle of friends and a debate club than a formally organized association. Whether public or private, actual or imagined, these groups are important because the rigor of Kharms's ideas is rooted precisely in the plurality that these groups represent. The question, who is Kharms? remains without a definitive answer. The dialogic principle, inseparable from the idea of plurality, brings into question the notion of a stable identity. On the one hand, a dialogic, plural self introduces ambiguity into the very notion of authorship, and on the other, it introduces fragmentation into the work. The initial impulse in my work on this book was not to explore the historical and biographical aspects of Kharms's work but to investigate its unique fragmentariness and its connections with the work of chance.

Toward the end of the fragment from which the epigraph for this introduction was taken, the ink gets smudged, making the last words barely legible. The scrap of paper on which this soliloquy is inscribed is the first item in the folder No. 338 of the Druskin Fund (F1232), held at the Manuscript

Division of the Public Library Saltikov-Schedrin in St. Petersburg, Russia. The folder contains fourteen items: loose pieces of paper, different in form and size, with textual fragments that range in length from a single line to a full page. The fragments are not summary descriptions intended for later use, and most of them don't appear to be abandoned beginnings of longer plays. Instead, they are pieces of dialogue that could easily fit anywhere in a hypothetically complete work. They are neither beginnings nor endings, but middles. They appear without warning, like solitary sparks in a vast darkness. There is no connection whatsoever between any two of the fourteen fragments. Most probably, they were scattered among Kharms's papers until someone decided to categorize the fragmentary manuscripts on the basis of their genre. According to this generic logic, all of the dramatic fragments should go into one folder. There are page numbers inscribed at the bottom of each paper in a handwriting that obviously differs from the rest of the text. These signs of order written in the broad margins of Kharms's notes could have been made by his friend Yakov Druskin, who saved his manuscript archive, or by some nameless librarian. Still, if we accept that this folder represents a unit of sorts, even a very loosely structured play, then the identity of the person who gathered together the miscellaneous papers is of no consequence. Namely, there is no organizing principle other than the form of dialogue that can be discerned from the "order" of the fragments. It is as if these leaves of paper were floating down the dusty stream of days and years, and were finally caught in the trap of a red cardboard folder. They were allowed to fall as they might. Kharms's collaborators on the "play" that is now "F1232, No. 338" were not only Druskin or the anonymous librarian, but even more significantly, history and pure chance.

Kharms's manuscripts are, to a larger or smaller degree, constellations of fragments. Some of them, like "F1232, No. 338," consist only of a few random scraps of paper. Others, like Kharms's most ambitious play, *Comedy of the City of St. Petersburg* (1927) (Kharms 1997b), are thick files that hold works in various stages of incompleteness, from notes and fragments of dialogue to drafts and revisions of entire acts. It is extremely difficult to establish clear boundaries between such loosely structured works. Whatever taxonomy is applied to them, they remain in a state of perpetual incubation. Long abandoned, these texts continue to ferment, forming connections and leakages. Themes, characters, formal inventions, and entire narratives spill from one work to another, then suddenly break apart or disappear. The agents of these migrations are the undetermined fragments, free radicals that could simultaneously belong to several works. For instance, the second fragment in "F1232, No. 338" features Vertunov, a character who figures prominently in *Comedy of the City of St. Petersburg* and is also the protagonist of the children's play *Circus Shardam* (1935) (Kharms 1997c). This fragment could belong to either play, but also to neither. "F1232, No. 338" is not only a constellation of paper scraps but, insofar as it consists of pieces of dialogue, a play in fragments and a play of fragments. Not a fragmentary play, but a fragment-play.

Kharms's manuscripts are not merely scrapbooks—herbaria filled with dried out, crispy leaves of paper. Among his writings, there are longer works that can be considered completed, such as the play *Elizabeth Bam* (1928) and the long story "The Old Woman" (1939). Also, there are edited volumes of his short works, such as *Events* (the 1930s).[1] Still, even the works that are at an advanced stage of completion have the fragment as their basic structural unit. *Elizabeth Bam* consists of nineteen loosely connected bits, and parts of "The Old Woman" are almost completely independent from the main narrative. Finally, Kharms's decision to include a piece in the anthology *Events* does not necessarily mean it is any more complete than other unanthologized fragments, as evidenced by Event No. 5:

> **Petrov and Mosquitov**
> PETROV: Hey, Mosquitov! Let's catch mosquitoes!
> MOSQUITOV: No way, I'm not ready for that;
> Let's better catch cats! (Kharms 2007, 51)

Kharms's notion of *sluchai,* which covers a broad scope of meanings (the most important of which are "incident," "case," and "event" or "happening") pertains not only to the subject matter of his miniatures but also to their form and their mutual relationships. Everything about an incident appears to be random: characters, their actions and conversations, and even its language. The piece cited above contains a linguistic co-incidence that is very easily lost in translation: the name of the first character, Kamarov in the original, is almost identical with the plural objective form of the Russian word for mosquito, *komar;* and the second couplet features the rough rhyme *gotov* (ready, or up for something) / *kotov* (cats). Kharms does not polish his fragments in order to capture the greatest possible meaning with the fewest possible words. Rather, he chips the meaning away from the fragment until it reaches the paradoxical state of lapidary crudeness. In all their laconicity and impenetrability, Kharmsian fragments stand as fractions, not only of narratives, but of meanings as well. They are self-sufficient in the sense that there is no whole that could contain them, there is no unity to which they refer, and they do not combine well into larger structures.

In that sense they are directly opposed to the ambitious fragments of Jena Romantics, best exemplified by Friedrich Schlegel's Athenaeum Fragment No. 24: "Many of the works of the ancients have become fragments. Many modern works are fragments as soon as they are written" (Schlegel 1971, 164). As Nancy and Lacoue-Labarthe clearly recognized, the fragment as conceived by the Jena Romantics is a genre insofar as the text becomes a "seed," a "statement of theory" that "strives to be absolutely self-posited" (Lacoue-Labarthe and Nancy 1988, 40, 41). In their attempt to define and delimit meaning, the fragments of Jena Romantics acquire aphoristic status. In comparison to them, a Kharmsian fragment is more reminiscent of an ancient fragment, but one that is not recognizable as such: a fragment that is abandoned and anonymous, with no reverence and no commentary, a mere splinter and leftover that has no means to evoke a larger totality. Kharms's fragment is not a component of a system, and in that sense, a "symbol of incompletion to which the will to completion is dedicated" (1988, 28). In other words, its function is not to point dialectically to an absent totality. Instead, in accordance with Blanchot's dictum, Kharms's is a nonaphoristic fragment: "what remains without remains," "beyond all fracturing," "radically unquotable" (Blanchot 1995, 33, 34, 37). This fragment points toward that which cannot be bound by discourse and delimited in meanings: not the fullness of language, but its *outside.* In his reflections on the writing of Maurice Blanchot, Foucault recognizes in the fragment the drama of the limit: "When language arrives at its own edge, what it finds is not a positivity that contradicts it, but the void that will efface it. Into that void it must go, consenting to come undone in the rumbling, in the immediate negation of what it says, in a silence that is not the intimacy of a secret but a pure outside where words endlessly unravel" (Foucault 1990, 22). That always-imposing annihilation removes any possibility of absoluteness or, for that matter, of the subject. Perhaps we should ask not who, but what, is Daniil Kharms? As we are going to see, he foresaw the possibility of that question.

So, the fragment-play "F1232, No. 338" involves much more and much less than the sum total of its parts. In this case, the "unfinished" and "fragmentary" also means the interminable. This is the work that has no beginning and no end. The fragments form fragile associations that always remain provisional. This tentativeness and unfixity affirms the plurality, not unity, of the work. In a constellation, the elements are not opposed to one another, and the work does not come into being by opposing other potentialities, other works. Blanchot writes that fragmentary work emerges "where opposition does not oppose but rather juxtaposes, where juxtaposition gives together what escapes all simultaneity, without becoming a succession" (Blanchot 1993, 154). This paradox of the fragmentary work is most readily observable in collage. It is not only a representation but also a collection; it consists not only of visual or linguistic signs but also of preexisting objects whose concreteness exceeds signification. The collage elements are connected not only through their edges but also through their entire surfaces. The main outcome of this combination and layering is not only the literalization of the three-dimensional space but also the higher juxtaposition of simultaneity and succession. "F1232, No. 338" is at the same time a repository and a collage, an accumulation, or a collage-collection. Like this sedimentary work, all of Kharms's works are collections of fragments that are only provisionally connected with one another. Kharms's texts tend to fall apart even as they evolve. The plurality of his works is recognizable in a myriad cracks and fissures that scathe their surfaces. The framing devices being either weak or nonexistent, the fragments pull in opposite directions or clash violently. The extreme fragility of this composition that, paradoxically, crumbles even as it evolves is one of the primary characteristics of the Kharmsian work.

Kharms's works are incomplete, fragmentary, and plural in more than one sense. First, due to external forces—the impossibility of publication—he either abandoned or perpetually revised and corrected his works. Second, internally, Kharms's texts are fragmentary due to the lack of a firm narrative framing. Their structure is further loosened by the frequent use of formal devices of interruption and metatextuality. Every one of Kharms's papers seems firmly attached to the basic material condition of writing. His texts are not narratives or arguments, but simple, unambitious traces of lead or ink on paper. His attentiveness to the material and visual aspects of writing often prompted him to abandon the linearity and intelligibility of the alphabetic text in order to devise a complex *mise en page*. However, Kharms's manuscripts are much more than a paper theater. These complete works that are never finished stand out as textual ruins. What is ruined in the ruins is the clear distinction between the inside and the outside. Gaps and openings are basic structural elements of a ruin: the outside is let in and the inside escapes out. A ruin is a holey place. It is a structure that consists equally of material, tangible elements and of immaterial, imperceptible outlines of nonexisting parts. Where the concreteness of brick and mortar ends, another concreteness, that of a schema, begins. This is not to say that material segments in any way precede the immaterial ones: while the former contain an outline of the latter, they are at the same time held together by that same outline. In other words, in the gaping holes of a ruin, the lines of tensions and suspensions are revealed. Picture a collapsed cupola: all that is left of the supporting walls are narrow strips of stone and mortar, arching elegantly, impossibly, toward the sky. Somewhere between them is the point, non-actual but real, that keeps the injured structure standing.

The secret of a ruin is transparency. Unlike a complete building, a ruin is never completely closed upon itself. Its structure remains exposed, partially visible and partially not, thus leaving open the possibility of looking through it, of seeing it break apart against its own physical surroundings as in a double exposure. This effect of double exposure is what ties ruins with the past. However, Kharms's ruins resist this atmosphere of decay and melancholy. There is a pervasive sense of crispness and clarity to these works. They belong to the category of what the American artist Robert Smithson describes as *ruins in reverse,* "the opposite of the 'romantic ruin' because the buildings don't *fall* into ruin *after* they are built but rather *rise* into ruin before they are built" (Smithson 1979, 54). What else is this construction into demise if not theater? Regardless of all the energetic attempts to give a theatrical production an appearance of completeness, it remains incomplete and unfinished. The elaborate structure of theater—from the specially assigned space within the city, to the building itself, to the stage, to the procedures of staging (reliance on the *fixed* text, rehearsal period, opening night, closing night)—is just a feeble attempt to contain that which is uncontainable, to impose on an event the solidity of the art object. This basic condition of incompleteness accounts for the theatricality of Kharms's work. His work in theater and performance (playwriting, acting, performance of poetry, performance in everyday life) is just a subspecies of this general condition of theater that pertains to all the rest of his work, whether poetry, musical composition, or drawing.

Performances

"The fragmentary imperative," writes Blanchot, ceaselessly dismisses the System, and, "in principle, the I, the author" (1995, 61). Approaching language from the outside, fragmentary writing does not, cannot, sustain confessional narrative. In short, it rejects instrumentalization of any kind. In the late 1930s, Kharms wrote simultaneously, often in the course of a single day, literature for children and for the drawer, made clean copies of the pieces he considered successful, maintained albums such as "Blue Notebook" (1937) (Kharms 1997b) and "Harmonius" (1930s) (Kharms 2002a), and recorded documentary notes in pocket-sized notebooks and loose pieces of paper, sometimes written from hour to hour. In the very act of capturing the present moment, the fragment bears witness to its destruction. Written in the moment of distraction, the fragment is the thought of the scatterbrain. It repeats, but does not re-collect. Kharms never even attempts to reminisce about his past. The few autobiographic texts that he composed were the result of either friendly invitation or violent enforcement. His NKVD questionnaire from his 1931 arrest constitutes his first official biography of sorts:

1. Family name: KHARMS (Yuvachev)
2. Name, patronymic: Daniil Ivanovich
3. Age (year of birth): 1905
4. Background (birthplace, parents, nationality, citizenship): Leningrad, son of court advisor, mother of noble origin.
5. Address (permanent, most recent): 11 Nadezhdinskaia Street, Apartment 8.
6. Profession (the last place of employment, occupation): writer, no state employment.
7. Family (close relatives, their names, addresses, profession before and after the Revolution): Father—Ivan Pavlovich, sister Elizaveta Ivanovna Gritzina. Abroad I know Nadezhda Aleksandrovna Nadejena, an editor of Russian papers, with whom I am in correspondence.
8. Property (of the interrogated and his family, before and after the Revolution): Not wealthy.
9. Education (primary education, high school, university or professional school, where when): High school and incomplete higher education.
10. Party membership, political orientation: no response
11. Evidence of socially engaged or revolutionary activity: No socially engaged activity.
12. Evidence of previous wrongdoings (before and after the revolution): None.
13. Service with counterrevolutionary armed forces: No.

> Statement about the case:
> I work in literature. I am apolitical, but when it comes to questions that are close to me, questions of literature, I state that I disagree with the politics of Soviet authorities in the field of literature and [illegible] I ask, contrary to the existing governmental regulations, for free press of my own work and also of the work of the writers that are close to me, who are together with me members of a literary group.
> Daniil Kharms
> December 11, 1921 [*sic*]
> (Sazhin 1998, 525)

The sketch from this interrogation can be supplemented by the list he produced in the opening sessions of the discussion group that gathered over the course of some two years (1933–34) in the apartment of Kharms's friends, philosopher Leonid Lipavsky and his wife, Tamara Meier-Lipavskaya. The Lipavskys recorded most conversations in a notebook entitled "Conversations":

> D. Kh. spoke about his interests. This is what interests him: Writing of verses and learning from them all sorts of things. Prose. Illumination, inspiration, enlightenment, higher knowledge, and everything that is related to it; the ways of reaching it; finding personal systems of reaching it. Various kinds of knowledge, unknown teachings. Null and nil. Numbers, especially those out of successive order. Symbols. Letters. Typography and manuscripts. Everything that is logically nonsensical and unpretty. Everything that provokes laughter; humor. Stupidity. Natural thinkers. Ancient signs and newly devised signs for no purpose. Miracle. Magic tricks (without props). Personal relations between people. Good tone. Human faces. Odors. Annihilation of squeamishness. Face washing, bathing, bath. Cleanliness and filth. Food. Preparation of certain dishes. Table manners. Arrangements of houses, apartments, and rooms. Clothes, men's and women's. Problems of dressing. Smoking (pipes and cigarettes). What people are doing when they are alone. Dream. Notebooks. Writing on paper with pen or pencil. Paper, pen, pencil. Daily recording of mental states. Recording of weather. Lunar phases, the appearance of sky and water. Wheel. Sticks, canes, batons. Anthill. Small short-haired dogs. Kabbalah. Pythagoras. Theater (personal). Singing. Church service and chant. Rituals of all kinds.

> Pocket watches and chronometers. Plastrons. Women, not of my favorite kind. Sexual physiology of women. Silence. (Lipavskii 2005, 308).

This list of interests is further appended by the inventory that Kharms recorded in his diary at approximately the same time:

> I like writing. I like looking at the people I like. I like observing beautiful women. I like to eat. I like smoking a pipe. I like singing. I like lying naked on a hot day in the sun by the water, surrounded by a lot of pleasant people, with many interesting women among them. I like small short-haired dogs. I like a good laugh. I like that which is not pretty. I like watches, especially the thick pocket ones. I like notebooks, pens, paper, and pencils. I like walking on foot through Petersburg, especially on these streets: Nevsky Boulevard, Mars Fields, the Summer Garden, and Troitski Bridge. I like walking in Catherine's Park in Tsarskoe Selo. I like walking by the sea, at Lakhta, at Olgino, at Sestroretsk, and at the resort. I like walking alone. I like being among delicate people. (I like women, but only of my type.) (Kharms 2002b, 20)

In his autobiographical and documentary writings, from police questionnaires to diaries, Kharms never tries to explain or even address extensively his arrests and the censorship of his works. He rarely, if ever, mentions politics in his writings. In the prospectus for his domestic journal "Tapir," politics is banned as one of the undesirable subjects, together with antireligious, liberal, anti-alcoholic, satiric, and parodic "things" (Kharms 2001a, 22). This ironic prohibition notwithstanding, Kharms and his friends were deeply aware of the magnitude of the historical break inaugurated by the October Revolution. Consider the following exchange between Yakov Semenovich Druskin (Y. S.) and Leonid Lipavsky (L. L.) in "Conversations":

> Y. S. Some anticipated the change in people that we are witnessing these days—it is as if the new race has emerged. But they all imagined this change in general terms, and they were wrong. Now we are seeing it with our own eyes. We should write a book about that, to leave a testament for posterity. Because later it will be impossible to reconstruct the change that we now see all too clearly.
>
> L. L. It reminds me of the writings that Marcus Aurelius made in his

> tent at the boundary of the empire to which he would never return; to which he had no reason to return. (Lipavskii 2005, 329)

Here they are: strange, sedentary nomads, traveling through history without moving an inch, pitching their tents at the precarious border between then and now. They are aware of the catastrophic proportions of the present they are witnessing, but they are not nostalgic for the past. They are equally aware that the present catastrophe brings about an even more catastrophic future: catastrophic insofar as it won't be able to recognize the true proportions of the catastrophe that shaped it. The catastrophe is neither the historical event nor its aftermath. It is of the same order as Blanchot's disaster that "ruins everything, all the while leaving everything intact." The boundary that Lipavsky talks about is imperceptible and ungraspable. It gives no ground for shelter. The disappearance of temporality that Kharms's friends recognize in their own time is the primary property of disaster. Again Blanchot:

> We are on the edge of disaster without being able to situate it in the future: it is rather always already past, and yet we are on the edge or under the threat, all formulations which would imply the future—that which is yet to come—if the disaster is not that which does not come, that which has put a stop to every arrival. To think the disaster (if this is possible, and it is not possible inasmuch as we suspect that the disaster is thought) is to have no longer any future in which to think it." (1995, 1)

It was the source of some confusion for literary historians that, even though they made the first literary steps in the artistic environment shaped by the pre-Revolutionary Russian avant-garde, Kharms and his circle resolutely rejected any critical association with Russian Futurists. Already in 1927, in one of his early plans for a publication of his poetry, Kharms writes to the editor: "before you include me among the Futurists of the last decade, read their work, and then mine <u>for the second time</u>" (2002a, 203, emphasis in the original). The following year this refusal of any parallel with the poetics of Russian Futurists was reiterated in the only public statement that Kharms and his friends made, "The OBERIU Manifesto": "Some people even now call us *zaumniki.* It is difficult to decide whether that is because of a complete misunderstanding or a hopeless failure to grasp the principles of literary art. No school is more hostile to us than *zaum.*"[2] Still, in one of the first references to OBERIU outside of the Soviet Union, Pavel Markov cites Kharms's group as one of the last Futurist groups in Russia (Markov 1969, 358). Misunderstandings concerning period and the literary style of the OBERIU persist to this day. However, some clarity has been established, at least when it comes to the Futurists. OBERIU's recognition of the demise of temporality is interpreted as part of the counter-Futurist reaction in Soviet literature. Alexander Nikitaev sums up the difference between these two consecutive generations of Russian literary avant-garde by saying that "while for the Futurists the world represents process, movement, and, in the last analysis, speed, for the Oberiuty it is the totality of objects, arrested phantasmagoria, a world deprived of causality and, consequently, of movement" (Nikitaev 1991, 7). In the late 1920s and into the 1930s, the literary establishment considered the absence of tropes such as movement toward the great goal, the struggle for progress, and leaping into the future more as an antirevolutionary attitude than an attempt to stay out of politics. What causes confusion is not only Kharms's and the OBERIU's poetics, but also their performances.

In the list of the things he likes, Kharms writes, somewhat enigmatically: "Theater (my own)."

1. Theater. This is fairly straightforward: together with his friends, Kharms worked on a number of theatrical and poetic performances. Many of them failed. Already in 1926, together with Vvedensky and Georgi Katsman, he formed the theatrical group Radix. According to Katsman's recollections, the members of Radix wanted to explore "non-emotional and anti-narrative" art, a pure theater of sorts. Radix rehearsed Vvedensky's play *My Mother All in Watches,* but this effort never resulted in a public performance.[3] The following year, the core members of Radix formed OBERIU, and they used some of the theatrical experience they gained from the rehearsals of *My Mother All in Watches* in their work on the largest public performance OBERIU ever had. It took place on January 24, 1928, in Leningrad's House of the Press (*Dom Pechati*). In accordance with the title "Three Left Hours," the evening was divided into three sections: poetry readings given by, among others, Kharms, Vvedensky, and Zabolotsky; a performance of Kharms's play *Elizabeth Bam,* which was directed by Igor Bakhterev, Boris Levin, and the author himself; and finally, a screening of the film *Meat Grinder* by Alexander Razumovsky and Klement Minz, followed by a public discussion. All three segments of the evening were marked by unexpected juxtapositions of scenic effects with the ultimate goal of eradicating meaning and any eventual didacticism. This insistence on theatrical nonsense is already present in the announcement for "Three Left Hours," in which it is stated that during the poetry reading, the master of ceremonies will "ride on a tricycle, making impossible lines and figures."[4] Some of the witnesses of that night's performance remembered a big, decrepit cupboard positioned center-stage, in front of which Kharms paced with a shiny top hat, smoking a pipe and reciting poetry.[5] The performance of *Elizabeth Bam,* already loosely structured, was repeatedly interrupted by such scenic actions as sawing a wooden log and flaunting a poster with the inscription "Entr'acte—Cataract." *Meat Grinder,* the only production of the OBERIU film section, did not survive. It was most likely composed of scraps of already existing footage, and opened, reportedly, with an "endlessly repeating shot of an approaching train."[6] The following day, on January 25, the evening edition of the *Red Gazette* (*Krasnaia gazeta*) published a review by Lidia Lesnaya, entitled "Ytuerebo"—Oberiuty spelled backward. The article begins with the rhetorical question "Unintelligible? Indeed!" and continues with the statement that "last night something unpublishable happened in the House of the Press."[7] She goes on to describe the provocations performed onstage, the anarchic atmosphere in the theater, and the altercations between the poets/performers and audience members. Finding the spectacle out of place and time, this critic effectively put an end to OBERIU performances and the group itself:

> Checkered hats, red wigs, hobbyhorses. A dark attempt at a grim circus show, without any good effects.
> The Futurists drew daisies on their cheeks, in order to
> Astound the bourgeois.
> In 1928 you are going to neither astound nor intimidate anyone with a red wig (150).

In spite of herself, L. Lesnaya captured the spirit of Kharmsian joyless clownery. That says more about the precision and assertiveness of the imagery used during the "Three Left Hours" than about L. L.'s perceptiveness. Not heeding attacks of this kind, Kharms continued devising hobbyhorsical performances. In the fall of 1928, he outlined in his notebook an evening that would include "literary lecture," "astronomical lecture," "OBERIU lecture," and would involve juggling and recitation of poetry (Kharms 2002a, 252). However, there was never a sequel to "Three Left Hours." OBERIU performances became smaller in scale, and eventually were reduced to poetry readings. In Kharms's notebook for March 1930 we find the following draft: "I. An evening of Kharms's poetry. Theatricalized debate. II. An evening of OBERIU poetry. No theatricalization" (2002a, 352). In the meantime, what Mikhail Meilakh called the "pogrom of OBERIU" continued (Meilakh 1987, 187). In 1931, during the debate in the Writers' Association, Nikolai Aseev described Kharms, Vvedensky and Zabolotsky as "futile" and "creative paralytics" and accused their poetic practices of being "alienated from the problems of building socialism" (187). Soon thereafter, both Kharms and Vvedensky were arrested and sentenced to exile in Kursk.

2. *My own.* Here we encounter the murmur behind the writing that eventually grew into the elaborate Kharms mythology. On the one hand, it seems that even during the period of the OBERIU public performances Kharms engaged in small private diversions reminiscent either of Nikolai Evreinov's "mono theatre" that came before it or of Fluxus events that came after.[8] In the aftermath of "Three Left Hours" Kharms outlined the following list of diversions:

> In restaurants:
> Coffee with cucumbers.
> Tea with eggs.
> Synchronized slurping of milk through straws.
> 7 cups of tea for three. . . .
> Read the alphabet.
> Black paper.
> Pour from paper.
> Sit with eyes closed.
> Throw the embroidered towel over the shoulders.
> Cut cucumbers with scissors. (2002a, 241)

On the other hand, and much more important for this study of his work, the writing increasingly changes in status from public to private. Instead of serving as a pretext for performance, writing blends with playing and becomes inseparable from Kharms's personal performances. Thus, his "personal theater" splits in two: small acts performed among the close group of friends and the solitary theater of writing.

Much of what Kharms wrote in the police questionnaires pertains to the last decade of his life, from July 1932 to his second arrest in August 1941. It is clearly discernable from his lists of interests and preferences that the notion of "poetry" recedes and gives way to "writing." Whereas in the 1931 interrogation Kharms states poetry as his profession, a year later he declares in Lipavsky's discussion group that, for him, versification is a way to learn and not a goal in its own right. From the practice of poetry as pure experimentation, the scope of writing broadens to prose, to daily writing, to all kinds of inscriptions with pencil and ink on paper, to the very materials for writing: pen, paper, notebook. Profession yields to vocation, trade to obligation. "Trade" is both in the sense of profession and of exchange: there is no more receiving, only giving. Kharms's meditations on the topics of gifts, errors, and miracles date from these years: the object cedes to concept. If the hobbyhorse disappears along with the other props of the OBERIU performances, the hobbyhorsical never ceases to prop up the rider.[9] Kharms was a hobbyist. On the one hand, there is the ever-present writing. On the other hand, there is evidence of many other pursuits, such as his interest in "natural thinkers," the interior design of apartments and homes, clothing, food, and erotica.

Kharms's performances provided raw material for the memoirs of the few survivors from Kharms's circle. Alisa Poret, a painter from the school of Pavel Filonov, writes about the games that they devised during this period, such as contrived dialogues in which an elevated tone is combined with crude content, or dressing up and posing for photographs (figure 2).[10]

Vsevolod Petrov explains that "natural thinker" is Kharms's name for various Leningrad eccentrics, many of whom he regarded highly, received into his home, and fed when he could.[11] "Personal theater" features an equal share of spectacle and intimacy. It turns away from the eyes of the broader public, often receding to utmost invisibility and unintelligibility. It is a pure, inexplicable passion—a hobby(horse) in the full sense of the word. No doubt, Kharms was a man of many passions. Presiding over them was the one for his girlfriend, later wife, Ester Rusakova. She was his first love and the first letter of his cryptography. He devised a monogram from the letters of her name, and called it a window. He also devised an idiosyncratic etymology of the name "Ester," which he imagined to mean star. In the final analysis, "Ester" ceases being simply a proper name or a poetic symbol and becomes a complex that joins everyday life (not only its performative and spectacular but also its sentimental and banal aspects), discursive writing, and visual symbolism together with a certain resistance to all discursivity. His parting with Ester was a prolonged affair: it lasted some seven years, from 1927 to 1932. The story of Kharms's love affair with Ester and their separation parallels the story of his passion for writing, and of his rise to the highest circles of Leningrad's avant-garde (Malevich, Filonov, Terent'ev)

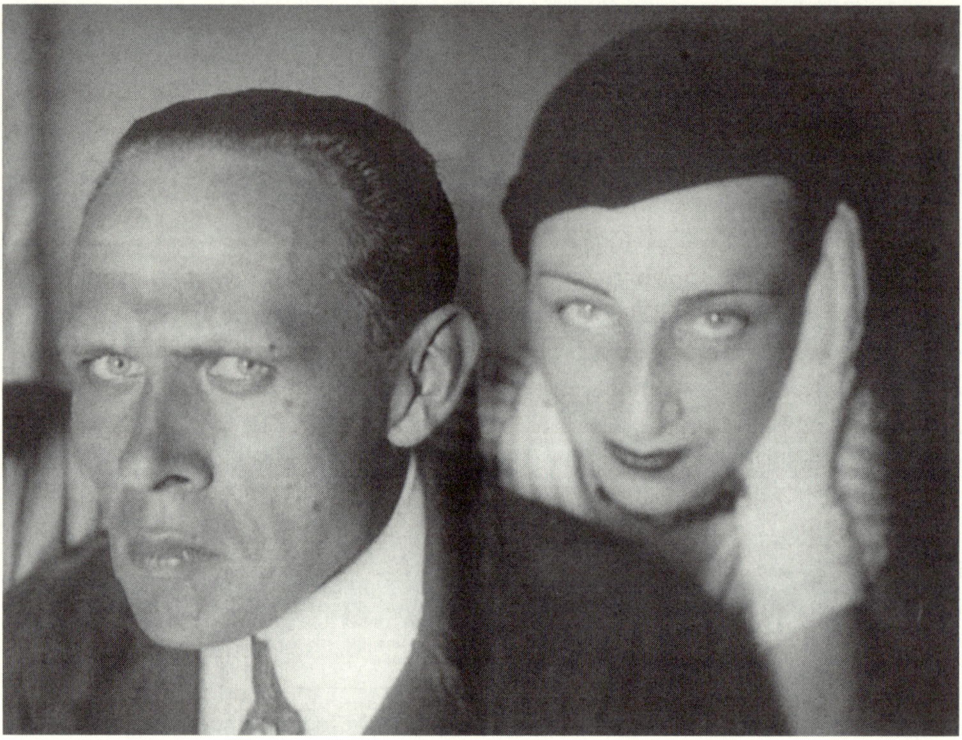

Figure 2.

Kharms and the artist Alisa Poret

and his fall to the very limit of biological survival. This falling out with the star is also falling from the star. "Falling out with" mirrors the linguistic paradox of "parting together": fall and separation here do not designate absenting. The star remains in the yellow glow of the dis-aster: "If disaster means being separated from the star (if it means the decline which characterizes disorientation when the link with fortune from on high is cut), then it indicates a fall beneath disastrous necessity" (Blanchot 1995, 2).

Events

Like Kafka's, the majority of Kharms's works were published posthumously. Whereas for Kafka death was slow in coming, Kharms was snatched from his apartment by the secret police. He didn't even have a chance to get dressed and put on his shoes, much less to leave instructions for the handling of his manuscript archive. Even though most of his major works remained unpublished during his lifetime, Kafka lived to see the publication of some of them, such as *Metamorphosis* and *In the Penal Colony*. Kharms published next to none. Only two of his serious poems—written for grown-ups and not for children—were published during his lifetime, both of them at the very outset of his literary career: "Incident on the Railroad" (1926) and "The Verse of Peter Yashkin" (1927). Also, like Kafka's, Kharms's manuscripts were saved without his knowledge. Kharms's Max Brod was Yakov Druskin, who in the month of October 1941, upon hearing that Kharms's apartment building at Nadezhdinskaia Street No. 9 was hit by an artillery shell,[12] made his way across the besieged and bombed-out Leningrad and carried Kharms's entire manuscript archive back to his home—a considerable exertion for someone who lived in a city where already scores of people were dying of starvation.

There is a certain pattern that emerged in the last decade of Kharms's life, which was also his most productive period. This pattern concerns the structure of the work, its spectacular and intimate sides. The spectacular is intelligible and memorable. Sooner or later, in one way or another, it enters the public sphere and joins history. During the 1930s, the first to join history were Kharms's children's books. The intimate, or hidden, side concerns two kinds of publications, which we can call utopian and coercive. I'll start from the latter. Ironically, the only anthology of works by Kharms and his friends was put together by the NKVD (the precursor of the KGB) for their internal use. In the KGB archives there is a neatly typed volume that, on the cover page, carries the official title "Case P-81210, Volume 2";[13] the descriptive subtitle, "The Collection of Counter-Revolutionary Works of the Illegal Anti-Soviet Group of Children's Writers"; and the names of the featured authors, "Daniil Kharms. Alexander Vvedensky. Aleksander Tufanov. Peter Kalashnikov. Igor Bakhterev." Most likely, the editor of this volume was A. Buzhnikov, a minor NKVD officer who was in charge of the interrogation of the "illegal group." After his 1931 arrest, the result of which was this "anthology," Kharms did not give up on the idea of writing for publication. He made elaborate plans—all of them utopian—for group publications, such as his 1929 proposal for *Archimedes' Bath*.[14] After this attempt failed, he kept writing and anthologizing his own texts into the collection *Events*. Finally, in the late 1930s, he drafted the outline for a fully utopian project, the domestic journal "Tapir," and even wrote his longest prose work to date, the story "The Old Woman" (1939). Each side of Kharms's work—the public and the private, the spectacular and the intimate—is tied with a different notion of disappearance. The spectacular disappears in the persistent murmur of history, the intimate in the silence of the unintelligible. The former belongs to memory, the latter to forgetfulness.

Forgetfulness and erasure make a deep cut in the history of Kharms's publications. His works, written in the late 1920s and 1930s, reached their initial, very limited publication in the late 1960s, mostly in *samizdat.* In the 1970s and 1980s, his works were smuggled abroad and published by Kafka Presse, a small imprint in Bremen, Germany.[15] During the period of glasnost an ever-increasing number of his works were published in Russia, a trend that culminated in the publication of his collected works in six volumes, completed in 2002.[16] This deferral and publication in stages was crucial for the reception of Kharms's works. As it turned out, the thirty-year period (1941–71) during which his work was completely forgotten turned out to be also the period of germination for the first critical performance dedicated to it. Yakov Druskin was one of the few members of Kharms's circle who survived the waves of Stalinist purges and the siege of Leningrad (1941–44), and for decades he was the sole proprietor of Kharms's and Vvedensky's and Lipavsky's manuscripts. As such, he is at the source of the two main tendencies that prominently marked the first decades of Kharms criticism and scholarship.

First is the biographical interpretation of the work. This interpretation makes the most out of Kharms's "personal theater." Here, the spectacular overwhelms the private. This interpretation relies exclusively on the authority of experience: "Kharms used to say to me," writes Druskin in his article "On Daniil Kharms," "that art for him took second place, second place to *making his life;* that is to say, making it just as poetry and music is made" (Druskin in Cornwell 1991, 85, italics in the original). This emphasis on the ephemeral art of "personal theater" is all too easily identifiable with the utopian genre of "life-making" devised by Russian symbolists at the turn of the twentieth century.[17] Ultimately, this approach makes Kharms's writing inseparable from something that is beyond and above the work itself. That something which is ungraspable and inexpressible is a life—biographical, anecdotal life—that can never be fully captured. This approach produced a minor strand of memoirist and anecdotal literature, such as Svetozar Shishman's collection of spurious anecdotes, *A Few Jolly and Sad Stories about Daniil Kharms and His Friends* (1991), and an all-but-spurious book of reminiscences by Kharms's second wife, Marina (Malich) Durnovo, *Moi muzh Daniil Kharms.*[18]

The second, absurdist, interpretation is much more productive. Having its roots in the personal writings of Yakov Druskin, it came to dominate

OBERIU scholarship in Russia and abroad. Trained as a philosopher, mathematician, and pianist, Druskin developed his own, as his brother Mikhail puts it, "highly personal and intuitive method" of thinking (Druskin 1999, 32). The intuitive part of Druskin's method could have originated from his philosophy professor Nikolai Lossky, who was the main proponent of Bergsonism in Russia. Druskin, who came from a middle class family of nonpracticing Jews, completed his study of philosophy just in time, before the removal of Lossky from Leningrad University in 1923. He had become close with Vvedensky and Lipavsky already in high school, and met Kharms in 1925. They remained close throughout the 1930s, and while Druskin never took part in any of their public activities, he actively participated in their private gatherings. He was one of the participants in "Conversations." Decades later, while talking about "Chinari," the informal group to which both Kharms and Vvedensky subscribed in the late 1920s and early 1930s, Druskin asserted that the word *chin* refers to rank both in its military and spiritual sense, so that whereas "OBERIU was an exoteric organization, Chinari was an esoteric group" to which, apart from himself and the two poets, Lipavsky and the poet Nikolai Oleinikov also belonged (Druskin 1998, 549). On the continuum of the circle members' spiritual interests—which ranged from Kharms's occultism, to Lipavsky's irrationalism, to Vvedensky's poetic mysticism—Druskin was the closest to the doctrines of Russian Orthodox theology. His path from nonpracticing Jew to practicing Orthodox Christian was facilitated by his interest in music and by his philosophy teacher Nikolai Lossky's combination of Bergsonism and Russian religious thought. Whereas in the 1920s and 1930s Druskin's religiosity took the form of a vague mysticism, after the war Orthodox Christianity came to occupy the center of Druskin's intellectual efforts. In the fifties and sixties he was writing down his religious meditations in complete isolation. Then, in the late 1960s he reconnected with another surviving member of their prewar circle, Tamara Meier-Lipavskaya.

A fascinating person in her own right, Tamara Meier had multiple ties with the circle: in the late 1920s she was married to Vvedensky, whom she divorced, and then married his friend Lipavsky. Also, she became Kharms's great unfulfilled love after his breakup with Ester Rusakova. Still largely neglected by Kharms and OBERIU scholars, she seems to have been much more than muse to the group of poets and thinkers. She participated in "Conversations" and worked on its recording and transcription. Later, in the 1960s and 1970s, she studied the unpublished manuscripts of her first husband. One of the most intriguing items in the OBERIU-related corpus of manuscripts held at the Saltikov-Schedrin Public Library is her "Dictionary of A. I. Vvedensky's Language," which consists of twelve boxes of index cards.[19] The cards are alphabetically ordered and cross-referenced, and each of them contains a word or a phrase from Vvedensky's poetry. (Should we read this catalogue as an analytical investigation, a statement of commitment, a continuation of legacy? Is it a disinterested work of classification? But why such attention to work that has never been published, and at the time still had no prospect of publication? Is it then a work of love? Of memory? Of dedication and commitment? Or of sadistic chopping of poems into basic units? Or rather, their rewriting?) In Meier-Lipavskaya's collaborations with Druskin, this practice of critical delinearization of literary text receives yet another form. Here, she spatially reorganized Vvedensky's dialogues into charts and diagrams, thus effectively demanding new reading(s) of the text.[20] In "Conversations," Leonid Lipavsky mentions several of his paralinguistic utopian projects, such as a dictionary of things' meanings and a dictionary of hieroglyphs, which would come not in a book form, but as a deck of cards (2005, 382). This idea is clearly recognizable in Lipavskaya's dictionary, and in that sense her critical work can be seen as a continuation of conversations between her friends and lovers. On the other hand, Druskin's critical project is a work of revision that takes place in the light of his own spiritual and intellectual transformations during the decades that intervened between the creation of Vvedensky and Kharms's work in the 1920s and 1930s and Druskin's return to them in the early 1970s.

At the outset of "The Star of Nonsense," his literary-philosophical investigation of Vvedensky's "A Certain Quantity of Conversations," Druskin places himself within the context of the creation of the work itself. He writes, for example, that Lipavsky personally related to him his theory of the hieroglyph (Sazhin 1998, 601), and that Vvedensky would certainly agree with his interpretation of his works (602). Calculated or not, this kind of self-insertion into critical investigation lends the authority of experience to Druskin's critical analysis. However, he does not stop at that. On several occasions in his essay, he asserts that for the purpose of publication he had corrected Vvedensky's idiosyncratic punctuation, which positions his work, both editorial and critical, as the *completion* of Vvedensky's poetic project.

"The Star of Nonsense" is a tour de force of Druskin's "personal and intuitive method" that brings together Losskian religious epistemology (or "gnoseology"), semiotics, medieval nominalism, musicology, and literary criticism. Taking the phrase "the star of nonsense" from Vvedensky's "A Certain Quantity of Conversations" for the title of his essay, Druskin argues that Vvedensky's and Kharms's literature constitutes a special case of nonsense that strives for "the deepest communicability,"[21] recognizable in the polyphony of Vvedensky's dialogues: it is "simultaneously the independence of each voice, and the connection and unity of all voices" (593). Nonsense, then, is an alternative meaning, not an absence thereof. Druskin then relates this concept of nonsense directly to Eugene Ionesco by introducing into his analysis the work of the Soviet semiologist couple O. G. Revzina and I. I. Revzin, "A Semiotic Experiment on Stage: The Violation of the Postulate of Normal Communication as a Dramatic Device." The Revzins' analysis of Ionesco's plays *The Bald Soprano* and *The Lesson* is based on the premise that this kind of drama subverts what they call the "eight postulates" that make possible normal human communication (Revzina and Revzin 1975, 256). Vvedensky, claims Druskin, postulates an entirely different level of communication based on the identification of the signifier and the signified (Druskin 1998, 624). On the one hand, this semiotization of the real goes hand in hand with Druskin's notion of "life-making." On the other hand, it props up his notion of "semiotic silence" as a certain apophatic communication that is based on faith instead of on exchange of information and, therefore, on shared knowledge in general. So, contrary to Ionesco's nonsense, which is irrational and anticommunicative and therefore a-communal, Vvedensky's nonsense is a-rational and negative, and as such aspires toward a completely different idea of sociality. Druskin claims that this communication does not take place on the everyday "I–I" level, or on the "I–You" level, but on the "I–You–We" level (628). In short, it is the mode of communication that takes place within the community of believers.

The first major critical study of Kharms's work came from the Swiss scholar Jean-Phillipe Jaccard in his 1991 book *Daniil Harms et la fin de l'avant-garde russe* (*Daniil Kharms and the End of the Russian Avant-Garde*). Much of Jaccard's book is an exquisite and groundbreaking work of literary historiography that rigorously contextualized Kharms's work for the first time: its main predecessors and influences, its biographical aspects, and its major developments and phases. In the final chapter, "From Real Art to the Absurd," Jaccard departs from this rigorous historiographic method in order to advance an argument that places Kharms even closer to the theater of the absurd. Whereas in his analysis of nonsense, Druskin relies on the Remzins' semiotic work, Jaccard borrows his critical framework from Robert Abirached's *La crise du personage dans le theatre moderne* (1978) which, much like Martin Esslin's classic some twenty years earlier, seeks to interpret the works of such authors as Eugene Ionesco and Samuel Beckett through the prism of mid-twentieth-century existentialism. Hence, instead of "semiotic silence," we now have metaphysical dread (Jaccard 1991, 244), and instead of alogism, the breakdown of causality under the weight of ideology (247–59). Even though he quite correctly places his entire discussion of Kharms and the OBERIU in the context of Stalinist terror, Jaccard, like Druskin, insists on the importance of communication in Kharms's work. Taking the performance of Kharms's play *Elizabeth Bam* as the defining moment of his work, Jaccard concludes that "it is evident" that "the problem of communication is at the center of Kharms's play" (245). In short, even though they employ different methodologies, reception and communication are decisive categories in these early and influential absurdist interpretations of Kharms and Vvedensky.[22]

During the period starting from Druskin's analysis of Vvedensky's *A Certain Number of Conversations* and ending after the publication of Jaccard's book first in French and then in Russian, OBERIU absurdism acquired the status of a received idea. This curiosity of literary criticism became the basis of a number of works that interpreted Kharms beyond recognition. The most recent and most radical in the series of exegeses of the Kharmsian absurd is certainly Dimitri Tokarev's 2002 comparative analysis of Kharms and Beckett, *Kurs na khudshee: Absurd kak kategoria teksta u Daniila Kharmsa i Samuela Bekketa* (*Worstward Ho: The Absurd as Textual Category in Daniil Kharms and Samuel Beckett*). Tokarev duly notes the absence of critical investigations of Beckett in Russian, but makes no serious attempt to change that situation. Instead, it seems that he is interested in Beckett only insofar as he can use his declared and much-commented-upon atheism as a dialectical prop for Kharms's alleged theocentrism. According to him, Kharms's "entire metaphisico-poetic concept" is based "on a single unalterable truth: there is a higher reality, immanent to God, which in the moment of creation turns from a transcendental force into a force that is transcendent and immanent to the poet" (35). He goes so far as to assert that "according to Kharms and Vvedensky," "the task of artistic creation . . . consists in the 'raising' of human words to the alogical level and turning poetic words into divine. Divine words don't explain and don't describe anything: they simply reflect the reality of Heaven" (123). What is truly unsettling in Tokarev's book is not so much the perpetuation of a limited critical model as its transition from an absurdist interpretation of Kharms to a total obfuscation of his work, which becomes evident in the 2003 work of Finnish scholar Jussi Heinonen, *Eto i to v povesti* Starukha *Daniila Kharmsa* (*This and That in Daniil Kharms's Story* "The Old Woman") and Andrei Rossomakhin's *'Real' Kharmsa: po sledam okkul'tnykh studii poeta-chinara* (*Kharms's 'Real': Following the Poet-Chinar's Occult Studies*) (2005).

The two approaches, biographical and absurdist, are only seemingly irreconcilable. First, they are both founded on the notions of existentialism that range from philosophic and literary to theological and mystical. Second, they both find it impossible to accept the fragmentariness and unfinishedness of the work at hand. In other words, both the biographical and absurdist interpretations see the fragment only in relation to the whole. They represent two variations of the kind of literary criticism that is so widespread and all-encompassing that it is customarily seen as the only one possible: the criticism of the whole. This criticism presumes a totality and completeness in order to make the fragmentary work comply with the Aristotelian notion of the work of art as "complete and of certain magnitude" (Aristotle 1987, 37). In the biographical interpretation what is supplemented is the "life-making," while in the absurdist interpretation it is the modern condition, most readily identifiable in the idea of the absurd. Not only that: this criticism often sees itself as a necessary and legitimate completion of the work. Third, both of these approaches involve certain notions of history. The "life-making" approach ultimately affirms something that could be described as hyper-history: this is the historicity of the lived experience that, paradoxically, surpasses any possibility of containment and communication. The absurdist approach sees its subject as a prehistory of a phenomenon that already has been fully examined and described: in that sense, it is a study of a historical variation. Finally, they both see as their noble mission, and rightfully so, the wrestling out from the past of the suppressed work that is under the threat of complete obliteration. The underside of this rescue mission is that the saved work is considered to be not self-sufficient. The ruins in reverse scattered across the landscape of modernism become increasingly obscured by the elaborate scaffoldings that are erected around them. Writing about an altogether different shipwreck of modernist theater, Jacques Derrida asserts that often the only accomplishment of critical rescue missions is the transformation of the ruins into cases:

> At the moment when criticism (be it aesthetic, literary, philosophical, etc.) allegedly protects the meaning of a thought or the value of the work against psychomedical reductions, it comes to the same result [as

a reduction would come to] through the opposite path: *it creates an example.* That is to say, *a case.* A work or an adventure of thought is made to bear witness, as example or martyr, to a structure whose essential permanence becomes the prime preoccupation of the commentary. (Derrida 1978, 170, emphasis in the original)

Kharms did not become a case[23] automatically upon his admission into the "psychomedical" department of one of the most efficacious bureaucracies of murder ever. And not all of the critical literature about Kharms is concerned with the elaboration of his case history. For example, in his work *Poetika "OBERIU" v kontekste russkogo literaturnogo avangarda* (*"OBERIU" Poetics in the Russian Literary Avant-Garde Context*), published in the year 2000, Alexander Kobrinsky undertakes a comparative analysis of Kharms and Vvedensky in relation to the leading representatives of the major Russian literary movements from the first decades of the twentieth century, such as Andrei Bely, Velimir Khlebnikov, and Nikolai Gumilev. Mikhail Yampolsky takes a different approach in his book *Bespamiatstvo kak istok: chitaia Kharmsa* (*Forgetfulness as Origin: Reading Kharms*), in which he looks at Kharms's work in the context of the renaissance of ontology in Western metaphysics (Iampol'skii 1997). His argument, centered on the idea that "Kharms's project is to replace memory with forgetfulness, to supplant the peace of knowledge with the peace of ignorance" (82), had a significant impact on the shaping of my project. Unlike most other scholars who wrote about Kharms, Yampolsky does not use his critical writing to complete Kharms's works, but instead accepts the work as it is: fragmentary, incomplete, visual as much as literary.

What attracted me initially to Kharms was performance, not theater—or rather, not only theater: not just his dramatic writings, not just Radix, not just *Elizabeth Bam* and "Three Left Hours"; definitely not only his poetry recitations and his performances in everyday life. As much as in these more or less conventional performances, I am interested in what happens on the page, in his manuscripts, drawings, musical compositions, and diagrams. The ideal example of such textual happening is certainly the following short text:

Blue Notebook # 10

There lived a redheaded man who had no eyes or ears. He didn't have hair either, so he was called a redhead arbitrarily.

He couldn't talk because he had no mouth. He didn't have a nose either.

He didn't have arms or legs. He had no stomach, he had no back, no spine, and he didn't have any insides at all. There was nothing to speak of! So, we don't even know who we're talking about. We'd better not talk about him any more.

January 6, 1937

(2007, 41)

This extraordinary work partakes, to some extent, in the adventurousness of "F1232, No. 338," the manuscript "drama" that I discussed earlier. It was composed on a loose piece of paper. Then, things change a bit. Whereas loose fragments of "F1232, No. 338" are committed to chance, the text about the redheaded man was committed as a clean copy to a notebook bound with hard covers lined in a blue silky material. It was the tenth item in the notebook that Kharms maintained during 1937, the year that gave him the foretaste of his horrible death. So, whereas the fragments from "F1232, No. 338" happened together, the fragment entitled "Blue Notebook No. 10" happens in relative isolation. Its eventness is not only a question of its form. Yes, it is anthologized and included in a small family of texts, but the somewhat bureaucratic numerical designation in its title still establishes a certain anonymity and isolation. Neither a story nor a poem, this is a fragment that doesn't want to narrate or explain or express. This writing has no ambition to grasp or preserve or communicate that which is outside of it. It is writing in which disaster happens: "The disaster, unexperienced. It is what escapes the very possibility of experience—it is the limit of writing. This must be repeated: the disaster de-scribes" (Blanchot 1995, 7). This is "writing which distinguishes itself by deleting from itself all distinguishing marks, which is to say perhaps, ultimately, by effacing itself (right away *and* at length: this takes all the time), for it seems to leave indelible or indiscernible traces," writes Blanchot (34). These are not textual traces, but events.

This book is not written from the perspective of Slavic studies or comparative literature, but primarily from that of the study of avant-garde performance. The main problem that emerged in the course of my work on this book was the limiting nature of the central paradigm of this study: performance. Even a cursory survey of various understandings of performance, as well as of the methodologies that contributed to the complex idea of performance that we now have—from theater studies (aesthetic performance), to ethnography (ritual, social drama), linguistic performance, gender studies, and efficiency analysis—reveals that the various meanings and applications of the idea of performance revolve around the notion of action and doing, and therefore of some sort of agency. Action in its multiplicity of forms—movement, interaction, presentation, perception—can be said to be the main focus of the study of performance. Kharms resists this methodology, at least as much as he resists absurdist or theological readings. Where does this resistance come from?

Of course, ontologically, performance and event have much in common. We can say that, while things exist, events and performances happen. Both events and performances are ephemeral entities. Aristotle's texts on poetry and language can be seen as the first indicators of the formalization of actions and their separation from the event. In *Poetics* this formalization is aesthetic. Aristotle makes sure to define tragedy as an "imitation of an action" and not of an "event." Since *Poetics* is concerned with the mimesis of action, or mimetic action, he does not dwell on the properties of the imitated action and its relation to the event. In *De Interpretatione,* however, he tends to consider actions together with substances, that is to say, physical objects and their properties. So, for example, in the first part of the text, "Categories," he writes that "a color . . . being numerically one and the same, cannot be black and white; nor can an action, which is numerically one and the same, be both vicious and virtuous" (Aristotle 1980, 7). While they don't accept opposite properties, substances and actions "admit of contraries of variation and degree. (Thus heating is contrary to cooling, etc.)" (20). Actions, like things, can be counted, described, situated in time and place, and therefore imitated and reproduced. Not so the events. Aristotle relegates events to the second part of *De Interpretatione,* dedicated to propositions, and here he talks about events in terms of truthfulness and falsity in relation to time, not space. He concludes that "if an event will neither occur nor fail to occur tomorrow, there would be no happening [tomorrow] in either of two ways, e.g., a sea fight would neither have to occur nor fail to occur tomorrow" (36). Aristotle then goes on to outline even more explicitly the limit between action and event. Elaborating on the logical impossibility of an event happening and not happening at the same time, Aristotle asserts that

> of things in the process of becoming, that which would be or which would come to be could not be in either of two ways but of necessity

> only one of them, in which case there would be no need to deliberate or take *action* with the expectation that, if we act in a certain way, a certain result will come about, but if we do not it will not come about. For nothing prevents one man from saying now that a certain event will occur ten thousand years hence, and another from saying that the event will not occur. (36)

What Aristotle seems to suggest is that there is not only a limit to agency, but also a limit to action. Event begins precisely where action ends. This distinction has been largely erased by the very branches of thought that claim to have originated from Aristotelian philosophy: formal logic and semantics.

The example I used earlier, "Petrov and Mosquitov," might create a false impression of Kharmsian incidents as purely linguistic events. If viewed as such, they would have nothing more to offer than an example of events as conceived by formal logic. Perhaps the most famous—and most contentious—example of this approach to events is Donald Davidson's essay "The Logical Form of Action Sentences" in which he tried to formally prove the existence of entities called events. He suggests that a simple action sentence, such as "Shem kicked Shaun," consists not of two names and a two-place predicate, but instead of three: Shem, Shaun and the event of kicking of Shem by Shaun. In logical notation, this proposition takes the following form:

$$(\exists x)\ (\text{Kicked}\ (\text{Shem, Shaun}, x))$$

Grammar seems to defy this attempt to isolate the event. Davidson's suggested translation of this formalized proposition into plain English reads: "There is an event x such that x is a kicking of Shaun by Shem" (Davidson 2001, 118). Certainly, many of Kharms's events don't lag behind the sadism that abounds in philosophical texts on formal logic: "Comrade Mashkin punched Comrade Koshkin in the head . . . Comrade Mashkin whopped Comrade Koshkin under the stomach and punched him once more in the back of the head," and so on (Kharms 2007, 70). Of course, that is not what makes them into events. Jonathan Bennett, one of the most lucid contemporary critics of formal logic's conceptualization of the event, argues that the language of logic is confusing facts and events: first, these two are not the same, and second, while facts can be stated in the form of propositions and are, therefore, subject to truth and falsity claims, no such thing is possible of the events.[24] The best language can do is point to an event, suggest it, and refrain from stating it in the form of a proposition, which is subject to truth-falsity valorization. "I am unperformable," says the event, and that unperformability, that resistance to enactment, comes from its openness to contingency. Rather than formal logic's understanding of the event, Kharms's work demands a different approach, which Michel Foucault outlines in *The Discourse on Language:*

> An event is neither a substance, nor accident, nor quality nor process; events are not corporeal. And yet, an event is certainly not immaterial; it takes effect, becomes effect, always on the level of materiality. Events have their place, they consist in relation to, coexistence with, dispersion of, the cross-checking accumulation and the selection of material elements; it occurs as an effect of, and in, material dispersion. Let us say that the philosophy of event should advance in the direction, at first sight paradoxical, of an incorporeal materialism. (Foucault 1972, 231)

Toward the end of this important paragraph, Foucault adds that "we must accept the introduction of chance as a category in the production of the events." In doing so he reminds us that the event has been one of the most overlooked ideas in the practice of the avant-garde and its longstanding engagement with the idea of chance. It can be traced to Mallarmé's "Igitur" (1869) and its myriad echoes in the culture of symbolism; to Tristan Tzara's formulation of the basic chance operation of cutting down a readymade text and its reassembling, to the Surrealist notion of objective chance and Artaud's demand for theater that fully embraces randomness, to Jackson Pollock's drip paintings, to John Cage's indeterminacies, to Happenings, Fluxus events, and situationist *dérives.* The avant-garde's discovery of chance has its own place in the history of Western culture. Historically, recognition of chance came together with the increasing demands for order and predictability, reflected in the birth of the new science of statistics.[25] Not surprisingly, the discovery of chance by the avant-garde coincides with the triumph of probabilistic thought and statistics as its main truth procedure. If, as Jacques Lezra asserts, the act can be seen as an attempt at formalization, aesthetization, and ultimately sublimation of events,[26] then the avant-garde's embrace of chance comes as a profoundly desublimatory gesture.

My objective in this book is not to establish the event as a new category of literary criticism. In no way am I suggesting that the event is the all-powerful tool for interpretation of Kharms's work, the new paradigm that supplants the absurd. Instead, it designates a certain method of reading. As such, all it allows me to do is to look at the radical fragmentariness of Kharms's works without the necessity of imposing an overarching meaning upon them. The event permits each of them to retain its own sense, and to talk to the multiplicity of other meanings. Therefore, if my investigation of Kharms's work begins with the plurality of the fragment, its central focus is on the singularity of the event. Let me return, for the last time, to the distinction between performance and the event. At one point in *The Fold,* Gilles Deleuze poses the problem in the following way: "A concert is being performed tonight. It is the event." Where does the performance of music end and the event of the concert begin? Deleuze continues: "Vibrations of sound disperse, periodic movements go through space with their harmonics or submultiples. The sounds have their inner qualities of height, intensity, and timbre. The sources of the sounds, instrumental or vocal, are not content only to send the sounds out: each one perceives its own, and perceives the others while perceiving its own" (Deleuze 1993, 80). The sounds are at the same time sounds and perceptions of sounds, or, as Alfred North Whitehead would have it, prehensions. On one side, there are objects or acts, and on the other their perceptions, which are also actions in their own right. Between them is the center of indetermination, the event. I am looking at Kharms's manuscripts as a (dis)concert of sorts, in which each text or image or mathematical formula is both the thing and the perception of the thing. It is the indeterminate, contingent event that makes their reading possible. This reading is not only a reading of texts, but also of images, diagrams, scores, mathematical formulas. For Kharms, an event emerges from language, but is not linguistic in itself. That is why he so easily and effectively switches to nonlinguistic forms such as music, gesture, and visual arts. In Kharms's work, images, words, gestures, objects, and musical notations are not visual, linguistic, choreographic, sculptural, or musical traces of the events. They are not representations, but eventuations. Representations capture events. Eventuations allow them to take place.

If we accept that Kharms's overall project is the replacement of knowledge with ignorance, then in his theatrical work it translates into a shift from representation to the event. First, then, I analyze Kharms's passage from representation to eventuation; second, I examine the event's status within the work, and then the ways in which the work adapts itself to the event. It would be imprudent to claim that Kharms turned to the event because he was prevented from producing theatrical performances. The opposite is true: his performances were oppressed because of their eventfulness. The specifically Kharmsian notion of the event is not elaborated only in his theatrical pieces or in his poetry and prose but also in his theoretical tracts and notes. Disobjectification is one of the primary characteristics of the Kharmsian event: neither purely material nor purely immaterial, it can perhaps be best described as incorporeal but real.

Kra kra krasi fasi perekosi. Object, object, object, object, object, object, object, object, object, object, object, object.

—Daniil Kharms (1933)

1. Against Metaphor

The OBERIU Situation of the Object

Man Ray's 1921 object *Cadeau* (*Gift*) is memorable for its simplicity and effectiveness: an ordinary domestic iron, propped upright, with a row of nails protruding from its flat bottom surface. This materialization of Surrealist anti-metaphor follows Comte de Lautreamont's famous dictum "beautiful as the encounter of a sewing machine with an umbrella on a dissection table." The juxtaposition of flat and sharp objects dominates both Lautréamont's image and Man Ray's object. Threatening spikes turn the functional part of the iron into a metal jaw, thus rendering the object useless. An umbrella ends with a point, an enlarged version of the sewing machine's needle. Nails, spikes, and needles are associated with piercing, scraping, and tearing apart, but also with much less destructive functions: attaching, piecing together, connecting. Even the word Man Ray used to name his object, *cadeau* (gift), sonically resembles the French word for another sharp object, the paradigmatic symbol of cutting and stabbing: *couteau* (knife). This, again, points toward the ambiguous etymological origin of the word "gift," which in the old Germanic languages had the double meaning of gift and poison.[1] In the lecture "Surrealist Situation of the Object" that he delivered in Prague in 1935, André Breton talked about Man Ray's idea of establishing a recognizable proof of authenticity: a seal, or trademark, for Surrealist objects. At this point, Surrealists felt this necessary because the "*fundamental crisis of the object*" that took place "in the wake of Surrealism" affected the entirety of Western culture (Breton 1972,

257, italics in the original). In his book Breton makes a bold assertion: since the dawn of Dada, the object—the artistic object, the industrial object, the object for everyday use, and even the dreamed and imagined object—has ceased to be reliable and even easily recognizable. We no longer know what an object is.

This discussion of the status of the object in one of the movements that defined the European avant-garde is pertinent to a discussion of Daniil Kharms and OBERIU for at least two reasons. First, while the Surrealist object and the OBERIU object share the basic premise of uselessness, in the case of the Surrealist object, the appearance of uselessness is overpowered by a much deeper sense of marvel and danger emanating from the object. Second, although some characteristics of the OBERIU object formally reflect the Dada spirit, which was crucial in the fermentation of the Surrealist idea of the object, the concept of the OBERIU object emerged from an entirely different crisis than the one cited by Breton.[2]

So, what is the OBERIU object? How is it distinguished from other concepts of the object that emerged from the crisis in the first decades of the twentieth century? What is Kharms's understanding of the object?

The most accessible source for answers about OBERIU is *The OBERIU Manifesto* (1928), the only collective statement published during the brief period of the group's existence. Some of the rather striking sections of this much-cited and discussed document are dedicated precisely to the question of the conceptual position of the object in OBERIU theater and poetry.[3] From the very outset, it is clear that the Oberiuty value the object for its concreteness and that they freely transpose this quality from the object to word and action. Each of the OBERIU members proposes a slightly different way to achieve this concreteness. In a brief personal, poetic "statement of purpose," Kharms evokes ideas about language and objects that are on the surface strikingly similar to Breton's definition of "convulsive beauty." While Breton talks about an object that is at the same time moving and arrested in place, Kharms is always interested in an object in action. Convulsive beauty is the motion at rest, arrested motion, and Breton illustrates it with the image of "a speeding locomotive abandoned for years to the delirium of the virgin forest" (Breton 1987, 10). In *The OBERIU Manifesto,* Kharms professes a pronounced interest in the "collision of a number of objects" (Kharms 1971, 198). Like Breton, he is not interested in the static object but in the object in action. He explains that "at the moment of action, the object assumes new concrete traits full of real meaning." Kharms is not interested in the simultaneity of stasis and movement but in the simultaneity of two kinds of action: the classical Aristotelian action and its reversal, "action turned inside out" (198). In the section of the manifesto dedicated to OBERIU theater, this "action turned inside out" is distinguished from the classical action by its alogicity. Much like other radical avant-garde groups of the first half of the twentieth century, OBERIU insists on the absence of a logical plot in its theatrical performances: while "until now [. . .] a play has been a story, told through characters about some kind of event," OBERIU introduces theater "that will interest the spectator, even if it takes place without any dramatic plot" (200–201). Much has been made of this plotlessness of the OBERIU theater, especially of the ways it plays out in Kharms's dramatic works.[4] However, the Oberiuty were ready to admit in the manifesto only this much: "We can only say that our task is to render the world of concrete objects on the stage in their interrelationships and collisions" (202). While the emphasis of this statement is, again, on the object and not on the plot, it doesn't offer a satisfactory explanation of the OBERIU object itself. The OBERIU object undergoes a profound transformation in Kharms's creative writing. Here, it is distinguished from the world of ordinary things by its uselessness. On the most basic level, resistance to any kind of utilization, application, or purpose of the OBERIU object comes from its magnitude. It can be an object of enormous proportions, such as the giant brick wall from Kharms's 1930 untitled narrative about an engineer who decides to immure the entire city of St. Petersburg. In this story, a small group of engineers decides to erect the wall in only one night. This considerable engineering feat is accomplished with the support of the city authorities: "The next day St. Petersburg is all in commotion. The inventor of the wall itself is depressed. What this wall is good for, he himself never knew" (Kharms 1997b, 19). Similarly, uselessness often results from the miniaturization of an everyday object. In another unfinished and untitled dramatic scene, one Petr Mikhailovich anxiously expects a visit from a girl. His elderly neighbor Ilya Semenovich comes in and destroys everything that Petr Mikhailovich has carefully arranged. The girl, Maria Ivanovna, arrives. The situation is tense and uncomfortable.

> Maria Ivanovna sits on the sofa. The old man takes a small hammer from his mouth.
> Petr Mikhailovich: What is that?
> Ilya Semenovich: A small hammer.
> Maria Ivanovna: What have you done? You took it from your mouth?
> Ilya Semenovich: No, no. I'm just killing time!

Maria Ivanovna: Is that a magic trick?
(Silence)
(Kharms 1997b, 391)

The same situation is repeated toward the end of the scene, after the old man leaves the apartment. This time, it is Maria Ivanovna who pulls a small hammer from her mouth. When Petr Mikhailovich inquires about the strange feat she has just performed, she points to her throat and explains that the hammer had been bothering her all day.[5] The miniature hammer appears in the place vacated by words. It becomes the material sign of aporia, of the absence of language and memory. Here, the OBERIU object emerges as a paradoxical object, a useless utensil. It is a concrete object, a tangible thing deprived of any symbolic value. It emerges from the mouth as a kind of speech that is tangible and inaudible. This object evokes Kharms's famous credo about the writing of verses that are as concrete as things, so that, if thrown at a window, they could break the glass.[6] However, the small hammer is not simply an objectified word. It is a piece of dead matter that is extracted from a living body: it gets pulled out from a mouth like an improbable tooth. This gesture points toward the idea of the intermingling and combining of living beings and inanimate objects. In Kharms's work, the line between dead matter and organic life is never clear: the frequent appearance of cripples, people on crutches, and, generally, of the human body in symbiosis with an object is just one way of unhinging the predictable relation between the animate and the inanimate. In these cases crutches, artificial limbs, and dentures do not appear as proper OBERIU objects. They still serve a function: supporting a failing human body.[7] The human body in the state of ultimate ruin becomes a formidable OBERIU object: a body that fails to continue living; a body that cannot be prompted anymore by any kind of prosthetic aids; and a corpse that shows signs of decay but that refuses to cease movement and lie down to final rest.

The cessation of vital bodily functions is traditionally recognized as a certain sign of death. The living organs turn into inanimate matter. However, this matter is, so to speak, still animated: the dead body twitches and writhes, thus escaping complete objectification. There is a movement unrelated to organic life that is perceived as an autonomous "life" of objects. Objects are independent of human beings. The horror of this simple realization is best communicated through the image of a dead body that continues to "live." A dead body animated by an inhuman movement, a corpse that adopts the life of an object, is a frequent image in Kharms's work. These crawling corpses are no less dead because they are moving: it is precisely this inanimate movement that makes their death categorical, concrete, and menacing. In the story "Cashier," a store manager seats a dead girl behind the cash register and puts a cigarette in her mouth in order to give her corpse "a greater resemblance to the living." The result is a deceptive and paradoxical object: "the dead woman sat there looking quite alive, except that her facial coloring was very green and one eye was open while the other was completely closed" (Kharms 1993, 121). This semblance between the living and the dead is inseparable from the sense of persecution: the heroine of Kharms's only completed and performed play, *Elizabeth Bam,* is accused of killing Petr Nikolaevich, who comes back to arrest her. This nonorganic life brings the sense of an impending menace with even more urgency in Kharms's longest prose piece, "The Old Woman." Even to a greater extent than in "Cashier" or *Elizabeth Bam,* in this tale the image of a life-like corpse evokes a pervasive sense of invasion. Here, an elderly woman enters the narrator's apartment and dies. The initial sense of annoyance swiftly changes:

> Maybe I only imagined it, but the sickeningly sweet smell of decay wafted in my face. I peeked around the slightly opened door and for a moment was frozen to the spot. The old woman was on all fours slowly crawling toward me.
>
> With a shout I slammed the door, turned the key, and jumped back against the wall opposite the door. (Kharms 2007, 99)

The moving corpse in Kharms's story is not animated by an otherworldly force. What is horrifying here is not the unknowable power of the living dead, but precisely the opposite: the aimless and senseless progression of the corpse unprotected by any kind of life in it. This moving matter embodies a determination without will and an unyielding indestructibility. It does not engage with other objects: this absence of interaction with the immediate environment is a sure sign that the life of the object is inhuman. Such inhuman motion amounts to an inert action; it is an action deprived of cause, effect, and meaning. Whereas the corpse of the old woman moves on its own, in "Cashier" the store manager puts a mushroom in the dead cashier girl's hand "for additional verisimilitude" to the living (1993, 121). However, this banal imitation of life does not prevent an inhuman, foreign life from entering the body. In "Water Tractatus" Leonid Lipavsky explains that the feeling of dread is associated with the image of spilled blood not because of the logical association of blood with pain but because of blood's gelatinous quality, its formlessness and coagulation as a postmortem reflection of life. The fear of spilled blood is the fear of "formless life," or a "life of emptiness" (Ostashevsky 2006, 209). The coagulating blood and decomposing corpse are porous entities. Their boundaries are infirm. Their shape is easily affected and changed by outside forces. The alternative to this death-in-formlessness, or lifelike death, is the geometrization of the body.

Kharms's 1929 tract "The Saber" is important for understanding his approach to work, creation, individuality, and agency. The entire piece, titled after an object, is centered on establishing a clear distinction between the self and the world of objects:[8]

> We stand here and say: now I've stretched out one arm in front of me, and the other arm behind me. And now, in front, I end where my arm ends, and in back I also end where my arm ends. On top, I end with the top of my head, on the bottom with my heels, and on the sides with my shoulders. Now, this is all of me, and whatever is outside me, is not me anymore. (Ostashevsky 2006, 86)

The image of the body as a unit defined by clear and firm physical limits is summed up in the next paragraph:

> The three pairs of our edges are as follows:
> 1. arm—arm
> 2. shoulder—shoulder
> 3. head—heels

This image of the body in outline, or the body reduced to its epidermis, the surface-body, recurs in Kharms's works in several different variants. As we progress, we will see that the body as a surface outline can be alphabetized, geometrized, diagrammatized, or transformed into a landscape. At this point, however, it is important to realize that Kharms's emphasis on the limits of the physical body is always shadowed by the limitlessness of thought. His tract "The Werld" concludes with such a double movement:

> Then I realized that, while I had somewhere to look, there had been a world around me. And now it's gone. There's only me.

And then I realized that I am the world.
But the world—is not me.
Although at the same time I am the world.
But the world's not me.
And I am the world.
But the world's not me.
And I am the world.
But the world's not me.
And I am the world.
And, after that, I didn't think anything anymore. (2006, 96)

The title of Kharms's tract is the wordplay based on the similarity of the word *mir* (world) spelled in the Russian Cyrillic alphabet as мир, and the word *my* (we), spelled мы. The combination of the two words results in the neologism мыр, which can be fairly accurately paralleled with the English "werld." In "The Werld," we encounter one of Kharms's favorite themes: division of the world into fragments. While in his other texts dedicated to the relation of parts to the whole Kharms investigates the problems of order, seriality, and causality, here he makes a stunning observation about the continuity of parts: "But then I understood that I do not see the parts independently, but I see it all at once. At first I thought that it was NOTHING. But then I understood that this was the world and what I had seen before was not the world" (95). In the manuscript, the title is accompanied by the figure ⦶. In light of the tract, this emblem becomes highly ambiguous: it is a circle divided into two halves, but it can also be seen as two semi-circles, or the two parts, fused into a whole. This title, which is both iconic and phonetic, informs the tract's ending in an interesting way. Like in "The Saber," the realization "I am the world" is based on the understanding of identity as based on the physical sense of being in the body that is distinct from the surrounding world of objects and other bodies. At the same time, the self is a world unto itself. The self is both limited and limitless. The repetition of the affirmation and negation "I am the world / The world is not me" ends, significantly, with the cessation of thinking. The thought does not simply vanish. It disappears into its own fullness, into the fullness of the world in which all fragments, including the one who thinks, are unified. We are the world: werld. This is not an expression of the new communal spirit. It is even less an affirmation of solipsism. The tract "Eleven Statements by Daniil Ivanovich Kharms," which opens with the assertion "objects are gone," ends with the following theses that, together with "The Werld," represent Kharms's full engagement in questioning the division between subject and object:

> Statement X
> One person thinks logically. Many people think FLOWINGLY.
> Statement XI
> Though I am alone, I think FLOWINGLY.
> (Kharms 1997b, 305)

The scope of the OBERIU object encompasses, therefore, the singular useless objects such as the miniature hammer or the giant wall, porous and amorphous bodies (cadavers) suspended between human and inhuman life, and perfect geometrical objects. Beyond that, Oberiuty were keenly interested in the form of matter that is transitional, a substance in flux, a medium that circulates and which is in the state of perpetual transformation. A perfect example of this form of viscosity of matter is, of course, water.[9] Kharms and his friends related the absence of structure and the relative formlessness of certain kinds of matter to the sense of pleasure. In a brief exchange between Kharms and Lipavsky recorded in "Conversations," Kharms proposes that air, as the most amorphous of all matter, should induce the most pleasure. Lipavsky's response reveals that it is not just the formlessness and fluidity of water that matters, but also its materiality: its resistance together with its complaisance makes water unique among various kinds of matter. Gas, however, simply "spreads about and disappears. It is as if it doesn't exist for us: it is not an elemental force, but an abstraction" (Lipavskii 2005, 410). Ideally, air is without smell and taste; it cannot be seen or felt. It cannot be sensed in any other way. Air is the state of neutrality itself, a nonobject. Things disappear and fly into the air.

Dissolution, spilling out, sudden vanishing, and, as it were, abstraction of the body occupy a prominent place among the various kinds of disappearance that occur frequently in Kharms's texts. His short story "Holiday" ends when the two draftsmen who are sitting on the rooftop "dissolve into the air" (Ostashevsky 2006, 118).

Similarly, the protagonist of the short piece "How One Man Fell to Pieces" bloats until he reaches the ceiling and then breaks into "a thousand little spheres" (Kharms 2007, 227). In his discussion of the sphere symbolism in Kharms's work, Mikhail Yampolsky points to the opening section of the short scene "The Mathematician and Andrei Semyonovich":

Mathematician: (removing a sphere from his head)
I removed a sphere from my head.
I removed a sphere from my head.
I removed a sphere from my head.
I removed a sphere from my head.
(Kharms 2007, 55)

Yampolsky finds it significant that the ball emerges from the head, which also has a spherical shape. The sphere not only resembles the globe of the head but also belongs to it. "The sphere," says Yampolsky, "like every other geometrical form, belongs to the world of the subject; it is not a natural object, but a pure concept" (Iampol'skii 1997, 207). However, he warns that the sphere still maintains a certain objectivity because it is always related to a subject: it remains halfway between an object and a concept.

Like the sphere, the OBERIU object is the physical, tangible thing conceptualized and separated from the world of everyday objects. Perhaps the most important aspect of the OBERIU object is that it brings into question the very idea of the object and, consequently, the subject. Moreover, it questions the very possibility of objecthood. In the text "On Phenomena and Existences # 1" Kharms imagines the artist Michael Angelo in the midst of a world so distorted that the meaning of the word "world" becomes questionable. It has to be a werld. The story opens with "Michael Angelo" sitting on a heap of bricks and eyeing a rooster. Leaving this pile of solid, heavy cubes, he goes to his wife, who is "very long, the length of two rooms." As he departs from the heap of sharp-edged, dusty bricks, the world around him loses its firmness. A sphere appears in the sky, and then it turns into a giant spoon that floats above Michael Angelo's head. The story ends with a remark about one Nikolai Ivanovich Stupin, who "has a theory that everything is smoke" (Kharms 2007, 191). By now we know that the Oberiuty saw the air as an essentially abstract idea, something that surrounds us, like time. Similarly, the inconsistent sphere that turns into a spoon makes it more an idea, an apparition, than a precisely defined geometrical object.

This is, however, only a preface to the radical de-objectivization attempted in the second part of the text. In "On Phenomena and Existences # 2" Kharms isolates an object, a bottle of vodka, and a subject, Nikolai Ivanovich Serpuhov, who drinks from the bottle.[10] This subject-object couple is surrounded by pure nothingness. "Behind Nikolai Ivanovich's back there isn't even any air-less space or, as they say, universal ether." The same nothingness is in front of Nikolai Ivanovich and even inside him. The subject emerges also as a concept, a fragile border between two voids. What remains is the concept of "outside" and "inside": "if we're saying that nothing exists neither inside nor outside then the question comes up: inside or outside what?" (2007, 193). Discussion of the subject-object relation turns into a question of pure interiority and exteriority, or, ultimately, into a question of the very possibility of the existence of the "object." And this is precisely the question that represents the crisis from which the peculiar OBERIU object emerged. This question points not to the Dadaist crisis of object's meaning, but the crisis of the very notion of the object, powerfully expressed in Kazimir Malevich's theory of nonobjective art.

Obscure Mirror

The encounter between Kharms and Malevich took place toward the end of 1926. The meeting remains shrouded in an aura of eccentricity and strange theatricality.

The immediate cause for the unlikely collaboration between the pioneer of painterly abstraction and the emerging poet was the proposal that Kharms and his friends from the theater group Radix submitted to Malevich, who was then the head of the Formal Theoretical Department at the State Institute of Artistic Culture (GINKhUK). According to one of the members of the group, Georgy Katsman, the word "radix" was chosen because, apart from its Latin meaning—the root, and therefore something basic, original, and fundamental—it is also a play on words, suggesting the radical nature of their theatrical experimentation (in Vvedenskii 1993, 128).[11] The proposal that ended up on Malevich's desk was designed like a collage, and it by and large confirms the mission of the group as stated by Katsman[12]: "We organized the theatrical group Radix with the intention to experiment in the field of nonemotional and nonnarrative art, and taking as our goal work on the pieces of pure theater that are not subservient to literature, in which all things that enter the production are rendered EQUAL" (in Jaccard 1991, 77; emphasis in the original). Igor Bakhterev recalls that he, Kharms, Vvedensky, and Katsman were in the Radix delegation that visited Malevich at GINKhUK in the late fall of 1926. They took off their shoes upon entering the building and proceeded barefoot: "when we entered Malevich's office, we went down on our knees. He stood up to greet us, and then also knelt. That is how, kneeling, we began our meeting" (in Meilakh

1987, 167). By the end of this strange summit, Malevich seemed interested in the young poets' project. According to Katsman, he told them: "I am an old hooligan (*bezobraznik*), and you are the young ones: let's see what is going to happen" (in Vvedenskii 1993, 130). Alexandra Shatskikh points out the possible double meaning of Malevich's utterance. The proper meaning of the Russian word *bezobraznik* is, indeed, hooligan, blockhead, thug, or brute. However, Malevich, who had a taste for creating neologisms based on his own idiosyncratic etymology, possibly chose this particular word because of its literal meaning (*bez,* without; *obraz,* form or image). He had already employed it in his writings as a synonym for "nonobjectivity" (Malevich 2000b, 38). It should be noted that Malevich's double entendre also neatly parallels the double meaning of the word "radix."

Radix started rehearsing the play *My Mother All in Watches*[13] as early as September 1926 in the apartments of the play's author, Vvedensky, and its director, Bakhterev. On October 18, the rehearsals were transferred to the "White Hall" of the GINKhUK; on November 10, "Radix fell apart," as Kharms and Katsman plainly stated in their list of rehearsals. It seems that out of all the members of Radix, Kharms remained the closest to Malevich. The painter presented the young poet with a copy of his book *God Is Not Cast Down.* The same winter, Kharms composed the poetic drama *Temptation,* dedicated to Malevich. This play speaks not only about Kharms's close ties with Malevich but also about his attempt to understand the painter's philosophy of art. The protagonist of the play is actually a group, a small chorus indicated as "Four Girls on the Threshold."[14] This quartet announces that their "legs are broken at the gate" (Kharms 1997a, 68). Already in this image dominated by severed earthly ties, Kharms hints at the suprematist idea of departure from the world of objects into the weightless realm of pure nonobjectivity.

God Is Not Cast Down: Art, Church, Factory was published in the spring of 1922 in Vitebsk, where Malevich served as the president of the council of professors of UNOVIS (the school's name is the abbreviation for *Utverditeli novogo iskusstva,* The Founders of New Art). *God Is Not Cast Down* was Malevich's most ambitious theoretical work to date, and it turned out to be his last theoretical work published in Russia during his lifetime. During the winter of 1921 to 1922, Malevich had an extraordinary outburst of theoretical and philosophical activity, which resulted in his magnum opus, *Suprematism: World as Non-Objectivity, or Eternal Peace.*[15] The booklet *God Is Not Cast Down* is a significantly condensed excerpt from this much longer manuscript. In *Temptation* Kharms addresses questions relevant to Malevich's understanding of the world as expounded in these treatises without summarily subscribing to them.

Temptation is a moment of decision. This decision marks an entrance into the realm of error and exit from the state of perpetual bliss. In *God Is Not Cast Down* Malevich talks about the Adamic fall from the "generic system," the perfect system in which every unit freely moves and yet is "unable to leave the system's limits" into the world of objects, of weight, and of limited and limiting forms. The fall, for Malevich, is the falling apart of the original Paradise. The world of objects, the historic world, is an Adamic engine that tries to forge its way back into the state of primordial unity and objectlessness. "Adam," says Malevich, "transgressed the limits of the system and its weight collapsed onto him" (Malevich 1968, 201). In this interpretation of the biblical story of origin, Adam's temptation is seen as a drawing of the line, establishing the boundary and thus the fragmentation of the limitless "generic system." Malevich reminds us that Paradise is not an enclosure, a hidden garden, but an open and all-encompassing space. Temptation, however, is still not the fall itself: it is the potentiality of the fall, the attraction, the brief moment that separates resistance from yielding. Temptation marks the point of indecision, the crossroads between the known and the unknown. It reveals the presence of a choice, of an alternative, of another world that has its own weight and gravity. It precedes takeoff and leads to the state of flight and weightlessness. Temptation is an attempt, an investigation, a tryout. A test.

The generic determination of Kharms's *Temptation* as a "poetic drama" is insufficient, to say the least. Like many others of Kharms's works, this hybridization of genres is not merely a drama in verse or a versified dialogue, but an attempt at a systematic overturning of the laws of dramatic representation. Each appearance of the Four Girls takes place in a different spatial arrangement. Five different "movements" are distinguishable according to these different situations of character in space. From the first (Four Girls on the Threshold—Four Girls off the Threshold) to the last (Four Girls Look Through a Microscope—Four Girls Disappear and Go Silent) each of the "movements" involves a visual frame or an optical device. *Temptation* is a drama about transition and flux, or about what Kharms names toward the end of the piece a "spatial draft" (1997a, 70).

Although each of the "movements" is set in a liminal position, the direction of the movement is unambiguous: the Four Girls move from inside, out. The couplet that Kharms uses as the leitmotif, "come out on that hillock / take the shirt off your shoulders" describes a double movement of exit from coercion: from an enclosed space and from clothes. The Four Girls move from the frame of the door to the larger space of an open landscape. This, however, is not a boundless space, since it is limited by what appears to be a frame of vision. The Four Girls (now described as "Four Girls in Perspective") undergo a transformation that doesn't proceed according to the conventional rules of linear perspective. The basic rule of perspective dictates that the closer an object is located to the vanishing point, the smaller it appears to be. As they slide into the landscape, the Four Girls are transformed in an unexpected way: "our arms are many-sided / our heads are gray / turning our eyes eastwards / we see delicate steps" (1997a, 68). Instead of appearing smaller, they become distorted and grow older. Whereas in linear perspective the origin of the image is located at the vanishing point, in the "perspective" of *Temptation* the origin is located in the east, where the original Garden of Eden was located. If the Four Girls look eastward, it means that they are located in the west, in the land of exile after the fall. The temptation from the play-poem's title does not lead to transgression and departure from paradise but to a return to this origin. In other words, the temptation that Kharms sings about is the temptation of the nonobjective world, of the absolute unity, of the world that is imperceptible not because it is unknown but because it has been forgotten. Instead of receding silently toward the horizon, the Four Girls, so to speak, explode into a realm beyond objective representation: "Four Girls Disappear: BOOOOOOM!" This is perhaps the finest disappearance in all of Kharms's works. Vanishing is one of the prominent themes in Kharms and, significantly, the first one that we find in his work is related to mathematics. In his notebook for 1924, he tries to work out the following problem:

> In time t, which leans towards [one] zero, the value α becomes identical to value β.
> If lim t = 0
> $\alpha = \beta$

The following day he returns to the same problem:

> β was for me a completely unknown value. I was not concerned with the observation of α. H—α—all the same! I think that β (A) acquired the speed C and ceased to exist, in relation to me, as matter. (2002a, 15)

This initial mathematical vanishing eventually moves to Kharms's poetry and prose. In *Temptation* it happens with the bang. It is followed by the movement "The Colonel in Front of the Mirror."

In *Temptation,* the image of the mirror brings together two motifs prominent in Kharms's work. The first one is the window. Both mirror and window are framing devices: they detach and isolate a fragment from the totality of the image. Kharms attaches a great symbolic value to the window as a figure of passage and transformation. In *Temptation,* the Four Girls proceed from threshold to windowsill to mirror, and then pass through it. The second motif is the reflective surface. In Kharms's works the surface of water most commonly takes over the function of the mirror. Still water's surface, that proto-mirror, reflects everything that surrounds it, but most prominently it mirrors that which stands opposite: the sky. If the window represents the point of conversion between the inside and the outside, then the water's surface symbolizes the inversion of up and down. And both divide the world in two: The window is an opening, a gap in the materiality of the wall, and it facilitates the exchange between the two spaces separated by that same wall; the water's surface and the mirror are characterized by their dual quality as material objects and immaterial reflections. Alexander Kobrinsky recognizes "mirror effect" or "reflectivity" as one of the central themes shared by the Oberiuty. In their works, asserts Kobrinsky, the mirror not only multiplies the material objects but also becomes the symbol of multiple worlds. He underlines that "all of those worlds are *equally real* and are not susceptible to any attempt at hierarchization" (Kobrinskii 2000, 69, italics in the original). Image or representation of any kind, including spoken and written language, holds the same ontological status as empirical reality: the original-copy duality breaks down. By and large, Kharms's entire project is informed by this principle.

Back to the colonel we left standing in front of the mirror. As he mechanically rehearses military exercises, what actually does he see in the mirror? What kind of mirror is he facing? And, after all, why the mirror in a play dedicated to an artist who during the first years of the modernist rediscovery of abstraction advanced one of the most compelling arguments against realist verisimilitude?

Academic realism and its insistence on the mirrorlike representation was one of the main targets of Malevich's attacks in his pre-Vitebsk writings. For example, in his 1915 essay "From Cubism and Futurism to Suprematism: The New Realism in Painting,"[16] Malevich observed that in the history of painting, the only change in the time span from antiquity, through the Renaissance, and up to nineteenth-century academic realism was the improvement of technique. According to Malevich, the masters of these epochs in painting "despite their colossal mastery . . . did not complete the savage's idea: the reflection, as in a mirror, of nature on canvas" (1968, 21). He located the main problem of naturalist art in the "idealization of form" and its emphasis on the subject matter, or, in other words, on its insistence on the representation of objects in painting. While in "From Cubism to Futurism and Suprematism" Malevich still allowed for the existence of nature, matter, and objects, in *God Is Not Cast Down* he asserted that objects and even matter as such don't exist. Instead, in opposition to the "savage idea of naturalism" Malevich was here arguing against "objective consciousness," which creates, as it were, such concepts as matter and object. "Objective thinking is occupied with building a mirror—seeing the world is the reason for matter itself" (211). This is the fundamental idea of Malevich's theory of nonobjective art: object is thought as such, not the other way around. His ideas about nonobjectivity, laid out on the hundreds of pages of the Vitebsk manuscripts, were summarized on the single page of the pamphlet "The Suprematist Mirror," published in the Moscow journal *Zhizn' iskusstva* (*The Life of Art*) in 1923. The central position of this single-page document is occupied by the following equation:

$$\begin{array}{l}\text{The World as}\\ \text{human}\\ \text{distinctions}\end{array} \left\{ \begin{array}{l} \text{God} \\ \text{The Soul} \\ \text{The Spirit} \\ \text{Life} \\ \text{Religion} \\ \text{Technology} \\ \text{Art} \\ \text{Science} \\ \text{The Intellect} \\ \text{Weltanschauung} \\ \text{Labor} \\ \text{Movement} \\ \text{Space} \\ \text{Time} \end{array} \right\} = 0$$

(1968, 224)

If we cast a glance at *Temptation* through a Malevichian lens, we will notice that the progression of the play's action is marked by the reduction of differences between the main characters. They start as what I have called a composite dramatic character. Soon, it becomes clear that the Four Girls are not only grouped in space (on a threshold, in perspective, and so on), but that they also go through identical transformations ("our arms are many-sided / our heads are gray"). Finally, their explosive disappearance can be seen as the final obliteration of distinctions that separate them. Upon losing their individual properties they inevitably disappear. They are invisible, but their voices come from behind.[17] They are separated from the colonel by a mirror that does not permit them to see the outside, and which does not offer reflection. This is the mirror of nothingness, of the absence of distinguishable forms, or, as Malevich has it, of "*the zero of form*" (1968, 19, italics in the original). The flat surface that the colonel faces is not the looking glass that separates the everyday world of proper coordinates from its inversed twin, as is the case in the famous fable of Lewis Carroll. The suprematist mirror does not reflect the world. It does not contain a reversed version of reality, an immaterial, upside-down, inside-out version of the world. The idea of the parallel worlds that Kharms shares with other Oberiuty can be traced to Malevich's radical widening of the notion of art. For Malevich, art is not the art of the works themselves, but a sovereign system of thought. As Boris Groys observed, if with Husserl's revolution in philosophical methodology the philosopher becomes more like an artist, then with Malevich's nonobjectivity the artist becomes more like a philosopher (Groys 1982, 362). Art, for Malevich, is not a subject of thought: it is the thought itself, an instrument for philosophizing.

The zero on the right-hand side of Malevich's equation does not designate the void. For him, the absence of matter, objects, and forms stands for the original unity and fullness.[18] In the concluding paragraph of his tract *God Is Not Cast Down* Malevich offers his vision of God as primordial creator who, having finished his creation, withdrew from the world of action. Malevich's zero is the zero of the absolute: "God . . . has entered rest; and it turned out that nothingness was God, and passing through perfection became nothingness. . . . God exists as 'nothingness,' as non-objectivity" (1968, 222). According to Malevich, the crucial characteristic of the absolute, of God—which he so often equates with Nature—is its wholeness, the absence of distinction and fragmentation. This strong emphasis on the ontological absolute both in his art and in his writing (which, as we are going to see shortly, often become indistinguishable) has been singled out by art critics as the crucial difference between Malevich and other early abstract painters. Jean-Claude Marcade, one of the most lucid readers of Malevich, points out that nonobjectivity has often been confused with painterly abstraction, which also "refuses all reference to any known thing in the perceptible world." Comparing Malevich's nonobjectivity with the abstraction of Kandinsky and Mondrian, Marcade concludes: "whereas abstraction wants to know the object in its essence, to interpret this essence such as we intuitively know it and not according to our normal eyesight, suprematist nonobjectivity refuses all reference to the world of objects and only recognizes *one world,* that of the abyss of being" (Marcade 1978a, 189; italics in the original). While other representatives of early abstraction in painting still recognized the separation between the internal world of man and the external world of nature, Malevich firmly rejects any such possibility. If God and Nature are absolute, indivisible, and infinite, then, says Malevich, "man's skull represents the same infinity for the movement of conceptions." He then asks: "Is not the whole universe that strange skull in which meteors, suns, comets, and planets rush endlessly?" (193). This same question echoes in the final section of Kharms's tract "The Werld": "But the world is not me / But I am the world." Malevich's skull is inseparable from his symbolism of perfection: it is the sphere as the perfect object, but also the skull located at the foot of the cross—the symbol of Adam before the fall and the destruction of the "perfect system."[19]

Already in his tract "From Cubism and Futurism to Suprematism" Malevich insisted that true artistic creation cannot and should not have anything in common with mere representation of nature. For him, "art is the ability to construct *on the basis of weight, speed, and the direction of movement*" (Malevich 1968, 24; italics in the original). The outcome of this construction is not the representation of objects, but of independent forms: "Forms must be given life and the right to individual existence." This rigorous rejection of the representation of natural and symbolic forms in Malevich's paintings and in his theoretical texts prompted Marcade to separate him from other "Russian painter-philosophers" as "the only one who has put into philosophical terms the question of being in his meditation upon art." Marcade goes on to say that "visual suprematism is the revelation proceeding from *Black Square* (1913–15), regarded as the generating primordial form of the abysmal being" (1978, 225–26). Indeed, Malevich's thinking about independent and primordial form, which is different from object and its representation, brings to mind Heidegger's meditation on the thing:

> An independent, self-supporting thing may become an object if we place it before us, whether in immediate perception or by bringing it to mind in a recollective re-presentation. However, the thingly character of the thing does not consist in its being a represented object, nor can it be defined in any way in terms of objectness, the over-againstness, of the object. (Heidegger 1971, 167)

Where Malevich talks about "individual forms," Heidegger is talking about "independent things." The object obscures, hides, and essentially annihilates the autonomous thing. Malevich and Heidegger seem to agree on the central point concerning the thing: it has not been destroyed by technology and science; instead, an essential destruction of the thing is a necessary precondition for the object's very existence. Where Malevich talks about "objective consciousness" as a broken mirror that reflects nature fragmented into a vast number of objects, Heidegger talks about the inability of thought to see things qua things. This annihilation of the thing, which results in the production of objects, says Heidegger, "has happened and continues to happen so essentially that not only are things no longer admitted as things, but they have never at all been able to appear to thinking as things" (1971, 171). The idea of the form qua form, form which is independent from the object and even opposed to it, is essential to Malevich's thought. So, what is Kharms's relation to Malevich's ontology?

His earliest attempts to formulate his own theoretical pronouncements coincide with his encounter with Malevich. During the period between 1927 and 1931, he produced some of his most intriguing theoretical tracts. Significantly, in these theoretical statements, Kharms is not addressing questions concerning art, but instead the ultimate questions about the existence and sense of objects, language, and actions. Some of these statements rest on Malevich's ideas. For example, the first of the "Eleven Statements by Daniil Ivanovich Kharms" is a clear tribute to the old nonobjectivist. It reads simply: "Objects are gone" (1997b, 304). As we have seen, in "The Werld" Kharms examines the idea of nothing as the blending of the "parts" into a universal whole. Unlike Malevich, Kharms leaves open the question of the absolute: the circle that accompanies the title is split in two. Differentiation of segments is still discernable on the surface of this continuous, unified world. In more than one way, this circle marks the difference between Malevich's and Kharms's projects. It points beyond the line inscribed in it vertically: while for Malevich the idea of nothing is an exclusively metaphysical category, for Kharms it remains tied to mathematics and mathematical logic. In the tract "Null and Nil" he distinguishes between the ideas of zero and nothing. He explains the general significance that this distinction holds for mathematics:

> 2) The notions of "more" and "less" are incorrect, as are the notions of "up" and "down." It is our personal idea to consider one number larger than the other, and following that principle we ordered the numbers, thus creating the Solar sequence. We only invented the order of numbers, not the numbers themselves. It will appear to many that the essence of a number depends on its position in the Solar sequence, but I dare to assert that number could be observed separately, independently from the system. Only that will be the true science of the number. (Kharms 1997b, 312)

In the broad metaphors that he develops in his Vitebsk writings, Malevich often borrows ideas and figures from astronomy, his favorite pastime. The metaphor of the "Solar sequence" for numerical order is the only trace of Malevichean thought in this essay. Kharms's approach to the idea of the number is closer to Pythagoras or Gottlob Frege, who conceived the number as a pure idea and not a tool for enumeration, than to Malevich or Velimir Khlebnikov. What definitively sets him apart from them is his identification of nothing and infinity:

> 4) I assume and even dare to argue that the learning about infinity will be the learning of nothing. I call nil, in distinction to null, precisely that which I mean by it.

Nine days later,[20] Kharms clarified this distinction:

> 5) The symbol of null—o. The symbol of nil—O. In other words, we will consider the circle the symbol of nil. (313)

Needless to say, Kharms's theses are mathematically unjustifiable. In every other way, poetically and philosophically above all, they are of great importance for understanding every line he drew during the last decade of his life. What does it mean that a number can be observed separately from the numerical system? What determines its value, or its "essence," if not its relation to other numbers?

The Fifth Meaning

By the time Kharms and Malevich met, the latter had already completed his major theoretical formulations on suprematism in painting. At that point, he was dedicated to pedagogical work at the State Institute for Artistic Culture. The most important part of his work with students at this period was devoted to the investigation of perception and the relation between the environment and artistic creation, which resulted in his theory of the "additional element" in painting. In November 1926 Malevich received an invitation from the Polish avant-garde magazine *Praesens* to give a lecture on his latest work. Toward the end of that year and in the first months of the following one, he was occupied with work on a series of twenty-two charts, which he used as visual support for lectures on the additional element in painting, which he was to give in Poland and Germany in the spring of 1927. The title of the Polish lecture was "The Analysis of Contemporary Trends in Art."[21] In Germany, the lectures were accompanied by the publication of Malevich's book *The Non-Objective World,* edited by the leaders of the Bauhaus, Walter Gropius and László Moholy-Nagy. In the first of the book's two essays, "Introduction to the Theory of the Additional Element in Painting," Malevich's comparative analysis of the form in paintings of different periods and styles results in the conclusion that "the work of art . . . comes into being independent of time, since art does not progress" (1959, 40). This might partially explain Malevich's inscription on the copy of *God Is Not Cast Down* which he presented to Kharms early in 1927: "Go and stop progress."[22]

The idea of the absence of progress stems directly from Malevich's ontology. One of the main empirical premises of his Vitebsk texts, informed by the disaster of the First World War, was the illusoriness of scientific progress. According to him, the idea of progress is foreign to all authentic art because there is no progression in the sphere of pure Being. The theory of the additional element in painting can be seen as a further refinement of this basic ontological position. Malevich tried to represent it schematically in the ninth chart of his lecture series, entitled "The Ideological Independence of New Art." In that simple diagram, Malevich's own *Black Square* is positioned between an icon of the Holy Mother and a realistic portrait. The icon belongs to the ideological sphere of religion, which is broader than the work of art (icon) itself. Similarly, the realistic portrait is framed by the plane of "good manners" and everyday life. In both cases the artistic form is subjected to content foreign to art. The black square is placed in the void between two planes. From it emanates another conceptual frame, that of nonutilitarian art, that cuts the icon and the portrait out of their ideological context. In his essay "Suprematism," Malevich compares the creation of this canvas with a departure to the desert of nonobjectivity. "No more 'likeness of reality,' no idealistic images—nothing but a desert!" (1959, 68). The desert is the place of the second temptation. Adamic temptation, as we have seen, leads to a terrible fall into the world of objectivity. The first temptation is marked by a clear dichotomy of the internal emptiness (bliss) of the First Man and the external fullness of Paradise. This first temptation, therefore, is a de-realization of the perfect state of being. The second temptation is diametrically opposed to the first one: here Christ, the second Adam, experiences internal fullness and self-reflection in the desert, which is the place of emptiness. The second temptation, the temptation of Christ by the devil, is the resuscitation of the fallen man. In his chart, Malevich points to the idea that the two "utilitarian paintings" are redeemed by the pure form of *Black Square,* which Malevich considered the originary gesture of painterly suprematism. An entire world has been born out of the desert: "The black square on the white field was the first form in which non-objective feeling came to be expressed. The square = feeling, the white field = the void beyond this feeling" (1959, 76). Critics such as Marcade and Groys unmistakably recognize the parallels between Malevich's and Heidegger's thought. Underneath Malevich's murky excursions about primordial, indivisible, and unmediated "excitement" and "nothingness," they correctly make out the outlines of a philosophy of Being. Groys asserts that, like Heidegger, Malevich is not trying to "offer a sign of transcendence, which is beyond all signification, but instead seeks the conditions for the existence of those signs." He adds, significantly, that "Malevich aspires to achieve in art that transition which thought does in its own sphere" (Groĭs 1982, 362). The basic suprematist forms, the white and black square, are not the absolute itself, but means of thinking of the absolute.

In "Suprematism: 34 Drawings" (1920) Malevich said that the suprematist white square stands for the action from which objects have been removed, or the pure action. This void of "white world building" is contrasted by the black square "as the sign of economy" (1968, 127). Marcade explains that Malevich ascribed two different meanings to the concept of economy: first, it is a principle and an instrument of rejection, and, second, a principle for reducing to being (1978a, 232). The pure action of the white square is the purity of nonobjectivity and the sharp clarity of the "desert."

The black square is the starting point, the initial gesture, of the new creation of the nonrepresentative and nonobjective symbolic forms. The purity of the white square is impossible without the operation of reduction to being in *Black Square.* "The black square determined economy, which I introduced as the fifth measure in art" (Malevich 1968, 127). Malevich's fifth measure brings art away from the world of objects and resemblances and closer to the question of Being. The same numerical designation appears in one of Kharms's central theoretical statements, "Objects and Figures Discovered by Daniil Ivanovich Kharms," written in August 1927.

Although in this tract the object is at the center of Kharms's attention, he does not show an inclination to follow Malevich in his repudiation of objects and, consequently, objectness. Moreover, his consideration of the subject-object relation seems to be in complete disagreement with Malevich's theory of nonobjectivity. Instead of the existence of a particular object in relation to the absolute (the thing, or the Being), Kharms's principal area of investigation is the object's meaning. Still, the assertions he makes do not ultimately pertain to a theory of language or a theory of meaning. His central insight weighs precisely upon the ontological status of the object.

Let's follow Kharms's line of reasoning:

First, upon stating his interest in the relation between the meaning of an object and its existence, he lists five different meanings that can be recognized in every object. The first four he declares as the "working meanings." Clearly, all of the working meanings concern the beholder's perception of the object. They are: graphic (or geometrical), utilitarian, and the emotional and esthetic meanings the object has for the observer.

Second, he sharply distinguishes the fifth meaning, which he calls "essential," from the four working meanings: "the fifth meaning is defined by the very fact of the existence of the object. It lies outside the connection between the object and man and serves the object itself. The fifth meaning is the free will of the object" (Kharms 1997b, 306). Clearly, the fifth, or essential, meaning of the object is at the center of Kharms's attention. The four working meanings belong to the beholder: they come from human consciousness and therefore are not specific to the object itself. As such, they correspond to Malevich's concept of "objective consciousness." These four meanings are not the locus of the object's authenticity, and they do not emanate from its thingness: they are the properties of thinking of the thing as an object. Through the four working meanings, says Kharms, "the object settles into the person's consciousness, where it then lives." The object, therefore, gives itself to the observer through its four working meanings.

Third, since the object gives itself to objectification and conceptualization through the four working meanings, we can say that these meanings are the means by which the beholder possesses the object. The fifth meaning is the line of flight. It is the avenue through which the object escapes the beholder's consciousness, conceptualization, and possession:

> The fifth, quintessential meaning is possessed by the object only outside of man, that is, by losing its father, its home, its native ground. Such an object "SOARS." (306)

The "quintessential meaning" marks the limit of thought, and Kharms's next step is to broaden its area of application from objects to gestures, actions, words, and thinking itself. In this final step, Kharms definitively departs from the ontological reduction that characterizes thinkers such as Malevich and Heidegger. His doctrine of the fifth meaning amounts to a claim that each object, each animal, each man, and even each gesture and action exists in its own unique and independent way. In Kharms's world everything is tentative; everything is in flux and in perpetual transformation. The fifth meaning asserts itself in its clearest and most poignant form in Kharms's writings from the late 1920s and early 1930s. It informs the "separateness of theatrical" gestures and events described in the "OBERIU Manifesto." Also, it animates the objects in the play *The Comedy of the City of St. Petersburg* (1927) and erases distinctions between human beings, plants, animals, and even letters and drawings in Kharms's other extraordinary dramatic work, *Lapa* (1930). Kobrinsky readily observed this strange tendency toward equalization in Kharms's works, characterizing it as "natural philosophy" and "infantilism" (2000, 120). It is not difficult to recognize in Kharms's doctrine of the "fifth meaning" the emergence of difference and a splintering of the totality of Malevich's nonobjectivity.

A large section of "Objects and Figures Discovered by Daniil Ivanovich Kharms" is dedicated to a consideration of the logical consequences of the fifth meaning doctrine. Kharms begins by investigating the possible impact of the reduction of the object's working meanings upon the beholder and asserts that if a beholder were to face an object that possesses less than four of its working meanings, he would "cease being a man."[23] Later, he adds that an encounter with the fifth meaning of the object would result in a similar dehumanization of the beholder (1997b, 307). In this particular instance, Kharms sees this loss of humanity as objectification.[24] The other two consequences directly pertain to his later work, and we can certainly trace a programmatic tone in the way they are laid out in "Objects and Figures Discovered by Daniil Ivanovich Kharms."

He recognizes that the concept of the five meanings results in a doubling of the object. It exists simultaneously as a concrete object and a concrete word:

> The fifth, essential, meaning of the object in a concrete system and in a discursive system is not the same. In the first case it is the free will of the object, and in the second case, it is the free will of the word. (307)

The word splits from the object, or from the idea. The signifier departs from the signified, which results in the demise of the process of signification. As a direct corollary of the principle of concreteness, there emerges the idea of a different, alternative, and nonhuman organizing principle of objects and words. Here we can find the explanation for Kharms's evasive reference in "Null and Nil" to an order of numbers that is different from the manmade "Solar sequence":

> 11. Any sequence of objects that interrupts the connection between their working meanings maintains the connection between their fifth, essential, meanings. The sequence of that kind is the sequence that is not related to man, and represents the thought of the objective world. If we examine such a sequence as a whole and as a newly created synthetic object, we can deduce new meanings, three in number: 1) geometric, 2) esthetic, 3) essential.

This new sequence differs significantly from the common sense of the observer:

> 12. If we transfer this sequence to another system, we will get a verbal order, which appears to man as NONSENSICAL. (307)

Concreteness, Case

In order to better understand Kharms's idea of concreteness in its relation to language, it would be useful to return briefly to Malevich. His attitude toward language is particularly intriguing because it is informed almost simultaneously by the Futurist search for the universal language and by an ontological mistrust in the signifier.

On the one hand, Malevich wrote of himself not only as a nonobjectivist (*bespredmetnik*), but also as a *besknizhnik* (Malevich 2000a, 134). The word "besknizhnik" is Malevich's neologism, created from the Russian words *bez* (non, less, or without) and *kniga* (book). If nonobjectivity renounces objects, this booklessness renounces positivist knowledge and scientific learning. For Malevich, however, the notion of booklessness contains a nuance of wordlessness, for there is no correct means of representation, linguistic or otherwise, of the absolute unity of Being. He dedicates large sections of "Suprematism as Pure Cognition" to attacks on falsity in science, painting, and literature. Although he does not dwell on the question of logos in relation to Being with Heidegger's persistence and power, he does not fail to mention that all naming conceals (2000a, 207–8). Malevich grants that nonobjectivity necessarily involves wordlessness and muteness because language and communication in general operate as a system of objectification. In his essay "On the Subjective and Objective in Art, or On Art in General" he states that communication annihilates subjective perception: from the moment of communication, of the transformation of thought into a coded sign, "subjective cognition becomes recognizable and hence deprived of its subjectivity" (1968, 33). Writing for Malevich has an ancillary function despite his claims that "one cannot attain with a brush what can be attained with a pen" (1968, 271). The point is that Malevich's brush is a pen. His suprematist canvases are tracts diagrammatized. The ultimate goal of his project is to find a symbol for the reduction to Being. *Black Square* is that privileged symbol.[25]

On the other hand, himself a poet, Malevich was actively engaged in the investigation of language undertaken by the Russian Futurists. In his 1919 essay "On Poetry," Malevich complains about "utilitarian reason" as an "indefatigable worker" on the transformation of "poetic steam" into "signs for its use" (1968, 75). His solution for outplaying and evading this ubiquitous work of reason is twofold: the first part of the solution is the creation of nonsensical words, "mad words" as he calls them, which is a poetic practice reminiscent of Futurist *zaum* ("trans-sense") poetry; the second part of the solution is a sort of direct bodily gesture that does not necessarily require codified language:

> The poet fears to reveal his groan, his voice, for in the groaning and the voice there are no things; they form pure, naked words, although these

> are not words as such, but only contained in words by virtue of letters. They have no substance, but there is the voice of the poet's being, true and pure, and the poet fears his very self.

Further on, Malevich adds that rhythm and tempo, the basic principles of all art, are expressed

> in action, in sounds, in clear signs that need no explaining, in pure movement, in the gesture tracing forms. (1968, 79)

Even after the period of his intense engagement with the Russian Futurist movement, Malevich remained convinced that *zaum* represented a viable solution for the problem of the exhaustion of language. In his Vitebsk manuscripts, there are attempts to incorporate *zaum* into his general theory of nonobjectivity.[26]

It is not difficult to recognize instances of *zaum* in Kharms's poetry. However, considering Kharms's closeness to the *zaum* poet Alexander Tufanov during his formative years as a poet, his lifelong admiration for Khlebnikov, and his association with Malevich, a surprisingly small number of Futurist innovations that include the use of *zaum* are detectable in Kharms's work.[27] Malevich's idea of "mad words," or language liberated from its ties with objects, is far from being the cornerstone of Kharms's poetic language. Instead, it is only one of the tools at the poet's disposal, a poetic device that Kharms often used in a playful and ambiguous manner.

While Malevich has the ambition of establishing a direct analogy between linguistic and visual representation in their relation to the object, Kharms sees this relation as infinitely more complex. As we have seen, through its four working meanings, the object enters consciousness and "lives" there. This transformation from concrete to conceptual object is so fundamental that the word achieves its own independent existence. According to Kharms, the word is neither purely objective nor purely conceptual. It has its own linguistic concreteness: "the word 'cupboard' and 'cupboard-concrete object' exist in the system of the concrete world together with other objects, rocks, and celestial bodies. The word 'cupboard' takes part in the conceptual system, together with words such as 'man,' 'sterility,' 'density,' 'passage,' etc." (1997b, 307). As a consequence, the fifth meaning of the object in the concrete system is different from the fifth meaning of the object in the "conceptual system" (language).

What indeed is this word, which is as concrete as an object and as immaterial as an idea? How can we comprehend the notion of the "free will" of the word? What could be the "essence" of the word if not to signify objects and concepts? And what about the idea that meaning obstructs communication? Malevich's prejudice against poetic language emerged precisely in response to the poet's subordination to the symbolic power of language. Since language by its nature is metaphorical, the poet is doomed to separation from his own being. Language obscures, rather than reveals, the innermost subjectivity of the poet. Unless he breaks language down into "mad words," he cannot move further than the dusty surface of conventional language: "the poet speaks only through the clothes about clothes, about those distinguishing marks necessary to reason and its provision-store, its pawnshop" (1968, 75). Language, as Malevich sees it, is reason at work: it is reason that deciphers itself, that expresses itself to itself. He therefore protests the very foundation of language: its self-sameness. More precisely, he opposes the fact that by its very nature, language imposes severe limitations upon creativity. Linguistics locates these limits of language at its metaphoric and metonymic poles. Himself a former Futurist, linguist Roman Jakobson is adamant about this point in his *Fundamentals of Language:*

> The development of a discourse may take place along two different semantic lines: one topic may lead to another either through their similarity or through their contiguity. The METAPHORIC way would be the most appropriate term for the first case and the METONYMIC way for the second, since they find their most condensed expression in metaphor and metonymy respectively. (Jakobson and Halle 1956, 90; original emphasis)

Sure enough, Malevich's attack on language is aimed not only at the metaphoric principle of substitution but also at the metonymic principle of contiguity. They are both based on the assumption of signification. Kharms's tract represents a bold attempt at departure from this widely accepted theory of language.

The "fifth meaning," or the "free will," of the word suggests that language is independent from human will and reason, and that the word has its own meaning that does not have to point to objects, ideas, or feelings, or, indeed, to other words. In one of his diary entries, Kharms talks about the power concentrated in words, most notably present in what he calls "language machines":

> The power contained in words has to be released. There are such arrangements of words in which the effects of this power become evident. It would not be advisable to assume that this power could move objects. Although, I am sure that the power of words could do even that. But, the most important effect of the power escapes definition. We can get a rough idea of the power through the rhythm of metric verses. Still, even such complex ideas as the impact of certain metric verses on the movement of certain body parts should not be discounted. That is the most obvious and the weakest example of words' power. Other effects of this power can barely be conceived. If we, however, look for the method of investigation of this power, it has to be entirely different from everything that was used in scientific research thus far. First of all, we can't use as proof facts or experiments. Neither can I say exactly how the conclusions should be proved or tested. So far, I know of four kinds of language machines: verses, prayers, songs, and spells. These machines are not constructed by way of calculation or reasoning, but by another way, which is called ALPHABET. (Kharms 2002b, 174; original emphasis)

This entry, written in May 1931, contains several statements important for the understanding of the notion of language's concreteness. For one thing, as Yampolsky observed, Kharms is not interested here in the word's power to communicate. He is not addressing the question of meaning or semantics but of the "pure energetics" of language (Iampol'skii 1997, 59). It is also interesting that he takes as examples of "language machines" those linguistic forms in which energy, either physical or psychic, takes precedence over meaning: the metric rhythm of verses is just as important as their meaning; similarly, songs depend on both rhythm and melody. In spells, the meaning of the words is often intentionally obscured; prayer is not exclusively a literary form, but even more, a form of address, a statement composed at the moment of utterance. Furthermore, writing as a process of mediation is altered or completely absent in all of the "language machines." Kharms claims that it is true that not only does the body dictate the language but also the other way around. He brings up the example of verses that bear on the body not through their conceptual meaning but precisely through their characteristics that escape the process of signification, such as meter and rhythm. This breakdown of semantics is also prevalent in the notion of "alphabetization." Here, the word as the primary signifying form is atomized and broken into letters, the meaningless rudiments from which it is composed. If the word's meaning emerges from the overall arrangement of letters, its power is stored in between the letters. In other words, if the word's sense rests in the arrangement of letters, its power comes from its de-composition, or as Yampolsky notes, from its fission and splitting into basic elements (Iampol'skii 1997, 59).

Kharms does not see alphabetization as a process that results in confusion and obscurity. It is quite the opposite, a process of simplification and clarification. The ideas of alphabetization and language machines are closely related to Kharms's idea of clarity, or purity. In his diary Kharms relates this category to the specific verses from his 1930 drama *Gvidon.* He remarks that "clarity has been achieved" in the following verses:

Monk:
The letter *yat'* comes to the gate.
Should I let it in?
Abbot:
Yes, yes, let it in.

And then he adds: "the monk and abbot are spoiling" (2002a, 444). A strange turn occurs in this passage from *Gvidon.* It seems as if the entire drama, the action itself, turns from the fictional characters, the dramatis personae, to the concrete characters, the letters inscribed on the page. If the notion of clarity, like alphabetization, implies a reduction to the letter, then its primary importance is not in a total destruction of meaning but in establishing an interaction between the meaningful and meaningless elements of the word. Alphabetization calls attention to the sonic aspects of speech, and to the material aspects of written language. It makes sure that the materiality of language is not repressed and erased by its meaning.

Kharms does not arbitrarily take *yat'* as the renegade letter that has to be fetched from the gate. Together with three other signs, the letter *yat'* was dropped out of the Russian alphabet in the orthographic reforms introduced in the aftermath of the October Revolution of 1917. In these reforms, the letters Ѳ, Ѣ, and і were replaced by Ф, е, and и. In his manuscripts from the late 1920s and early 1930s, Kharms often used the Greek Ѳ from the old Cyrillic orthography instead of the new Ф. Curiously, in this passage of *Gvidon* he chooses to spell out the letter "ять" (*yat'*) instead of writing out the sign ѣ directly from the old orthography. The brief exchange Kharms cites as the example of clarity follows the Abbot's monologue in which he addresses the play's protagonist, Gvidon:

Your bliss is full of sadness
blue vanities and the moon
it's to the letters *a b c d*
that your capons gallop
it's reason racing bravely
that produces that wild scream
our thought's continent
spirit's hawk and body's lion
so love from the depths of the body
flames up like a fire
and love's mighty cedar
holds a banner over common sense
here doubt appears
the frightening ditch of the world's gift
the scimitar of nature the thunder of confusion
the stomach's fungus the cover of passion
the rivers of our learning are drying up
a herd of quick gazelles
gallops in our majestic skull
filling the air with cries
full of bliss. It's a sin
the skull will crack like a nut.
(1997b, 466)[28]

The conflict between reason and emotions is the central theme of this monologue. In the opening stanzas, the nocturnal imagery of silence and contemplativeness is confronted by the figures of speed and action. At first, it comes as a surprise that they are adjoined by the alphabet (*a b c d*). However, as the monologue progresses, it becomes clear that Kharms associates letters with the emotions, body, and raw expression, which clash with the conceptual powers of the mind. The traditional split between the feelings and intellect, body and mind, subjectivity and the outside world, is joined by the pairs alphabet/language and letter/word. Midway through the monologue, the body seizes the advantage over reason: the banner rises high on the pole made of the precious cedar wood.[29] In this play, the name of the protagonist, Gvidon, comes from Pushkin's fairy tale poem *The Tale of Tsar Saltan, of His Son Glorious and Mighty Knight Prince Gvidon Saltanovich and the Fair Swan-Princess.*[30] Pushkin's poem and fairy tales related to it share some prominent motifs, such as swan and star, with

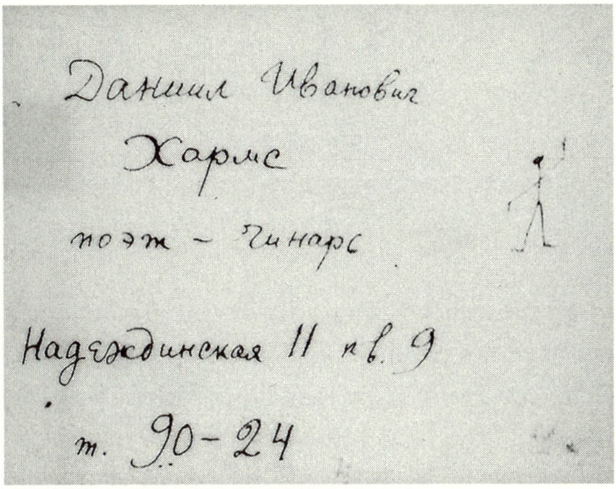

Figure 3.

Kharms's homemade calling card

Lapa, another Kharms play from this period. However, in choosing "Gvidon" as the name of his play's main character, Kharms reaches beyond Pushkin's poem. The raised banner could easily stand as a reference to the Italian word for flag holder, *guidone.* As we are going to see, Kharms associated poetry with heights and flag-raising. The main characters of the play, Gvidon and Lisa, stand for Kharms himself and his wife, Ester Rusakova, to whom he dedicated the play.[31] If we now return to the monologue, we will find that this thinly disguised self-reference is followed by the image of a skull that becomes dominant in the final stanzas. The skull is progressively hollowed, until it is reduced to an empty shell that falls down, like a walnut. In *Lapa* a decapitated body becomes a letter. The exchange about the letter *yat'* can be seen as another instance of alphabetization of the body. In the debates that surrounded the orthographic reforms, the conservatives argued for preservation of this sign because of its "sacredness." The Futurist poet Vassily Kamensky retorted that he saw the *yat'* sign not as a cruciform symbol, but as a skeleton (Janecek 1984, 18).

Alphabetization always involves a double movement. On the one hand, it is, as Yampolsky recognized, a "de-figuration" and removal of the meaning conventionally attached to signs (Iampol'skii 1997, 59). On the other hand, together with this literalization comes the affirmation of the pictorial aspect of the letter and its form. Quite playfully, Kharms associates this form with the shape of the human body. On his handmade calling card, the name, address, and profession ("poet-chinar") are accompanied by a schematic drawing of the human body (figure 3).

Figure 4.

The code from Arthur Conan Doyle's story "The Dancing Men"

Kharms had a pronounced interest in cryptography and hieroglyphics, which is evident in the marked similarity between the drawing on his card and the secret code deciphered by his favorite literary character in Arthur Conan Doyle's story, "The Dancing Men"[32] (figure 4).

By bringing together body and letter, alphabetization turns writing into choreography. Kharms assigned a considerable importance to the material aspects of the text, to its congruity with the hand that writes. It seems that he thought about the manual aspect of writing not only in terms of graphology, that is to say, as a tic or a symptom—something that unwillingly betrays the writer's character—but also as a discipline. At least, that appears as the primary significance of the notion of "clarity." The observation about clarity in verses from *Gvidon* is followed by another entry on the same issue:

> It is necessary to go through the path of purification (*Perseveratio, Katharsis*). It should start exactly with the alphabet, i.e., with letters. (2002a, 444)

Kharms's ideas about the concreteness of language and its congruity with the body complement Lipavsky's theory of language, which he formulated in the essay "Theory of Words," and in several sections of "Conversations."[33] The starting premise of Lipavsky's theory is that a letter, not a word, represents the basic unit of language. Lipavsky narrows down this point of origin even further, to consonants, which he calls a "word's seeds" (Lipavskii 2005, 211). A seed develops into a word through a series of transformations: accumulation, repetition, combination, and "rotation,"[34] all of which produce sound as the primary carrier of language. Here, Lipavsky is generally in agreement with Ferdinand de Saussure's linguistics (Saussure 1966). However, already at the next step, his theory radically diverges from structural linguistics. In contrast to Saussure's theory of signification, according to which a signifier (spoken or written word) refers to the signified that is an object or a concept, Lipavsky believes that words primarily designate what he calls "elements," or basic conditions, and only later do they name objects, actions, and concepts.[35] Lipavsky attaches great significance to the notion of an elementary state, or basic condition. He explains this concept by evoking the surviving remnants of an "elementary world-view," such as the phenomenon of odor, which is not an action, has no form, and cannot be acted upon but instead seems to possess some kind of sovereign existence: "We similarly understand heat, cold, and many meteorological phenomena and psychological states; they exist independently, they spread out, they can absorb each other, they have a certain intensity (density or strength) and at the same time they are not objects" (228). The elementary state is the basic condition, the condition of baseness, or simply an unconditioned condition.

Lipavsky's "Theory of Words" is based on the premise that language, like nature, operates according to the principle of total expenditure. Conversely, Saussure's linguistics is based on the principle of exchange and of hearing-oneself-speaking: released from the speaker, voiced language has to have a recipient, a goal. The purpose of the voice is to be heard. The breath is, as it were, saved and preserved by the ear. Such a teleological and utilitarian view of language is completely foreign to Lipsavsky's theory of language, which is based on the principle that can be described as feeling-oneself-speaking: "Words are not born from perception of sounds, colors, or odors, but from muscular strength. The basic sensation in speech is the sensation of the speech apparatus, and not its aural perception" (258). This is the language as absolute excess: speaking-oneself-speaking, or giving oneself in speech. Meaning is formed through physical activity, not through perception: "The point of origin is breathing, the final point—the world of solid objects in which we live; meaning goes through such a laborious and long journey" (226). There is no such thing as arbitrariness of the signifier in Lipavsky's theory. Quite on the contrary, there is a certain permanence and absoluteness to language. If its main principle is expenditure, language has to have a certain totality that is released and lost. For Saussure, communication is provided by the reciprocity of breathing and hearing, voice and ear; for Lipavsky, language is produced by muscular activity and "projected" not to an organ of hearing, but onto the world, which is only an outline, a drawing that receives the word. Language is a stream that flows out from the speaker and into the world that is its receptacle.[36] This is the stadium of language Lipavsky calls "projection on fluid." The "fluid" that Lipavsky talks about is neither a fresh running stream nor stagnant receding water. It is a dense matter that can be formed and molded. In *Water and Dreams: An Essay on the Imagination of Matter,* Gaston Bachelard talks about the viscosity of clay, an admixture of water and earth. This paste, he says, is a "duration associated with work," with a molding hand. Clay, the unformed matter, invites work and therefore "produces the dynamic hand." He associates this special kind of fluid with the force of projection: "Here there is a natural projection. Here we have a particular case of projective thought that conveys all thoughts, all actions, all reveries from man to things, from worker to the piece of work" (Bachelard 1983, 108). Bachelard is more direct in his analysis of reverie than Lipavsky in his analysis of the word. The muscular strength that produces language is another name for work aimed at the unformed, viscous world. Words are concrete and absolute, not abstract and arbitrary. And language is a muscular effort, a physical labor.

Lipavsky looks for the proofs for his bold theoretical statements in the structure of words, in their history and origins. For instance, he deduces the principles of the "projection on fluid" from the analysis of the words *rech'* (word) and *reka* (river). This intuitive procedure of word analysis was promoted by the Russian Futurist poet Velimir Khlebnikov, and it had a great impact on Russian poetry in the first decades of the twentieth century. Lipavsky readily admits his indebtedness to Khlebnikov on several occasions.[37] Kharms's notion of the free will of the word, Lipavsky's theory of language, and Khlebnikov's investigations of word origins are all based on a belief in a certain authentic force and sovereignty of language. Consider the following word analysis by Khlebnikov:

> In the words *tak* [thus] and *tot* [that], we find the iron immobility of heavy [*tiazhelye*] things; we feel the presence of fettered angles fixed so firmly to the ground that no tremor can shake them, while in the particle of doubt, *li,* we find the separation of the personal principle itself from the universal, a kind of upward flight on the wings of the wind. It would seem then that fact is the essence of the force of gravity. Freedom from this force is called *li,* while rootedness, submission to it, is expressed by the adverb *tak.*
>
> This conjunction of cognitive forces and the forces of gravity is remarkable. It would seem that the principle we call language knows more about gravity than we do. (Khlebnikov 1987, 268)[38]

The principle we call language is not a utility or a communication tool, but something more than that. Each word has its own knowledge and its own history. Khlebnikov and Lipavsky are investigating not only the meaning of the word. There is much more to meaning than the play of words, they seem to say. What we perceive as a language game is actually a strictly determined network of rules. We are not playing with words: they are interacting with each other, acting upon each other, thus forming chains and entire genealogies, families, and societies. Words have their own integrity and their own force. And, above all, they are perceived, but are also perceiving one another. Khlebnikov's idea about words' knowledge of the world, and therefore of one another, strongly resembles Whitehead's idea of "prehensions" as "*uncognitive apprehensions*" (Whitehead 1967, 69). Prehensions are unities, or, as Whitehead calls them, prehensive events: "each event is an individual matter of fact issuing from an individualization of the substrate activity" (70). Lipavsky, Vvedensky, and Kharms understood very well Khlebnikov's epochal intervention of removal of the agent from poetic language. In "Conversations" Lipavsky talked about him as a "reformer of humanity" (2005, 325). This reform concerns the transformation of writing from the mere use of language into an interaction and active collaboration with it. For Kharms as well as for Lipavsky, words are not empty shells, "dusty clothes" that are filled with different meanings. Similarity between words, then, does not reveal the emptiness and relativity of their meaning, but precisely the opposite: it indicates their non-arbitrariness. Lipavsky concludes: "in language there is no such thing as a metaphor" (240).

There is no trope as contrary to Kharms's notion of the "fifth meaning" as the metaphor. It is based on transferring, carrying over—*metapherain*—meaning from one term to another. Meaning seems to always reside outside of metaphor. The transfer displaces the meaning outside of the word, which indeed turns into the "dusty clothes" that Malevich disapproves of so energetically. Metaphor is made possible by the transferability of meaning, the same process by which its very terms are rendered disposable.[39] It rests on the idea that the word, not the world, is an outline, a sketch that needs to be filled out and colored by meaning. Nonmetaphorical language envisioned by Lipavsky is projective, while metaphorical language is introjective. In his only mention of modern literature in *Of Grammatology,* Derrida points to Kafka's despair over writing that cannot avoid using introjective language that is dependent on the outside, nonliterary, world. Derrida implies that the most modernism can do is protest against the metaphor because "literature, which lives by being outside itself, within the figures of a language which is primarily not its own, would die as well through a reentry into itself by way of the nonmetaphor" (Derrida 1976, 272). Literature thrives on the metaphor's restlessness and approximation of meaning, on the imprecision and elusiveness of poetic language: "a precise and exact language should be absolutely univocal and literal [proper]: nonmetaphorical" (1976, 271). Unlike Kafka, Kharms does not complain and protest against metaphoricity: he plainly rejects it. What does it mean, then, to write with an eye toward the "fifth meaning" of the word? Does it mean to renounce writing? To give up writing?

Yes, if we consider nonmetaphoricity as the exactness of meaning. Kharms shows that the rejection of metaphor is neither a question of style nor despondency over language. It is the question of allowing things to happen in language, not only in the process of writing but in the text itself. What I have called concreteness refers back to "Objects and Figures Discovered by Daniil Ivanovich Kharms" and the assertion that the word is the thing. In his examination of the semantics of the word "thing," Heidegger goes to the Roman word *causa* and its original meaning as that which is the case: "only because 'cause,' almost synonymously with *res,* means the case, can the word 'cause' later come to mean cause, in the sense of causality and effect" (1971, 175). The soaring object, or word, is exempt from the chain of cause and effect. It effects itself. Kharms explains that the series formed by the fifth meaning appears to man as nonsensical. The fifth meaning, therefore, is not the cause but the case in the sense that it has no relation to anything else. It is the case. The case is incidental only insofar as it doesn't comply with rational logic.

First: If you call all objects statues, then OK.
Second: I would have called stars or immobile clouds statues. As for me, I would have.
Third: I am running to God—I'm a runaway.
Second: I know that I killed myself.

—Alexander Vvedensky, "A Certain Quantity of Conversations" (1936–37)

2. Writing Without Difference

Clarity of Order

There is an apparent contradiction that emerges in the analysis of Kharms's ideas about language and writing. On the one hand, there is a strong resistance to metaphorical language, revealed most prominently in his pronouncements about language machines, the concreteness of the poetic text, and, as we are going to see, the perfect gift. And in "Blue Notebook No. 10" he provides an exquisite proof that such adherence to the nonmetaphor does not have to end in the destruction of the discursive text. On the other hand, this resistance to the metaphoric nature of language often proves to be too difficult a doctrine to maintain. That is why Kharms resorts to the desemiotization of alphabetic writing, its spatialization, and to the transformation of words into pictorial signs akin to hieroglyphs.

Kharms hardly ever deals with the question of style and only generally with aesthetics. In his theoretical texts, he expresses more interest in problems of mathematical logic than in those of literary style. In his other writings, mostly in plays and prose pieces, he often resorts to citational techniques of pastiche and parody, and seems to gladly embrace textual models and even clichés. One of his favorite ways to begin a narrative is, as is obvious in "Blue Notebook No. 10," with the phrase "there was" (*byl,* or *zhil-byl*), which is customary for children's tales and fables, and is also often used in everyday storytelling and even gossip. He also borrows the form of nonliterary narratives, such as mathematical problems. The opening sentence of the story "The Hunters" sounds almost exactly as if it came from an elementary school textbook in mathematics: "Six men went hunting, but only four returned" (2007, 72). An untitled text begins in a similar way: "The streetcar is running. There are eight passengers in it. Three of them are sitting: two on the right and one on the left" (1997b, 24). Finally, another noticeable characteristic of both his prose and plays is the laconic tone of narration and dialogue. We need only remember the story "Events," in which the inventory of senseless deaths ends with the laconic conclusion: "All good people but they don't know how to hold their ground" (2007, 42).

One of Kharms's rare remarks on the issue of style in writing appears in his letter to Claudia Pugacheva, dated November 4, 1933. Even on this occasion, he addresses the question of style only to change the statement he had just made. Not surprisingly, this correction is aimed at the purging of a metaphor: "I visited Marshak and told him about you. His eyes were so shiny, and his heartbeat was so on fire. (See, an entirely inappropriate and unpretty phrase sneaked in again. Such rubbish! Marshak with flaming eyes!)" (Kharms 2001a, 84).[1] We can read the parenthetical comment as evidence of Kharms's writerly discipline. It results in a Kharmsian text with characteristic brevity and rudimentariness. Kharms never engages in a lengthy explanation or psychological motivation of an action. He never ventures beyond the surface of an event. As superbly exemplified in "Blue Notebook No. 10," instead of capturing an event, the language becomes the event itself. In Kharms's work, there is no introspection driven by a consciousness that observes, merges with its surroundings, experiences, and endures. In this respect, Kharms is the exact opposite of Joyce. All stylistic qualities of Kharms's writing, from its laconicism to the excision of interiority, can be seen as aspects of the larger project: the purgation of metaphor. And this intolerance of metaphor comes from Kharms's seemingly endless confidence in the word. This confidence does not originate in the mastery of language and its full possession, but, conversely, in the conviction that it cannot ever be fully or even sufficiently owned. There is a limit to the use of language. At a certain point, the word withdraws into itself. For Kharms, writing is not about the utilization of language, but rather collaboration with it. There is no "style" in writing: only ordering, sequencing, and spacing words. Kharms returns to the question of order in his last extant theoretical text, "A Tract (More or Less) According to a Synopsis of Emersen [*sic*],"[2] written in February 1939. We have seen that in "Objects and Figures Discovered by Daniil Ivanovich Kharms" he establishes an essential duality of the object: it gives itself to an observer through its four working meanings, and it resists and withdraws through its essential fifth meaning. Consequently, a group of objects, or a series, in which the linkage of the "working meanings" has been disturbed reveals the alternative connection of the fifth meaning. In "On Gifts," the first section of "A Tract (More or Less) According to a Synopsis of Emersen," Kharms employs a similar line of reasoning to talk about "perfect" and "imperfect" gifts. The imperfect gift is the object lost in the chain of utility: an inkwell lid that asks for an inkwell; or an inkwell with a lid that asks for a support such as a table, which asks for a chair, and so on, ad infinitum. Conversely, the perfect gift is a self-contained object or an object that disrupts the chain of utility: a lid becomes a perfect gift if the recipient already owns an inkwell. "Decorations of the naked body such as rings, bracelets, necklaces" are perfect gifts, and so would be "a stick [. . .] to the end of which has been attached a wooden ball and to the other end a wooden cube. Such a stick can be held in the hand or, if one puts it down it doesn't matter at all where. Such a stick is no use for anything else" (2007, 249). If the imperfect gift disappears in the chain formed by its own usefulness, the perfect gift disrupts such a series by its self-sufficiency and futility. A series of imperfect gifts is based on the principles of linearity and progression. The perfect gifts form a strange series based on difference, or on the principle of disjunctive synthesis.

The notion of order is most commonly related to the numerical progression of real numbers. In "The Werld" Kharms rejects this kind of order as a concept that is forced upon numbers. That does not mean that he summarily dismisses the model of the numerical sequence in which real numbers progress by the simple addition of one. For example, the additive sequence represents the most evident organizing principle of Kharms's texts. Also, he uses enumeration in the internal structuring of the texts, especially theoretical tracts that are, as a rule, divided into enumerated short paragraphs. Although the numerical progression sanctions linearity, Kharms also uses it as a means of creating nonlinear narratives.

Two enumerated texts stand out. Both of them are addressed, in one way or another, to a philosopher,[3] and in both of them a series of seemingly unrelated events is brought together by an invisible series of causes and effects. In the first segments of "The Connection" (1937), a group of hooligans attack a violinist and knock off his hat; the segment outlines a series of seemingly unrelated events that takes place over fourteen years, until in the twentieth fragment the sons of the violinist and one of the hooligans are riding in the same tram, completely unaware of one another and their connection. In "Five Unfinished Narratives" (1931), the possibility of the series and its demise are related directly to the notion of thinking. The series begins with smashing a head against a wall:

> 1. A certain man, having taken a run, struck his head against a smithy with such a force that the blacksmith put aside the sledgehammer he was holding, took off his leather apron, and having smoothed his hair with his palm, went out on the street to see what happened. 2. The smith spotted the man sitting on the ground. The man was sitting on the ground and holding his head. 3. "What happened?" asked the smith. "Ooh!" said the man. 4. The smith went a bit closer to the man. 5. We discontinue the narrative about the smith and the unknown man and begin a new narrative about four friends and a harem. (1993, 90)

The series of narratives begins with the smith and head-smashing, and ends with a philosopher and the flowing of thoughts:

> 8. There was a barrel of beer and next to it sat a philosopher who contended: "This barrel is full of beer; the beer is fermenting and strengthening. And I in my mind ferment along the starry summits and strengthen my spirit. Beer is a drink flowing in space; I also am a drink, flowing in time. 9. When beer is enclosed in a barrel, it has nowhere to flow. Time will stop and I will stand up. 10. But if time does not stop, then my flow is immutable. 11. No, it's better to let the beer flow freely, for it's contrary to the laws of nature for it to stand still." And with these words the philosopher turned on the tap in the barrel and the beer poured out over the floor. 12. We have related enough about the beer; now we shall relate about the drum. (1993, 90)

The additive sequence is but a vehicle for a powerful assertion regarding a different kind of series and the spatialization of text. On the one hand, the story about the beer barrel and the philosopher can be read as a reference to Heraclitus's idea of flux, but it also points to Kharms's own idea of the "flowing thought," which is opposed to logical thinking.[4] On the other hand, thought is not the only thing that flows: writing, like a numerical series, proceeds by adding one letter to another, one word to another. Linear progression does not apply only to numerical order and the order of words, but also to the organization of objects: namely, to the series of imperfect gifts. Curiously, Kharms chooses the inkwell as an example of both a perfect and imperfect gift. An inkwell together with the lid, a closed ink container, is an imperfect gift. A perfect gift would be an object that rounds up and completes the open inkwell.[5]

For Kharms, writing equipment represents the concreteness and materiality of writing. His narratives often conclude with a turn to a metatextuality that identifies the end of the narrative with the end of writing. For example, the story "Knights" ends in the following way: "with this the author is finishing the narrative, since he cannot find the ink-pot" (1993, 140). This self-reference is also potentially a beginning for a terrible series of imperfect gifts: from author to the pen, from pen to page, from page to the table, and so on. This kind of additive progression obstructs the flow. Writing is not in-scription in the sense of arresting but precisely the opposite: an outpouring and a flow. Paradoxically, this flow emerges from the collapse of the linear progression. Writing flowingly, like thinking flowingly, is not logical. The demise of logic, according to Kharms, has the virtue of revealing the order formed according to his doctrine of the fifth meaning, or a series based on the principle of disjunctive synthesis.

The archaeology of Kharms's work, either in manuscript or in published version, often yields surprising pieces in which similar figures, situations, or narratives are used to produce completely different models of thought. So, in an untitled text we find the principle of the additive (. . . and . . .) series combined with the notion of spatial ordering:

> Here I am sitting on a chair. And the chair stands on the floor. And the floor is part of the house. And the house is on the earth. And the earth extends in all directions, to the right, and to the left, and in the front, and in the back. And where does it end? (Kharms 1998b, 32)

The same idea is used in sections two and three of "A Tract (More or Less) According to a Synopsis of Emersen" to approach the notion of disjunctive synthesis (either-or). Kharms begins the second section, "The Correct Way of Surrounding Oneself with Objects," by outlining an additive series. He offers the example of a "completely naked" person who, settling into an empty apartment, furnishes his dwelling with a chair, which requires a desk, which demands a lamp. The process of addition is endless because, Kharms writes, every point of the system could potentially branch into a subsystem:

On the round table one would want to spread a napkin, on the napkin place a vase, and in the vase one would want to stick a flower. This way of surrounding oneself with objects whereby one object clings to another is incorrect because if there are no flowers in the flower vase then such a vase is rendered meaningless, and if one is to take away the vase then the round table becomes meaningless. (Kharms 2007, 249)

The additive series is organized according to the usefulness of objects that enter its structure: the connectivity refers primarily to the utilitarian aspect of the object. Conversely, the disjunctive series does not depend on the utility of its members: it can be formed by either this or that object precisely because the objects don't have any purpose or use value. The absence of meaning, or of common sense, is the organizing principle of Kharms's disjunctive series. Although in "Objects and Figures Discovered by Daniil Ivanovich Kharms," he asserts that the "fifth meaning principle" is revealed in nonsense, in a letter to Claudia Pugacheva he describes the same idea as the "*clarity of order*" (2001a, 79, italics in the original). Yampolsky explains that the disjunctive series is at the same time transcendental: "in this case 'clarity' stands for the unrelatedness of the order to myself. . . . 'Clarity' does not belong to the group that I am manipulating, but to the world" (Iampol'skii 1997, 353). So, if the objects in an additive series are easily rendered meaningless, then its initiator is also easily rendered meaningless. That is why Kharms recommends the reverse procedure:

If the naked superintendent were to dress himself in rings and bracelets and surround himself with spheres and celluloid salamanders, then the loss of twenty-seven objects would not change the essence of the thing. Such a system of surrounding oneself with objects is the correct system. (2007, 249)[6]

The naked body is the body without physical shelter, but also the body without protection from human relations and feelings, including the feeling of shame. Nakedness is the original state. In one of his pseudo-autobiographical narratives about his own birth, Kharms says that he was born in the reeds and describes his encounter with a frog while lying naked in the water. He converses with the frog and they wonder, "why should we be ashamed of our fine bodies, given us by nature, when we are not ashamed of the vile acts that we ourselves perpetrate?" (Kharms 2007, 210). The body itself is the gift. Nakedness is not a state of vulnerability and incompleteness, but of self-sufficiency and perfection. Clothes and possessions indicate the needs of an incomplete, vulnerable man. Jewels and adornments on the naked body are not a response to utilitarian needs. They are an addition, always in excess. The purpose of this extravagance is not utilitarian but purely ornamental. In *A Thousand Plateaus,* Deleuze and Guattari associate writing with tools, and jewels with weapons. Work is an organized activity, and in order "for there to be work, there must be a capture of activity by the State apparatus, and a semiotization of activity by writing" (Deleuze and Guattari 1987, 401). If semiotized writing designates the operation of capture and fixing of an activity, ornamentation and jewelry designates its release. However, they warn that jewelry and ornamentation do not represent proper writing, "even though they have a power of abstraction that is in every way equal to that of writing" (401). Deleuze and Guattari are not trying to show that ornamentation is the same as writing. Ornamentation, unlike writing, has an extremely limited communication value. It is not a transcription of a spoken language. It resists decipherment. Jewelry and adornments constitute "an affective semiotic," a "text that is ornamental rather than scriptural, 'an invention with little utility, half aborted,' a substitute writing" (402). It is important to point out that ornamentation is not posited as a system capable of completely replacing alphabetic writing or as a predecessor of the phonetic sign.[7] It does not contest the alphabet, but instead complements it.

Kharms's advice about the correct "system of surrounding oneself with objects" is followed by the section titled "The Correct Way of Annihilating Surrounding Objects." This is the central segment of the five-part tract, and it is dedicated, as its title suggests, to the removal of peripheral objects. We have seen that the connections Kharms establishes between the object and the word lead inevitably to the question of writing: the notions "concreteness of the case" and "clarity of order" unambiguously pertain to writing. Writing seen as an interaction with and an attitude toward the world receives its final shape in the notion of the perfect gift. The perfect gift is not only a useless object but also a useless symbol, a sign without signification. The main characteristic of this meaningless sign is its resistance to logos.

The first cardinal way in which the meaningless sign defies logos is by obliterating not only the form, but also the function, of the written word. In the third part of the tract, Kharms presents, in effect, a concept of writing that subverts itself. The "system of perfect gifts" does not perform a utilitarian function of any kind, and it does not contain information or any other kind of symbolic meaning. It neither communicates nor stores information. It is a cipher without a key. It is the writing that forgets. This forgetting is not a loss of the memory of things previously known, experienced, learned, or imagined. It pertains to the memory of memory, or that which Deleuze describes as "transcendental memory" and "essential forgetting":

> Transcendental memory . . . grasps that which from the outset can only be recalled, even the first time: not a contingent past, but the being of the past as such and the past of every time. In this manner, the forgotten thing appears in person to the memory which essentially apprehends it. It does not address memory without addressing the forgetting within memory. (Deleuze 1994, 140)

Not surprisingly, Kharms's writing falters in the sections that follow the central paradox of the perfect gifts. His difficulty with developing the idea is still further evidenced in the manuscript, which contains the three false starts of the tract's fourth section. In the first attempt, entitled "The Correct Way of Annihilating Oneself," Kharms tries to respond to the hypothetical offer to take the place of Henry Ford's grandson "and be happy"; the second, much shorter, version is entitled "World Without Objects"; the third attempt at the fourth section is so heavily scratched over that it turns into rows of ink blots on the page.[8] It could be argued that this series of ink stains represents the only consistent way of continuing the tract about the appearance of forgetfulness. In the final version of the fourth segment, Kharms breaks away from the idea of the perfect gift and transforms it into a discourse, "On Approaching Immortality." Paradoxically, then, the more Kharms departs from the question of the perfect gift, the less his tract adheres to Emerson.[9]

Hieroglyphics

The propensity for hieroglyphism nurtured by Kharms and his friends was first noted by Yakov Druskin. According to him, the idea of hieroglyphism does not pertain to pictorial writing of any kind, but instead represents the practice of fashioning broad poetic symbols and their complex usage. He asserts that Lipavsky's "hieroglyph" has its proper and improper meaning. The former is literal, while the latter "can't be determined exactly and unequivocally; it can be transferred only *metaphorically,* poetically, sometimes by putting together logically incompatible notions, that is, through antinomy, contradiction, nonsense" (Druskin 1998, 551, italics added). So, metaphor finds its way into this definition of the OBERIU (or Chinari) hieroglyph. It should be noted that Druskin's idea of hieroglyphism differs from Tamara Lipavskaya's practice of it. Namely, she seems to rely on the notion of nonlinear and hieroglyphic writing in order to distribute Vvedensky's "A Certain Quantity of Conversations" on a grid. This manipulation makes it possible to read the linear text both vertically and horizontally. Again, in "The Star of Nonsense" it is hard to tell where Lipavskaya's interventions end and Druskin's interpretation begins. It is certain, however, that his doctrine of hieroglyphism as a critical tool is hardly applicable to Kharms, whose *mise en page* includes both pictorial and phonetic writing. It is not surprising that the two kinds of writing, pictorial and alphabetic, not only complement but also interpret one another. The symbol appears both as an image and a word. But that is not all: it seems to go back and forth quite liberally, and it even takes a prominent role in the formation of much larger structures, such as the writer's personal cosmology. In order to understand Kharms's notion of the hieroglyph, we should begin with his engagement with Ralph Waldo Emerson, who took the practice of modern hieroglyphics beyond the mere imitation of the ancient ones.

In "Nature," his first published work, Emerson sees words as "natural facts" transformed. However, "It is not words only that are emblematic; it is things which are emblematic. Every natural fact is a symbol of some spiritual act" (1950, 15). In "The Poet," the opening essay of the Second Series, Emerson reiterates and broadens this idea: "Nature offers all her creatures to [the poet] as a picture-language. Being used as a type, a second wonderful value appears in the object, far better than its old value;" he also states, "Things admit of being used as symbols because nature is a symbol, in the whole, and in every part" (1950, 325). The poet is "the Namer" and "the Language-Maker" insofar as he is capable of reading the natural emblems offered to him. He is "the Sayer" of nature because he "sees the flowing or the metamorphosis" (1950, 329). In short, Emerson vigorously affirms the idea of the two Divine books, two non-manmade revelations: the Bible, written in phonetic language; and Nature, written in a picture-language of hieroglyphics. His own writing can be seen as an attempt at translation, a kind of metamorphosis of the enigmatic hieroglyphs of nature into a phonetic, discursive language.[10] This work of decipherment of already existing ideas, laws, and phenomena results not only in the rapid movement of thought characteristic of Emersonian text, but also in a sense of the anguish and constraint of the phonetic language in which this text is written. This translation, this decipherment, is, in a sense, the work of forcing the multidimensional flow into a linear series of words. The propensity toward hieroglyphism is the most profoundly Emersonian feature of Kharms's tract.

More important, after rejection of metaphor, hieroglyphism can be seen as Kharms's second cardinal strategy in defying the logos. Certainly, the Kharmsian hieroglyph radically differs from the Emersonian one. In Kharms's language there is none of the Romantic symbolism that abounds in Emerson's texts and represents the basis for his very idea of hieroglyphics. Emersonian text is monodimensional and uniformly phonetic. Its flow and spatiality emerge from the relentless pursuit of deeper meanings of the concept-emblem and from the poetic mastery of the metaphor. The most unusual and striking of Kharms's perfect gifts, a wooden stick with a wooden sphere and cube attached to its ends, can be considered the exact opposite of the Emersonian symbolic hieroglyph. While Emerson establishes numerous analogies between the hieroglyph and word, Kharms insists on the neutrality of his "perfect gift." A wooden stick with a sphere and cube attached to it is not only useless as an object but also, as a form, does not have a definitive meaning. It is not a symbol that points to other symbols, and does not include other signs. It is an assemblage of pure geometrical forms.

Lipavsky produces an intriguing geometric hieroglyph in the opening passages of his works "Water Tractatus" and "Investigation of Horror." Both tracts are written in the dialogic form:[11] in the first, one of the participants, "champion," threads a steel string through an apple; in the second, an unspecified dialogist pierces an apple with a needle. In both cases, the assemblage is, in geometrical terms, a sphere pierced by a line. In both tracts, this geometrical form is taken as a self-sufficient unit. "Here is a world," says Lipavsky, "a world which exists, but which does not have a purpose or meaning." According to him, this world is positioned below the "lowest border of human language" (Ostashevsky 2006, 205). It represents a preverbal, prelinguistic world: "it is extremely difficult to define [it] by words, like a landscape or a trumpet sound. It attracts attention enormously, but who knows what is exactly the case here" (Lipavsky 2005, 18).

This world is impossible to describe and define because it is unlike anything else. However difficult to define in words, a landscape or a sound are phenomena that are repeated in countless variations organized around a set of distinctive rules that make a sound describable as a sound and a landscape describable as a landscape. A sphere penetrated by a line is precisely the opposite: it is a basic situation without repetitions and variations. It is a world in becoming, a world without simile, likeness, word, or voice. The only thing certain about this world, says Lipavsky, is its shape, its outline. And this three-dimensional geometrical form follows, as much as possible, one of the most startling conceptual bodies dreamed up and calculated by modern mathematics. It is the sphere devised by Georg Riemann, one of the leading proponents of non-Euclidean geometry:[12] a sphere whose cardinal points are 0 and ∞. Using projective geometry and the theory of complex numbers, Riemann developed a geometry based on this model in which every straight line is a circle. This geometry explains the function $1/x$ in which, when x goes to zero, $1/x$ gets bigger and goes to infinity, which is the basis of the mathematical idea of singularity. We can safely assert that Lipavsky's "world" approximates, as far as such approximation is at all possible, the idea of mathematical singularity. As we are going to see, some of Kharms's works can be seen as intricate theaters of singularities. Before we get there, we have to look at some of his more conventional hieroglyphs.

Lipavsky considered devising an alphabet of objects. The elements of this alphabet would not be subsemantic, like elements of the phonetic alphabet. He asserts that the objects in this alphabet would be "neither symbolic nor allegorical." Instead, they would represent a "crystallization of world principles" (2005, 368). In other words, the elements of this objective alphabet-dictionary would be three-dimensional hieroglyphs. Figurative language is here replaced by a language of objects, or, quite literally, of figures. Lipavsky's objective is to examine the essence of objects and their mutual relationships. In "Conversations" he also asserts that these hieroglyphs form their own order and their own "hierarchy," which is not completely random but which is less rigid than the phonetic alphabet. "I would like to make a deck of hieroglyphs like a deck of cards," says Lipavsky (382). A deck of cards is essentially an unbound book. It resembles the endless book Malevich talks about in *God Is Not Cast Down.* It is also a concept that relates to Kharms's idea of the cyclical book, "Malgil."[13] Also, among Kharms's papers there are examples of hermetic symbols inscribed on separate cards, similar to Lipavsky's deck of hieroglyphs.[14] Each card, each element or page, does not have a fixed position in the deck. The deck can be mixed and rearranged according to the properties of each card. If a book and a linear text are organized by the law of sequence, a deck is organized according to the law of combination. This combination is not independent of the value and meaning of the elements. Here, everything is at play: the internal properties of each card and the rules of the game in which they are used, as well as the exception from the rule—the chance order of the cards. The linear order of the phonetic text is completely foreign to this complex textuality.

This flexible and nonlinear alphabet of hieroglyphs corresponds to Andre Leroi-Gourhan's concept of prephonetic writing. In his book *Gesture and Speech,* Leroi-Gourhan argues against the idea of pictography as a "primitive" predecessor of phonetic writing. Instead, he proposes the concept of two languages that emerged simultaneously: the language of hearing and the language of sight. The former corresponds to the functional pair face-and-language, and the latter to the pair hand-and-tool. The prevalence of phonetic over pictographic language is the outcome of the separation of face and hand: "the invention of writing, through the device of linearity, completely subordinated graphic to phonetic expression. . . . An image possesses a dimensional freedom which writing must always lack" (Leroi-Gourhan 1993, 195). According to Leroi-Gourhan, a long period of human literacy that preceded the invention of phonetic notation was dominated by a multidimensional and heterogeneous mode of writing. It combined image, speech, and action. The remnants of this mode of writing are still recognizable in Egyptian hieroglyphics, which combine images and phonetic signs. Therefore, this alternative to phonetic writing is multidimensional in two senses: instead of the linear sequence of signs, it uses groups of images that progress in all directions, a characteristic that prompted Leroi-Gourhan to call this form of writing "radial"; it is an essentially dual language of hand (image) and face (speech) in which neither one is subordinated to the other. Due to this multidirectionality, the object described in this kind of text is provided with an unstable and unfixed meaning that Leroi-Gourhan calls a "halo," which is "much wider than the narrow meaning words have assumed in linear writing" (1993, 205).

In Kharms's manuscripts there is an evident propensity toward the spatialization of text. Even in his more conventional texts, such as the typescript of his play *Elizabeth Bam,* there is a clear tendency toward a departure from discursive language. In a number of scenes, phonetic writing is intertwined with musical notation. At one point, toward the end of the play, the heroine's mother suddenly makes an utterance in the language of mathematics: "3 × 27 = 81" (1993, 182). These instances of nondiscursivity have the effect of obscuring the overall meaning of the play. This is, however, only a minor example of Kharms's emblematization of writing. In some of his tracts, alphabetic writing almost disappears behind the point-

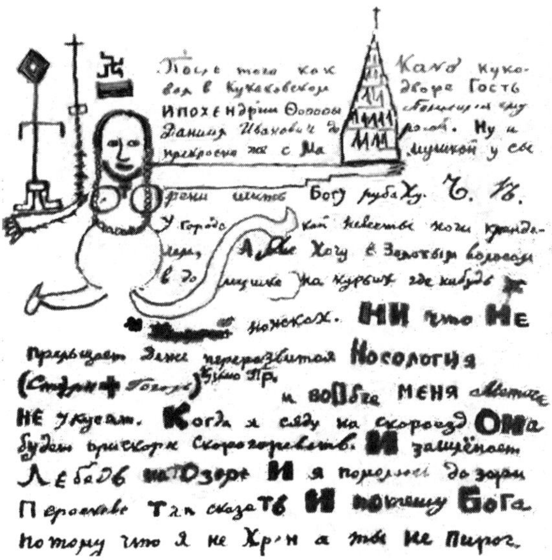

Figure 5.

Kharms's visual poem. The translation of the opening verse is "After that as how . . ."

edly radial mathematical formulas. In others, however, the images, symbols, and letters form an intricate image. In figure 5, the "halo" of nonlinear writing turns into a complex *mise en page.*

This *mise en page* combines visual and discursive elements into a single "text" that resists the conventional techniques of reading. In one of his most characteristic works of this kind, Kharms seems to combine all four of his "language machines" on the single page: In its use of hermetic symbols and colored inks it resembles a spell; in its invocation of God, a prayer; in the composition of its textual part, a poem; and in its emphasis on the sonic quality of words, a song. At the same time, however, all of the "language machines" seem to undermine one another. The alphabetic text begins abruptly. The beginning of the sentence is agrammatical, and then it turns into a purely visual text, followed by the invocation of the author's name: "After that as *how cuckooed in cuckoo court* the guest of IPOHENDRdrii Θoθoθoθы grew fond of dear Daniil Ivanovich." This initial incompleteness and abruptness suggests that something has been already said by the image that precedes the text. The relation between text and images is literal and metaphorical. The sentence that begins at the fingertips of the girl's extended hand starts with the letters ь and ъ, written in calligraphy and capitalized. The letters are followed by periods, which suggest that they represent the initials of a proper name. However, in the Russian alphabet these two signs have the function of soft and hard signs, and are in some cases added to consonants in order to specify the pronunciation. In other words, there is no specific sound that corresponds to the letters ь and ъ. So, the sentence with its grammatical subject of unutterable initials refers directly to the image: "ь. ъ. in the city of the girl with the legs like pretz*els, and* I *want with the golden hair* in a little home."[15]

The girl with the pretzel-like legs dominates the composition. In this crude drawing, the head and bust are rendered relatively realistically, while the extremities are drastically distorted. The name that appears in the first line, IPOHENDRdrii Θοθοθοθы, has a vaguely feminine form. It resembles nicknames by which Kharms called his second wife, Marina Malich. In his poems from the mid-1930s he refers to her as "Fefyulin'ka" (Фефюлинъка) and Fefyu (Фефю). Also, a similar feminine name appears in his poem from 1936 "On Boring Firfafusa Gomina" (the first name is spelled in Russian Cyrillic letters as: Фирфафуса).[16] With her right hand she supports two crosses: the one next to the very edge of the paper combines anthropomorphic and geometric shapes, and the second floats in space above the girl's shoulder and "bleeds" smaller red crosses. The third cross, in the shape of a swastika, is positioned directly above the girl's head.[17] The girl's left hand extends midway through the page, and on her palm she holds a pointed structure that could be a temple or the "city" mentioned in the text. The entire three-piece composition points strongly to the symbolism of the last chapters of the book of Revelation, in which "the holy city, the New Jerusalem" (21, 2) descends from heaven to become "the bride, the Lamb's wife" (21, 9). Clearly, Kharms is not making just an illuminated text. The pictorial symbols are not just illustrations of the phonetic text, which, for its part, does not represent an interpretation or a commentary on the images. This combination of phonetic text and images results in a rebus, a form of writing that emerged, as Benjamin suggests in *The Origin of German Tragic Drama,* from the attempts of the Renaissance humanists to restore the sanctity of writing (Benjamin 1998, 169). He explains that, traditionally, the relation between phonetic and hieroglyphic text has been seen as hierarchical. A hieroglyph was considered "older" not only in a chronological but also in an ontological sense:

> The sanctity of what is written is inextricably bound up with the idea of its strict codification. For sacred script always takes the form of certain complexes of words which ultimately constitute, or aspire to become, one single and inalterable complex. So it is that the alphabetical script,

as a combination of the atoms of writing, is the farthest removed from the script of sacred complexes. These latter take the form of hieroglyphics. The desire to guarantee the sacred character of any script—there will always be a conflict between sacred standing and profane comprehensibility—leads to complexes, to hieroglyphics. (175)

On the one hand, these complexes accomplish a personification of words and letters in images (186), and on the other, organize fragments into elaborate allegories. Both of these tendencies are evident in Kharms: we have seen a personified letter *yat'*, and in the torso of the pretzel-legged girl, we find the fragmentation of the image characteristic of hieroglyphics, which Benjamin likens to a rune (176). However, Kharms approaches allegory in the same way he does its compacted version, metaphor. Namely, he reduces the allegory to a mere "dry rebus" that no longer has a discernable meaning. In the case of the untitled work under discussion, this de-allegorization is accomplished through the mutual subversions and clashes between the visual and phonetic sides of the text. Furthermore, certain sections have the quality of a *zaum* incantation. Consider, for example, the use of the phoneme "ka" in the opening line of figure 5: "*posle togo kak kako koval v kukavskom dvore.*" While this text seems rather exceptional in its use of pictorial symbols, orthography, and themes, there are other characteristic examples of Kharms's hieroglyphism that also feature this combination of sacred symbolism and *zaum*-like poetic practice. That, however, does not necessarily suppress allegory. Consider the following drawing (figure 6), dated November 1931.

Here, the complexity and number of symbols are paralleled by the relative simplicity of the *mise en page:* a column of symbolic images is flanked by two columns of phonetic text. In the previous image (figure 5), there was a physical contiguity between image and text, organized in linear and horizontal order. If we compare the spatial layout of the two texts, we will see that the first has the quality of a prose piece, and the second that of a poem. This contrast in the physical orientation of the text should not be disregarded as mere formalism. The date of the column of hieroglyphs (1931) coincides with one of the most significant shifts in Kharms's writing: from poetry to prose. In his notebook for 1930, he wrote that "prose has the laws of proportional relations and sense material" whereas "verses" those of "the word material" (2002a, 331). In other words, prose relies on the ability of language to create meanings, and poetry on its sound quality. The following year, the form of narration typical of his *Events* begins to emerge in his

Figure 6.

Column of hieroglyphs, dated November 1931

writing. This kind of simple prose narration never completely suppresses his poetry. In another notebook entry, he wrote that prose and poetry have their own clarity of order (2002b, 54). As Agamben suggests in *Language and Death,* "the verse (*versus,* from *verto,* the act of turning, to return, as opposed to *prorsus,* to proceed directly, as in prose) signals for a reader that these words have always already come to be, that they will return again, and that the instance of the word that takes place in the poem is, for this reason, ungraspable" (1991, 78). Kharms's earliest excursions into prose came through dramatic writing, the most significant of which is his play *Elizabeth Bam,* written between 1927 and 1928. Already then he was aware that it is nonsense in prose that corresponds to the ungraspable quality of verse. His later prose acquires a nonsensical quality that is quite distinct from that which he used in *Elizabeth Bam.* Kharms's experiments with visual (or hieroglyphic) writing during 1930 and 1931 intervene between these two phases of his prose.

The symbols used in the visual poem with the "pretzel-legged girl" (figure 5) are limited to this work only. Conversely, most of the symbols from the column of hieroglyphs (figure 6) reappear with significant persistence throughout Kharms's manuscripts. For example, the Egyptian cross, the flower, and the square divided by a horizontal line are inscribed on separate cards, and the entire column without the accompanying text exists in another version.[18] Another point of difference is that in contrast to the text in figure 5, in figure 6 the phonetic text closely follows the symbols in the column. The inscription to the right of the column reads:

I am O, I am *sir,* I am *is*[19]
I am a triad, teach me how to
read. We say
    that is I
    I
    present you
    the key,
    so that you
    say
    I.
    I take the key
    when, as our grannies
    taught us, I find

a fern flower
that blooms
only once a
year, on the eve of
Ivan Kupala Day.

But, where to find that
flower? It grows
in the forest under the tree
that stands upside
down.

You go to the big
slumbering forest, but
there is not a single tree
that grows upside
down. Then you should
choose the most beautiful
tree and climb it.

Then take a rope and tie one
end of the rope to the branch
and the other end to your
leg. Then jump off
the tree
and you will hang with your legs
up, and you will see
that the tree stands upside
down.

Before you go to the tree
look at the window
to check the weather.

* * *

I am looking through the window and see
there ends the street, there begins the
field, there runs the river, and there on
the bank is the tree.

(1997a, 214)

The text to the left of the column of hieroglyphs, aligned horizontally with the image of the flower, begins with a reference to the opening of the sixth seal in the Book of Revelation: "then the sky receded as a scroll when it is rolled up, and every mountain and island was moved out of its place" (6:14):

> The sky rolls
> into a scroll and falls on
> earth; earth and water
> rises to the sky;
> the whole world turns upside down.
> When you see all of that,
> then the flower in your chest
> opens and blossoms.
> I say: that is the end
> of thc old world, for I
> have seen the new world.
> (1997a, 212)

If the relation between the phonetic text and pictorial symbols in the "pretzel-legged girl" text is characterized by playfulness, here it becomes formalized. The phonetic text provides an interpretation of the hieroglyphic complexes, but in its "profane comprehensibility" it also limits their meanings, confining the entire group to its own narrative, linear mold. In this regard, the two columns of phonetic text seem to be in opposition: while the one on the right limits the symbolic range of the hieroglyphs, the text on the left, with its biblical references and prophetic tone, adds to them an additional layer of ambiguity.

Here, I am interested neither in the general interpretation of this intriguing series[20] nor in the *mise en page* employed in it, but in the origin and development of a particular hieroglyph and its use in the more complex structures. That is the hieroglyph located at the bottom of the column. For the sake of clarity, I will limit my discussion of the other elements to their most prominent traits.

There are at least three basic layers of meaning to this text: the narrative layer of the text on the right, the prophetic layer of the text on the left, and the symbolic layer of the column of pictorial signs positioned, significantly, at the center of the page. The top four symbols can be grouped in two pairs. The first pair is brought together by the principle of triplicity. The cryptogram on the top consists of three emblems,[21] and the phonetic text next to it asserts "I am a triad." The Ankh, or Egyptian cross, located immediately beneath the cryptogram is the only pictogram that Kharms borrows directly from Egyptian hieroglyphics. His interpretation of this hieroglyph as the "key of life" is basically correct. However, he does not stop at adopting an Egyptian hieroglyph. In the tract "On Existences" he outlines this key's tripartite structure as "Heaven–World–Heaven" (2001a, 37). This formula is symmetrical[22], and it remains unchanged if read from left to right or the other way around. This reversibility of order seems to foreshadow the principle that couples the next two hieroglyphs: the turning.

The flower is positioned at the very center of the series of symbols. Its prominence is affirmed in both columns of the phonetic text: the loose narrative of the poem that opens with "I am O, I am *sir,* I am *is*" is centered on a popular belief related to the pre-Christian deity of the Eastern Slavs, Ivan Kupala, that came to be identified with St. John the Baptist. The "night of Ivan Kupala" was celebrated during the summer solstice. It was believed that the fern blooms during this shortest night of the year, and "the person who picks the flower gains the ability to see all treasures hidden under ground, and to understand the language of beasts and plants" (Voloshina and Astapov 1996, 145). In the inscription to the left of the column, the flower "opens" and "blossoms" in the chest, the place of the heart—that is, the center of the human body. In both the right- and left-hand columns, the blooming of the fern flower is closely associated with the turning of the world upside down. Yampolsky notes that in Kharms's symbolism, the flower is almost certainly related to the idea of the chakra, wheel, from Hindu tradition (Iampol'skii 1997, 330).[23] The turning wheel at the center of the column is coupled with the figure of the upturned tree with a man hanging from its crown. The image of the hanged man comes from the twelfth card of the Tarot's Major Arcana. Kharms was familiar with the traditions of both the Tarot and Cabbala, and, as Yampolsky suggests, in this case, the figure of the upturned tree is most likely related to the cabalistic symbolism that ties this image with the process of creativity (1997, 319). In an intriguing way, the notion of creativity is also related to the symbol at the base of the column.

Kharms was quite liberal when it came to the sources from which he borrowed his favorite symbolic figures: as we have seen, he drew on the New Testament, Egyptian hieroglyphics, Russian religious beliefs and folklore, Tarot, and Cabbala. In this regard, the square divided by a horizontal line stands out from all other symbolic images. Kharms reveals its origin and meaning in a letter to Raisa Poliakova, written about the same time as the column with symbols (the column is dated November 1931, and the letter November 2, 1931). He confesses to Raisa that the only person he loved prior to her was his wife Ester Rusakova:

> She was not only my wife, whom I loved, but also something else that entered all of my thoughts and deeds. I didn't converse with Ester in Russian, and I spelled her name with Latin letters: ESTHER.
> Then, I made a monogram out of them, and got ⊟.
> I called it a window, through which I look at the sky and see a star. And that star I called a heaven, albeit a very distant heaven.
> And suddenly I realized that the sign ⊟
> resembles a window.
> (Kharms 1988a, 459)

Monogrammatization is the compression of the word into a single, unified sign: what is obliterated is the spaces between letters, not the letters themselves. It is, quite literally, writing without difference. If, as Derrida claims in his essay "Differance," phonetic writing depends on assimilation of nonphonetic elements such as spacing, the monogram can be seen as phonetic writing in the strict sense of the word (Derrida 1973, 133). At the same time, it is a kind of play with the signifiers, and as such belongs to what Derrida calls "protowriting without a present origin, without an *arche*" (146). For, as we are going to see, the window is the sign not only of Ester but also of the place of absencing. The letters are piled one on top of another so that the word occupies as little space as possible. As the end result of this process, not only the word's spatial aspect is eliminated but also its duration in time. This detemporalization sets up a simultaneous perception: The glance passes through a window; and in its turn, the window limits, narrows down, and focuses the field of vision. We have already encountered the window in the series of visual devices deployed in *Temptation.* However, in the evolution of the window sign, Kharms quickly dispenses with its relation to sensory perception.

The window as a literary figure appears in Kharms's earliest works, such as the 1925 poem "From Babushka to Esther." The years 1930 and 1931 are a period of radical reconceptualization of this figure. The following diary entry represents one of Kharms's most intriguing window-texts from 1931:

> Before coming to see you I will knock on your window. You will see me in the window. Then I will stand in the doorway and you will see me

in the doorway. Then I will come into your house and you will recognize me. Then I will enter you and no one, apart from you, will see or know who I am.

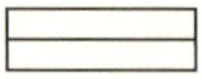 You will see me in the window.

 You will see me in the doorway. (Ostashevsky 2006, 105)

Whom is Kharms addressing here? On whose window is he knocking? Who sees him? Where or what is he entering? The addressee of this note remains out of sight. Upon entering, the author also disappears. That much is clear. It is also clear that he makes a distinction between the window and the door. If the door is the place of passage, then what is the window? Is physical passage different from the passage of the glance, or what might be termed a visual passage?

The window monogram compresses not only the letters of the proper name Ester (or Esther, as Kharms sometimes wrote it), but also several strata of meaning. I will briefly outline the most discernable ones.

First, the monogram points beyond the name Ester to the body to which that name refers. If, for Kharms, the disaster is departure from the star, then this departure has a somatic starting point. In his notebooks, Kharms recorded his arguments with Ester in great detail, which date to the early days of their relationship. The reason for their first breakup was banal and of a sexual nature. On September 30, 1925, he writes: "I was bold to ask an flc from you  and now I am punished" (Kharms 2002a, 52). Throughout his notebooks, the window sign is closely related to fellatio and to oral sex in general. The window sign, then, is not only the proper name (Ester) compressed into a symbol (star), but also a graphic representation of her bodily openings: mouth and vagina. In his poem from 1930 entitled "To My Wife" Kharms adds another layer to the standard Freudian interpretation of oral sex as pleasure and nutrition:

For a long time I haven't written at the table,
The pen falls
From my limpid hand
As my woman sits on me.

There follows an account of pleasuring a woman orally, which again turns to writing:

Now it's enough! Where are the pens?
Where is the ink and paper?
The scent is escaping through the window,
And my dear looks in fear.
At the table, I write everything
Let the letters serve me well
Let the string of sense ring
Let the thoughts weave together. (1997a, 113–14)

Here, the table serves as a dual arena of writing and passion, and the window becomes the bodily organ that literally gags the writer's mouth. In doing so it redirects all of the powers of symbolization toward the body, which is, on its part, enraptured and out of control. This body, reduced to the mouth, occupies the very border of discursivity, and in that sense repeats the condition of the textual fragment. Therefore, the window represents at the same time the compression of letters and the fragmentation of the body.

Second, as Kharms's relationship with Ester deteriorated, the window became detached from its primary symbolism and its association with the mouth.[24] It seems that this double transformation was quite intentional. In 1932, Kharms writes in a somewhat programmatic manner:

To make a figure out of the window ⊟
I postulate.
My mouth is shut.
II postulate
Mouth is open for the highest wisdom, power, and light. (2002a, 22)

The window, then, is the figure that brings together mouth and light. This light is related to a distinct form of visibility. In another fragment from 1930, a character named Vid recites: "a door to the right, a door to the left, a door ahead, a door below, a door aslant, a door by the side, a door on the rear, and a door across" (1997a, 311). *Vid* in Russian means "appearance" or "view," and it is also at the root of the words *videt',* to see, and *vidimost',* visibility. There is a door in all directions. Wherever the glance wanders, there is a passage. With every movement, one might step into a door. The situation is different with the window. It is not a simple passage, nor is it a simple framing device. Kharms tries, as much as possible, to disassociate the figure of the window from the notion of physical perception and the sense of sight, and transform it into a place of transcendence.

In his letter to Raisa Poliakova, he abruptly abandons his story about Ester and starts telling her about his suffering through a sleepless night. He complains that he could not continue to lie awake in bed, nor could he spend the night just walking around his room. Then:

> I sat at the table and wanted to write. I put a notebook in front of me, and I took a fountain pen, and started thinking. I knew I had to write something, but I did not know what.
>
> I did not even know if I was supposed to write verses, or a story, or some argument, or simply a single letter. (1988a, 460)

He goes on to describe the futility and horror of his vigil. The entire night passes without his being able to write a single letter. At dawn, he leaves the table and approaches the window:

> I suddenly said to myself: here am I, sitting, looking through the window at . . .
>
> But, what am I looking at? I recalled: "a window, through which I see a star." But now I am not looking at the star. I don't know what am I looking at right now. That which I am looking at is the letter I can't write. (1988a, 460)

The window is the square of gentle morning brightness that breaks apart the gloomy darkness of night. However, this brightness and clarity cannot itself be penetrated, known, and represented. The lightness and brightness of early morning come from the inexperience of a beginning. For a window to be a window, there has to be nothing in it.

The traumatic story confessed in the letter to Raisa Poliakova is repeated in the prose piece "The Morning." Kharms also talks here about the torments of the blank page in front of him:

> I couldn't fall asleep for a long time. I wanted to know what I was supposed to write. In my mind I combed through all forms of literary art,

> but could not find my own form. It could have been a single letter, but possibly, I was supposed to write an entire book. I asked God for a miracle so that I could understand what I was supposed to write. (1997b, 29)

This wish is not granted, and the torture continues through the night. He goes back to bed, extinguishes the lamp, and tosses from one side to another. It seems that a light sleep finally overcomes him:

> I look through the window and see the superintendent sweeping the yard.
> I stand next to the superintendent and tell him that, in order to write something, it is necessary to know the letters that are supposed to be written. (30)

Again and again, the window sheds light on the insight that there is a kind of writing that is more direct and immediate than the alphabet. The interior of the room figures as the place of obscurity in both the letter to Raisa Poliakova and in "The Morning." The atmosphere within is dark and hallucinatory. Darkness and insecurity linger on the page of the open notebook until it catches the early morning light from the window. In both cases, the window opens to the outside world, infinitely more real than the world of the insomniac locked up in the room. And both times, facing this reality, he finds himself lacking language.

Third, the formation of the window monogram amounts to the erasure of writing: the word folds into a monogram, which then unfolds into a blank surface. The mouth survives as a deep memory of the symbol, its unconscious. As such, it does not represent the voice, but the primary tracing made by the mouth. This notion, strongly present in all of Kharms's writing on the window, is clearly illuminated in Mallarmé's early poem "The Windows." A dying old man confined to a hospital bed gazes at the window in order to escape the dullness of his final days. He leans toward the windowpane:

> And fevered, greedy for deep azure, the mouth,
> As, youthful, it would breathe its wealth away,
> A virgin skin of long ago! befouls
> With a long, bitter kiss the warm, golden panes.
> (Mallarmé 1982, 9)[25]

The dying man presses his bloodless, dry lips to the clear glass, smearing it with the moisture from his own breath. In the window he tastes himself. It becomes a strange mirror of recollection and reflection. In his brilliant exegesis of Mallarmé's poem, Robert Greer Cohn duly observes the ambiguity of *glace* as window glass and as ice, solid water (*eau gelee*). This sucking on the *glace* reduces the dying man to a child clinging to the "virgin skin" of the maternal breast (Cohn 1977, 25). This is what Mallarmé's dying man/child discovers in the window:

> His gaze, gorged on the horizon of light,
> Sees golden galleys, beautiful as swans,
> On a ruddy, perfumed river, cradling to sleep,
> The tawny, rich light of their echelons
> In a vast nonchalance charged with memories! (9)

In a gesture that limits the metaphor, Kharms looks through the window only to find a distorted, upturned world:

> I am looking through the window and see
> there ends the street, there begins the
> field, there runs the river, and there on
> the bank is the tree.

And the tree is turned upside down, and the sky rolled into a scroll that descends to earth, and earth and water rise into the sky. Or he sees the letter that he does not know. Mallarmé draws on the strange materiality of the window: this smooth and invisible surface is firm, rigid, even warm. This reminds us powerfully that there is no *glace* in Kharms's window frame. This opening is not filled with solid matter, not even with the paradoxical *eau gelée.* It is the place of loss, not of recollection. This window is not a source, but an abyss. It lets not only one's gaze pass through it without resistance, but also one's saliva, and one's entire body. In a verse fragment "[Where did I lose my arm?]" Kharms laments:

> Danya![26]
> How will you undress before bed,
> take off your boots
> and put them in the dresser.
> Put yourself to sleep. Cross.

Turn around. How to dream?
How to wake rested the next day,
look through the window and spit?
(1997a, 125)

And in his diary he makes a note for a story that will open with "Mikhail Ivanovich pressing a notebook on the wall and spitting in it four times" (2002a, 503). Perhaps Danya lost his arm when he pushed it through the window/page. In the story "The Notebook" he relates that he was sitting by the window when he heard a whistle: "I leaned through the window and was slapped in the face" (1997b, 135). By now we should not be surprised to find out that Kharms relates this episode to another one, in which he receives a notebook as a gift and is subsequently asked to tear out the pages containing his writing. The loss that occurs in the window is peculiar. In his insightful analysis of the idea of the window in Kharms's work, Yampolsky describes this loss as a "defiguration" that is based "not on similarity, but on difference" (Iampol'skii 1997, 54). He points out Kharms's drawing of the window in which a standing human figure is shown from the waist up, suggesting that it is positioned inside, in the room, but at the same time an open landscape behind it suggests that the figure is outside. These conflicting details can only designate the paradoxical situation of the window, which opens simultaneously to an interior and exterior. The window, then, does not separate inside from outside, near from far. I mentioned earlier that Kharms relates the window sign to the notion of transcendence. It would be more accurate to say that although it points toward the beyond, it never delivers. The central significance of Kharms's window is that its beyond is either false or nonexistent. Kharms privileges this symbol not because of the multitude of meanings it contains but precisely because of its vacuity: the absence of any accurately identifiable content. It is the place where near and far, writing and meaning, collide.

Fourth, it is an architectural element. This simple observation gains an added importance if we take into consideration Kharms's obsession with drawing floor plans. His notebooks and diaries are peppered with drawings of blueprints for apartments. In his manuscript collection, there is a separate folder that contains drawings of the floor plans on loose pieces of paper.[27] Most of these apartments are Kharms's inventions, but among them there are also drawings of existing homes.[28] Some of the floor plans are crude sketches; others, elaborate drawings. In some of them, it is still possible to discern light lines in pencil that trace the movement from one

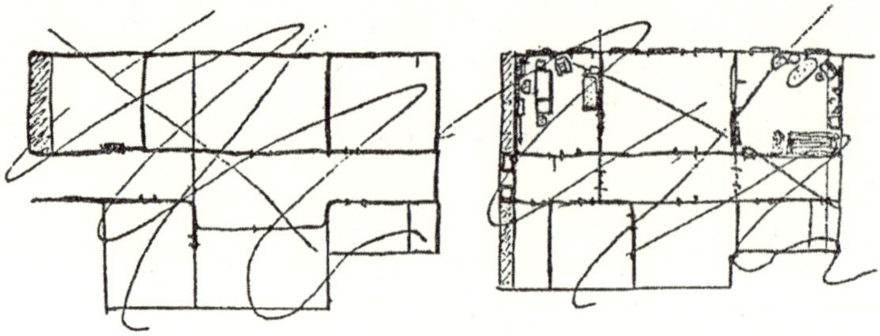

Figure 7.
Floor plans from Kharms's diaries

room to another. Kharms rarely wrote about his passion for this kind of drawing. It gave him comfort: on October 4, 1937, as he was starving, Kharms wrote: "If you could only sit in your room, knowing that you are safe and provided for, and just draw the apartments" (2002b, 195). A few years earlier, he wrote in his diary: "Since long ago, I have liked to draw apartments and make up the interior design for them. Once, I drew a private residence with 80 rooms, and another time I liked an apartment with two rooms. Now I would like to have such an apartment" (209). The note is accompanied by two sketches (figure 7).

In the drawings and doodles of this kind, the window loses its spatiality and becomes an element of architectural notation. It is a sign in the form of writing, or more precisely, tracing, which Bernard Tschumi described as non-mimetic and non-representational (Tschumi 1994, 8). Unlike writing, architectural notation does not program meanings but movements: "For any organized repetition of events, once announced in advance, becomes a program, a descriptive notice of a formal series of proceedings" (Tschumi 1996, 127). However, what distinguishes this architectural programming is that the events themselves de-scribe the notation. As Tschumi puts it pointedly: "Architecture and events constantly transgress each other's rules, whether explicitly or implicitly. These rules, these organized compositions, may be questioned, but they always remain points of reference. *A building is a point of reference for the activities set to negate it*" (133, italics added). What attracts Kharms to the window and to architectural notation is their resistance to discursivity. It is their blankness, their empty space, and their nothingness that lends significance to these forms.

In the process of monographization, letters are not only compressed but also piled up on one another. In this piling up they are forced to comply to one form that is common to all of them. So, compression turns into a projection along a single axis. This centrality becomes paradoxical once it is assigned to the wall, which always belongs to the periphery and the outer limit. Kharms detaches the window from the notion of the margin and focuses on its central emptiness. From the proper name, to the monogram, to the pictorial symbol, back to the word transformed into a broad concept, the window finally ends up at the center of the universe conceived by Kharms. The window is not material, but it is not completely separated from matter, either; it is not formless, and yet it changes form. Kharms does not stop at contemplating the window: he is sitting in its hollowness, leaning and looking through it. He is also talking to it and listening to it. In 1931, he wrote two poetic plays that feature the complex figure of the window. The first one, entitled simply *The Window,* is an exchange between a young student and her dominant teacher. The teacher forces her to understand the "secret temperature of steam-formation," and, as the piece progresses, becomes increasingly aggressive. The girl never reaches an understanding of the concept, but instead inhabits it and brings her body temperature to this "secret temperature." At that point she disappears, and the character named Window suddenly pops out and declares:

> I opened suddenly
> I'm a hole in walls of buildings.
> The soul spills out through me.
> I'm the air-vent of enlightened minds.
> (2007, 151)

The same character appears in the conclusion of a related piece, entitled *Oknov and Kozlov,* and delivers the same text, save for the penultimate line, which has been changed from "through me the spirit spilled" into "everything in the world obeys me" (1980, 21). Like *The Window* (*okno* in Russian), *Oknov and Kozlov* is a drama of interrogation, in which Oknov takes the role of the student and Kozlov of the sadistic interrogator. The colossal increase of the window's significance and power originates from Oknov's confession:

> This is a serious question.
> To my mind, matter's a dummy,
> its monotonous architecture
> can't set itself in motion.

Would but spirit touch it gently—
then the cork of movement pops away,
from dark chasms sharks of heat,
molecules, race away in fear,
the egg of the universe breaks open with a bang,
and we, falling to our knees, see God's face.
The same one that's in the pocket of fate,
the servant of sin, and reason's slave,
expires before the expiration date,
defeated by the poker.
Defeated by the poker.
(1997a, 192)[29]

The Window that "everything in the world obeys" is clearly related to the idea of the "egg of the universe." This phrase appears only in one other place in Kharms's papers, safely housed at the center of his diagram of the universe (figure 8).

In this system of concentric circles, the outermost ring is designated the "Earth's crust, on which we live." It is followed by two more layers, the "sea of lava" and the "circle of fire." The regions of magma and fire are followed by what appears to be a further increase of heat, the ring marked as the "proto-stars." A strange inversion happens at this point: after the stars comes the "void." As we progress toward the center of the schema, it becomes increasingly clear that the stars form a curious internal heaven. The penultimate circle is described as the "fluid rainbow," and it envelops the very core: "The World's Egg, or Nil." Nil, for Kharms, is nothing, which is different from zero, insofar as it is related to infinity. It is symbolized by the circle, not by the oval that stands for zero. The circle that symbolizes nothing, the nil, is the epicenter, the bull's eye, the eyeball, and the sun. Kharms doesn't miss out on the association between the eyes, the sun, and the window as sources of light (2001a, 175). The central circle, finally, turns into the axis of the wheel-shaped figure entitled "REAL" (figure 9).[30]

It would be a mistake to explain the formidable plasticity of the window sign by unhinging the meaning from the sign, or in terms of the complete absence of identity in any of the forms designated as "window." Precisely the opposite explanation emerges from a careful reading of Kharms's window texts: namely, the variety of forms and functions that this sign takes is made possible by the stability of its central meaning. We are going to find out that it is not at all surprising that this core, or the World's Egg, is nil, or

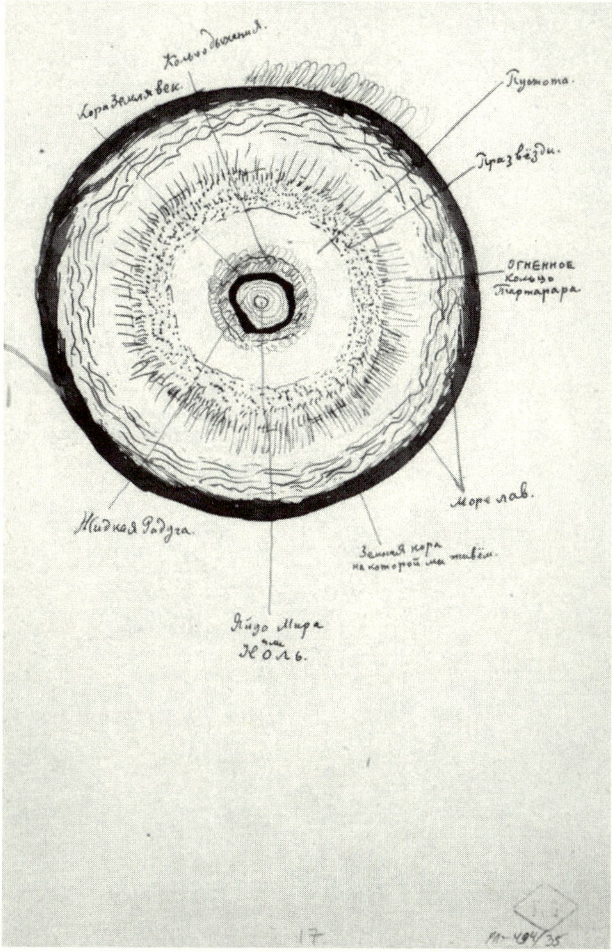

Figure 8.

"The World's Egg"

nothing. The perpetual variation of the window's forms around the vacuous center also indicates Kharms's intimacy with the symbol. It is not accidental that in the notes for an early draft of *Oknov and Kozlov,* Kharms and Window take the place of these two characters. One of the notes reads:

> the loss of reason[31]
> and O and A
> descending into the stomach
> and E and U
> here's the jar of the train engineer

Figure 9.

"Real." This symbolic drawing was executed in red pencil and titled in English.

and here the hut of Dr. Karasev
there the cart and the plate
there the street of ink
here umbrellas, don't you see, umbrellas[32]
(1980, 174)

There are several aspects to Kharms's intimacy with null and nil. They are the subject of the next chapter.

Discovery—that's light giving birth to the eye.

—Leonid Lipavsky, "Conversations" (1933–34)

3. Infinity—Letter—Event

The Tropical Sensation

One of Kharms's drawings that probably dates from the early 1930s features Leonid Lipavsky, Tamara Lipavskaya, and Kharms himself (figure 10).

It is a depiction of an encounter: Lipavsky holds his wife's hand, and they face Kharms. That turns our attention to bodily postures. Lipavsky's body opens toward Kharms, who leans slightly forward. Tamara Aleksandrovna bows, exposing her leg up to her thigh. The drawing is a caricature and a diagram that depicts the set of relationships within a triangle: Kharms is superior, Lipavsky diminutive, and Tamara Lipavskaya submissive. The woman bows, and as she tips forward, she looks like she may lose her balance at any moment and fall on the chest of the giant. It is by no means an innocent situation. As Kharms's seven-year relationship with Ester drew to an end, he turned to Tamara Aleksandrovna. His letters to his friend's wife contain some of the most humorous prose he ever wrote. It is hard to tell when he adopts the role of rejected lover and when he actually is one:

> Leningrad, August 20, 1930
> Tamara Aleksandrovna,
> I have to tell you that I understood everything. Stop pretending and writing your stupid letters to who-knows-whom. You think: he is dumb. He won't get it. But Daniil Kharms is not dumb. He gets everything. . . . I will tell you calmly and boldly: I am furious. (Kharms 2001a, 57)

Figure 10.

Kharms's caricature of himself and the Lipavskys

And so on, lividly. Then, a few months later, a complete change of tone:

> Leningrad, December 5, 1930
> Dear Tamara Aleksandrovna,
> I love you. I wanted to tell you that yesterday, but you told me that I have spots all over my forehead and I felt uncomfortable. But later, as you were eating a turnip, I mused: "All right, I don't have a pretty forehead, but Tamarochka is not a goddess either." I said that to myself in order to calm down. But essentially, you are a goddess—tall, beautiful, intelligent, a bit cunning, and priceless. (59)

The second drawing betrays the promise of the first one. Instead of falling into Kharms's lap, Tamara Aleksandrovna turns her back and leaves together with her minuscule husband (figure 11).

In 1933 and 1934, both Kharms and Tamara Aleksandrovna participated in the informal discussion group that was documented in "Conversations." Only one of their direct exchanges is recorded. On that occasion, Kharms told the story of his birth, which is one of the most amusing narratives of this kind he ever produced.[1] This is the only one in which the infant is radically transformed, or, better yet, deprived of form and turned into a slimy, undifferentiated mass. Even though Tamara Aleksandrovna took up Kharms's challenge, she could not stop the slimy story from oozing through her fingers and getting to its apparent destination: Leonid Lipavsky.

Lipavsky was a philosopher with very few works. His entire philosophical oeuvre easily fits into an average-size volume.[2] It consists of a number of rather long drafts and compilations of notes, such as "Explanation of Time," "On Transformations," "Vertigo," and "Dreams." His only longer, and apparently complete, work is "Theory of Words." As already noted, in the mid-1930s Lipavsky initiated and facilitated a discussion group that he called "The Club of Ignorant Scholars." The exchange of ideas that took place in this "club" is in many ways related to his two texts from the mid-1930s that constitute the kernel of his philosophical legacy, "Investigation of Horror" and "Water Tractatus."

Both "Investigation of Horror" and "Water Tractatus" are written in the form of philosophical dialogue, and both of them feature four participants. In "Investigation of Horror" they remain nameless, while in "Water Tractatus" they are designated as champion, captain, diminutive Greek, and the fourth speaker. Both texts are fragmentary. "Investigation of Horror" consists of seventeen numbered sections, two of which also have titles: the

Figure II.

"The Lipavskys Leaving"

fourth section is entitled "Water, Hard as Stone" and the subsequent, fifth section is "Blood and Dream." "Water Tractatus" has four sections, one for each of the dramatis personae. Here, the sections are not numbered, but they all have titles: the title of the tract, "Water Tractatus," can also serve as the title of the first section; the second section is "The Champion's Tale," the third "Investigation of Horror," and the last "The Tale."[3] "Water Tractatus" is considerably shorter than "Investigation of Horror," approximately one third of its size. As they are both undated, it is hard to tell whether "Water Tractatus" is a condensed version of "Investigation of Horror" or if "Investigation of Horror" is an expanded version of "Water Tractatus." The sequential or chronological order of these two texts is further complicated by significant repetitions and overlaps between them. They share characters, themes, entire sections of texts, and even titles: the most significant overlap of this kind is the section "Investigation of Horror" in "Water Tractatus." The two texts dovetail and intersect, rather than follow one another in any strict chronological order of creation.

Both the tractatus and the investigation begin with the mental image that sets the tone of the entire piece. In "Investigation of Horror," one of the four men gathered around the table pierces an apple with a long needle, announcing: "Here is the world which has no name" (2005, 18). In "Water Tractatus," it is the champion who runs a steel wire through an apple and proclaims: "Here is," of course, "a world which has no name. It lies under the lowest border of human language" (Ostashevsky 2006, 205). As we have seen, "Projection on Fluid" is the phase in the history of language that is characterized by "nonobjectivity" and "nonsubjectivity," that is to say, by nondifferentiation and the absence of form. This same formlessness is at the center of "Water Tractatus" and "Investigation of Horror." In "Water Tractatus," Lipavsky's interest in the formless is clearly related to his philosophical concern with the questions that were of primary importance to him: time and fear. The subsection of the tractatus that bears the same title as "Investigation of Horror" opens with the captain's story about a maid who got panicked at the sight of jelly trembling on a plate. The foursome seated at the table proceed with a discussion of the interconnectedness of formless matter and fear.

In the essay "Investigation of Horror," Lipavsky goes into much greater detail about the anamnesis of the formless. He relates formlessness to the absence of distinction, to non-separation, and, ultimately, to non-individualization. Water and fluidity are important to him because they exemplify that which is primordial and undifferentiated (2005, 22). Plasma is closely related to water and fluidity; it vacillates between "determination and indeterminacy," between the state of "individuality" and the process of "individualization" (29). Indeed, this ambiguity is, for Lipavsky, the most important aspect of formlessness, and it culminates in the loss of distinction between life and death. Of course, the absence of form is easily identifiable with the absence of organic life. It is enough to think of sludge, dirt, sand, or snow. However, it would be wrong to think that the definiteness of form is the defining characteristic of organic matter. In "Conversations," Lipavsky talks of the living organism as something that evolves, absorbs its immediate environment, spreads, swarms, and spills out (395). The formless, then, inhabits the very boundary between the animate and the inanimate. Lacking definition, it could be either living or dead. It is the region of indecisiveness in which the animate absorbs the inanimate, and death invades life. For Lipavsky and his friends, formlessness designates not only the absence of physical shape but also undifferentiated movements, sounds, psychic states such as neurosis or melancholia (386, 412), and, in short, any kind of amorphousness. The power of the amorphous is best exemplified by blood.

Initially, Lipavsky offers the image of blood dripping from a wound, slowly forming an undefined, incessantly spreading stain. But, the blot represents only one aspect of the formlessness of coagulating blood. As it leaves the body, the life-giving liquid seems to begin another life, a life of its own. In "Water Tractatus," the champion speaks of the "unindividuated life" of blood. In "Investigation of Horror," the line of inquiry related to death extends to the corpse.[4] A dead body is not frightening just because it is no longer alive but because it is alive differently. It is possessed by a life other than human. The familiar rhythms of breathing, heartbeat, and gait are replaced by the swarming, arrhythmic, crawling movement of decomposition and rotting. Indeed, for Lipavsky the formless is primarily related to spilled, non-concentrated, unindividuated, and ambiguous life. At one point he produces a long list of examples of formless matter: "dirt, swamp, fat—especially liquid fats such as fish and castor oil—mucus, saliva (spittle, expectoration), blood, all glandular excretion, and in that sense all seminal fluids, protoplasm in general" (2005, 29).

"Spittle is, finally, through its inconsistency, its indefinite contours, the relative imprecision of its color, and its humidity, the very symbol of the formless, of the unverifiable, of the non-hierarchized": that is how Michel Leiris concludes his entry "Spittle" in the seventh issue of *Documents,* published in 1929 under the editorship of Georges Bataille (*Encyclopae-*

dia 1995, 78). Almost simultaneously, on two sides of Europe, two groups of young thinkers and artists were engrossed in similar questions without having any awareness of each other. In particular, the similarities between Lipavsky and Bataille are astonishing. Both of them were conveners and facilitators, Lipavsky of the discussion group and Bataille of *Documents,* then "Acephale," and finally "College of Sociology." Both harbored a fascination with idiosyncratic taxonomies and classifications: whereas Bataille initiated the Dictionary as a distinct section within the magazine *Documents,* the section that he later described as "anomalous," Lipavsky entertained ideas of a dictionary of physiognomies (2005, 212) and an "alphabet of things' meanings" (368). And even more specifically, within this shared interest for "anomalous" encyclopedic projects, both Bataille and Lipavsky were intrigued by hieroglyphics: Lipavsky dreamt of compiling a "deck of hieroglyphs" and Bataille wrote about coins and the language of flowers. A pronounced mistrust of rationalism marked both the Frenchman's and the Russian's thought, best exemplified in their unyielding anti-Cartesian attitude. This incredulity toward rationalism and positivism propelled an intense interest in that which challenges reason; that which is irregular, atypical, unintelligible, unsystematic; that which one identified with heterogeneity and the other with horror. This shared obsession with the formless and with base, low matter becomes uncanny in Bataille's and Lipavsky's writing on the big toe. Bataille speaks of the "clamorous waves of [man's] viscera" that are just as uncontrollable as the pain in his big toe. The pain interrupts his highest thoughts and reminds him that "he has feet, and these feet lead an ignoble life, completely independently of him" (Lebel and Waldberg 1995, 92). Says Lipavsky, "The less specialized the bodily part, the less it resembles a working mechanism, the more assertive becomes its independent life. Because of that the female body is more terrifying than the male, legs than arms, and that is especially evident with the big toes" (34).

It would be quite compelling to pursue this investigation of the correspondences between Bataille and Lipavsky, and further, of the ideas generated within their intellectual circles. However, my point is not to prove that Lipavsky was a Bataillean thinker without being aware of it, or the other way around. More telling than the similarities are the differences between the two thinkers. Namely, fear and time, the two themes that dominate Lipavsky's thought, are completely absent from the Bataille of the *Documents* period.[5] Fear and time as points of divergence between Lipavsky and

Bataille are exceptionally important because they participate in a certain idea of the formless that is completely foreign to the latter thinker.

"*Base materialism* is the principal weapon in the battle Bataille wanted to wage against idealism," writes Yves-Alain Bois in "The Use Value of 'Formless,'" thus reminding Bataille's readers of the polemical and political nature of his heterology (Bois and Krauss 1997, 29, italics in the original). Indeed, in his dictionary entry "Materialism," Bataille openly condemns traditional philosophical materialism, including its dialectical variant, as "senile idealism." "Most materialists," he wrote, "have situated dead matter at the summit of the conventional hierarchy of diverse types of facts, without realizing that in this way they have submitted to an *ideal* form of matter with a form that approaches closer than any other that which matter *should be*" (58, italics in the original). In Lipavsky there is no trace of such a polemical tone, and no attempt whatsoever to politicize the base matter.

Evert van der Zweerde points out in his excellent survey, *Soviet Historiography of Philosophy,* that by 1923 the last vestiges of non-Marxist philosophy were removed from Soviet universities. During the 1920s fierce debates ensued around the idea of materialism that ended with interventions from high party circles and the establishment of dialectical materialism (*diamat*) and historical materialism (*istmat*) as the basis of the official philosophy of the Soviet Union. As Zweerde points out, *Dialektika mifa,* the last non-Marxist philosophical book in the Soviet Union, was published in 1930, then promptly banned, and its author Nikolai Losev was condemned to ten years of hard labor (Zweerde 1997, 34). The purpose of this brief look at the professional context of Lipavsky's philosophizing in the early 1930s is not to lament his fate as a "crypto-philosopher." Rather, its primary purpose is to illustrate his circle's complete isolation from ongoing philosophical practice in the Soviet Union, and consequently, their radical separation from the philosophical tradition in Russia, Marxist and non-Marxist alike. As we have seen, Lipavsky and his friends were keenly aware that between them and the past there was a radical and unbridgeable gap, a historical discontinuity that left them as shut away from the past as they were shut down in the present. They responded by creating highly personal thought. In this philosophical endeavor, they felt free to get rid of the constraints of professional philosophy, such as systematicity and rigorous adherence to certain philosophical schools, and to include things utterly foreign to professional philosophy: humor, narrativity, speculation, and eclecticism. Consequently, it is hard to say that Lipavsky is a materialist philosopher, even of a Bataillean brand.

In order to further investigate Lipavsky's understanding of base matter, we have to return to his philosophical narrative "Water Tractatus." As we have seen, it begins with a model of the world, a thought model manifested in an apple pierced by a piece of steel wire. A brief contemplation of this world below "the lowest border of human language" is followed by "The Champion's Tale," in which Lipavsky discourses on what he calls "the tropical sensation." This easily could be subsumed into another correspondence with Bataille and the ethnographic tendencies of *Documents*.[6] But we need to look more carefully.

What is "the tropical sensation"? Lipavsky shuns the conventional philosophical procedure, and instead of a definition, he offers a story. In a shift that effectively pulls in the reader, the mode of narration turns from third to second person. The philosophical argument suddenly acquires the quality of poetry in prose. You walk through a forest on a hot summer day, "grasses surround you, long like hair. You walk and recall a song. Ants run over your route. Grasshoppers dart, flying sideways from under your feet" (Ostashevsky 2006, 206). And you walk further: flowers smell strongly, there is no sound, it is hot as in a bath. We are all familiar with the sensation when we lose awareness of our body and are reduced to a head floating over the landscape. We glide:

> Space itself swims toward you to spread under your feet. You walk thus for a long time across the meadow or the sparse forest. Ants run over your route.
>
> Suddenly you are gripped by the premonition of irremediable misfortune: time prepares to stop. The day falls upon you like lead. The catalepsy of time! The world stands before you like a member. You look around: how dead is the bloom everywhere! With horror and dread you wait for the explosion. (206)

"The tropical sense" is an experience of nature that is intimately tied with the experiences of terror and temporality (through its suspension). Then comes formless matter:

> [Y]ou entered Dead Water. Dead Water is dense water that closes over your head like a rock. You walked easy as song. You entered an overcrowded day, where light, smell, and heat are at a limit. They stand

> like thick rays, like horns. There is no division there, no motion, no sequence. This water is hard as a rock. (206)

Lipavsky employs two distinct ideas of the formless: that which is undifferentiated or unindividuated, and that which is overwhelming. In "Investigation of Horror," the section about "Dead Water" ends with a brief discussion of "tropical melancholy" and "snow melancholy."[7] Clearly, this suggests that panicked fear emerges from the contemplation of those aspects of nature that are overwhelming. "Dead Water" stands not only for fluidity and viscosity, but also for a vast and continuous space that overwhelms imagination. We also find the imagination cringing in fear before the prospect of its own collapse at the center of the "Analytic of the Sublime" in Kant's *Critique of the Power of Judgment.*

The first book of the Third Critique, "Analytic of the Beautiful," proceeds through four moments, or categories: quality, quantity, relation, and modality. Kant asserts that these same categories are applicable to the categorical investigation of the sublime.[8] They may be applicable but they are not sufficient, for he adds to the latter an additional division: mathematical versus dynamic sublime. Kant defines the sublime as "that which is absolutely great" (Kant 2000, 131). It is that which is great beyond any comparison (132), and therefore that in relation to which everything else is small (133). The formlessness of the sublime comes from its size. The sublime requires the greatest extension of the mind insofar as it is something that is comprehensible but not imaginable. The section toward the end of the discussion of the mathematical sublime is of particular interest:

> The measurement of a space (as apprehension) is at the same time the description of it, thus an objective movement in the imagination and a progression; by contrast, the comprehension of multiplicity in the unity not of thought but of intuition, hence the comprehension in one moment of that which is successively apprehended, is a regression, which in turn cancels the time condition in the progression of the imagination and makes simultaneity intuitable. (142)

In effect, Kant describes a collapse of the sense of time though imagination's sudden fall from a successive progression of parts to the totality of the whole. In the sublime, the reason that posits the infinite is in conflict with the imagination, which fails to represent it.

This operation of making the imagination meet its own limits is familiar to members of Lipavsky's circle. We can recognize it in Alexander Vvedensky's contemplations on time. He participated in Lipavsky's discussion group, and in one of the sessions he proclaimed himself the inventor of the "poetic critique of reason." This is in reference to his poetic understanding of the world, but also a hint at his namesake, Alexander Ivanovich Vvedensky (1856–1925), Russia's greatest proponent of neo-Kantianism. In his *Grey Notebook* Vvedensky writes:

> If we were to erase the numbers from a clock, if we were to forget its false names, maybe then time would want to show its quiet torso, to appear to us in its full glory. Let the mouse run over the stone. Count only its every step. Only forget the word every, only forget the word step. Then each step would seem a new movement. Then, since your ability to perceive a series of movements as something whole has rightfully disappeared, that which you wrongly called a step (you had confused movement and time with space, you falsely transposed one over the other), that movement will begin to break apart, it will approach zero. The shimmering will begin. The mouse will start to shimmer. Look around you: the world is shimmering (like a mouse). (Vvedenskii 2002, 12)

This picture of the world no longer held together by our powers of representation points toward the dynamic sublime. Whereas the mathematical sublime is the result of the conflict of reason and imagination, the dynamic sublime emerges from the mind's encounter with nature. If it is impossible for human mind to take in the infinite at once, without progression, then it is equally impossible for it to square off with the power of nature. The dynamic sublime is overpowering nature that "has no dominion over us" but nevertheless arouses fear (Kant 2000, 143). Kant provides a number of examples of the dynamic sublime, from "threatening cliffs" and "thunder clouds towering up into the heavens" to volcanoes and the "boundless ocean set into rage" (144). What is significant about the dynamic sublime is that the sight of threatening nature "becomes all the more attractive the more fearful it is, as long as we find ourselves in safety" (144). The absence of form in the dynamic sublime comes from nature's immeasurability. It is this boundlessness of nature that emerges as our own limit.

It is important to keep in mind that Lipavsky's main interests are fear and temporality, not the sublime and infinity. That fact alone can be said to be enough to keep Kant and neo-Kantianism at a safe distance from Lipavsky's poetic philosophy. Scholars who looked at Henri Bergson for intellectual sources of the contemplation of time by Lipavsky and his friends are justified by Kant's own conventional approach to the question of time.[9] In the *Critique of Pure Reason,* he sets up time as an a priori category that is objective and inseparable from space. And, most important, he takes causality as the prime evidence of temporal progression. In short, time of the First Critique is the transcendental schema that is the condition of possibility in relation to thought, and, as such, cannot constitute its proper subject. Over the years, this understanding of time was one of the main targets of Kant's critics. This criticism intensified in the late nineteenth century with the clash between neo-Kantianism and Bergsonian vitalism. This rivalry had resonances in the Russian philosophy of the early twentieth century.[10] Still, it makes the resonance between Lipavsky's thinking on time and Kant's additional insights into this question that emerged from his considerations of the aesthetic and the sublime all the more significant.

Kant is interested not only in the definition of the sublime but also in its operations. He asks not only what it is but also what it does, and finds the work of the sublime in its demand for the suspension of temporal progression. In doing so, the sublime brings about the breakdown of causality. It is this collapse of temporal order that makes time perceptible in a certain very limited sense—as an intuition. But what is the effect of this intuition? According to Kant, intuition is a property of imagination and not of understanding or reason. He suggests that by intuiting the possibility of time's collapse, imagination does violence to its inner sense—for this inner sense maintains that nothing can stop time. Then he adds that "the very same violence that is inflicted on the subject by the imagination is judged as purposive for the whole vocation of the mind" (142). The purpose of the sublime is in the vocation of the mind. But what is this vocation? What is the nature of this summons? We can also rephrase this question and ask: what does nature summon? In his discussion of the dynamic sublime, Kant asserts that the sublime in nature "raises the imagination to the point of presenting those cases in which the mind can make palpable to itself the sublimity of its own vocation even over nature" (145). The imagination, elevated to its very limit, calls the mind to overcome that which is most powerful, nature. And it is in this very movement of elevation and calling that nature itself collapses.

Nature plays a prominent role in Lipavsky's investigations of terror and time. However, it is never an elemental and powerful nature, but instead always a nature in the state of collapse: dead water, midday stillness, liquid animals, spilling intestines. As in Kant, it is a nature that is losing its form-giving properties, a de-natured nature in which no object can keep its form. The sublime clearly belongs to this nature deprived of forms. In order to help us hear its voice, I will summon an insightful reader of Kant. In his *Lessons on the Analytic of the Sublime,* Lyotard warns that the sublime does not belong to the world of phenomena. Like Lipavsky's model of the world, the sublime is outside language, that is, beyond representation. "Sublimity," he writes, "does not predicate the thing but the *Geistesstimmung,* the disposition of thinking that experiences or reflects on itself when it represents the thing to itself" (Lyotard 1994, 81). Lyotard leaves Kant's word *Geistesstimmung* in the original in order to preserve the connotations embedded in the proper meaning of that word: disposition. Already in his introductory lecture, dedicated to the discussion of Kant's "Analytic of the Beautiful," Lyotard warns that the German word *stimme* holds a number of senses that exceed that of the French *voix,* and, for that matter, English *voice:* "it evokes the accord of voices, and the mood of a soul (*Stimmung*), and the beginnings of its determination as destination (*Bestimmung*)" (18). It is important to note that it is precisely the term *Stimmung* that in early modernism establishes the bridge between artistic and clinical practice. The Surrealists borrowed it from de Chirico, who again adopted it from Nietzsche in order to designate a certain mood of apophany similar to the "praecox feeling" characteristic of the early stages of a psychotic break. Schizophrenic patients describe this feeling as a mood in which "everything is totally and uncannily transformed: the fabric of space seems subtly changed; the feeling of reality is either heightened, pulsing with mysterious, unnameable force, or else oddly diminished or undermined" (Sass 1992, 44). In it, we can easily recognize Lipavsky's "tropical sense." Indeed, the "catalepsy of time" can be seen as the encounter with the sublime that designates the very limit not only of imagination but of thought itself, reason and all. Something remarkable happens at that very moment when thought threatens to lose its form and, to use Lyotard's locution, ceases to feel itself thinking. Back to "Water Tractatus": we are caught in the caesura of time. The bloom is dead everywhere. With horror and dread, we are awaiting the explosion:

> And the explosion comes.
>
> "The explosion comes?"
>
> "Yes. You hear your name called. (Gogol talks about that.)"

> They all had a drink. And the diminutive Greek asked: "Why?"
> They smiled. (Ostashevsky 2006, 206)

The voice booms like an explosion. Remember, for Lipavsky, the origin of words is the muscular action of breathing: inhaling and exhaling. The voice is inscribed in the body. Now, it collects the body and tears it away from the state of undifferentiation. The undifferentiation here pertains no longer to dead matter, but to the death of reason. In this undifferentiation, the mind is overwhelmed, it loses its clear boundaries. It is at the point of spilling out and being invaded by its surroundings, at the point of losing its distinction from nature, and therefore, of losing itself in surrounding nature. It is the voice, *Stimme,* that breaks the *Stimmung.* In doing so, it pulls the mind back from the brink. Who is calling? Is this reason summoning the overwhelmed imagination?

We should not forget that this drama of individuation unfolds in a narrative: four buddies sitting in a restaurant, having a drink and contemplating an apple pierced by a steel wire. It is a model, a thought experiment, a pure schema. The Champion constructed this simple assemblage right in front of their eyes, but it is also a given, an a priori model of singularity. From it, the narrative ensues. Unlike Kant, Lipavsky not only discusses time but actually engages time through the narrative he unfolds. As Paul Ricoeur points out, the fundamental trait of narrative is that it brings together chronological and nonchronological dimensions (Ricoeur 1981, 174). The chronological dimension is the sequencing of instances and of fragments, their plotting and ordering, which is in Lipavsky emphasized by enumeration. The nonchronological dimension is the coming together of the story, which Ricoeur also describes as "the act of the plot" and "eliciting pattern from a succession" (174). Nonchronological is, then, also atemporal, but not in the sense of the absence of time—rather, in the sense of the disturbance of a linear understanding of time. It is a temporal jolt that suspends succession and brings forward the present moment.

On one occasion, "The Club of Ignorant Scholars" was joined by Vladimir Propp, who at that point had just finished his *Morphology of the Folk Tale,* which would eventually bring him worldwide scholarly recognition. Lipavsky grilled this then-still-young and timid scholar about the significance of his analysis of fairy tales. Propp laid out his theory from *Morphology* in a condensed version: the functions of characters are expressed in actions, which themselves have a strictly determined place within the larger narrative structure (Propp 1968, 21). Lipavsky retorted that these principles are not limited to fairy tales and could be found in any narrative, from traditional rituals to American film comedies. Propp then resorted to the *Egyptian Book of the Dead* in order to explain his idea that each character is a "soul," like Osiris, who chants "I am Osiris" (Lipavsky, 2005, 366–67). Propp's defense strangely echoed Kharms's poem from the column of hieroglyphs. However, he was not persuasive enough, and his ideas did not find their way into Lipavsky's narrative philosophy. He laid out his own idea of the narrative in one of the ensuing sessions of the club. It merits full citation:

> L.L.: The chessboard should also be included in the list of sacred objects. Because it represents an autonomous, hermetic world, alternative to our world. It also has time, but its own; space, objects, resistance—everything its own. It has mechanics, precise and no worse than ours, which we study on earth and in the sky. And with this autonomous world we can make a decisive experiment: to dematerialize it.
>
> We should start by replacing the visible figures with what they really are, the lines of force on the board. Then we cut the chess table into sections, assemble the deck, and play out a game of chess as cards. Then replace this deck with a table of signs chosen according to a corresponding system; turn it into a single formula in which, with the change of any one sign, all the rest undergo a change. Determine the final form of this formula—what's called "check-mate" in the game—and deduce the laws that govern the formula's transformations from the initial to the final form.
>
> In this way one of these worlds will transform itself into an auto-unfolding story about no one knows what. (Lipavskii 2005, 412)[11]

Whereas Propp is interested in morphology, Lipavsky searches for the formless; whereas Propp insists on function, Lipavsky affirms uselessness; whereas Propp limits narrative to its chronological aspects, Lipavsky unleashes nonchronological jolts; whereas Propp finds a limited number of narrative combinations, Lipavsky opens up infinite permutations; and whereas Propp affirms action, Lipavsky posits its breakdown and its replacement by the event. Formless, useless, nonchronological, infinite, evental: this list easily could be applied to Kharms's works. Indeed, his ideas and those of the other members of "The Club of Ignorant Scholars" are closely related to each other, especially the ideas concerning infinity. At the same time as he wrote love letters to Tamara Aleksandrovna, Kharms wrote philosophical letters to her husband.

Theaters and Xs

Many of Lipavsky's ideas—and one of Propp's—can be found in Kharms's *Lapa,*[12] which is certainly one of his most intriguing manuscripts. This work, composed between June 24 and August 17, 1930, teems with curiosities: It opens with a long poem that functions as a prologue and summary; continues in a prose dialogue interspersed with verse, a long section in *zaum* language, and a drawing; and ends hesitantly, with several alternative endings. The variant of the window sign, inscribed between the title of the play penned in calligraphic letters and the first verse of the prologue, indicates an ambiguous dedication to Ester. *Lapa* is Kharms's only dramatic work that opens with the window monogram. It is also his only dramatic work that contains an elaborate *mise en page,* and in that sense the emblem is not just an extra-textual element, a sign of the dedication of this work to Ester Rusakova, but instead it actively engages with other parts of the work. Finally, it is the only instance when another emblem is inscribed within the window. This figure is in the shape of a trident, or the letter Ш ("sh") in the Russian Cyrillic alphabet.

In their comments on *Lapa,* Anna Gerasimova and Alexander Nikitaev assert that the trident-shaped symbol resembles the Cyrillic letter *t* as it appears in Kharms's handwriting from his early manuscripts. In this case, this letter is turned upside down, which points toward the dynamic and interchangeable nature of the letters *t* and *l* in the semantics of Velimir Khlebnikov.[13] In his analysis of the worlds *let* (flight) and *tiazhest'* (weight), Khlebnikov argues that the letter *l* can be seen as "a marker for self-instigated motion towards an immobile point, and *t* as motion-dependant on an external cause going from the point of origin toward an immobile point" (1987, 267). Gerasimova and Nikitaev recognize the connection between the trident-shaped sign and Khlebnikov's transformation of the letter *t* into *l,* which represents both the sonic leitmotif and the predominant theme of the play: from the very title (*Lapa*), to the flight (*let)* as the leading idea of the play, to the one of its endings which is located in an iceberg (*lednik*) (Gerasimova and Nikitaev 1991, 27).

If the letter Ш is indeed a reference to Khlebnikov, then the window in which it is inscribed represents, in this instance, a sign of intertextuality, or a place of passage from Khlebnikov's to Kharms's work. It seems that Kharms even wants this passage to be physical: in the second part of *Lapa,* Khlebnikov appears in an allegorical scene in which he rides a horse, then a bull, a cow, and a piece of paper (2001b, 96). Also, it is anything but accidental that the window suggests a linkage between texts that is not only metaphorical but also physical. We have observed that Kharms transforms the window into the space of writing, and then into the text's locale, the blank page. Khlebnikov rides a page as if it were a magic carpet; at the same time, he is framed within a window, arrested in the moment of passage between one space and another. Kharms associates Khlebnikov with immortality: as early as 1926, he wrote a couplet dedicated to the deceased poet, "With his legs crossed / Velimir sits. He's alive" (1997a, 60), and in *Lapa* Khlebnikov appears riding a bull, an animal that is related to life after death in ancient Egyptian mythology. As a poet who greatly influenced Kharms's understanding of poetry, Khlebnikov is in Kharms's works always associated with writing.[14]

Lapa is a continuation of Khlebnikov's story "Ka" through drama. Whereas *Lapa* opens with a window, "Ka" concludes with the image of one of its principal characters, Layla, bursting violently into a room through a closed window:

> Suddenly, in the nighttime window that looked out into Kamenoostrovsky Boulevard, the glass shattered, it fell everywhere, and through that window appeared the head of Layla, lying peacefully stretched out like a box of vegetables. She seemed dead. (Khlebnikov 1989, 73)

Khlebnikov's windows are barred and glassed; they promise an opening and liberation, but instead deliver death. Conversely, Kharms's windows are always hollow and open. If Khlebnikov associates his windows with death, Kharms relates his to liberation, passage, and flight. In his pronouncedly autobiographical and hermetic untitled poem from 1931, he writes about the bird Ester who flies high as he calls her through the window (1997a, 191), as if he were attempting to reverse Layla's fateful landing in the shattered window glass.

The close association of the window with flight is not at all surprising. In *Lapa,* the window monogram prefaces the dramatic action of flying out into the sky and reaching a star. This is a curious flight: it is not presented as a teleological journey, but as a compendium of symbols compressed into a fragmentary narrative. This fragmentariness is underscored by the seemingly effortless passage from one genre to another within the same work. Furthermore, in the verse prologue, the theme of flight is already related to a dream, and, more specifically, to a prophetic dream. A gaze directed upward, into the heavens, often symbolizes a look toward the future. Interestingly, here this gaze is also turned inward. In the prologue, Kharms invokes a statue made of tin, bronze, cobalt, and iron, which later takes on a prominent role in initiating the flight of the protagonist, Landman[15] (Kharms 2001b, 90). The statue made of four different materials occupies a central place in the first part of the Book of Daniel, the Old Testament prophet after whom Kharms was named.[16] According to the Old Testament, Daniel was one of the three young Jews who lived in the court of the Babylonian king Nebuchadnezzar, who was tortured by prophetic dreams he could not remember. After the best astrologers and magicians of his kingdom were unable to uncover and interpret his nocturnal visions, they were revealed to Daniel in his sleep:

> (31) You, O king, were watching; and behold, a great image! This great image, whose splendor was excellent, stood before you; and its form was awesome. (32) This image's head was of fine gold, its chest and arms of silver, its belly and thighs of bronze. (33) Its legs of iron, its feet partly of iron and partly of clay.

In the biblical story, the "image" of the statue crumbles, symbolizing the gradual decline of the kingdoms that succeeded the great Babylonian Empire. Kharms departs from the biblical prophecy in two important ways. First, he replaces the regressive order of metals gold-silver-bronze-iron with a random sequence of nonprecious metals: tin, bronze, cobalt, and iron. Second, whereas the prophet Daniel is able to "see" the king's dream and then interpret it, *Lapa*'s protagonist is trying to reach the star Agam in order to be able to choose *not* to see his dreams. So, while the biblical statue endows the seer with knowledge of the future, the statue in *Lapa* initiates a blind(ed) man on a journey in search of forgetfulness (blinded because, echoing the biblical story of Tobias, Landman's eyes are covered with wax at the outset of his journey). As Landman reaches the sky, the wax melts and he opens his eyes. In an unusual turn, the progressive loss of memory is paired with the clarity symbolized both by the reversal of blindness and Landman's elevation toward the star.

Kharms is the poet of heights. He is powerfully, irresistibly, drawn upward. Rising, flight into the sky, navigation of the heavens, climbing onto roofs, levitation: up, up, by any means necessary. What is important, for Kharms, is the departure from earth. Unlike his other works about flying, which usually feature either an isolated instance or a single symbol of flight, *Lapa* is an ascensional tour de force. Landman climbs on a roof, is propelled upward by a statue, and then goes from one elevated plateau to another. This upward journey is marked by symbols: from the verticality of the statue, to the first heavens marked by an entire menagerie of birds, then to the bizarre image of a girl-tree who converses with angels, and finally to the cool breeze of an iceberg. Almost all of these symbols of elevation and flight can also be found in Kharms's works that precede or immediately follow *Lapa.* What sets this work apart is that the accumulation of symbols results in a flight that strives ever higher. The elevation is always related to transcendence, and Kharms makes sure to note this orientation of the journey: when, at a certain point, the flight seems to come to a standstill, "a cry is heard from beyond the horizon," at which point the flight resumes (2001b, 93). This flight, which strives ever higher, ever toward the beyond, finally results in the disappearance of the sky.

Lapa progresses in an unusual way. The main dramatic action unfolds through symbols. However, unlike the symbolist drama proper, the purpose of this deployment of symbols is not to give the play universal import. Quite to the contrary: Kharms obstructs this universalization by juxtaposing poetic with visual symbols. Both kinds of symbols appear as prominent signposts of an extremely fragmented dramatic action. The goal of Landman's journey is to reach the star Agam the Swan from the constellation of the Northern Cross. He takes off into the sky, reaches a place called "The Bird House" that is a filthy chicken coop, abducts a swan, and returns to the earth. Kharms makes sure to underscore that he does not plummet back to earth but instead goes into a gentle descent. Landman's landing is not depicted symbolically or dramatically, but physically: the *mise en page* of this return is in the form of a column of *zaum* words. From this point on, the idea of flight is taken over by another character, Utiugov, who, through a dialogue with Khlebnikov, surges upward. The improbability of this departure is underlined by the very name of the character, which comes from *utiug,* the Russian word for a heavy metal iron. For Utiogov, the sky is a creaky tin roof. Instead of giving shelter, this roof stands as a banal, makeshift cover.

Utiugov: Oh! I am tired of the sky
It hangs overhead
Leaking if the rain
knocks upon it from above

The Landman's journey pierces the "tin" of the sky. This breakthrough affects not only the sky but also all other spatial relations:

> Depth and dove transformed one into the other
> The constellation of the Swan was carried on
> the brain's rudder and memory's oar.

There is a strong correspondence between the imagery of *Lapa* and Kharms's hieroglyphic column (figure 6). Inversion, captured in the column by the image of the upturned tree and the paraphrase from the Book of Revelation, is here depicted as a "transformation" of depth into a bird, and vice versa. This transformation amounts to a complete loss of orientation. Lightness and disorientation make the language superfluous. Just as the song is liberated by the cessation of speech, so the removal of the sky has to be revelatory.

> The sky has vanished.
> Oh sky sky, now striped
> now blue just like a flower
> now long like cat tails
> now fast like skis.
> (2001b, 96)[17]

The sky is doubled: "Oh, sky sky." There is another sky behind the sky that is the tin roof. Beyond the gray metallic sky, there is a blue weightless sky. This empty, azure sky attracts objects, pulls them upward into itself. They give themselves to the sky and dematerialize. Later, we are going to see that, for Kharms, rising is a mathematical operation just as much as it is a poetic image. But, for the time being, let's follow this path into the azure, into the Sky beyond sky. In his meditations on the upward progression into the azure sky, Bachelard writes that "there is an imaginary beyond, a pure beyond, one without a within. First there is *nothing,* then there is a *deep* nothing, then there is a blue *depth* (1988, 168, italics in the original). This beyond "without a within" designates not only the absence of the interior but also of reserve. Whatever reaches the azure Sky beyond sky spills out and dissolves. This beyond "without a within," this complete expenditure and loss, is the ultimate destination pointed to by the window sign. "Before a sky from which the objects have been banished, there will be born an imaginary subject whose memories have been banished," concludes Bachelard in his investigation of the blue sky (1988, 168).

It is important to note that, within the structure of *Lapa,* Utiugov's speech about the nothing within and nothing without does not represent a completely new insight, but the repetition of an earlier realization, stated in a much more roundabout and complex way. While delivering his speech on the vanishing sky, Utiugov is waving a Primus portable stove. As Kobrinsky explains, in the Soviet Union of the late 1920s, the alcohol-burning Primus had been largely replaced by the gas cooker as a more efficient kitchen utensil. Although a pronouncedly unpoetic object, "primus" entered Russian poetry and came to signify something that is outdated, banal, and out of use (Kobrinskii 2000, 115). In Kharms's play, this meaning is paired with the literal meaning of the Latin word *primus* as the ordinal number one. Both Utiugov's attribute of *primus* and Landman's name point to the first man, the man made of earth, who dwells on earth, but whose proper home is in Paradise: Adam. Before Utiugov reaches the objectless sky, Landman has his encounter with nothing. Like his return to the earth, this encounter involves a complex interplay of text and image.

After the statue catapults him on his aerial voyage, Landman quickly traverses the distance from Russia to Egypt. At this point, a section entitled "Description of the Nile" interrupts the linear progression of the play. The description is both textual and pictorial. The textual section speaks of a coffin in which lies a man "green with death," who, in order to appear alive, incessantly recites recipes for soup preparation. "Essentially, this was the Nile," writes Kharms. "Amenhotep swam in the Nile. He wore shorts and a cap" (2001b, 92). And then he adds: "Here is the diagram of Amenhotep" (figure 12).

The diagram appears as a rough outline of a headless human body with outstretched limbs. At the same time, it resembles a map of an urban intersection. Amenhotep's bodily parts are marked in the following way: the right leg is designated as the "finite leg," the left leg as the "cisfinite leg," the torso as the "street of fibers," and the outstretched arms as the "streets" of the left and right arms. The round form that resembles the head detached from the body is located between the "street of the left arm" and the "cisfinite leg," and it is marked "Bukak E."

The window sign and the Amenhotep diagram are the most prominent examples of graphism in *Lapa.* In relation to the window sign, a double shift occurs in the Amenhotep diagram.

First, the window facilitates a horizontal, theatrical view, which with the "Description of the Nile" changes into a vertical, aerial view from above. This ninety-degree rotation of the angle profoundly affects the entire per-

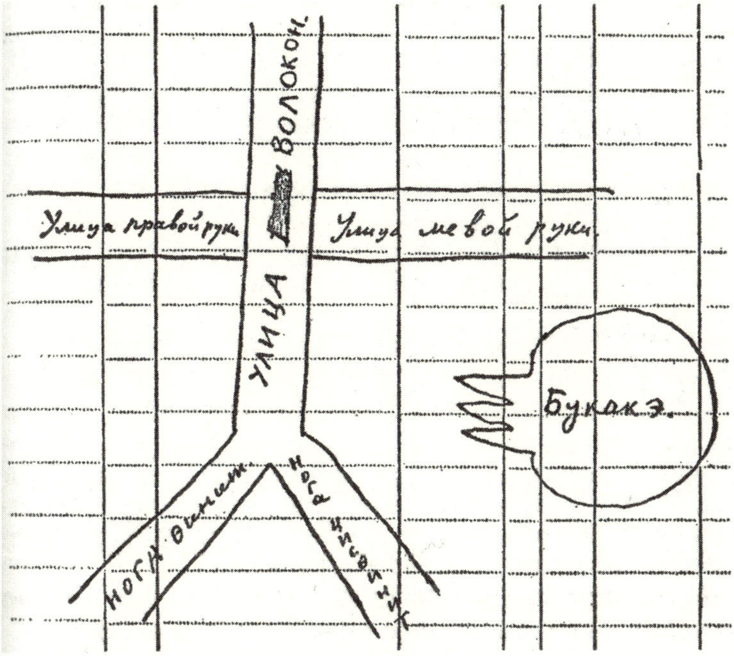

Figure 12.

Diagrammatic drawing of Amenhotep from the manuscript of Kharms's play *Lapa*

spective of the play. The horizontality of theater is inseparable from its frontality: the spectacle takes place at the horizon, which theatrical representation brings closer and enlarges. The horizontal gaze is the gaze that surveys, scrutinizes, and examines. The theatrical point of view moves laterally and proceeds methodically, step by step. It progresses through links and passages; it forms networks of intersecting lines and paths of uniform succession. Each knot leads to another juncture; each observation becomes a vista for a new sight. Horizontality searches for clarity. It is the position of contemplation, and it provides continuity and permanence. If horizontality proceeds though a network of logical connections, verticality is characterized by, more than anything else, the breakdown of the system of cause and effect, or of logical procedures in general. While horizontality signifies distribution, verticality signifies simultaneity. The vertical axis disturbs the flow of linear time and establishes an order free from the constraints of temporality—the order of pure transcendence.

The second shift from the window monogram and the Amenhotep diagram is manifested in the flattening of horizontality's relief and volume into a two dimensional, planar world facilitated by the view from above. In his essay "The Labyrinth," Yampolsky observes that "the map enters the realm of language which borders on silence; linguistics here changes into hieroglyphics, into cipher" (Iampol'skii 1996, 111). He adds that the map always represents a trajectory of the bodily movement, and in this regard, the manuscript represents a map of writing. In his aerial survey of the landscape, Landman assumes the point of view of a writer working on his text. The Amenhotep diagram is not only a *mise en page,* but also a *mise en abyme:* the landscape that Landman beholds is identical to Kharms's text depicting Landman observing the landscape. *Page/abyme.* Nothing is placed in it.

Kharms has Amenhotep quite literally stand on the convergence of two worlds. His left leg is marked "finite," referring to finite numbers, materiality and objectivity; and the left leg as "cisfinite," referring to the numerical order based on zero that Kharms devised at the time of his work on *Lapa.* Being based on zero, cisfinity implies nonmateriality and nonobjectivity. It also implies the absence of weight and, consequently, refers to flight. In his poem "To Ring—To Fly (The Third Cisfinite Logic)" (1930) Kharms celebrates a universe liberated from weight and the pull of gravity:

And horse to fly.
And house to fly.
And period to fly.
A forehead flies.
A chest flies.
A stomach flies.

Kharms, perfectly attuned to aerial symbolism, accurately detects the sound of flight in the ringing of bells:[18]

The house rings.
The water rings.
The rock nearby is ringing.
The book nearby is ringing.
Mother, son, and garden ring.
A rings.
B rings.
THAT flies and THAT rings.
(Ostashevsky 2006, 94)

Resting simultaneously on the rock of finity and on the ether of cisfinity, Amenhotep is neither on earth nor in the air; he is neither purely material nor purely immaterial, neither an object nor an idea, neither dead nor alive.

In the final analysis, Amenhotep represents an incomplete and impossible body. As depicted in the diagram (figure 12), Amenhotep's body is missing all of its extremities. The outstretched arms and legs of the headless body open into the empty surface of the page. This hollow, shuttle-like body floats in the water, levitates in the air, and rolls in the sand. It cannot assume an erect position because it is missing its base, its footing, hands and feet, paws. The text of *Lapa* (the paw) begins where Amenhotep's arms and legs end. The paw, as well as the foot and the hand, is the organ that makes traces and imprints. Landman's itinerary resembles the movement of a paw: he departs from the ground and returns to it. The paw and Landman belong both to the earth and to the heavens: they bring the two together and produce traces, imprints, signatures. The text of *Lapa* emerges as Amenhotep's footing—his feet and support: it is the missing organ of his schematized and diagrammatized body.

The lack of extremities, the organs with which the body ends, points to the region where it begins, to its center. The two legs marked by the abstract concepts of finity and cisfinity join the torso, to which the two streets/arms are perpendicular. The round-shaped figure that resembles a head detached from its body is marked with a combination of a word and a letter, "Bukak E.," which might be read as a first name with the initial of the family name. "Bukak" is Kharms's neologism, probably derived from the word *bukva* ("letter" in Russian), to which the suffix *ak* lends the meaning of a "letter-being," or "letter-man," or "letter-beast."[19] The concept of the letter-being, word-being, or alphabetized self is closely related to naming, and therefore to the writing of the proper name. Although Kharms often varied his pseudonym when signing his works, thus creating new names for himself such as "Khorms," "Khkharms," or "Charms"—he very rarely distorted his given name. We have seen that the reference to the Prophet Daniel, after whom he was named, already appears in the opening of *Lapa*. Kharms's first name is contained in the "Description of the Nile." In the only modification of his first name that I was able to identify, Kharms singled out the word "nile" contained in the Russian spelling of his name: *DaNiil* (1997a, 47). The use of that word in *Lapa* is complex. In Russian, the Nile is a homonym of the word zero (*nil*), which partially explains

Kharms's remark that the Nile resembles a coffin. The Nile, however, also refers to the first name of the creator of the play, DaNiil.

Whereas the window sign is the monogram, or the compressed name "Ester," the "Description of the Nile" can be seen as a strange spatialization of her lover's name. It repeats the linguistic formula used in the formation of "Bukak E.": a given name plus the initial of the last name. The former is suggested by the name of the river Nile, and the latter is easily recognizable in the diagram of Amenhotep, which resembles the Cyrillic letter X (Kh), the first letter of the author's last name spelled in Russian Cyrillic letters: Хармс. I have already noted that *Lapa* is dominated by the figure of Khlebnikov (Хлебников), whose story "Ka" Kharms used as the source text for his play. One of his most notable borrowings is the character Amenhotep, whose name Kharms changed in the play. While Khlebnikov in "Ka" used the name Amenofis (Аменофис), Kharms opted for Amenhotep (Аменхотеп), a slight variant of the same character from ancient Egyptian history. In this variation, the letter X is located at the very center of the word.

This letter is also a variant of the cross symbol, St. Andrew's cross, which was until the October Revolution featured on the standard of St. Petersburg. The flag is one of Kharms's most subtle auto-references,[20] and here it is paired with a cross, the traditional symbol that appears in Kharms's works with great regularity. In *Lapa,* Kharms places the cross in a privileged position. It plays an important role in the dramatic action of the play: Landman departs on his journey to reach the new star Agam the Swan, located in the constellation of the Northern Cross. But that is not all. The central position of the cross is also reflected in the conflation of the two points of view employed in the play: the horizontal point of view through the window intersects at a right angle with the vertical point of view of the flying Landman, thus forming the shape of the cross. Furthermore, the itinerary of the play originates from the window-star-heaven symbol, continues in the earthly episode that precedes Landman's departure, and then reaches up, toward the region that I described earlier as the Sky beyond sky, or heaven. This diagram of the movement to and from the earth follows Kharms's own symbolic schema of the cross. According to him, all existence is conditioned by difference, or by distinction between "this" and "that," which are made possible by a separating point or an "impediment" (2001a, 31). Kharms, then, sees the cross as a symbol of the manifestation of this principle in the doctrine of the trinity. He defines the cross as "the symbolic sign of the law of existence and life," and then offers his schematic reading of the Egyptian cross as Heaven-World-Heaven (2001a, 36).

One of the most striking characteristics of Kharms as a thinker and writer is his boldness in the literary application, or concretization, of his most abstract theoretical ideas. The tripartite structure of Heaven–World–Heaven is clearly reflected in an early draft of *Oknov and Kozlov,* entitled *Oknov–Kharms–Okno* (1980, 173). This version of the cross schema is slightly asymmetrical because of the difference between "Oknov" and "Okno,"[21] and, as we will see before this chapter ends, such disequilibrium in Kharms's work is anything but accidental. The association of the cross and the principle of trinity is also strongly asserted in the drawing of the girl with pretzel-like legs, who has three crosses inscribed above her right arm and head (figure 5). These are unusual crosses: the first from the left has its vertical axis planted on the pedestal that resembles a human pelvis and legs, and is crowned with a square- or diamond-shaped form, while its horizontal bar is broken at both sides, suggesting human hands; the middle cross that bleeds smaller crosses can be seen as a crucifixion; the third cross is in the form of a swastika, the Hindu symbol of movement and infinity, and it is underlined by a blue-and-red stripe. The grouping of three crosses, as stated earlier, points to the image of Golgotha, where the crosses of the two thieves flank Christ's cross. Christian symbolism often associates these two crosses with the duality of the Tree of the Knowledge of Good and Evil and Christ's cross, which is always in the middle, with the Tree of Life. Kharms's schema, Heaven–Earth–Heaven, is obviously informed by this kind of symbolism, and it is interesting that in this triadic structure one of the crosses is topped with a square. In his consideration of the geometric and numerical symbolism of the cross, Rene Guenon asserts that "the cross naturally represents the tetradic principle . . . in its dynamic form, while the square represents it in its static form" (Guenon 1996, 36). Be this as it may, it should be noted that for Kharms, the window and the cross are related, but not identical, symbols. The cross can be inscribed in the square frame of the window. At the same time, being the symbol of the star and heaven (Ester), the window appears at the cardinal points of the cross schema. This results in an overwhelming impression of a dynamic relation between the two symbols: they frame one another and are framed by one another at the same time.

If we read Kharms's text/drawing (figure 5) the same way we would read an alphabetic text, starting from the upper left corner, we would find that it opens with the three crosses. If we continue our reading in the "key" provided by the crosses, we will find, for example, that throughout the text the letter X is consistently capitalized, regardless of its position within the word and sentence. With its ambiguous status as both alphabetic letter and pictorial symbol, the cross brings about a decay of grammar. Apart from this agrammatical and nonalphabetic use, the cross is also employed as a mathematical symbol in the sentence that translates roughly as "Nothing incites a greatly overdeveloped Nosology (Sterne + Gogol) Kozma Pr." The use of the parentheses and plus sign turns the entire phrase into a strange formula in which the numbers are replaced by Kharms's favorite writers: Laurence Sterne, Nikolai Gogol, and Kozma Prutkov. The portion of this literary/mathematical phrase isolated by parentheses represents a short additive series that consists of only two members.[22] Still, this series is long enough to bring about yet another relation between the cross and the window sign in Kharms's work: if the former establishes an additive series, then the latter sets up a disjunctive series. Further, it affirms separation and difference as a relation of disjunction, and not as a total disengagement and absence of relation. According to Kharms, all existence is reducible to the notion of difference as relation.

The basic premise of Kharms's logical procedure in the tract "On Existence, Time, and Space" is that, in order to exist, the world has to consist of different parts. The total number of parts in any existing whole is reducible to two, or "this" and "that" in Kharms's terminology.[23] Following this logic, he establishes that, in order for "this" and "that" to exist, there has to be an "impediment" that separates them. In temporal terms, the impediment is the present moment, the "now," that distinguishes the past from the future. Kharms then proposes that, like the pure difference, the "present" cannot be said to exist: "the present appears only as the 'impediment' in the transition from the past to the future, and past and present appear as *that* and *this* in the existence of time" (2001a, 33). In the tract "On Existences," Kharms establishes the same logical procedure, this time outlining a diagram in which "this" and "that" are represented by a horizontal line, and "neither this nor that" or the "impediment" by a vertical line. The diagram, of course, is in the form of the coordinate system, or the cross. The coordinate system originates from the nodal point of the cross, the zero in both time and space. That is, for Kharms: the instant.

This schematization of time, space, and existence, with its simplicity and its emphasis on the nodal or zero point as the origin, is of major importance for Kharms. Considered in relation to his works, it clearly plays a major part in his departure from the symbol and his movement toward the event. This break is nowhere as clearly recognizable as in the dramatic poem "An Instant from Signs" (1931). Like *Lapa,* this piece talks about an unusual flight into the heavens. Here, however, the flight does not follow a winding path of aerial symbols but instead explodes in an austere, almost geometrical itinerary. Simply, a carrot shoots straight up from the ground and goes "beyond the clouds," where it converses with an entity named "The Son of All" (1997a, 203). Although it is still shrouded in esotery reminiscent of *Lapa,* the symbolism of "An Instant from Signs" is drastically simplified. The earth from which the carrot is catapulted stands for preservation, excavation, and the past: as it flies, the carrot complains that it spent forty years in the hole and that it "needs air" (202). The sky is the exact opposite of the earth: it symbolizes expenditure, disappearance, and the future. The carrot is a root that has a noticeably elongated form, which makes its underground habitat aerodynamically absurd. It belongs neither to the earth nor to the sky, neither to the past nor to the future. In that sense, it can be clearly identified with the idea of the impediment from Kharms's logical texts. In one of these texts, the poem "The Third Cisfinite Logic of the Infinite Non-Being" (1930), Kharms meditates on the progressive partition of time until time itself disappears into an instant: "Not all parts of the hour have always been, and now they are not" (1997a, 175).

So, what is Kharms's instant? Is it a negation of time? In *Sophist* and in *Parmenides,* Plato advances the idea of the instant as nonbeing in relation to time. In the latter text, he assumes that the unity consists of "is" and "is not," to which Kharms's "here" and "there" are clearly comparable. In relation to this unity, the instant emerges as a strange sort of being, which neither "is" nor "is not." If "is" and "is not" are seen as dialectical opposites, such as movement and stasis, the instant becomes the transition from one into another, without itself occupying any time. Plato further shows that the instant is the general category of transition, from likeness to unlikeness, from plurality to unity, from here to there. Kharms's notion of the instant and of not-being is certainly not of this Platonic order. It should be noted that he always relates the instant to affirmation, not negation, from the double negation in "Third Cisfinite Logic of the Infinite Non-Being" to the notion of conflation instead of transition in "On Existence, Time, and Space." The instant corresponds much more closely to Deleuze's understanding of nonbeing, or "(non)-being" and "?-being" in his notation, as "the *differential element* in which affirmation, as multiple affirmation, finds the principle of its genesis" (1994, 64, italics added).[24] Kharms's instant, or the impediment, is much closer to the notion of pure difference than to the Platonic notion of transition that bridges difference, and makes possible the notions of the *same* and the *similar.* So then, how does this understanding of the instant play out in Kharms's writing?

In *Lapa* (1930), a statue sends Landman on a windy road into the sky; in "An Instant from Signs" (1931), another earthly creature, the carrot, shoots up like a self-propelled projectile; in "The Falling" (1940), the direction of the flight is reversed:

> Two men fell from a roof. They both fell from the roof of a five-storey newly erected building. Seemingly a school. They had moved down the roof in a sitting position to the very edge and at that point started to fall. (1993, 145)

In *Lapa,* flight is intimately related to dreams, and more precisely, to prophetic dreams; "An Instant from Signs" concludes with an evocation of the idea of the eternal return[25] (1997a, 205–6); finally, in "The Falling" the prophecy is replaced by prolepsis, and eternal return by simple repetition. Here, the plummet starts unexpectedly and remains unexplained. But, as in Kharms's other stories about falling,[26] it quickly turns into a spectacle. The two falling men are first spotted by one Ida Markovna, who was "standing at her window in the building opposite and was blowing her nose into a tumbler" (1993, 145). As they continue to fall, another girl, also called Ida Markovna, sees them. The two Ida Markovnas are oblivious to one another: the abyss of the two falling bodies is the only thing that briefly brings them together. The schema of "On Existence, Time, and Space" is clearly discernable in the story: Ida Markovna and Ida Markovna correspond to "this" and "that," connected and separated by an impediment. The impediment takes a vertical position in relation to the horizontality of "this" and "that." Ida and Ida see the falling men from their apartment windows. Here again, as in *Lapa,* the story is centered on the intersection of the two gazes, the horizontal view through the window and the vertical view from above. These two perspectives are by no means identical.

The observers of the fall, the two Ida Markovnas, initially approach their windows, and then run away. The second Ida Markovna tries to open the window and then, remembering that she had nailed it shut, runs to grab the pincers from a stove located in the far corner of the room. The first Ida Markovna rushes to the window and then realizes that she is naked. She becomes excessively self-conscious, jumps away from the window, and hides "behind the wicker tripod on which there had at one time stood a potted plant" (1993, 146). We are already familiar with the situation of a naked tenant who is trying to surround himself with objects. In "A Tract (More or Less) According to a Synopsis of Emersen" Kharms uses exactly the same situation to illustrate the imperfection of the additive series of "if there are no flowers in the flower vase then such a vase is rendered meaningless, and if one is to take away the vase then the round table becomes meaningless," and so on. "[T]he negation of a single object destroys the entire system" (2007, 250). The two men are falling, but so is the system in relation to which they are moving. Ida Markovna looks through the window, and what does she see? And another Ida Markovna looks through the window, and she sees the same thing. The two falling men complete the disjunctive series.

Cisfinitum

Kharms's identification of the difference, or impediment, with zero is a curious logical move. The impact of zero radically changes, depending on its function in an equation: If added to a number it doesn't change anything, and therefore represents sameness; if a number is multiplied by it, then it turns into zero, thereby changing the number in a most drastic way. Zero is not only a paradoxical number, but also a concept that separates arithmetic from all other kinds of quantifying uses of mathematics. For example, Frege uses the concept of zero as the basis for his argument against empiricism in mathematics (Frege 1968, 11). Ultimately, he comes up with the notion of number as pure thought:

> The basis of arithmetic lies deeper, it seems, than that of any of the empirical sciences, and even than that of geometry. The truths of arithmetic govern all that is numerable. This is the widest domain of all; for to it belongs not only the actual, not only the intuitable, but everything thinkable. (1968, 21)

In the tract "Cisfinitum: The Falling of a Stem" (1930), written in the form of a letter addressed to Leonid Lipavsky, Kharms proposes a "category E" that pertains only to the "creative disciplines" and resists all "noncreative disciplines" such as "formal logic" and "The Laws of Thought" (1997b, 309). In the course of the initial elaboration of the "category E," he pushes aside even the pioneers of formal logic, George Boole and Charles Sanders

Peirce (310).[27] This exclusion is of great significance for our understanding of Kharms's project.

From its publication in the mid-nineteenth century until well into the twentieth century, including the period when Kharms's tract was written (1930), Boole's book *An Investigation of the Laws of Thought* was considered the seminal work in the discipline of formal logic and pure mathematics. It dealt with the mathematical operations that are not concerned with measurement and enumeration, but instead with processes formulated as conditional "if . . . then" statements that are fundamental to thought. Frege's concern with what is thinkable and not calculable can be traced to Boole's *Laws of Thought.* This book brought to a turning point the thinking of the second logician Kharms excludes from his tract, Charles Sanders Peirce. His approach to the calculation of chance and probability was significantly altered by Boole's logical algebra. The "laws of thought" helped him realize that the only way to take chance into account—to master, or "tame," it, as Ian Hacking[28] put it—is to fully embrace its ubiquity, to consider it an event that is not isolated. Peirce is interested not in the philosophical investigation of chance, but in its logical probability and in the soundness of logical argument:

> The strength of an argument is only the frequency with which *such* an argument will yield a true conclusion when its premises are true. Hence probability depends solely upon the relative frequency of a specific event (namely, that a certain kind of argument yields a true conclusion from true premises) to a generic event (namely, that that kind of argument occurs with true premises). (Peirce 1984, 22, italics in the original)

Kharms is interested in a specific, isolated event, not in a series; in randomness, not in randomization. He is not interested in the "laws of thought" but, precisely, in that which escapes these laws: in that which is unpredictable, incommunicable, weak to the point of disappearance and in that which is ignored, dismissed, and considered unverifiable by logical algebra. In other words, he is engaging in what Vvedensky calls the "poetic critique of reason." This critique comes from the position of an extreme subjectivity that is mistrustful of the ways in which things relate to one another. Says Vvedensky, "My predominant feeling has to do with the disconnectedness of the world and the fragmentation of time. And since it opposes reason, it means that reason does not understand the world" (in Lipavskii 2005, 323). In the tract on Cisfinitum, as in his quasi-Emersonian essay, Kharms is interested precisely in intervals between things, in gaps and disconnections, and not in linkages and continuities. That interval, that gap, is chance as a singular event. Not surprisingly, in the diagrammatic schema outlined in "Cisfinitum: The Falling of a Stem," this event is presented as an impediment in the form of a vertical line.

So, turning away from the procedures of logical algebra, Kharms asks the addressee of his tract/letter to conceive of "category E" as the base for a strange series of verticals, the stems that "stand" on each other while resting on the "category E." "We are going to turn the postulate E into an *original* stem," says Kharms: "The stem E will then stand on the new postulate ρ" (1997b, 310, emphasis added). Each "stem" added to this series becomes its primary unit, while at the same time providing support for the one that precedes it. The origin of the series, therefore, is not fixed. In other words, it does not begin from a defined point and then extend into infinity, but the other way around: it comes from infinity and continues toward the point of the entire series' "fall" or termination. This point of origin/support/termination is unreachable. The direction of such a series is irrelevant and interchangeable:

> So, in the endless movement ρ and the subsequent ρ1, ρ2, ρ3, . . . the stem grows, or rather, falls into the unlimited field of postulation, which takes the form ρ1, ρ2, ρ3, . . . , ρω. We can name the new stem Sω. Also we should note that, if we want to create the field (ρ1 . . . ρω), we have to, in turn, explore each ρ. Let's agree to mark such examined field with the letter α. (1997b, 310)

We should pause for a moment to look at Kharms's mathematical terminology. The German scholar Anke Niederbudde, who studied the use of mathematics in early-twentieth-century Russian art and philosophy, asserts that for Kharms, "postulate" is not only a mathematical but also a discursive notion. It is related not only to Euclidean axiomatics but also to naming in general (Niederbudde 2002, 201). Indeed. If we look at Kharms's postulation of the number we will see that it does not stop at its mathematical and linguistic, but goes on to include its visual properties. He makes permeable the boundaries between algebra and geometry, poetry and trigonometry, and ultimately creates a mathematical poetics that goes far beyond the conventional understanding of this discipline.[29] For example, in his tract "The Saber" he writes that "1 is a special number" in the "natural, or countable, number sequence. . . . It can stand to the side as a sign of the absence of count" (2007, 87). He goes on to say that "we represent the one by using a sign in the form of a little stick" (88). This sign is, he says, a matter of convenience. But that is not all. In "Null and Nil" he writes that "one of the ways to discover the real properties of a number"—namely, properties that go beyond its numerical value—"is to pay attention to its anomalies. The number 6 would be a particularly interesting case in point" (1997b, 313).[30] If the anomaly of number 6 is that it easily turns into 9, then the anomaly of number 1 is that, being a stick, it is a portion of the line, which is, as Kharms asserts in his tract "On the Circle," infinite by definition (314). It is, then, not surprising that Kharms relates number one to the representation of the line most commonly found in nature: the tree. In his meditation on numbers he writes that they are not closely connected because "in nature there is no such thing as pure equality: . . . in their natural uniqueness two trees can never be equal" (2001, 16). An untitled dialogue that ends up with the assertion "Numbers, such an important part of nature! And growth and work, all is number," begins with one Khvilischevsky peeling bark off a tree (1997b, 42). Last but not least, the diagram of the universe that has the nil at its center is depicted in the form of a cross section of a tree (figure 8). It is not only Kharms who relates numbers to trees and trees to numbers. Consider the powerful finale of Nikolai Zabolotsky's 1933 long poem "The Trees":

> Further on, the trees lose their contours,
> Appearing now triangular, now semi-circular—
> These are already abstract concepts.
> Here, the Sphere Tree reigns over the others.
> The sphere Tree is the sign of the infinite tree,
> The sum of all numerical operations.
> Mind, do not look for them among the trees:
> It is among them, and to the side, both here,
>   And everywhere.
>   (Zabolotsky 1999, 106)

Taking all of this into consideration, we should keep in mind both meanings of the word "stem": a mathematical sequence, but also a tree trunk. If we go back to his tract on Cisfinitum, we will see that Kharms's insistence on the pure verticality turns the stem into a branchless tree, a pole, a log. In falling, it does not follow the trajectory of a felled tree, which comes down with its longer side toward the earth. Instead, the "tree trunk" moves in a straight line: it is perpendicular to the flatness of the ground. The letter α describes the area into which the trunk is falling/rising. According to Kharms's hypothesis, it cannot fall beyond its own circumference. The series of operations that describes this curious fall proceeds in an orderly fashion: from E to $\rho 1, \rho 2, \rho 3, \ldots, \rho\omega$; from $\rho\omega$ to $S\omega$. It is important to note that Kharms describes $S\omega$ as an "endlessly diminishing field": it shrinks, contracts, and recedes toward zero. Kharms separates this endless diminishing toward zero from the rest of the procedure of "the falling of a stem" by introducing the new "unit of support" in the place of $S\omega$:

> The new unit of support will be o (zero).
> $\alpha (\rho 1 \ldots \rho\omega) = 0$
> (1997b, 311)

So, finally, the trajectory of the "falling of a stem" takes the following shape:

$$E \rightarrow \rho 1, \rho 2, \rho 3, \ldots, \rho\omega \rightarrow S\omega \rightarrow 0 \text{ or } 0 \leftarrow S\omega \leftarrow \rho\omega, \ldots, \rho 3, \rho 2, \rho 1 \leftarrow E$$

The trunk, this straight vertical line, is falling/rising into itself. In the schema of the universe (figure 8), the innermost circle is described as "nil," or "The Egg of the World." Here, the basic point of support amounts to zero. This is the point where null and nil coincide. However, this nil does not signify emptiness: the entire process of "the falling of a stem" is a reduction that endlessly approaches zero. The final outcome of this vertical reduction is the point, which in "On the Circle" Kharms describes as the "infinitely nonexisting figure." He goes on to say that "we represent to ourselves a point as an infinitely small pointlet. But that is a false pointlet" (1997b, 314). The dot never fully disappears into pure nothingness and nonexistence. The zero is an approximation of the infinitely small and the endlessly receding point of support. This point of support holds the "original stem" and all other "stems" devised from it.

Nil is the nodal point. Like Amenhotep, nil is a spatial paradox. This nodal point determines the position of the vertical and horizontal lines that intersect it, not the other way around. The nil is an X, an undeterminable point. This indeterminacy is transferred to all orientations: as in the case of the red-haired man, we can talk about horizontality and verticality only "arbitrarily" (*uslovno*). Kharms writes in a couplet about nil:

But the zero I noticed in the grass
lay with a horizontal line across.
(1999, 448)[31]

The investigation of the idea of Cisfinitum can be narrowed down to the disjunctive series of zero and one. What is the impediment, we should ask, for "this," which is zero, and "that," which is one?

Zero, First

The liberty Kharms takes in the tract "Cisfinitum: The Falling of a Stem" is to think in mathematical terms about nonmathematical issues, or to turn logical investigation against itself. The consequences of this liberation of thought run much deeper than is apparent at first glance. It runs directly against the principal Pythagorean maxim and the first law of mathematics, according to which everything in nature resembles everything else. The same law of analogy permeates both mathematics and literature. [32] As we have seen, in "Cisfinitum: The Falling of a Stem," Kharms conceives of nil as an infinitely shrinking support, as the origin that permanently withdraws into itself. He imagines the vertical line that is neither infinite nor finite. This reduction to nil, the inward movement of an infinitely falling axis, Kharms calls "Cisfinitum." In Latin, the prefix *cis* designates the zone located on the near side of a barrier, and as such it is the opposite of *trans* (beyond).[33] Cisfinity may be understood literally as the zone on this side of finity, as self-nearness and self-proximity. This self-proximity is marked by the void, emptiness, infinite reduction, cancellation, and, as Kharms would put it, annihilation in the sense of making-nothing, as in "annulling," a *mise en nul* (*unichtozhenie*). In Kharms's poem about Cisfinitum, "To Ring—To Fly," we have recognized this idea of an object set against nothing in the Blue Sky, or Sky beyond sky. The verso of the poem's manuscript contains a diagram (figure 13).

The first line represents the conventional diagram of the infinite progression and regression. On the right-hand side of the continuum the values endlessly increase, and on the left-hand side they endlessly decrease. This continuum can be formed by the simple addition of the number 1, thus forming the progressive sequence 1, 2, 3, 4, 5, with the presumption that there is always a number higher than the last one in the series. The progression can be geometrical, 1, 2, 4, 8, 16, . . . or organized in a particular series such as that of Fibonacci, in which each member of the series equals

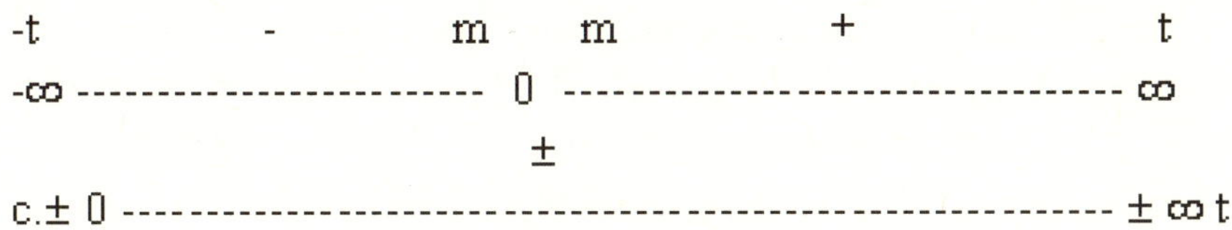

Figure 13.

Kharms's diagram that presumably represents his idea of Cisfinitum. It is on the verso of his 1930 poem "To Ring—To Fly."

the sum of the two previous members: 1, 1, 2, 3, 5, 8, 13, 21, . . . What is important is that it always remains a system of ordered numbers: the way in which the sequence is defined is less important than the fact that it is definable. Such a continuum is the basic premise of all fundamental mathematical operations. Zero divides the two sides of the continuum into two symmetrical halves. The two infinities, positive and negative, are equivalent, or analogous: for each value on the positive side of the continuum there is a corresponding value on the negative side.

The continuum on the lower line of the chart is actually a dis-continuum. Here, displacement of the zero to the left side of the continuum disturbs the analogy between infinities of positive and negative numbers. This shift renders impossible an ordered sequence: the values between zero and infinity are both negative and positive. The continuum proposed by Kharms is not completely amorphous and chaotic. Instead of being a starting point for the sequence that progresses in two opposite directions, zero becomes the starting point of a general progression (the order of this "sequence" is unknown) of numbers that unfolds toward infinity. This starting point is marked by the letter "c," which most probably stands for Cisfinitum. The opposite side is marked by the infinity symbol (∞). In his tract "On the Circle," Kharms talks about the perfection of this figure, which comes from the fact that there always remains something unknowable about it: "if the thing in question could be completely explored, it would cease to be perfect, because perfect is only that which does not have an end, i.e., the infinite" (1997b, 314). Infinity is not only the endless progression (or regression) of numbers, but also the concept of an endlessly unfolding universe that escapes knowledge and conceptualization: it is nil because there is nothing excluded from it. Therefore, while the left-hand side of Kharms's continuum is the area of Cisfinity (null, zero), the right-hand side is the area of the infinity (nil, nothing).

The only text that can be considered an accompaniment to the graphic schema is the poem "To Ring—To Fly (The Third Cisfinite Logic)." Although they are related, the poem and the graphicon do not explain one another. This leaves without proper definition the symbols "m," on the upper line, and "t," which appears on both of them. Nikitaev and Gerasimova propose that the symbol "t" might refer to Transfinitum, the concept discovered and elaborated by the German mathematician-philosopher Georg Cantor (Nikitaev and Gerasimova 1991, 35). Nowhere in his writings does Kharms discuss Cantor at any length. However, his name appears in his earliest preserved notebook, alongside the name of George Boole (2002a, 13). Cantor's idea of the Transfinitum was an important part of the wide-ranging polemic regarding the notion of "actual infinity," which involved mathematicians, philosophers, and theologians of the period just prior to Einstein's hypothesis about the finite universe, curved in time and space.[34] On the one hand, if the symbol "t" indeed stands for the Transfinitum or transfinite numbers, the way it is presented and used in the graphic schema is mathematically problematic.[35] On the other hand, if considered in relation to the concept of the Transfinitum, Kharms's idea of the Cisfinitum acquires a certain depth—but of a symbolic and ontological nature, not a mathematical one.

The scholastic argument against the use of infinity as a value in mathematics was based on the notion of the "annihilation of numbers." According to this argument, if there are any two natural or finite numbers *a* and *b* that are greater than zero, any attempt to introduce infinity into a calculation would simply "annihilate" the finite number: $a + \infty = \infty$. While agreeing that it is impossible to determine the largest possible number in the series of natural numbers 1, 2, 3, 4, . . . (first generation), Cantor proposed that it is indeed possible to think of a new number ω that expresses the regular order of the entire series (set). His choice of symbol for the new number was not accidental, as ω is the last letter of the Greek alphabet. Therefore, the theory of transfinite numbers effectively rejects the impasse of the "annihilation of numbers" and introduces the principle of the first generation into the creation of the series of the second generation: $\omega, \omega + 1, \omega + 2, \omega + 3, \ldots$

As Joseph Dauben points out in his excellent study of Cantor's work, "instead of introducing a single point at infinity, Cantor was prepared to produce an unending succession of actually infinite numbers and to show that they possessed identifiable and determinate number-theoretic properties" (Dauben 1979, 96). The transfinite number ω is not the largest number in the series of natural numbers, but a number of a different order. (Cantor energetically rejected the notion of "actual infinity" in mathematical operations and argued for its replacement with the transfinite numbers: that is why Kharms's use of both "t" and "∞" on the first and second line of his graphicon would be impermissible in Cantorian mathematics.) As Matila Ghyka explains with brilliant simplicity in his *Philosophie et mystique du nombre,* "in the kingdom of the transfinite a part can be equal to the whole, which is not the case with the finite numbers and sets" (Ghyka 1952, 114). It is important to emphasize that Cantor's concept of Transfinitum introduces an entirely new order of numbers in the same way that the idea of a negative number's root introduces the order of imaginary numbers. However, although imaginary numbers, quite surprisingly, found their application in the physics of electricity, transfinite numbers remain abstract and mark the very limit of the thinking of number.

It is clear that in his initial writings on the topic, Kharms already considered Cisfinitum a certain order of numbers. He returned to that idea three years after he wrote "Cisfinitum: The Falling of a Stem" and the poems on cisfinity. In his diary entry from September 19, 1933, the notion of cisfinity appears closer than ever to Cantor's transfinity. It is presented in this entry as an unending succession of cisfinite numbers:

> In the beginning, the numbers do not end with the zero. But, the system of negative numbers is an invented system. I was proposing a formation of the numbers smaller than zero—Cisfinitum. However, that was also incorrect. The zero contains within itself the numbers unknown to us. Perhaps, it would be correct to consider those numbers as certain categories of zero. In that fashion, a decreasing sequence of numbers would acquire the following pattern:
>
> . . . 3—category III
> 2—category II
> 1—category I
> 0—category 0
> category two 0s
> category three zeros
> category four zeros
> . . . , etc.
> (2002b, 177)

It is quite interesting that in this consideration of Cisfinitum as the category of zero, the null itself becomes the first member in the series: the "category of one 0" would represent a simple repetition of "0—category of 0." Cisfinitum is the realm of thinking in which zero becomes one—in which the non-number turns into a number, the only number, while the first natural number disappears. In the final analysis, the idea of Cisfinitum is not just a playful refashioning of the solid mathematical laws. It is not a mere game of fantasizing on the topic of mathematical series. Something much more important occurs in Kharms's attempt to define the mathematical order that is not based on natural numbers. The proportions of this event will perhaps become more comprehensible if we briefly return to Cantor's Transfinitum.

In order to define the first transfinite number, Cantor had to elaborate on his original idea of the Transfinitum and to introduce and define other new concepts. He developed the idea of the number ω into the concept of the "cardinal number," with the help of which he was able to introduce to mathematics the new notion of "power," crucial for defining transfinite numbers:

> We call the "power" or "cardinal number" of M that general concept which is derived from the set M by the help of our active powers of thought. The concept is abstracted from the character of the various elements *m* and from the order in which they occur in M. (We denote the result of this double act of abstraction, the cardinal number of the power of M, by M.) (Cantor in Dauben 1979, 171)[36]

This operation of "double abstraction" enabled Cantor to define the first transfinite cardinal number in the following way:

$\aleph 0 = \{\bar{\nu}\}$ (where ν = the entire sequence of natural numbers)

So, the first transfinite cardinal number is named "aleph zero." Cantor did not want to use the customary Greek and Roman letters as symbols for the new order of numbers he discovered. Instead, he used ℵ (aleph), the first letter of the Hebrew alphabet. Dauben explains that Cantor gladly adopted this symbol "since the Hebrew aleph served simultaneously to represent the number one and the transfinite numbers, as cardinal numbers were themselves infinite unities" (1979, 179). "Aleph zero," the first transfinite cardinal number, is entirely unrelated to natural numbers. Having no value and no "object" and "quantity" to support it, it is a pure concept. However, Cantor proves that in contrast to the concept of the infinite number, the transfinite number still complies with the mathematical laws applicable to natural numbers. The crucial difference between the natural and the transfinite number is that the latter is not based on the real—measurable and countable—value. It is based purely on what Cantor calls the "power" or the "active power of thought." If nothing else, the concept of transfinite numbers represents an amazing shift in which the number becomes divorced from value and completely dependent upon our intellectual ability to conceive a number. While keeping the mathematical operations intact, it introduces a new notion of number, and inevitably changes mathematics itself.

Kharms's Cisfinitum resembles Cantor's Transfinitum insofar as it marks a shift to a new structure. It is, in that sense, an event.[37] The tree trunk simultaneously falls and rises. Being in this paradoxical double movement, it is simultaneously multidirectional and indeterminate. It is, as far as possible, unrelated to any other field of action. It coincides, as far as possible, with the "fifth meaning" doctrine. The point here is not to prove the consistency of Kharms's thought. Not at all. What is truly important is to realize that such ideas as the "fifth meaning" and Cisfinitum are independent from any materialization in the sense of utilitarian application. They are not paradigms or examples, either. They resist instrumentalization in the way that, as it turned out, even Cantor's Transfinity couldn't.[38] It is not entirely justified, for example, to think of them as the "core," or the center. Such ideas, unlike the "center of gravity," have nothing to center and nothing toward which to gravitate. The falling tree trunk outlines the impossible core stripped of all other materialities and meanings. The tree trunk is not an object, and not even a diagram or a representation. It is a line of force, an event. It is not actual: it comes from nowhere and goes nowhere. In an untitled essay written during his exile in Kursk, Kharms proposes the "first theorem" of the difference between "nothing" (nil) and something, or cisfinity and finity: "that which nowhere begins, ends nowhere, and that which begins somewhere, ends somewhere" (2001a, 12).

In *The Logic of Sense,* Deleuze sets in opposition to Chronos a different concept of time: the empty time of Aion. Like Kharms's stem, the Aion is a "straight line and empty form." This pure event is never actual and in the present:

> Just as the present measures the temporal realization of the event—that is, its incarnation in the depth of acting bodies and its incorporation in a state of affairs—the event in turn, in its impassibility and impenetra-

bility, has no present. It rather retreats and advances in two directions at once, being a perpetual object of a double question: What is going to happen? What happened? (1990, 63)

The question here, however, is not only what Deleuze can tell us about Kharms, but also the other way around. At one point, Deleuze compares the Aion to a sage who thinks in the way an archer shoots an arrow. As it flies in a straight line, an arrow creates its own target. "The sage waits for the event," Deleuze writes: "*understands the pure event* in its eternal truth, independently of its spatio-temporal actualization, as something eternally yet to come and always already passed according to the line of the Aion" (1990, 146). There is no sage, no archer, no knower in Kharms's idea of the falling trunk/stem. It is infinitely passing though the bull's-eye not because its initiator understands the event but precisely because, being indeterminate and without origin, it is always in between the "eternally yet to come" and the "always already passed." The Kharmsian event does not oppose, but instead complements, Deleuze's pure event. Needless to say, like the sage's arrow, the stem is the full affirmation of chance.[39]

We should keep this complementarity in mind in pursuing Deleuze's notion of the event. In *Difference and Repetition,* Deleuze introduces the important opposition between what he calls the Idea, or "structure-event-sense" (or "the accident, the event, the sense"), and the representation, explaining that the latter turns the former into a possibility. As we have seen over and over again, this opposition is clearly identifiable in Kharms's conception of the event/chance. The true complementariness emerges at the point of Deleuze's claim that "the Idea is not the element of knowledge but of an infinite 'learning,' which is of a different nature to knowledge" (1994, 192). His elucidation of this difference is of great importance for understanding Kharms's theater:

> By contrast, the Idea and "learning" express that extra-propositional or sub-representative problematic instance: the presentation of the unconscious, not the representation of consciousness. It is not surprising that, among many of the authors who promote it, *structuralism* is so often accompanied by calls for a new theatre or a new (non-Aristotelian) interpretation of the theatre: a theatre of multiplicities opposed in every respect to the theatre of representation, which leaves intact neither the identity of the thing represented, nor author, nor spectator, nor character, nor representation which, through the vicissitudes of the play, can

> become the object of a production of knowledge or final recognition. Instead, a theatre of problems and always open questions which draws spectator, setting and characters into the real movement of an apprenticeship of the entire unconscious, the final elements of which remain the problems themselves. (1994, 192)

As they do in the case of the Aion and the Cisfinitum, Deleuze and Kharms approach the same point from different directions: whereas the former talks about "infinite learning," the latter strives toward what we can call infinite unlearning. One is not any more demanding than the other. However, in Kharms's theater there is no place for sages, neither in a Deleuzian nor in a Brechtian sense. If, as Yampolsky rightfully asserts, Kharms's project is the "replacement of memory with ignorance" and "supplanting the peace of knowledge by the peace of ignorance" (Iampol'skii 1997, 82), then in his theater chance is affirmed through an infinite forgetting, an infinite unlearning, and an infinite unknowing. As we are going to see shortly, the state of tabula rasa is just as unreachable as the full possession of knowledge.

It is unusual, to say the least, to think of Kharms as "structuralist." Still, there is an intricate structure to his paradoxical "new theater" in which the lessness of knowledge is gained infinitely. The search for that theater leads us back to the second constant from the tract "Cisfinitum: The Falling of a Stem": α.

α

Alpha. The first letter and the first number. One, first: the first real number and the first natural number. The basis and the root. For Pythagoreans the number one, *monad*, signifies the principle of identity: "that which is and which can not at the same time and in the same sense not exist" (Ghyka 1952, 93). The number one separates that which is from that which is not. As we have seen, in his essay "The Saber" Kharms likens number one to the stick, a full vertical line. While the self that is unrealized through work, Kharms says, resembles a hollow pipe, the self at work is a saber (Ostashevsky 2006, 85). The pipe receives, the saber cuts. The cross section of the pipe is a circle, an empty set, zero. The generative set of Kharms's series, and indeed the only series that matters for him, consists of only two members: 0, 1. That is the first step: from zero to one. It is not counting, or an additive series (zero added to one equals one). That is not the way this series is organized: "zero, one" is a disjunction, not an addition. In the same way, Cisfinitum is a disjunctive series. The overlapping of positive and negative numbers on the lower line of Kharms's graphic schema (figure 13) suggests that the series cannot return to zero: 7 can come before or after 8, and it moves by means of the "measure" of 1, but it doesn't return to 0, to the origin of the series.

Like the number one, the trunk is a vertical line. Its field of support, the cross section, is α. Alpha, the first letter, is the foundation and the beginning: one, first. Among Kharms's works, the same symbol emerges in an unlikely place. The symbol α appears in the poem "An Evening Song to She Who Exists by My Name" (1930), written several weeks before the tract "Cisfinitum: The Falling of a Stem." The poem "opens" with the window sign, positioned, as usual, between the title and the first line of the poem. The Greek "alpha" unexpectedly appears in the middle of the fifth line of the poem's second stanza:

> The steam bath of your faces
> the steam bath of your faces
> foreto opening memory's window take a look around what is situated in the distance
> take a count of the moving and the restless
> and count out on your hand α those restless ones
> those restless ones foreto taking from movement accepting life
> long to move and yet still sleeputh
> or quick say: from movement comes life
> but in stillness death. (2006, 97)[40]

This poem of extraordinary beauty and force is an address to Eve. It is also an experiment with language in which Kharms attempts to mimic the old Slavonic language used in religious services of the Russian Orthodox Church. The tone of invocation is strongly emphasized, and the poem reads as a prayer. It is actually one of the earliest in the series of prayers and invocatory poems that Kharms composed in the 1930s.

"An Evening Song to She Who Exists by My Name" is not only a supplication to Eve, but also an account of the defining moment in history: the beginning. The fateful event is mentioned in the very beginning of the poem. While in the first stanza, Kharms clearly addresses the foremother Eve, in the second stanza, he seems to address the original couple as a unified whole. The break and fragmentation comes precisely with the insertion of α in the verse "and count on your hand those restless ones." Alpha is the first natural number contained in five (*penthad*), the number of the fingers of one hand and the exact half of the perfect number, ten (*decad*). It is the beginning of the series, the starting point of genealogy, the fall from grace. The state of grace, heavenly existence before the Fall, cannot be equated with earthly existence: earthly life is inseparable from the idea of death, which does not exist in the Garden of Eden. Kharms sees the Fall as the first movement, the first step—and the shift to life from the original state as the "acceptance of life." The one who has accepted life is the one who has accepted work and perpetual movement. Like the number one, Adam is the measure of all men: he is contained in everybody, and nobody can return to him. The condition of man is therefore the condition of excess.

It seems that for Kharms, Alpha, Aleph, and Adam signify principles that are closely related but not identical. A strange figure that brings together these three ideas surfaces in Kharms's diary notes of the mid-1930s. In the entry dated December 23, 1936, Kharms writes: "Alaph! Today I didn't manage to tell you anything. All day long I felt like only eating and sleeping. I am very flaccid and not interested in anything." The next day he writes: "In view of the small hour, I am not going to start writing now, but tomorrow, Alaph, listen to me, and you Ity, help me" (Kharms 1992, 495). A curious *turn of writing* occurs in this supplication to Alaph: as he writes, Kharms turns the Russian words "and you" (*i ty*) into a proper name "Ity,"[41] suggesting that each word, as it touches the paper, tends to turn itself into yet another name for Alaph.

This naming in writing is an event. An event of this order can be related to "clarity," which Kharms considered the highest principle in writing. As we have seen in the previous chapter, he took as the prime example of this principle the instance of the detachment of the letter *yat'* from the text. In his letter to Claudia Pugachova, Kharms relates the idea of clarity to the power of primary experiences:

> I was thinking, how beautiful is everything that is first! How beautiful is the primordial reality! Beautiful is the sun, and grass, and stone, and water, and bird, and beetle, and fly, and man. (2001a, 79)

We can easily imagine such a romantic exaltation coming from the mouth of Dostoevsky's failed suicides and "monomaniacs." But this is nothing like that. In the continuation of the letter, Kharms proclaims his conviction that the "clarity" of the first, primordial reality can be found precisely in the place that is considered secondary and a replica of the first reality:

> It is this very clarity that penetrates all arts. When I write verses, the most important thing for me is not the idea, or the content, or form, or the hazy notion of "quality," but something even hazier and unfamiliar to the rational mind, but familiar to me and, I hope, to you dear Claudia Vasil'evna. That is: *the clarity of order.*
>
> This clarity is the same in the sun, grass, man, and verses. True art stands in the order of the first reality, it constitutes the world and is its first reverberation. It is inevitably real. (79, italics in the original)

There is no event of the second order. The truth of the event is that it represents the point of detachment from everything that precedes it and everything that eventually follows. There is virtually nothing that separates an event in writing from an event outside of the text. When, later in the same letter, Kharms invokes his famous idea that, if taken from the page and thrown at the window, the verses should be able to break the glass, he is not talking about the materialization of writing but about its *eventuation.*

We have already seen Kharms's various strategies of naming that which is the first in the character Landman, in the *primus,* in *yat',* Ity, and Alaph; we will see it again in his texts about Adam. In his note about Gustav Meyrink's novel *The Golem,* Kharms writes: "Golem lives in a room without doors. Whoever wants to look through the room's window, falls down. Athanasius Pernath's mind—the closed room. He would go out of his mind if he looked at it."[42] The hero of Meyrink's novel leaves his room through the iron door that was previously locked at all times: in order to make his way *up* to the doorless chamber, he descends *down* into the labyrinth under the Prague Ghetto, and in order to reach *inside* his own mind, he goes *outside* of the security of his own dwelling and into the uncertainty of the catacombs. In the desolate chamber, Pernath discovers a pack of Tarot cards. The first card he looks at is the pagad, a card that features a figure of a man whose left arm points up and the right one down. This figure is also featured on Kharms's calling card (figure 3). It represents Aleph, the first letter of the Hebrew alphabet, which, as Gerasimova and Nikitaev suggest, in Tarot symbolism stands for "man," or "active principle, initiative, movement, energy, the self" (1991, 48). Rising up is paired with falling down into one's own self. Obviously, what captivates Kharms the most about Meyrink's novel is the primordial scene of doubling.

His Alaph is the Alpha, the first letter, the first word, or the word that turns into a proper name. It is also Aleph, the self, or an othered self: the double. And Alaph is Adam, the one who is made from earth and the one who works the earth: the etymological connection between the name "Adam" and the Hebrew word for earth, *adamah,* pertains to the matter from which the first man was created as well as to his fate. Adam is a triple bridge between heaven and earth: in his origin as God's creature, in his fall, and in his work. The only story Kharms managed to relate to Alaph is the one about a curious fall:

> There is only one thing left to a man who is in the state of a sordid fall: not to look around, but to keep falling. It is important to do that energetically and with interest.
>
> I used to know a watchman who was interested only in vices. He narrowed down his interests and focused only on a single vice. And when in that vice he discovered his specialty, he felt like a new man. A sense of self-esteem appeared in him, erudition was required, he started looking at bordering fields, and he began to grow.
>
> That watchman became a genius. (2002b, 189)

There is always a guard in Kharms's narratives about falling or rising. In the conclusion of "The Falling," "a big-nosed caretaker" takes over the center stage, shoving people around and trying to move the crowd so that the two falling men won't hurt anyone (1993, 146). Kobrinsky rightfully comments that, throughout Kharms's work, the figure of the caretaker/watchman/militiaman represents an oppressive force (1991, 151).[43] So, Kharms confides to Alaph the story about a fallen man who falls still further. On the first reading, such a narrative might appear to be an illustration of Carpocratian Gnosticism, which harbored beliefs about the possibility of attaining perfection through sin.[44] However, something entirely different is at stake here. Kharms's narrative, unlike any of his other stories about falling, is an examination of the complexity of the fall. For one thing, the fall is inevitable, and there is no use in trying to prevent it. Second, any attempt at slowing down, suspending, or somehow evading the fall is doomed. The final, and the most stunning, realization that emerges from this narrative is that the fall is not passive, but instead demands work. Here for the first time the central problem of the fall is posed with crystal clarity: the question is not how to stop the fall but how to transform it—how to fail the fall. This transformation turns the fall into work, passivity into activity, impartiality into interest, a vital interest, a question of life. This turning is the most profound and the most dramatic instant: it changes death into life.

The turn does not bring the fall to a sudden halt, nor does it simply change its direction. The fall, as we have said, cannot be tried out, repeated, retraced, or reversed. In this narrative it becomes obvious that, for Kharms, every fall is related to the original Fall. It is a violent separation from an origin and a departure into an unknown Outside. Just as every fall essentially represents a repetition of the original Fall, so every sin is related to the original sin. As Paul Ricoeur asserts, "the fundamental symbolism of sin expresses the loss of a bond, of a root, of an ontological ground" (1967, 71). Being given to sin—or as Kharms has it, to vice—is exposure, unprotectedness, and uprootedness. The fall is a state of essential danger, not because of the vulnerability of the one who falls, but precisely because of the oblivion of the fall. The fall takes in and swallows the whole being. In proposing the interchangeability of falling and rising ("growing"), Kharms does not by any means suggest an easy way to redemption, that double of sin and a kind of reversed elevation. No, the turn that Kharms proposes is not a quantitative (if we can use that word) surrender to sin: there is no such thing as excess in falling. The narrative from Kharms's diary represents the turn from multitude to singularity. It is a clearing and a reduction exchanged for the profundity of the fall. In the story addressed to Alaph, as well as in the poem "An Evening Song to She Who Exists by My Name," there is an urgent realization that the only salvation from the disaster of the fall is the fall itself. But how are we to understand this salvation by falling, this preservation by expenditure?

The insight that Friedrich Hölderlin makes in his hymn "Patmos" is pertinent to this question: "But where danger is, grows / The saving power also" (Heidegger 1977, 28). Heidegger considered this turning of the "danger" into a "saving power" one of the insights central to the question of Being. If we consider it in relation to Heidegger's essay "The Turning" (1962), we will realize the primary importance of Kharms's idea of reduction to the single, most *dangerous* of all dangers. Not only in his address to Alaph, but in a number of his other works, Kharms voices the opinion that the most dangerous is at the same time the most essential: knowledge, experience, learning, and memory are absolutely excluded from the turning of danger into salvation. As Heidegger would put it, "when the turning comes to pass in the danger, this can happen only without mediation."

This is so, he goes on to explain, because this essential reversal represents turning toward the inside, an in-sight, in-turning:

> The turning of the danger comes to pass suddenly. In this turning, the clearing belonging to the essence of Being suddenly clears itself and lights up. This sudden self-lightning is the lightning-flash. It brings itself into its own brightness, which in itself both brings along and brings in. When, in the turning of the danger, the truth of Being flashes, the essence of Being clears and lights itself up. Then the truth of the essence, the coming to presence, of Being turns and enters in. (Heidegger 1977, 44)

In Kharms's diary entry, such an instance of in-turning, of this sudden flash, is the act of addressing, supplication, turning to Alaph. However, it also becomes clear that this address is also the danger, or "vice," Kharms talks about. "The Being comes to presence," it "turns," it "enters in" in a diary entry. In the same gesture, writing brings about and obliterates this flashing in-sight. That is why Kharms's addresses to Alaph are tormented by a simultaneous swiftness and slowness: the invocation of Alaph, the thought that rings "*i ty Ity*," comes together with the always hopelessly belated act of writing. For Kharms, in the instant of turning, the fall becomes a painstaking endeavor. This profound work of the falling becomes slow and laborious. Heidegger asks, "toward where does in-turning bring itself to pass?" and answers instantly: "toward nowhere except into Being itself" (1977, 44). For Kharms, the direction of the inverse fall is somewhat different. In order to discern this direction, we have to briefly reconsider his graphic representation of the Cisfinitum:

c.± 0 -- ± ∞ t

It is a strange diagram, indeed: the cardinal points of the continuum are zero and infinity, an empty set and a circle. The former marks maximum reduction, while the latter designates maximum expansion and the absence of limits; the former is related to falling and the latter to peace and stillness. The zone of finity, populated by random numbers, separates these two points. The three zones—cisfinity, finity, and infinity—are interrelated in a peculiar fashion. If we use Kharms's own terminology for zero and infinity, we can say that the left side of the continuum is marked by null and the right one by nil. The is a strange order to this image: it forms a less-than-perfect symmetry, a relation that is slightly asymmetrical, where the sides are not analogous to each other. The nature of this imperfect symmetry becomes clearer if we think of the three zones as mathematical sets: Cisfinitum as an empty set (of zero members), Finitum as a set with a measurable quantity of members, and Infinitum as an endlessly large set. The Finitum then becomes the point that separates two different infinities, similar to the way in which zero separates positive and negative values in the continuum of natural numbers. The two cardinal points of Kharms's continuum are similar, but they are neither identical nor equivalent. We have already encountered this slight disequilibrium: "Oknov–Kharms–Okno" and "Heaven–Earth–Heaven." All of Kharms's tripartite schemas are characterized by a slight discrepancy between the two poles, a difference that can't be easily determined. This kind of discrepancy Kharms calls a "small error," to the concept of which he, together with Druskin, ascribes a great significance.[45] In his note "Various Examples of the Small Error" (1930s), Kharms lists the epitomes of this principle found in the fields of literature, music, history, and architecture. The principle of the small error points to questions of order and disorder, regularity and irregularity, symmetry and asymmetry. Actually, the question of (a)symmetry is a point of exigency and shared concern for disciplines as varied and dissimilar as music and geometry, physics and poetry, biology and arithmetic.

The German mathematician Hermann Weyl points to examples that further indicate the universality of this principle, such as the assertion that symmetry "signifies rest and binding," and asymmetry "motion and loosening;" "the one order and law, the other arbitrariness and accident, the one formal rigidity and constraint, the other life, play, and freedom" (Weyl 1952, 16). In his comparative investigation of asymmetry in art, biology, and mathematics, Weyl finds that this concept makes inroads into various explanations of the origin of life. He cites Louis Pasteur's discovery of optically active crystals, as well as Pascual Jordan's assertion that "the beginnings of life are not due to chance events which, once a certain stage of evolution is reached, are apt to occur continuously now here and there, but rather to an event of quite singular and improbable character, occurring once by accident and then starting an avalanche by autocatalytic multiplication" (1952, 32).[46] (This prompts the mathematician to conclude that "there is some truth in the story of Adam and Eve, if not for the origin of mankind then for that of the primordial forms of life.") The significance that Kharms assigns to the principle of the small error, however, pertains not only to the origin of life but to the general state of the universe. Quite the opposite of Jordan, he holds that chance events *do* occur "continuously now here and there." However, these events are entirely singular. In his story "On Equilibrium" (1934), a Fairy appears to a steam-engine stoker who is quietly sitting in a restaurant. This causes a general turmoil. He rushes home and relates his discovery to his wife: "There's no equilibrium in the world. It's just an error of some kilogram and a half over the universe as a whole, but it's really a surprising thing, Ekaterina Petrovna, totally surprising!" (1993, 99).

Asymmetry is not a complete absence of symmetry: it is symmetry disturbed, a relation of formal equilibrium corroded by a variation that departs from the strict order of symmetry. It is a breakdown of repetition, that basic principle of formal symmetry, and an affirmation of difference. It is also an interruption of reciprocity. As we have seen, Kharms's idea of the "perfect gift" is exemplified by an asymmetrical object: "a stick to the end of which has been attached a wooden sphere and to the other end a wooden cube." Like the perfect gift, the perfect giving is an asymmetrical relation. The gift is not earned, but given and received. Also: the return of a gift cancels the giving. That is why Kharms and Lipavsky in "Conversations" describe a gift as a "minor miracle" (Lipavsky 2005, 408). This asymmetry in actions and in words is the fundamental procedure of Kharms's aesthetics. But that is not where it ends.

The "small error" is something unfathomable, often even hardly noticeable. Error resists knowledge, and as such, the phrase "small error" is a pleonasm: infinitely small or infinitely large, an error is a break in regularity; it is a rupture, a cleavage that is unknowable. Furthermore, an error or a mistake cannot be mastered, regardless of the degree of skill or the amount of effort put forth. It is, by definition, unpredictable. An error, in the sense of a mistake or an accident, never comes by design. An accident made according to a plan cancels its own unpredictability and, with it, its own nature. It offers yet another layer of meaning to the word *sluchai:* an incident or an event as something that is unfathomable, a disturbance of order that happens in an instant, a lightning-flash that opens limitation and order toward infinity. For Kharms, the incident represents a miracle of the lowest order and an example of the very possibility of a miracle. This promise of a miracle is usually overlooked, ignored, and vigorously suppressed. However hard it seems to be, the elimination of incidents and errors is much easier than their active pursuit, which is exactly what Kharms tries to accomplish. Here is narrative No.19 from the anthology *Events:*

The Meeting

Now, one day a man went to work and on the way he met another man, who, having bought some Polish bread, was heading back home where he came from.

And that's it, more or less. (Kharms 2007, 65)

Kharms's note "Various Examples of the Small Error" is accompanied by a group of five drawings, "Architectural Examples of the Small Error" (2001a, 18). They are followed by a shield which can be seen as an application of the small error principle to heraldic symbolism (figure 14).

The upper and lower sections of the shield are interconnected in an interesting way. The upper half features the Latin maxim *Quaedam aequi-*

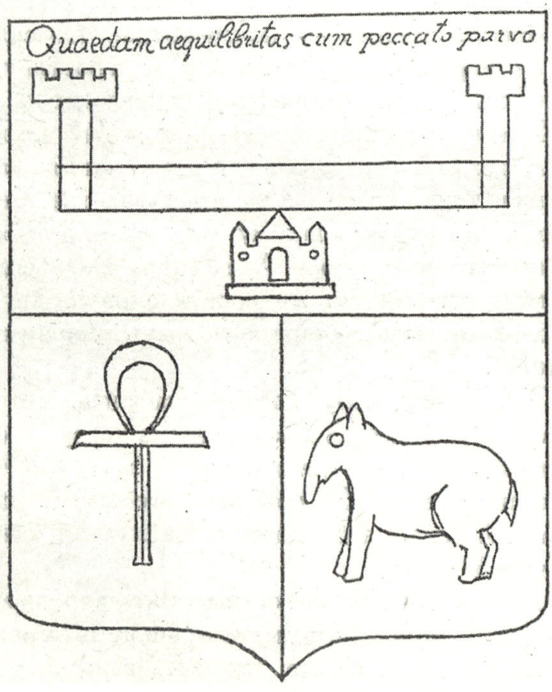

Figure 14.

Shield illustrating application of the small-error principle to heraldic symbolism. From a series of drawings titled "Architectural Examples of the Small Error."

libritas cum peccato parvo inscribed over two towers on either end of a crossbar that is balanced on the pointed roof of a small castle. The motto in Latin translates roughly as, "Some equilibrium with a small error." The error in the drawing is truly small: a single extra tooth on the top of the left tower. On the bottom left field, corresponding to the "strong" tower, is the Egyptian cross, or "the key of life," as Kharms calls it. We are already familiar with this symbol and the schema "Heaven–World–Heaven." The figure of the tapir featured on the lower right side of the shield that corresponds to the "weaker" tower comes from Kharms's unrealized utopian project, the "domestic magazine 'Tapir.'" In old French, the verb *tapir* means to hide. Kharms was certainly aware of this meaning. His story "Predestination" contains a list of animals that includes a tapir, who runs into the woods in search of hidden places where he can save his life. "He sits in the hole and covers himself with dirt and dry leaves. He sticks out only his long and narrow nose so that he can breathe" (2001a, 261). The image of the tapir represents Kharms's hidden and fearful life. The domestic magazine "Tapir" and the idea of the small error emerged in the late 1930s, after Kharms had gone through imprisonment and exile in 1931 and through the bout of hunger in 1937. This hidden and fearful life in the late 1930s is the inversion of his public and bold life in the late 1920s. In the late 1920s, there was OBERIU and "Three Left Hours." Ten years later, there was the secret "Order of the Equilibrium with the Small Error."[47]

Kharms cites as an example of a small error from the field of plastic arts the "antique marble statue of Venus with a beautifully sculpted marble wart on her beautiful leg" (2001a, 17). It brings to mind the climactic moment from Thomas Mann's novel, *The Magic Mountain.* Before he falls asleep from exhaustion during a skiing expedition, the novel's hero, Hans Castrop, meditates on the crystalline beauty of the snowflakes. As he admires the regularity of the ice crystals and the endless variations of their symmetrical shapes, he realizes that their "icy regularity" betrays their "antiorganic" and "life-denying" character. "Hans Castrop felt he understood now the reason why the builders of antiquity purposely introduced minute variation from absolute symmetry in their columnar structures" (Mann 1964, 85). Perfect symmetry is the complete arrest of form, absence of movement, and death. Exclusion of irregularity eradicates life. We find the last mention of "small error" and *peccato parvo* in the 1941 NKVD file No. 2196-41, which documents Kharms's second arrest.[48] Following the abduction from his home on August 23, Kharms was taken to Leningrad's central prison. On September 2 he was transferred to a psychiatric hospital for evaluation.

The report from the psychiatrist states that he is able to orient himself in space and time, but that he "has ideas about fantastic inventions," such as the "way to remove small error, or *peccato parvo*" (Sazhin 1998, 598). He was diagnosed with a "mental disorder of schizophrenic type" and declared unfit to work.

I am interested only in "nonsense;" only in that which has no practical meaning. I am interested in life in its most awkward manifestations.

—Daniil Kharms, *Diaries*, October 31, 1937

4. Theaters of Terror

Incub-Ator

Kharms was also a children's writer. He was a regular contributor to the Leningrad children's magazines *Ezh* (*The Hedgehog*) and *Chizh* (*The Siskin*) from their inception—in 1928 and 1930, respectively—until his arrest in 1941.[1] In addition to publishing original prose and poetry, Kharms engaged in the field of children's literature, doing translations from German of writings by Wilhelm Busch and editorial work, mostly devising new columns and themes for children's periodicals. Kharms's only theater piece staged during his lifetime, apart from *Elizabeth Bam,* was a marionette play for children, *Circus Shardam,* which opened in October 1935 in Leningrad's Marionette Theater. Among Kharms's papers, there is a hardcover notebook that contains examples of children's literature that he copied in several languages, among them a selection of verses in English entitled "Alice's Adventures in Wonderland by Lewis Carroll."[2] There are also extant drafts of Kharms's attempted translation into Russian of the poem "Twinkle, Twinkle Little Bat" from *Alice's Adventures in Wonderland* (Kharms 1980, 215).

The choice of this particular poem is hardly accidental. Here, the little star of the nursery rhyme has been replaced by the "little bat." The star, Ester, is the window: an opening, a passage that provides light and visibility. It is now blind as a bat. A bat, a hedgehog, a siskin, a tapir. This menagerie tells us that we are firmly on the weak side. The weak one is either a child or an animal, inarticulate and helpless. That which is weak is not readily understood. It elicits curiosity and violence.

In Kharms's works we find children who burn and fly into the sky; we find a father who compares his newborn's chest to a reed, its nose to a faucet, and mouth to a pan; also, we hear that children are afraid of sadness; they are thrown into a cesspit and then splashed with quicklime; they are sprayed with turpentine and nitric acid; they are torn apart by mad dogs; they break their skinny legs; they are poisoned, calcified, and deemed worse than corpses; they are considered disgusting when they play; they are screaming and scabby; a newborn has a watch dial instead of eyes; a child falls from a bench and breaks both jaws, another is beaten with a tub, and yet another has its face rubbed against a brick wall; a young boy eats filth from a spittoon; the rat is considered a useful animal because it bites infants in their cradles.

Such gratuitous violence is reminiscent of the kind of humor that Artaud recognized in the Marx Brothers' films: humor that goes beyond the ordinary cruelties of slapstick comedy to reach that "poetic quality" that "would fit the definition of humor if this word had not long since lost its sense of essential liberation, of all reality in the mind" (Artaud 1958, 142). And, as Artaud knew very well, this kind of humor does not provoke a benign comic effect, but precisely the opposite: an invasive sense of Danger.[3] The "dangerous aspect" of humor, writes Artaud, emerges in the exercise of "the poetic spirit," which "always leads toward a kind of boiling anarchy, an essential disintegration of the real by poetry" (1958, 144). It is precisely this sense of danger that puts the Marx brothers in the same category as the bloodbaths of Elizabethan tragedies and the incestuous orgies of their Romantic progeny. In Kharms's writing, the double edge of comedy and danger emerges most profoundly in the violence toward the weak that slashes so suddenly, so inexplicably, throughout the work of this children's author.

Disconcerted and irregular diary entries from the late 1930s are pierced by statements of this kind: "I don't like children, old men and women, and reasonable elderly people"; or, "It is cruel to destroy children. But, there is nothing else that can be done with them"; or, "Old women imbued with reasonable thoughts ought to be hunted down with a lasso"; and, finally: "Every snout of reasonable style provokes in me unpleasant feelings" (1997b, 88). This gives us a pretty good idea of why Kharms sees elderly women falling from windows, or why they continue to wiggle slowly, stubbornly, and blindly even after they die. He is not irritated by the unreasonableness of the elderly, what one could imagine as their superstition, or by their stench, ugliness, frugality, and fear of death. On the contrary, it is their caution, prudence, cleanliness, and sense of measure that annoys Kharms, who voices his distaste for the experience, wisdom, and measure of old age. He seems to suggest that reason and good sense are the last remnants of a life exhausted of energy. The reasonable old people are incapable of excess and are, therefore, reduced to moderation. However, even this radical rejection of reasonableness could be easily discounted as a stereotypical attitude of a young rebellious soul, were it not for the strange pairing of children and the elderly.

Nowhere did Kharms display animosity toward children as aggressively as in "The Article (for the Journal 'Tapir')." The single surviving article written for the unrealized homemade journal extols the decision of the emperor Alexander Vilberdat to isolate children and their mothers from the general population of the cities under his rule. "The great emperor Alexander Vilberdat . . . knew very well that children are, at the very best, just cruel and capricious old men. Inclination towards children is almost the same as the inclination towards the embryo, and inclination towards the embryo is almost the same as inclination towards excrement" (2001a, 23). This observation about the capriciousness shared by children and the elderly contradicts Kharms's diary entries on the repulsiveness of reasonable old ladies. How are we to understand this simultaneous charge against reasonableness and capriciousness? Why this equalizing of man as a four-legged and three-legged monster from Sphinx's riddle? What, indeed, does a newborn share with an old man?

Children and the elderly stand at opposite ends of the life cycle. Both are in proximity to the events without representation: birth and death. Children and the elderly have no memory and no language. For Kharms, the cliché of the wise old man is just as improbable as that of a child-sage. Children are innocent, just as the elderly are sclerotic, and that makes them disengaged from the symbolic—and every other—exchange. They receive without offering anything in return. And not only that: they demand. Their weakness is often experienced as the utmost aggression. Their "cruelty" and "capriciousness" come from their essential absence of commitment. It is detachment of a kind, or what Emerson in another context calls "neutrality."[4] This neutrality is also applicable to sexual differentiation: the newborn and the elderly are androgynous: they have not yet acquired or have already lost the outward and obvious marks of their gender. As a matter of fact, Kharms insists on this pregenital condition of babies. "The Article" continues: "It is foolish to boast 'I am a good man because I like an embryo or because I like to take a dump.' It is equally foolish to boast 'I am a good man because I like children'" (2001a, 23). Their neutrality is also the neutrality of matter.

In *The Logic of Sense,* Deleuze proposes yet another understanding of neutrality, this one different from noncommitment, androgyny, or objectness: he talks about "neutral energy" which is "pre-individual and impersonal, but does not qualify the state of an energy which would come to join a bottomless abyss" (1990, 213). Neutrality, for Deleuze, characterizes language as a surface effect, language separated from the body. It is an extension of the Freudian notion of "desexualization," a "desexualized energy" that nourishes the death instinct and conditions the mechanism of thought (208). Opposed to the surface language, or the "pure surface of thought," is the noise of the body, the cry of depth. The Kleinian analysis of children's sexuality is crucial for Deleuze's consideration of depth-surface opposition. According to the schema devised by Melanie Klein, the mother's body is fragmented into partial objects and introjected into the infant's body. What follows is an exchange between depths and heights:

> Introjected morsels are like poisonous, persecuting, explosive, and toxic substances threatening the child's body from within and being endlessly reconstituted inside the mother's body. The necessity of a perpetual re-introjection is the result of this. The entire system of introjection and projection is a communication of bodies in, and through, depth. Orality is naturally prolonged in cannibalism and anality in the case of which partial objects are excreta, capable of exploding the mother's body, as well as the body of the infant. . . . In this system of mouth-anus or aliment-excrement, bodies burst and cause other bodies to burst in a universal cesspool. (Deleuze 1990, 187)

Deleuze calls this drama of bodily depths "the theater of terror," a categorization certainly applicable to Vvedensky's *Christmas at the Ivanovs'.* This catastrophic play features a cast of children that includes "Petya Petrov, one-year-old boy," "Volodya Komarov, twenty-five-year-old boy," "Sonia Ostrova, thirty-two-year-old girl," "Misha Pestrov, seventy-six-year-old boy," and "Dunya Shustrova, eighty-two-year-old girl."[5] When the "thirty-two-year-old girl" boasts about the size of her breasts, Dunya Shustrova, the nurse, scolds her wisely: "Again you are bragging. You were bragging about your buttocks, and now about your breasts. You ought to fear God" (Kharms 1971, 164). The nurse decapitates Sonia Ostrova, and by the end of the play this crime snowballs into a bloodbath and the extermination of the entire cast. What creates the sense of disturbance in Vvedensky's play is not so much the paradoxical age determination of the characters, or their sadistic attitudes toward each other. Confusion and cruelty result from the destabilization of birth and death as the cardinal points of life. Life that begins before birth and continues after death is highly reminiscent of language. Only the memory of language reaches back beyond the moment of birth. Says Petya Petrov, a one-year-old boy: "I'm the youngest of all. I wake up earlier than anybody. Two years ago I couldn't remember anything the way I remember things now" (181). The terror of this theater is the terror of undifferentiation, and its passion is the struggle of separation. The undifferentiated state is characterized by the permeability of the boundaries between self and other, animate and inanimate, past and immemorable. Kharms also sees birth as a point in life that is far from being absolute. In his birth-narratives, the "theater of terror" turns into a comedy of miscarriages and rebirths.

During the decade between 1927 and 1937, the most productive period of his life, Kharms created several birth narratives of different forms and lengths. They include schemas, oral narratives, poems, and pseudo-autobiographies. All of them invariably feature themes of miscarriage, abandonment, and rebirth. The one that is most prominently marked by the fetus/excrement partial object is the 1935 two-part piece "How I Was Born/My Time in the Incubator."[6] The unraveling of this coming-to-life story begins way before the moment of birth. The act of conception, considered purely accidental and therefore beyond human design, is in this case despoiled by the father's intention to have his child born on January 1. As if the coming into the world itself were not enough of a beginning, Kharms devises a story about his own birth in which the father tries to arrange it so the birth comes on the first day of the first month of the New Year. The father calculates that for this to happen the conception should take place on April 1, thus making the point of origin deceitful and buffoonish. However serious in his designs, the family planner can't restrain himself from playing an April Fool's joke on his wife, who in turn gets angry and rejects him. The year after, she is still angry. Finally, the conception is successful on the third attempt, but the delivery comes four months too early. "Dad threw such a fit that the midwife who had taken me out was flustered and started shoving me back into the place I'd just crawled out of" (2007, 211). The progenitrix disputes this reversed birth, asking for her baby, and only after she receives anesthesia is the baby delivered again. This "shoving back" and pulling out of the baby does not amount to a proper birth: the father protests that the baby is not a human being but a "semi-fetus." It is placed into an incubator, from which it emerges four months later, on January 1. "That's how I was born for the third time, if you like," concludes Kharms (213).[7]

The theater of terror is the painful transformation of the guttural sound of the bottomless abyss into the intelligible sign inscribed on the surface, and so much so that it can be safely assumed that the more clean and aseptic the surface, the more combustive the abyss. In her exquisitely humorous essay "De Stijl, Its Other Face: Abstraction and Cacaphony, or What Was the Matter with Hegel?" Annette Michelson throws light precisely on this moment of passage from an inarticulate sound into a poetic sign. Focusing on the wide range of avant-garde poetic strategies that sprang up across Europe in the first decade of the twentieth century, Michelson recognizes strong parallels between the crisis of the verbal sign, or what she calls "a loosening of signifier from signified," and the crisis of the self. For instance, Marinetti saw in *parole in liberta*[8] "a renewal of language" that "was to proceed through the destruction of the I, that is, of psychology" (Michelson 1982, 14). Michelson observes a similar tendency in "the linguistic utopia of Russian Futurism" and its poetics of *zaum,* which, she proposes, may be seen as "the radical challenge of the *Logos* as *ratio* within the Western metaphysical tradition" (15). This avant-garde renewal of verbal (and not only verbal) expression was marked by an analytic movement that was often recognized as a regression to infantilism and primitivism. Michelson observes that, in their focus on the phoneme as the "linguistic atom," a large number of poets, irrespective of national, cultural, or ideological background, returned to precisely those phonemes which, as linguists have observed, mark the primary stages of language acquisition: "The velar sign *k* and its twin *g* emerged at a particular stage, detaching themselves and in opposition to the dental sound *d* and its twin *t. Dada* and *kaka* or *caca,* then, are linked in the paradigm of the secondary stage of language formation" (1982, 23). This "common speech of European modernism" offers itself, naturally, to a Kleinian analysis of anal eroticism. Or, as Deleuze puts it bluntly, "speaking will be fashioned out of eating and shitting, language and its univocity will be sculpted out of shit" (1990, 193).

Now, even though Kharms was not as accomplished a "cacaphonist" as Kamensky or Khlebnikov certainly were, explosions from the "pan-European nursery" still detonate through his poetry.[9] It is enough to look at the instances of *zaum* in his work, such as the refrain "kur kir kar" that appears in the play *Places,* or the intertitle "KaHavaHa" from *Lapa,* the play that, for that matter, paraphrases Khlebnikov's story *Ka.* However, much more important than "cacaphony" is Kharms's notion of birth as a dual event. Biological birth does not coincide with the beginning of life. Instead, it is a continuation of the undifferentiated life that belongs to the bottomless abyss. At the same time, telling and writing of this event assigns it to the regime of language. Birth, then, becomes the site of multiple dualities: it is formless and structured, biological and symbolic, immemorial and recollected. Infancy can't be remembered, only figured. Itself mute, the infant is given to language. Once it acquires language, it can't speak its muteness. In Kharms's works, the birth is, as Yampolsky asserts, connected with forgetfulness through a paradoxical remembering: "birth is an impossible recollection about a forgotten loss of memory" (Iampol'skii 1997, 86).

"I spent four months in the incubator," writes Kharms in "My Time in the Incubator": "I only remember that the incubator was made of glass, was transparent and had a thermometer. I sat inside the incubator on cottonwool. I don't remember anything else" (2007, 213). And there is a diary entry that seems almost like an appendix to the story about the triple birth: "They say, there goes an incubus. He strangles kids. Incub-Ator" (2002b, 128). In medieval mythology, an incubus is a male demon who seeks intercourse with sleeping women, mostly nuns. The name of the lusty demon is the Latin word for nightmare, which shares the same root with *incubare,* to lay upon or weigh upon. Kharms's incubus not only begets witches, demons, and deformed offspring with sleeping women, but it also strangles children. Incub-Ator is at the same time a surrogate womb and the worst nightmare. Half-machine, half-monster, it both protects and endangers, nurtures and destroys. In the Incub-Ator, the theater of terror becomes an actorless theater in which the theatrical space, that false womb of cotton and glass, is a villain that devours infants. The only escape from incubation is yet another birth, yet another expulsion, out of the deceptive security of infancy. As early as 1927 Kharms proposed the following plan in "The Founding Manifesto of Daniil Ivanovich Kharms":

> [3]. Schema of my art or of the birth of the artistic things is as follows:
> Man's birth.
> Life.
> Birth of the poet.
> Confirmation of the poet in life.
> (Kharms 1992, 444)

This is only a fragment of a more complex schema, which Kharms eventually discarded. However, the first three stages remain unaltered in all of his nativity stories. The most striking is the one that he related to Tamara Alexandrovna Meier, recorded in Lipavsky's "Conversations":

> Daniil Kharms: I was born from caviar. And that is when a sorry misunderstanding happened. Daddy came to visit right after spawning, and mom was still lying exhausted. He comes in and this is what he sees: a cradle full of caviar. And he loved a good bite. He spread me over a piece of buttered bread, and even poured a glass of vodka. Luckily, they managed to stop him before it was too late; then it took them a long time to collect me.
>
> Tamara Aleksandrovna: How did you experience yourself in that form?
>
> Daniil Kharms: I have to admit that I can't remember: I was in the state of unconsciousness. I only know that for a long time my parents avoided putting me in the corner because I used to adhere to the wall.
>
> Tamara Aleksandrovna: And for how long did you remain in this unconscious state?
>
> Daniil Kharms: Until the end of high school. (Lipavsky 2005:331)

The order of successive births forms a pattern of becoming that is repeated throughout Kharms's work with the regularity of a personal myth. (As we are going to see, this pattern is readily available to him for projection on a cosmological level.) So, between the first and second birth stretches the gray zone of "unconscious" existence. The first birth is always a mistake, an accident, which yields a formless, undifferentiated being. In this case, existence in the gray zone is unmistakably likened to caviar. It is a formless mass that consists of moist, black, minuscule eggs. It is an unstable and impermanent grouping that cannot support itself. It leaks and smears. This fragmented self is hardly alive. It is vulnerable to a strange transformation that is neither death nor disappearance, but spilling and disintegration. In the story "How One Man Fell to Pieces," Kharms writes about a man who swells until he reaches the ceiling, and then spills into a countless number of small spheres. Then "Panteley the janitor came by and swept up all those balls into the dustpan that he usually used to gather horse manure, and took the balls away to some distant part of the yard" (Kharms 2007, 227). Kharms's nativity story about caviar, therefore, re-establishes the familiar connection between food, fetus, and excrement. This time it is clear that the granular, preconscious self is already stamped with an identity mark: caviar is the formless mass that consists of minuscule spheres. We know that Kharms used the word *shar,* sphere, as the root for one of his pseudonyms, "Shardam." He signed some of his most adept texts with this pseudonym, including the poem "On Kazimir Malevich's Death," the children's story entitled simply "The Story," and, as we have seen, an entire private anthology of literature for children. In caviar, the sphere, *shar,* is far from being an active self. There the sphere is endlessly replicated and fragmented, thus constituting a formless, inert body that is permanently exposed to danger. This granulated self does not act, but instead suffers action. Passivity and exposure are the main characteristics of the gray zone between the two births. Spheres grouped in caviar form a directionless and truly endless series reminiscent of the "passive synthesis" that Deleuze describes in *Difference and Repetition.* The passive synthesis produces a series populated by "larval subjects" and "passive selves":

> Passive selves because they are indistinguishable from the contemplation of couplings and resonances; larval subjects because they are supports or the patients of the dynamisms. In effect, a pure spatio-temporal dynamism, with its necessary participation in the forced movement, can be experienced only at the borders of the livable, under conditions beyond which it would entail the death of any well-constituted subject endowed with independence and activity. (1994, 118)

In the gray zone, "at the border of the livable," dread reigns supreme. In the theater of terror, the one who suffers is the infant, who is forced to regress to the border of the livable. In the monologue "They Called Me the Capuchin," the infants are beaten to a pulp and thrown into an infant cesspit of sorts (Kharms 1993, 135). While being "patients of dynamisms," or, simply put, on the receiving side of sadistic thrashings, baby caviar and infant puree correspond to Lipavsky's notion of terror, exemplified by the fear of blood. The spilled blood coagulates into a gelatinous mass that creates the impression that it can live on its own. While it circulates in a living organism, blood supports life; once it is spilled, it becomes an ambiguous mass, neither animate nor inanimate. Lipavsky describes this equivocal state as an "unindividuated life," life without form, rhythm, and symmetry (Ostashevsky 2006, 207). The fear it provokes is the "fear of uncontained life" (Lipavskii 2005, 24). In the final analysis, the granular self is in danger and poses a threat. It scares and is fearful at the same time.

The danger that besieges the granular self does not come only from without, or, to use Kharms's imagery, it is not only the father who spreads caviar on buttered bread. Caviar, the formless granular self, is always readily available to the active "conscious" self. The second birth is, paradoxically, always a double delivery: it is a knot, a juncture, from which emerges not only the differentiated self (active and "conscious") but also the granular, unconscious, and passive self. The former can't exist without the latter. The granular self is a fertile ground and the guarantor of identity and coherence for the active self. It is important to note that here the notion of "fertile ground" does not imply an ontological relation between the granular and the active self. There is no relation of precedence or "grounding" between them, neither in a chronological nor in an existential way. They are coexistent and coterminous. The granular self of the gray zone is a residue that simulates the source. In Kharms's work, it takes the role that the basic phoneme has for the "cacaphonists." The crucial difference is that Kharms does not aim to universalize and objectivize the notion of source/residue. Instead of providing a connection with "the universal language of modernism," this source/residue forges a private language that often remains inaccessible and obscure. However, a closer scrutiny shows that there is no such thing as a successful and complete withdrawal from the circulation of meaning.

The Kharms Effect

With Artaud's poetry of the Rodez and post-Rodez period, "cacaphony" reached the grounds untouched by the Futurist and Dadaist poets. In the essay entitled, simply, "K," Allen Weiss considers the instances of "cacaphony" in Artaud's glossolalia a linguistic anomaly that appears in prophetic utterances ("speaking in tongues") and children's gibberish, as well as in the language of schizophrenics.

And shit on psalmody,
  bomba fulta
enough seeking the true poetic psalmody.
  caca futra
  ça suffira
  mai danba
  debi davida
  imai davidu
by repeating **I annul . . .**
  (Artaud in Weiss 1990, 56, emphasis in the original)

In his investigation of poetic-schizophrenic glossolalia in Artaud's writing, Weiss argues that, while Artaud's howls and screams are "the image of language inscribed in its excess, at the threshold of nonsense," they "never fall below the threshold of meaning" (1990, 56, 59). Sense and meaning do not coincide. Unlike sense, meaning does not depend on codified language, syntax, and grammar. The scream as a "nonmaterial double of excrement" is not an expression of the mouth and of reason, but of the entire interiority of the body. So, if meaning is boundless, then what about sense?

While logicians would suggest that the same sort of thing cannot be said of an *object* and a *concept* without disturbing the sense of the statement, Deleuze locates sense at the border between language and things, a pure surface. He suggests that, first, "sense is both expressible and the expressed of the proposition" (1990, 22), and, second, being located between propositions and things, sense can be understood as the event, "*on the condition that the event is not confused with its spatio-temporal realization in a state of affairs.*" He adds: "We will not ask therefore what is the sense of the event: the event is sense itself. The event belongs essentially to language; it has an essential relationship to language" (22, italics in the original). Like sense, the event is positioned between propositions and things, or between language and bodies. Like the event, sense is marked by duality: "it subsists in language, but it happens to things" (24). In Carroll's work for children, the proximity of the two series, the series of propositions and the series of objects, short-circuits into instances of nonsense. Deleuze observes that Carroll's nonsense emerges from the confusion of the two series, the series of words and of things. Kharms, however, tends to see these two series as discrete: in "Objects and Figures Discovered by Daniil Ivanovich Kharms" he proposes the "fifth meaning" of objects, words, and even acts and gestures. Each phenomenon organizes its own series, according to its own "fifth meaning," which is independent of human reason. Taking this doctrine into account, we can say that nonsense in Kharms's works does not emerge from the short-circuiting of the two series, but from the existence of a great number of disconnected series.

This proliferation of series and their interplay is exemplified with greatest clarity on the weak side. "The Story," published in 1935 in the seventh issue of the journal *Chizh,* features the boy Vanya, who tries to narrate a story, and the girl Lenochka, his listener. Vanya makes three attempts to compose a story, and every time, Lenochka rebuffs him by saying that such a story already exists. Each of the boy's narratives teems with violence and speed. For example, his third story is about a blacksmith who was hammering a horseshoe so hard that the head of the hammer detached from the handle, went on a flight during which it hit a number of things, and, having completed the whole circle at light speed, returned to the handle without the blacksmith's noticing anything unusual.[10] In the course of its improbable flight the hammer head hits one Karl Ivanovich Shusterling. Not surprisingly, Kharms used this pseudonym to sign the story "Tiger on the Street," published in the same journal. The hammer head makes a full circle, and so does "The Story." When, in the end, Vanya proposes to write a story about himself, Lenochka informs him that that story has been already written, and that he can read it in the journal *Chizh,* number seven.

Vanya purchases that issue of the journal and reads "The Story." What, actually, does he read? The story about himself trying to write a story, which ends with him buying the journal and reading the story. The story revolves in on itself and ends in its own beginning, thus creating a *mise en abyme.* In the *mise en abyme,* the language refers to itself: the story is about another story, which is itself. In that respect, the *mise en abyme* represents language detached from "things." The causes that make Vanya try to write the story are the same ones that force him to read it. These are, of course, the quasi-causes that originate in language itself. *Mise en abyme* is a machine of repetition, a narrative *perpetuum mobile* that produces self-perpetuating narratives, or stories that write themselves in an endless loop. The Kharmsian *mise en abyme* is distinguished by the author's insertion of himself into his self-perpetuating story. The author's body is the impediment, the point of disjuncture.

By pointing to the story published in issue number seven of the journal *Chizh,* the author implicitly points to his own signature underneath the story: D. Kharms-Shardam, the name that, as I already pointed out, suggests a spherical or cyclical shape. The author is implied in the narrative, but he also appears explicitly as Karl Ivanovich Shusterling. If we follow the circular path of the narrative, metaphorically represented by the flight of the hammer head, we will find the author at the center and at the periphery of the circle: he hurls the iron and is hit by it. The narrator incorporates the narrative, and the narrative fictionalizes the narrator. The materiality of writing surges ever upward, preventing sense from becoming completely detached, entirely immaterial. It is not only the textual iron that hammers the author. The text itself is hammered, which gives an entirely different meaning to the notion of thinking with a sledgehammer. Blows and slams represent not only critical[11] but also physical force. Writing becomes hammering, literally. And it brings about literariness of meaning.

In "On How an Old Lady Was Shopping for Ink," the materiality of writing intervenes in the *mise en abyme* in a much more intricate way than in "The Story." Both pieces were written for children's journals, both are about writing, and, interestingly, their protagonists are children and elderly people. While Vanya is trying to compose a narrative, the old lady embarks on a journey through the city in search of ink, which she needs to write a letter to her son. Whereas in "The Story" the question of writing is reduced to the invention of a narrative, in "On How an Old Lady Was Shopping for Ink" this question pertains to all the elements of writing, from material tools to writing as a physical gesture, to memory, and to the search for a subject for the story.

The old lady spends her days sipping tea and writing letters to her son. When it comes to laws, customs, and the mechanisms of day-to-day life, she appears to be a tabula rasa: just as Carroll's Alice does not understand the rules of Wonderland, the old lady does not comprehend the mundaneland in which she lives. Then, one day, she decides to leave her home on Crooked Street No. 17. Once out on the street, she asks the caretaker where she can buy some ink. Not getting an answer, she continues her journey and eventually wanders into a crowded market. There, she engages in a series of unsuccessful exchanges: her plea for ink is regularly misunderstood, and she gets offers of food in return. Ink and food. Is the old lady actually looking for the wrong thing? What if the merchants are correct and the old lady is actually starving? Could she be starving *and* looking for ink? As we are going to see, the transaction of trading food for writing is much more sinister than it appears at first.

Back to the wandering old lady: she stumbles back to the street and runs into a circus parade. The noise scares her, and she turns the corner into a quiet alley, which leads to a broad, narrow street crowded with cars and trams. Figuring that there must be some ink in the proximity of books, she starts looking for a bookstore and drifts toward a building with huge glass windows filled with books. She goes through a turnstile, and someone directs her to a "cupboard" which starts going up. Having reached the top floor, the "cupboard"/elevator stops and the old lady enters a huge, bright, crowded room. Writers are hammering on their typewriters, and "it is as noisy as in a smithy" (1997c, 145). There she meets an odd couple: a short and stocky man joined by a tall and skinny one. The stocky man is talking about a story he has written, and his companion responds that he himself cannot think of anything to write about. The old lady asks them for ink, and the skinny writer agrees to give her a bottle of ink in exchange for the story of her wandering through the city. At long last, there is a successful transaction. The lady gets her ink, and the tall, skinny writer writes down the title: "On How an Old Lady Was Shopping for Ink."

The itinerary of the old lady's travels is particularly interesting. As her journey progresses, the topography is progressively less specific: she departs from a place determined by a specific address, Crooked Street No. 17, and arrives at a fantastic place with a strange revolving door and a "cupboard" that rings and goes up and down. However, her travelogue is narrated from a double perspective. Two pairs of eyes are engaged in the depiction of the journey: one, the old lady's, which look from within, and the other, the tall writer's, that look from without. What appears as a deterioration of the landscape's legibility when seen from the point of view of the tabula rasa, from the point of view of the "tall and skinny" man who writes down the story emerges as precisely the opposite. The name of the street on which the old lady lives is an adjective that describes a street that is not straight, and it is also suggestive of a curved line, or an unreadable, illegible word. The old lady wanders from this indeterminate place into a labyrinth of a crowded market, then into city streets with identifiable sites and landmarks: the image of the street crowded with cars and trams is recognizable as the Nevsky Prospekt section of St. Petersburg, and the large building with revolving doors fits the description of the House of Books, which on its top floor houses the editorial office of the children's journal *Ezh* (*The Hedgehog*). This time, instead of hiding behind one of his pseudonyms, Kharms appears nameless, but clearly recognizable in the physical description of the "tall and skinny" writer who takes over the story of the old lady's adventures in her search for ink. Finally, the transaction works out: ink for the story, the story for ink. Both sides involved in this exchange are at the brink of extinction: the lady is old and can hardly survive in the world she no longer understands; the writer lacks ideas and much else (unlike his friend, who is "short and stocky" *and* has just finished writing a story).

The exchange finalizes the journey and initiates writing. It closes the circle between things and words. The *mise en abyme* appears as a vortex that spins around all of the elements of writing: from ink, to the crooked line or scribble, to the story of the old lady and her strange search for writing equipment, to the writer in search of a story. At the critical point in the development of the narrative, the old lady's forgetfulness coincides with the writer's lack of inspiration: at the center of the *mise en abyme* appears a blank spot. Not surprisingly, it leads to ink and a crooked line. After all, it turns out that ink is the best nutrition for a starving writer. I have said that in the *mise en abyme,* sense emerges as a pure surface effect, as the ability of language to represent not things but the language itself. However, as this story shows, in Kharms's writing this pure surface of sense is never perfectly horizontal. It seems to be slanted: the plane of sense appears at a certain angle, causing it to sink into the gray zone of what I have called "the granular self." However, it does not remain arrested in this zone of undifferentiation and illegibility, but emerges from it and makes another circle, another loop, only in order to fall back and collapse once again. But what causes this repetition, and what is its ultimate purpose?

In both "The Story" and "On How an Old Lady Was Shopping for Ink," repetition is caused by interruption, which is one of Kharms's primary narrative devices. It is enough to recall such creations as the playlet "An Unsuccessful Show," in which an actor appears onstage, tries to make an utterance, hiccups instead, throws up, and leaves—and each subsequent actor's attempt brings the same results; or the story about a man who tries to buy some carpenter's glue, but each time he leaves the house a brick falls on his head until he completely loses his memory; or the dramatic miniature *Pushkin and Gogol,* in which the two bards of Russian literature trip over each other as they cross the stage. Examples of such violent interruptions are numerous in Kharms's work. He seems to never get enough of interruption. Henri Bergson relates the comic in general to interruption and repetition. They are, according to him, the result of the "fundamental absentmindedness" in persons and events (1999, 95).[12] The "fundamental absentmindedness" (*distraction fondamentale*), that deepest source of laughter, comes from the mismatch of the mind and the world.

If the memory trips over matter, it does so because matter escapes the intellect. If we carefully reconsider the two stories that I just analyzed, we will see that in them the interruption appears not only as a comic effect but as a departure into the unknown. On the one hand, both Vanya and the old lady are deprived of some fundamental and seemingly ordinary knowledge: each time Vanya begins a new narrative, Lenochka seems surprised that he is unaware that his story already exists; and each time the old lady asks for ink, her interlocutors concur that she behaves as if she has fallen from the moon. On the other hand, Vanya is inventing his narratives out of nothing, and the old lady searches for ink in no particular place: essentially, nowhere. As so many of Kharms's characters do, Vanya and the old lady depart from a certain physical location, most often home, and then they drift away, forget what they were looking for and who they were, disappear, and end up forgotten. They seem like strange amnesiacs able to hold onto only what happens in the moment. This moment, precisely, is the nowhere: anagrammatized, this nowhere becomes here-now. It is the present moment of production and consumption of the text, the privileged moment shared by writer and reader, the moment that defies the certainties that we take for granted, such as birth and death. Each here-now is a new interruption that brings about repetition. This is not an exasperating flight in place, a movement without departure, but a strange progression through demise. And that is the diagram of Kharms's writing: progression through demise. In this *mise en abyme,* repetition appears as the outcome of obliteration, not its source. Artaud's chant "I repeat in order to annul" transforms into the formula "I repeat because I fail," or, by extension, "I advance through regression." That is why Kharms uses the device of the *mise en abyme* only in isolated cases, and, even then, in a form adapted to his basic principle of progression through demise. The exemplary case of this progression through demise is actually the story "Blue Notebook No. 10": "There lived a redheaded man who had no eyes or ears. He didn't have hair either," and so on. If the extensivity of sense is named the "Carroll effect,"[13] then I will call this catachrestic progression through erosion, or advancement toward disappearance, the "Kharms effect."

The Kharms effect outlines a paradoxical spatial situation: a placing into nothingness, *mise en néant.* In his diary entry that inaugurated the term *mise en abyme* into literary and art criticism, André Gide borrowed this expression from heraldry: *abyme* is the center of the shield, the area that British heraldic experts determine as "escutcheon" or "inescutcheon." Therefore, *mise en abyme* is the heraldic operation of placing a miniature image of the shield at the center of the shield itself. *Mise en abyme* always refers to a replication of an image within an image, or a narrative within a narrative, as in the nursery rhyme that opens the second act of Beckett's *Waiting for Godot:*

A dog came in the kitchen
And stole a crust of bread.
Then cook up with a ladle
And beat him till he was dead.

Then all dogs came running
And dug the dog a tomb . . .

And wrote upon the tombstone
For the eyes of dogs to come:

A dog came in the kitchen
And stole a crust of bread . . .
(Beckett 1954, 37)

In Kharms's use of the *mise en abyme,* the placement of the narrative within the narrative is not as important as the *dis*placement of the end of the story to its beginning. This overlapping of the beginning and the end suggests not only the collapse of cause and effect but, more importantly, the collapse of the intelligible into the unintelligible, of the linear into the nonlinear, and of sense into nonsense. This return to the beginning does not only represent the launch of an endless narrative loop, but also the plunge into the "gray zone," or the zone of birth. This slippage from the plane of sense is precisely the place in which interruption and collapse occur. In short, Kharms's *mise en abyme* can be seen as a complex choreography of sense and nonsense.

The story "On How an Old Lady Was Shopping for Ink" was published in 1928, the year of *Elizabeth Bam.* The play is also marked by circular narrative: it opens with an attempt by Petr Nikolaevich and Ivan Ivanovich to arrest Elizabeth Bam, and by the end, we learn that she is persecuted for the murder of one of the persecutors, Petr Nikolaevich. And again, this cyclical surface is slanted: this time, not downward toward the "gray zone," but upward, toward an equally ambiguous place described by Ivan Ivanovich and Petr Nikolaevich as their "poor hut" on a hill, a place in which "*no one resides*" (1993, 175, italics added). In the small wooden house on a hillock, "only mice rub flour between their palms," "the anchorite cockroach [sits] on the stove," and a lamp burns with an unearthly flame, without beginning or end, never lit and yet inextinguishable. This is how Petr Nikolaevich elaborates on the paradox of the lamp that burns by itself:

There is an infinite movement,
the breathing of the lighter elements,
planetary motion, the earth's rotation,
the crazed alternation of day and night,
the combination of remote nature,
the anger and strength of untamed beasts

and the subjugation by man
of the laws of light and wave. (1993, 176)

Kharms assigns to the figure of a hillock or an elevated place an important and deeply ambiguous symbolism. As we have seen in the analysis of *Temptation,* the crucial stage in the process of the Four Girls' disappearance is their placement on a hillock in a landscape.[14] There is a pronounced correspondence between depths and heights, between the "incubator" and the "hill cabin." I have said that the granular self, identified with the "incubator period," is simultaneously in danger and dangerous, that it is frightened and frightful at the same time. Similarly, the hill cabin is identified with infinity, circular movement, and eternal light, but at the same time it houses the cockroach that, like formless matter, represents the fear of the inhuman and of impersonal movement.[15] While the incubator is associated with birth, the hill cabin is associated with death. Kharms readily transfers the symbolism of birth and death to the cosmological level. Among his diary notes, there is a chart that follows the pattern of multiple births outlined in Kharms's "Founding Manifesto" and in his nativity stories:

	God the Father HEAVEN	God the Son WORLD	God the Holy Spirit HEAVEN
1	emptiness	existence	emptiness
2	past	present	future
3	rest	movement	rest
4	creation	action	destruction annihilation
5	religion	materialism	art
6	innocence	sin	innocence
7	birth	life	death
8	exit from heaven	(world) sinking into ground	return to heaven

(Kharms 2002b, 107)

The tripartite structure of this chart corresponds to the fundamental pattern that Kharms develops in the tract "On Existence, Time, and Space": this–impediment–that, or its variations, Oknov–Kharms–Okno, or Heaven–World–Heaven. The latter trinity is the schema of the Egyptian cross, the key of life, depicted on the "strong" side of the shield (figure 14).

Animals, children, and the elderly are relegated to the weak side. Helpless and speechless, they all reside at the border of the livable.[16] The granular self is mute and defenseless. In his intriguing essay "Mainmise," Jean-François Lyotard establishes a structure of double birth that, exactly like Kharms's schema, is equally applicable to an individual and civilization. The double birth is hinged on the notion of *infans,* that which is without language: "By infancy, I mean that we are born before we are born unto ourselves. And therefore we are born through others, but also born to others, handed over defenseless to others" (Lyotard 1992, 420). For Lyotard, childhood is not a period in life but a state without the shield of representation, language, and reason: "For the infant, everything is a wound, the wound of a pleasure that is going to be forbidden and withdrawn. Both the suffering that results from it, and the search for an object, an object in some way analogous to emancipation, emerge from this wound" (420). Kharms also shows, too, how the order of cause and effect turns upside down, and how vulnerability brings about the Danger. A cut produces the knife of humor. And each wound brings about a stab.

On Kharms's shield (figure 14), an exotic animal is juxtaposed with an ancient symbol: the Egyptian cross is inscribed on the "strong" side, across from the tapir. There is a small error, an infinitesimal discrepancy between that which is simply living and the key of life. As in the towers on Kharms's shield, there are two peaks and a valley cut into the key. There are no peaks and valleys on the weak side: just a flat, slightly tilted surface. The blind bat instead of the winking star. Is the small error, then, in heaven? If so, why small? Doesn't heaven make a big difference?

In his supplication to heaven, Kharms seems to assert that it does.

Ester is a star, and a star is "a heaven, albeit a very distant heaven." We remember that Kharms makes a confession about his seven-year-long love for Ester in the letter dated November 2, 1931, and addressed to another woman, Raisa Poliakova. The date on the letter, as well as the content, establish connections between this letter and two other texts: "The Morning," written a week before the letter, on Sunday, October 25, 1931, and the column of five hieroglyphs from November 1931 (figure 6). In the text accompanying the column, Kharms offers the apocalyptic image of heavens rolling up into a scroll and coming down to earth while land rises up. In this reversal, heaven and earth seem to touch. Whereas in the poem the heaven-scroll comes down, the letter to Raisa seems to be dispatched in the opposite direction. Raisa spells out heaven in much more unambiguous terms than Ester. Kharms relates the name Ester to a series of complex passages: from the proper name to its Latin meaning, then to a monogram, its visual symbolism, and the final metaphorical sign of heaven. Conversely, in Raisa he recognizes a direct correspondence between the proper name and heaven. She is nicknamed Raia, which in Russian also means heaven (*rai*):

> I came to know you and learned that you go by the name of Raia. I began thinking a lot about you, about Heaven. The thought of You became my most predominant thought. And I hung the inscription above my bed:
>
> Think about Heaven.
>
> My main thought, besides You, is the thought of heaven, and You understand that, for me, you are no longer a woman I love, but a part of all of my thoughts and deeds. (1988a, 461)

It seems that in this letter Kharms makes it his primary task to excise from his notion of heaven everything vague and intangible. He writes that he looks through the window and sees not a star, but her, Raia, in a bathing suit (1988a, 460). If Ester is a symbol of heaven, then Raia is its embodiment. The torturous night described in "The Morning" ends with a voice that announces to the insomniac that he is finally asleep. The letter to Raia concludes with a phone call:

> Today you called me on the phone when I started writing this letter.
> I positively recognized your voice at once, but did not know what to say, and kept asking all the time: who is there? (1988a, 462)[17]

Where does the call come from? What causes the sudden aphasia? Who is there? Where is Raia? Across the street, in the window, wearing only a swimsuit. In November? All the way up north, in Leningrad? How are we to read the letter to Raia? There is a strange temporality to it. Kharms first starts writing the letter, then receives the call; he recognizes the voice, but, having forgotten the words, he retrieves only the question, who is calling? The caller is unknown, but she has a name: Raia, *rai,* heaven. He can only respond to this call later, in the letter, which was already half-written before the call came through. The response comes either too soon or too late, before or after the call. It is never on time, during the call. The affair with the letter is reducible to a simple syllogism: if the caller is unknown, and she is Raia, then Raia is unknown; if Raia is heaven, then heaven is unknown.

The subject of heaven receives a radical revision in one of Kharms's most intriguing "vaudevilles," entitled *Adam and Eve.*[18] (A number of Kharms's short dramatic works are described as "vaudevilles" without having any formal properties of this genre.) In the first act of this short play, Anton Isakovich declares to Natalia Borisovna that he is fed up with being who he is, and that he wants the two of them to become Adam and Eve. The only thing more curious than this wish is the way in which he plans to accomplish their transformation: "It is very simple!" Anton Isakovich explains to Natalia Borisovna: "We will climb onto the writing desk, and when someone enters the room, we will bow and say: 'Allow us to introduce ourselves: Adam and Eve'" (2001a, 245). The first visitor "falls as if stricken by lightning" when they bow, perched on the writing desk, and introduce themselves. The remaining three acts are as brief as they are phantasmagoric:

> Second Act
>
> On the streets the people are jumping on three legs. A violet wind blows from Moscow. Curtain.
>
> Third Act
>
> Adam Isakovich and Eve Borisovna fly over the city of Leningrad. The people fall on their knees and pray for mercy. Adam Isakovich and Eve Borisovna smile benevolently.
> Curtain.
>
> Fourth and Last Act
>
> Adam and Eve sit on a birch tree and sing.
> Curtain. (2001a, 246)

Unlike Kharms's early aerial pieces such as *Lapa,* this piece, written in 1935 at the outset of the great purges, has a sinister underlying tone: The not-quite-red wind blowing from Moscow lifts the couple above Leningrad, whose citizens kneel down in fear; the flying couple gain hybrid names, composed of their old family names and new first names, Adam Isakovich and Eve Borisovna; the tree on which they sit is not exactly one of the Edenic plants, but an ordinary birch tree—perched on a tree, they continue their flight, as it were, by other means. Whether they are poetic or political, all of these aerial stunts are countered by the overwhelming banality of the initial situation: an average man and woman decide to become the first couple by simply stepping into the realm of the symbolic. Kharms further emphasizes the crudeness of the imposition of everyday banality upon the presumed sublimity of art by appending to the title and generic description yet another completely useless paratextual bit of information: "Price 30 rubles" (2001a, 245).

The writing table is a dais from which the speakers address the auditors. More important, it provides them with a plateau for transformation. There is something scandalous in climbing onto a writing desk and making a simple and direct claim of altered identity. Yet every signature amounts to precisely this claim. Kharms never fails to acknowledge the incompleteness of the passage and the exposure to the danger of banality as the occupational hazard of those who climb onto writing desks. At the same time, he never stops responding to the call. The story of Ester/Eden, Raia/*rai*—the story of love found, and lost, and regained, and lost—is the story of vocation and of the emergence from a larval state. Of a second birth. The writing desk is the platform and the shield. However, there is nothing definite and secure about emergence from the primordial ooze. The platform is not a firm ground. It is a floating surface, like the iceberg featured in the last scene of *Lapa,* at the conclusion of all of the flights and landings, vertiginous ascensions and plunges. It is a flat, creaky surface that splits and cracks. Walking on it amounts to jumping from one ice block to another. The blocks are shaky and infirm. They are floating on the invisible, powerful undercurrents that force them apart, and, in the opposite direction, against one another. And still, this provisional ground is not completely indeterminate. We might say that it suffers from a surplus of determination. Following Kharms's image of the iceberg, we will find this landscape of flat and fissured vastness at the cardinal points of the globe, where the compass points only in one direction: the opposite pole. For Kharms, this is not an existential situation. It is a textual strategy, and, as such, it abounds with comic effects. Rarely did Kharms stage this cracking more provocatively and effectively than in yet another short play on the Edenic theme, *The Fall from Grace, or the Knowledge of Good and Evil.*[19]

Unlike the 30-ruble piece with which it shares the principal characters, *The Fall from Grace* does not point only to the famous couple from the Book of Genesis. The source of this play is the rich literary, theatrical, and artistic tradition based on 1 and 2 Genesis, generated during the Middle Ages and the Renaissance. Kharms the medievalist? This notion almost automatically invokes Mikhail Bakhtin's book on carnival, the work that was, as the hypothesis goes, inspired as much by Rabelais as by the Leningrad avant-garde.[20] If we pursued this hypothesis, we would find Kharms at the end of the procession, taking up the role of jester, luring and teasing onlookers and security guards. He fooled around, and he paid dearly for that. Leaving this hypothesis aside, I want to investigate *The Fall from Grace* not as a prop in an elaborate buffoonery but as a platform, a shield: How are foolishness and the text related? Or foolishness and the fall?

Kharms's play begins as a close adaptation, almost an extended citation, of one of the earliest extant medieval plays, *Ordo repraesentationis Adae,* dating most probably from the latter part of the twelfth century and composed in Anglo-Norman and Latin.[21] Whereas Kharms indicated vaudeville as the genre of *Adam and Eve,* in the case of *The Fall from Grace* he invented the genre of "*didascalia.*" The Greek word *didascalia* (didascaly) has a dual theatrical usage: in the Renaissance, it was a term for catalogs of ancient Greek tragedies; the same word is still used today as a technical term for stage directions. Beyond theater, *didascalia* holds the meaning of teaching and instruction. In its literal sense, *didascalia* can be seen as a reference to *Ordo repraesentationis Adae* which, being an extension of a liturgical service, opens with a sermon. Moreover, in the introductory stage directions, the medieval playwright refers to the play that is about to be seen as a "lesson" (*lectio*):

> Let paradise be constructed in a prominently high place; let curtains and silken hangings be placed around it at such a height that those persons who will be in paradise can be seen from the shoulders upwards; let sweet-smelling flowers and foliage be planted; within let there be various trees, and fruits hanging on them, so that the place may seem as delightful as possible. Then let our Saviour come, clothed in a dalmatic, and let Adam [and] Eve be stationed before him. Let Adam be robed in a red tunic, Eve in a woman's white garment with a wimple of white silk; and let them both stand before the Figure [of God]—Adam somewhat nearer, with peaceful countenance, Eve on the other hand not quite sufficiently humble. (in Bevington 1975, 81)

Then, the "lesson" begins with a reading of 1 Genesis and the responsory in Latin. When Adam appears onstage, the dialogue switches to the Anglo-Norman dialect. Historians of medieval drama agree that the bilinguality of *Ordo repraesentationis Adae,* together with the indication that the acting space is in front of a church, situates this play midway between liturgical drama and popular theatrical entertainments of the time.[22] In his rendition of the play, Kharms preserves a single Latin word and the reference to the church, which is reduced from the dominant structure of the total setting to one of several stage elements:

> An alley lined with beautifully groomed trees represents the garden of paradise. In the middle stand the Tree of Life and the Tree of Knowledge of Good and Evil. In back to the right is a church.
> Figura (pointing at a tree, speaks):
> Here is the Tree of Knowledge of Good and Evil. You can eat the fruit from other trees, but from this tree do not eat the fruit.
> Adam (pointing at the tree):
> Here is the Tree of Knowledge of Good and Evil. We will eat the fruit from other trees, but from this tree we will not eat the fruit. You, Eve, wait for me, while I go pick raspberries. (Leaves.)
> Eve:
> This is the Tree of Knowledge of Good and Evil. Adam forbade me to eat the fruit from this tree. But how does it taste, I wonder. (2007, 194)

Whereas the medieval stage directions evoke an image of plenitude, in Kharms's play the original fullness is replaced by the geometrical beauty of groomed trees ordered into strictly planned alleys. Kharms alters many of the stage descriptions but retains the character of Figura, whose name he spells in the original Latin instead of Cyrillic letters.[23] Such a selective citation calls attention to Figura as a representational device. According to the conventions of medieval drama, Figura is a metatheatrical element of the performance. It designates the noncharacter of a priest who, wearing ceremonial dress, steps out of the church and onto the theatrical stage in order to deliver the lines that the scripture assigns to God. Seen in this way, Figura represents the mark of citation. In his rendition of the medieval play, Kharms takes Figura out of its original context. Figura's words are echoed by Adam and Eve. By consigning the scriptural text to Figura, Kharms acknowledges its originary status. In many ways (literary, spatial, ceremonial, and symbolic), Figura attaches the medieval play to its complex theological background, thus allocating originary significance to the entire episode of the fall. Kharms's citation of "Figura" is equivocal.

First, it not only provides a connection to its literary source but also establishes a distance from it. This citational double gesture is characteristic of parody. In his essays on parody from the 1920s, Yuri Tynianov, one of the most prominent members of the OPOYAZ group, proposes that the essential trait of parody is its dual structure, in which the literary text, while following its own narrative logic, simultaneously points toward the parodied model (Tynianov 1977, 214). Parody is, according to this view, a repetition and variation of an already existing model, and it does not necessarily have to be comic. Tynianov sees parody as one of the main agents in the evolution of literary genres. It is not a faithful citation, and it does not necessarily mock the source text: it takes up and repeats only certain aspects and sections of the model.[24] Kharms choice of sections from *Ordo repraesentationis Adae* leads us to the second point, which pertains to figura as a trope.

Erich Auerbach recognizes that the change in the meaning of the Latin word *figura* coincides with the establishment of Christianity as a dominant religion. From its original meaning of "form" and notions related to it, such as the cognate of the Greek *schema* in philosophy, "plastic form" in the visual arts, and even "copy" and "dream image" in literature, in the early Middle Ages, *figura* received the new sense of something that is at the same time "real" and "spiritual." Auerbach recognizes in passages from the Acts of the Apostles and the Pauline epistles, repeated attempts at interpreting events from the Old Testament as "prefigurations" or "confirmations" of Jesus as the New Messiah, revealed in the New Testament. So, according to the new reading of the Book of Genesis, Adam is not only the forefather but also a *figura Christi.* Auerbach contends that figures "point out not only to the concrete future, but also something that always has been and always will be. . . . This eternal thing is already figured in them, and thus they are both tentative fragmentary reality, and veiled eternal reality" (Auerbach 1959, 59). Further, he recognizes that literature benefited from the figural interpretation of history because it made legitimate the new sense of realism in multilayered works that drastically departed from the classical ideals of harmony and unity. The new understanding of *figura* brings closer than ever the elevated style, *sermo sublimis,* and the low style, *sermo humilis:* "realism of a coarser grain begins to thrive, and varieties of mixed style, of the blunt juxtaposition of Passion and crude farce develop" (Auerbach 1953, 159). Kharms opts for *sermo humilis.* What in his play seems to be crude parody, actually already exists in *Ordo repraesentationis Adae:*

Devil:
Don't be afraid.
For a long time I have known
All the secrets of paradise.
One part of them I'll tell you.

Eve:
Begin, and I will listen.
Devil:
Will you listen to me?
Eve:
I'll do so, all right,
Nor anger you in any way.
Devil:
Will you keep a secret?
Eve:
Yes, by my faith.
Devil:
Will it be revealed?
Eve:
Certainly not by me.
Devil:
I will put me in your trust.
I wish no further assurance from you.
Eve:
You can certainly trust my word.
Devil:
You have been to a good school!—
I have seen Adam, but he is too much of a fool.
(Bevington 1975, 91)

Kharms retains from the original the intricate game of seduction woven from carefully chosen questions and lightly made promises. He alters, with no apparent explanation, the identity of the seducer:

Master Leonardo:
Listen, Eve! I learned all the mysteries of paradise long ago. I can tell you something.
Eve:
OK, talk. I'll listen.
Master Leonardo:
Will you listen to me?
Eve:
I won't disappoint you.

Master Leonardo:
You won't betray me?
Eve:
No, believe me.
Master Leonardo:
What if it comes to light?
Eve:
It won't through me.
Master Leonardo:
All right. I believe you. You went to a good school. I've seen Adam, he's a dummy.
Eve:
He's a bit crude. (2007, 195)

So, Adam, once the fool, is now relegated to the role of dummy. Such a slight change can be explained as a loss in translation. But what about the Devil and Master Leonardo? What is the purpose of the replacement of the Edenic tempter with the Renaissance master? Why would Kharms have Leonardo take the role of the antagonist in the drama of the fall?

There is something of a figural interpretation in the connections that Alexander Nikitaev establishes between Kharms's miniature play *Pushkin and Gogol*[25] and a minor incident that took place during a session of the St. Petersburg Religious-Philosophical Society held on April 18, 1902. The transcript of this session, published a year later in the journal *Novi Put',* contains, among other discussions, Dmitri Merezhkovsky's argument about the relevance of Pushkin and Gogol to the advancement of Russian religious thought, followed by V. A. Ternavtsev's response, which can be summed up by his claim that Gogol "tripped over Pushkin" (Nikitaev 1994, 49). Nikitaev presents this anecdote as a probable source of Kharms's mini-play. It adds to the play an obscure underlying sense and proves the author's close familiarity with the thought of Merezhkovsky, a novelist and religious thinker who greatly influenced Russian symbolist poets.

If Kharms, as Nikitaev attempts to prove, read Merezhkovsky's religious and philosophical works, then there is no reason to doubt that he was aware of his novel *Vosskresshie Bogi: Leonardo da Vinchi* (*Resurrected Gods: Leonardo da Vinci*).[26] In this historical-biographical novel, Leonardo is recurrently associated with paradise. The irrigation system that he designs for the Duke of Milan turns the swampy lowlands of Lombardy into “God’s Paradise”; at the center of this artificially created cornucopia is Duke Moro’s garden: “formal, laid out in geometrical design, with alleys of clipped box, laurel, and myrtle; with covered ways, labyrinths, loggias, and arbors of ivy”; one of the attractions of this paradise is “a little private theatre” (Merezhkovsky 1928, 88). Merezhkovsky also pays close attention to Leonardo’s drawing of Adam and Eve and to his design of an elaborate theatrical allegory that contains geometrical representations of heavenly bodies and is entitled *Paradise.*

The most obvious similarity between Kharms’s play and Merezhkovsky’s novel is the very form of Leonardo’s name: in both works, his interlocutors address him as “Master Leonardo.”[27] Even more to the point, Kharms’s description of the Garden of Eden as “an alley lined with beautifully groomed trees” is much closer to Merezhkovsky’s description of the Paradise that Leonardo created for Duke Moro than to the stage instructions in *Ordo repraesentationis Adae.* It is not hard to imagine Kharms’s play performed in the small open-air theater at the center of Leonardo’s garden: after all, the last *didascalia* is spoken by Leonardo, who appears to be the master of this modest entertainment. Most important, the one major discrepancy between the dramatic plotline of *The Fall from Grace* and its medieval source can be traced to the novel about Leonardo. In the opening scenes of *Ordo repraesentationis Adae,* devils tempt Adam three times, only to meet with resolute refusal. They bounce back, regroup, and attack Eve, who also resists. Only then does the play make recourse to the crucial twist of its biblical source:

> Now the serpent was more cunning than any beast of the field which the Lord God had made. And he said to the woman, “Has God indeed said, ‘You shall not eat of every tree of the garden’?” (Genesis 3:1, New King James version)

In the medieval version of the story, the temptation scene is rendered as a silent mime:

> Then a serpent, artfully constructed, arises alongside the trunk of the forbidden tree. Eve will incline her ear near to it, as if harkening to its counsel. Hereupon Eve will accept the apple, and offer it to Adam. (Bevington 1975, 92)

Kharms turns the same scene into a screwball comedy:

> Eve:
> Oh, look, how funny—the he-pheasant is riding the she-pheasant!
> Master Leonardo:
> That's exactly it.
> Eve:
> What is it exactly?
> Master Leonardo:
> It's love.
> Eve:
> Then it's funny. And you? You want to ride me too?
> Master Leonardo:
> Yes. I do. But don't tell Adam.
> Eve:
> OK, I won't.
> Master Leonardo:
> I see you're a good girl.
> Eve:
> Yeah, I am a tough broad.
> Master Leonardo:
> And you love me?
> Eve:
> I wouldn't mind if you gave me a ride around the garden.
> Master Leonardo:
> Climb up on my shoulders. (Eve mounts Master Leonardo, and he gallops with her around the garden.) (2007, 195)

In Merezhkovsky's novel, the image of the mounted master emerges in the long-winded question addressed to Leonardo by his friend Niccolo Machiavelli:

> Do you know the old fable of how the philosopher Aristotle, at the whim of a wanton woman, with whom he was hopelessly in love, did, in the presence of his pupil Alexander the Great, get down on all fours and put her on his back,—and, all naked and shameless, she did ride the sage, even as one rides a mule? (1928, 435)

Of course he does. Among Leonardo's drawings, there is a sketch of an old man ridden by a plump young woman. Like many other medieval and Renaissance artists, Leonardo depicted the scene from the popular medieval fable about Aristotle and Phyllis. *Lai d'Aristote,* one of the most elaborate versions of this didactic story, was written by the thirteenth-century poet Henri d'Andeli, and it belongs, together with *Ordo repraesentationis Adae,* to the rich corpus of Anglo-Norman literature. In Andeli's fable, Aristotle advises his pupil Alexander the Great against spending too much time with his beautiful wife Phyllis so that he can concentrate on his studies. Upon learning of this, Phyllis slips into the garden next to the philosopher's chamber, where she sings and dances barefoot and unbelted, with her hair loose. Unable to resist her charms, Aristotle reaches through the window, grabs her, and declares his desire for her. Phyllis responds by testing the old man: she asks him to obey her in order to have his wish granted. Aristotle submits: riding on his back, Phyllis sings: "Master Silly carries me / Love leads on, and so he goes, / by Love's authority."

In the final analysis, Kharms's play is not a parody of a single source but a collage comprising various sources, which include medieval literary works, Renaissance drawings, a modernist novel, and perhaps even a transcript of a scholarly debate. In this way, the story of the original sin becomes a patchwork of fragments. Kharms replaces ontology with an anthology, and in doing so shifts the emphasis from the question of Being to the question of connections. Clearly, there is a similar concern, a central theme that brings together the stories of this assemblage: it is the idea of temptation as a trying out. The central theme finds its expression in the setting as much as in the action. Namely, *The Fall from Grace* is a garden play, and it is drawn from garden stories: the Garden of Eden, Duke Moro's garden, Aristotle's garden. This is not Kharms's only garden play, nor is it his only play that features the mysterious character of "Figura." They both appear in the play *Grandpa and a Turnip,* a parody of a well-known children's fable, subtitled "ballet." This is one of Kharms's most explicitly political writings from the late thirties. A group of dancers struggles to pull a gigantic turnip from the ground. After they finally succeed, a huge Red Army soldier emerges from it. This piece was most probably written between 1935 and 1938, the period during which Kharms was plagued by deprivation and hunger. The enormous turnip, eaten from within and hollowed out by a human parasite, appears as an extremely personal response to the political situation in Russia during the second five-year plan.

It is unnecessary to overemphasize the parallels between garden and page, plowing and writing, and between the cultivation of land and language: texts are gardens, plots of land stitched together.[28] *The Fall from Grace* is at the same time an *anthologia,* a collection of flowers, and a *didas-*

calon, a table. The table onto which Anton Isakovich and Natalia Borisovna climb to become Adam and Eve is at once a writing and an acting table. The differences between the non-place of language and the concrete space occupied by bodies have been erased in a single bold move. This is a paradoxical table on which words and things merge and confuse, akin to the table that Foucault imagines, inspired at the same time by mad juxtapositions of modernism and the rational taxonomies of classicism: a place for a fortuitous encounter between disparate things, the operating table as a site of the chance encounter between a sewing machine and an umbrella, "and also a table, a *tabula,* that enables thought to operate upon the entities of our world, to put them in order, to divide them into classes, to group them according to names that designate their similarities and their differences—the table upon which, since the beginning of time, language has intersected space" (Foucault 1970, xvii). Foucault's invocation of the beginning of time is not accidental, for it coincides with the beginning of human language, or the fall of the miracle that was the Adamic language, an innocent language, language deprived of knowledge. In his play about the fall, Kharms does not attempt to capture this absolute beginning. Instead, *The Fall from Grace* is a play about a perpetual beginning. It is positioned in a strange space of multiple beginnings and multiple endings, intersections, breaks, and overlappings.

On the one hand, the pronounced indeterminacy of the Kharmsian text makes it open for anthologization. Kharms's texts have to be anthologized, organized into cycles and series, either externally by editors and the publishing industry, or internally by the author. I am interested in the latter form of anthologization. *The Fall from Grace* is a text written by a collector, not by a medievalist. What makes it intriguing is that this collector is an independent agent, so to speak: he does not have a club membership, and there is no other collector like him, which makes his collecting an odd activity that does not involve exchange, any kind of assessment, or value in general. Conventional collection is built through accumulation and addition. Not so with Kharms. In his diary entry "On Collecting," he extols collecting that does not have as its organizing principle "objective value, rarity, and quality," but rather "personal taste and wish" (2002b, 151). He is a disjunctive collector, a gatherer of useless things that don't fit together, a paradoxical hobbyist who collects through giving, losing, and abandonment. These collections have no recognizable organizing principle, no law that orders a group into a series. An anthology has no memory. Kharms's most famous collection, "Blue Notebook," is suitably subtitled "In the

Album." "Album": whiteness, blank page, an empty notebook. Kharms's table is a tabula rasa, a clear board without a structure outlined in advance, receptive not to words, but to entire phrases, large chunks of text.

The necessity of anthologizing Kharms's works comes together with the impossibility of finding any one way of ordering these free-floating fragments. Take, for instance, *The Fall from Grace.* It easily fits into several possible series. First, it could be grouped together with other works based on well-known literary sources, such as *The First Act of "King Lear," Arranged for Messengers and Beetles* based on Shakespeare's play, or *Don Juan,* which follows Alexei Tolstoy's variant of the popular story, or *Comedy of the City of St. Petersburg,* in itself an anthology of Russian literature, from Pushkin's *Bronze Horseman* to Dostoevsky's *The Idiot.* Second, whereas all of these plays remained unfinished, *The Fall from Grace* is a complete dramatic miniature in prose, similar to such a series of dramatic miniatures as "Pushkin and Gogol," "The Mathematician and Andrei Semenovich," "Makarov and Petersen," and "An Unsuccessful Show." Third, the ambiguous generic description of *didascalia* places it in a series based on generic uniqueness, a disjunctive series based on the principle of difference, not similarity, which includes works described as pasquil, sonnet, ballet, symphony, or passacaglia. Fourth and finally, we should not fail to mention that *The Fall from Grace* also belongs to a series formed by the signature Daniil Dandan. The pseudonym Dandan comes most likely from the title character of Moliere's ballet-comique *Georges Dandin.*[29] It appears under seven texts written during the summer and fall of 1934, including, chronologically, the following: a diary entry dated August 2, 1934; the prose pieces "On Equilibrium" and "On Phenomena and Existences," dated September 18, 1934; *The Fall from Grace* dated September 27; the poems "What Should We Do?" and "Romance," written on October 15; and the cantata "Salvation," composed between October 31 and November 4. This end point of the "Dandan" series is also the centerpiece of the series of Kharms's musical works. So, the proliferation of series continues, it seems, ad infinitum: any poem, story, play, and even fragment belongs simultaneously to a multitude of series that run in all directions, along the fissures and cracks that open on an empty surface.

But *The Fall from Grace* represents one of those rare instances in which the crack runs through the center of a single work. Here, the fissure does not only break open in between the anthologized texts, but also between the texts and the basic law of anthologization. An anthology is a collection of equal items. Its constituents are not ordered hierarchically. The space of anthology is flat and horizontal. The idea of the fall is foreign to it. In this space, the fall becomes a crack. The singular event is replaced by a multiplicity of fissures, openings, and breaks. And that is where the main slippage, the main drama, takes place: not between higher and lower levels, but between this and that platform. In between is the impediment. It is the point of disruption: an eruption, a break. Eve tastes the apple and gets caught in the crack. She blanks out. She is a blank.

> Eve: Oh, this tastes so good! Wait, but what's going on? You disappear all the time and then reappear again. Wow! Everything disappears and then everything comes back again out of nowhere. (2007, 197)

Eve and Adam experience temporary blindness. And so does Landman, who is Adam's namesake.[30] The blank opens up where the language disappears. It lays bare and opens the naked surface. The tabula rasa yawns suddenly. The crack is a momentary experience of muteness, forgetfulness, and senselessness. It is a loss of control in which the mind gives way and matter takes over, launching a Bergsonian general disturbance of things. That is why at the cracking point, the laughter breaks out. Interruption: Entr'acte—Cataract. The crack cracks us up. It is a gap, an opening, or a point of uncertainty. Like the scream, it decouples language and sense. It is the means of expression of the nonspeaking body.

Dummy

In *The Fall from Grace,* Eve/Phyllis tests the tester, and he fails. She comes out on top, and "the most cunning," "the sage," and "the philosopher" on the bottom, as a dimwit. So much for feminine foolishness. Eve/Phyllis positively joins Ester and Raia, and the most we can say about Adam is that he is hard-headed. But what about Master Leonardo? Clearly, his stupidity is not the same as Adam's. Is he outsmarted, or just plain dumb?

Merezhkovsky portrays Leonardo as an early herald of the age of reason. He mechanizes art by studying perspective, by scrupulously measuring pigments to get the exact color shades, and by creating moving sculptures, the crude automata.[31] In his novel about another great mind of the Italian Renaissance, Merezhkovsky wrote that "Dante's living wings—these interior wings, are completely opposite to the mechanical, exterior wings of Leonardo and our own" (Bachelard 1988, 54). It seems that Kharms and his friends shared this opinion about Leonardo. In "Conversations" they talk about him as a "genius" who never brought to completion any of his projects, a fact to which Merezhkovsky often returns in his novel. Furthermore, the Renaissance master is invoked in a discussion on the subject of technology, and, more precisely, flying. Here, Lipavsky asserts that in a distant past, "flying held a higher meaning, which is now unknown to us," and that advances made in the technology of flying resulted in the fact that "*a stupid man flew*" (Lipavsky 2005, 360, italics added). Science that enables man to take off into the air actually banalizes the dream of flight and effectively grounds the flight of imagination.

Chapters 2 and 3 of Genesis can be read, among other things, as a beautiful allegory about stupidity. According to Genesis, the entire process of creation culminates with the first human couple. The first humans are above the rest of the animals because they are in possession of the *logos*. This language has nothing to do with intelligence. In their relation to language, as in their relation to everything else, they are neither children nor adults: they speak but don't know; they are innocent but invulnerable. Kierkegaard suggests that the original innocence is "not a perfection one ought to wish to recover," and it is not "an imperfection with which one cannot be content to stop but must go further"; instead, "innocence is ignorance" (Kierkegaard 1957, 34). This definition of innocence reflects a uniquely Christian commendation of ignorance. This ignorance is not simple foolishness, stupidity, or madness. According to this schema, innocence is the absence of thought and reflection. It is pure inwardness: "the lack of inwardness is always a consequence of reflection," asserts Kierkegaard (126). The destruction of inwardness comes with temptation. The pure interiority crumbles at the mere acknowledgment of the outside. The outside, the other, tempts Eve; she yields, and is stung. The sexual symbolism of temptation that leads to the original sin is obvious.[32] In the moment of the fall, the innocence is lost, but no perfect knowledge is gained. Instead, the pure thought of innocence is disturbed by a certain animal craving, which is often seen as stupidity. By replacing the Serpent with Master Leonardo, Kharms alters the entire parable about the animality of stupidity. Master Leonardo does not hold Eve in much higher esteem than Adam, who is a "dummy." Indeed, he counts on her ignorance when he points to the empirical example of the "he-pheasant" mounting the "she-pheasant." Leonardo possesses mastery over things. If ignorance is pure inwardness, then stupidity turns outward; it is always the other who is stupid.

In the case of Master Leonardo, the animality of thought does not appear as what is often called the "intelligence of the body," or as an instinct. Instinct, like reflex, is characterized by sharpness and precision. Inasmuch as it is often seen as autonomous and trustworthy in its instantaneous accuracy, it is opposed to imagination and reflection, which are seen as predisposed to stray, wander aimlessly, and, in extreme cases, lose their objective and become idle and dumb. Master Leonardo's thought is not marked by innateness, or indeterminacy, or aimlessness. Quite the opposite, it is active, determinate, and, to use bureaucratic lingo, "goal-oriented." It seems that this kind of stupidity comes from the dulling of instincts by reason. It is a curious stupidity of reason, stupidity that comes not from the body, but from the mind itself. Paradoxically, this thought is not "genital" enough. So, we come to discover a certain kind of stupidity, a certain absence of thought that is buried deeply in thought itself. It is an empty form of knowledge, thought without insight, a stale thought content with itself, comfortable in language, and self-satisfied within its own limits. The stupidity of reason uses false inwardness and false movement as decoys. It is hard to interrogate because its main procedure is the interrogation itself. This interrogation is recognizable in the catechesis that Kharms almost literally quotes from *Ordo Repraesentationis Adae:* "Will you listen to me?" "You won't betray me?" "What if it comes to light?"

The interrogator fires a barrage of questions, without ever posing a problem. His goal is not to challenge the interrogated into reaching a new insight, but to have her submit to his own line of reasoning. The entire dialogue between Master Leonardo and Eve replicates the standard master-pupil situation: the teacher already knows all the answers, and his questions serve to constrain the student's thinking rather than to lead it to a crisis that might spark a flash of new insight. So, this lecture is not a questioning in the true sense of posing a problem, but a demonstration of an already familiar hypothesis. Stupidity defuses the problem and forecloses the unknown. At any point, any dialogue can turn into a questioning and then into a sadistic interrogation. *The Fall from Grace* echoes much more violent lecture demonstrations: there is a whole series of Kharms's works in which young girls are examined by superior teachers. More often than not, these examinations turn into violent demonstrations of an already existing knowledge; and, as a rule, they lead to an unforeseeable, sometimes fatal, outcome.

Kharms's dialogic lesson pieces[33] are centered on the encounter between two orders of thought. Here, the process of teaching is not only violent and coercive, but also makes learning impossible. It always turns into a teaching in reverse: as the lecture advances, knowledge regresses. Kharms's lessons are never far from torture. In an untitled verse dialogue, a teacher coerces a girl into meditation about a sphere as a geometric figure. Midway through the lecture, the girl helplessly admits "it is clear to me / simply, I am stupid" (1997b, 234). The Kharms effect, progression through demise, seems to be nowhere as pertinent as in the subject of questioning. In the playlet *Comprehensive Examination,* one completely healthy Ermolaev comes in for a checkup and perishes from the barrage of questions from his doctor (124). In the poetic play *The Window,* a process of intense examination ends with the girl turned green and speechless. The dangerous procedure of questioning results either in death or thoughtlessness. The absence of thought can be said to be a gap in the thought process. This gap is the failure of memory, a blank. How does it differ from ignorance and stupidity of reason?

The latter amounts to no more than a rehearsal of the already known. In other words, it restrains thought from positing the unknown. Its main principle is certainty; its main tool, the false question. Deleuze asserts that if the false question always reasserts a certain kind of established knowledge, then the true question-problem posits the objectivity of what is unknown. He calls the objectively unknown "a non-knowledge," which is different from insufficiency, stupidity, or animality. Instead, it is the enabling limit of learning (1994, 180). Excluded from the rehearsal of the known, the non-knowledge neither presents a problem as being unsolvable and impossible, nor does it point to the certainty of an already confirmed solution. Non-knowledge is precisely the new, that which is unrecognizable, that which is not similar to anything:

> The new, with its power of beginning and beginning again, remains forever new, just as established was always established from the outset, even if a certain amount of empirical time was necessary for this to be recognized. What becomes established with the new is precisely not the new. For the new—in other words, difference—calls forth forces in thought which are not the forces of recognition, today or tomorrow, but the powers of a completely other model, from an unrecognized and unrecognizable *terra incognita.* What forces does this new bring to bear upon thought, from what central ungrounding which strips thought of its "innateness," and treats it every time as something which has not always existed, but begins, forced and under constraint? (Deleuze 1994, 136)

The answer is hard to voice because it always causes the greatest of misunderstandings. Within a problem, non-knowledge does not represent an error but a transcendental limit of thought. Deleuze is careful not to confuse non-knowledge with stupidity as he defines it in the same work. Whereas stupidity "constitutes the greatest weakness of thought," non-knowledge represents its highest strength; stupidity forces thought to think, but non-knowledge is the force of thought.[34]

Kharms is not as cautious in naming different categories and degrees of the absence of thought, from ignorance to stupidity, thoughtlessness, and non-knowledge. His interrogators (teachers/torturers) are endowed with bestial thought; the thought of their victims, the interrogated students, is always extremely tense, constrained at the point of breakdown. The primary characteristic of the former is violence, and of the latter, absence of mind, logic, and reason.[35] Torturers can take the torture because it is justified by the task of driving sense into their victims' minds. As long as the tortured ones resist, they remain dense and stupid.

Even a cursory look points to an intriguing relation between nonsense and stupidity. Deleuze explains it by saying that "the mechanism of nonsense is the highest finality of sense, just as the mechanism of stupidity is the highest finality of thought" (1994, 155). What does it mean that nonsense represents the highest finality of sense, and stupidity the highest finality of thought? Can we assert that if nonsense produces its own sense, then stupidity thinks its own thought? Stupidity does not represent a kind of thought somehow deprived of knowledge but a kind of thought that disregards its other, the *terra incognita* of non-knowledge. Stupidity has to be considered from the standpoint of thought, which, as we have seen, has to be grounded in order to exist. To ground is to represent: by thinking, thought represents. It is grounded precisely in that which stupidity does not have: memory. Memory, the pure nonmaterial past, is the ground. Stupidity is ungrounded and indeterminate. It has no past to recollect and no future to foretell. (There is a certain unsettling universality and timelessness to stupidity. It belongs to no time, no epoch in particular.) On the one hand, stupidity is passive and static, and that is why it is coercive; that is why thought perishes in it, and is, finally, forced to escape from it. On the other hand, having no memory and no determination, it is light and formless. Whenever he refers to the absence of reason, to what I have called "pure stupidity," or non-knowledge, Kharms is focusing on the aspect of stupidity I just mentioned: stupidity as forgetfulness, lightness, and transparency. As we have seen, in his poetic drama *Gvidon,* Kharms relates that "the rivers of our learning are drying up / . . . in our majestic skull" (1997b, 466). The idea of the ungrounding of knowledge can hardly get more precise: knowledge does not evaporate into the air, but escapes down, oozes through fissures and cracks in the soil, and sinks into depth. The emptied surface is clear, silent, and translucent, as in the closing stanzas of the poem "Hnyu":

> Hnyu answered: "I was born
> A fool only to sit in a haystack,
> The noises of a full day's keyboard
> I cannot bear to hear.
> And if the butterflies can hear the crackling of sparks in the burdock,
> And if beetles carry in their tiny knapsacks the notes of vegetable voices,
> And if water spiders know the name and patronymic of the gun the hunter lost,
> Then I must confess that I am just a stupid little girl."
> "That's how it is," said her companion,
> "The highest priority of categories
> Exists in the complete ignorance of the surroundings.
> And that, I confess, I find terribly pleasing." (2007, 164)

And in the prologue to *Don Juan,* Kharms juxtaposes joy with stupidity and reason:

> Spirits:
> To be is to have been
> and the one who was, will be.
> To be is joy
> and the one who wants to be will be. . . .
> Spirit Firmapelius:
> To the one who wants to be and came into being,
> Stupidity is always befitting.
> Spirit Bustabalius:
> To be means to be in reason.
> And the one who wants to be,
> will be reasonable.
> Spirit Firmapelius:
> And the one who wants to be and is
> at that very moment is overcome with stupidity.
> Spirit Bustabalius:

I hold and maintain:
To be is not to be stupid.
And you, my friend Firmapelius,
are making a big mistake.
(1997a, 319)

I have to interrupt this spirited debate and question, for the last time, Kharms's notion of stupidity. We know with whom he sides in this debate. All of his major theoretical and poetic assertions are at the same time pronouncements against rationality. In this particular instance, what is opposed to reason is not the clarity of order, or a perfect gift, or the fifth meaning, but stupidity. Additionally, this stupidity is paired with joy. What is Kharms suggesting here? Could he be simply saying that ignorance is bliss?

Kharms's interest in joy is not surprising. Joy is the opposite of weariness and heaviness. The latter crushes and pulls downward, the former eases and elevates. Joy is the experience of lightness. In joy, lightness is inseparable from the sense of confidence. In the flight of lightness, the ground disappears. In joy, it is not the ground that provides safety and shelter. Joy means severing ties with the heaviness of the ground and entrusting oneself to the lightness of something that is even less material than air: to the event. Jean-Luc Nancy relates laughter to joy and asserts that this pure presentation still preserves a sense of direction: "In the end, there is no more object of desire, and consequently, no more subject; it is no longer a desire: it is something that burns, and it is joy" (1993, 384).[36] Joy is the end of desire and the loss of the self. As an experience of internal emptiness, it is easily related to the loss of knowledge and memory, and the sense of selfhood. So, for Kharms, stupidity is indeed bliss of sorts. Now, what is truly significant is that his only explicitly stated principle of literary style is directly related to this form of stupidity. This principle is clarity: in his letter to Claudia Pugachova it is the "clarity of order" in poetry, and in the poem "Hnyu" it is the "clarity of categories."

However, the fragment of the poetic drama *Don Juan* suggests that, for Kharms, the notion of stupidity goes even further than that. In itself, *Don Juan* represents one of the most intriguing instances of intertextuality in Kharms's work. This unfinished play consists of a long list of characters, a complete prologue, and the opening lines of the first act. It is a parody, in Tynianov's sense, of Alexei Tolstoy's romantic tragedy.[37] Tolstoy's *Don Juan* opens with a celestial prologue: a group of spirits—soon joined by picturesque characters such as Passing Clouds, Blooming Flowers, and Lakes and Rivers—conduct a dialogue on elevated themes declaimed in an appropriate tone. Kharms borrows the eccentric characters, alters the subject, and shatters the tone of their conversation. It seems as if the concern with stupidity leaks into this prologue from yet another intertextual and unfinished play, *The Comedy of the City of St. Petersburg,* which teems with literary references and citations.[38] One of the most striking instances of Kharms's citation of literary sources comes from Dostoevsky's novel *The Idiot.* The hero of Dostoevsky's novel, Prince Myshkin, travels by train to Russia from Switzerland. Kharms replaces the train with an airplane, and his Prince Meschersky flies across Mont Blanc. The differences between the source text and Kharms's parody are perhaps even more telling than the similarities: whereas in Dostoevsky's novel Prince Myshkin is the principal character, the prince is not the principal character of Kharms's play; although Myshkin returns to Russia after the completion of his medical treatment in a Swiss clinic, Meschersky asserts that he was invited to return to Petrograd/Leningrad; most important, Myshkin suffers from the "falling sickness" but there seems to be nothing wrong with Meschersky's health.

In her penetrating investigation of the idea of stupidity in philosophy and literature, Avital Ronell recognizes in *The Idiot* a particular kind of stupidity that originates in the afflicted body. She writes that "idiocy has something to do with the nearly existential fact of being stuck with a body or, to put it differently, with the fact that the body has claims upon us" (Ronell 2002, 180). Dostoevsky's Prince Myshkin suffers from epilepsy, the mysterious illness that approaches the limits of the sacred. Kharms removes signs of both illness and sacredness from his citational character. When Meschersky asks for an explanation for his urgent recall to Petrograd/Leningrad, he receives a crude answer reminiscent of the rumors that perpetually surround Dostoevsky's Prince Myshkin: "Your mind is in great demand" (Kharms 1997b, 208). Unlike Myshkin, however, Kharms's Meschersky jumps on the opportunity to display his intellectual abilities. In short, Kharms assigns to the idiot an altogether different model of dumbness, which Ronell opposes to idiocy:

> The stupid subject is fortified, defended, lives within a calculated economy of compensation and disavowal, holds it in and keeps it up. He subsists on a system of denial that does not deny itself a thing. The Idiot, well, the Idiot can't hold anything down or be sure of very much; there is little material consolation, in any event, and the confidence

> for which his simplicity allows falls on empty spaces. He lives on the edges of nihilist temptation, a permanent evacuee who cannot be said to appropriate much of a thought "sprung spontaneously from his own brain," nor do we witness him eating. (Ronell 2002, 219)

Kharms sees the "stupid subject" as, first and foremost, a babbling body. The subjectivity of a dimwit (*durak*) appears to be somehow lost between the assertive body and the words that incessantly pour from it. For Kharms, logorrhea is the symptom of stupidity. In his diary, he explains his revulsion for the elderly as a reaction to their long-windedness, and notes that verbosity is the mother of inaptitude. His sketch of the stupid subject is based on those premises:

> A neck stuck out from the collar of the fool's shirt, and on the neck was a head. The head was at one time closely cropped. By now the hair had grown out like a brush. The fool talked about a lot of things. No one listened to him. Everyone thought: when will he shut up and leave? But the fool, noticing nothing, continued talking and laughing. (2007, 187)

For Kharms, logorrhea does not signify evacuation and emptying, but precisely the opposite. The stupid subject is strangely self-sufficient: there is no listener for the words he emits. Ultimately, he ends up being his own audience, drowning in his own verbal content. This closed circuit of words parallels constipation. Kharms sees both the stupid subject and the idiot as "stuck with a body," albeit in ways that are completely opposed:

> Two friends lived in Kiev
> Amazing people
> The first was from the south
> And the other, the other way around
> The first was a big glutton
> And the other an idiot.
> The first died from constipation
> And the other, the other way around. (2002b, 97)

With its air of a nursery rhyme, this simple poem revolves around the trope of contrariness, "the other way around" (*naoborot*). If the first friend comes from the south and the second "the other way around," then the logical assumption is that the latter comes from the north (Leningrad?). The second pair of opposites is less obvious: idiocy is "the other way around" from gluttony. Finally, what is "the other way around" from death caused by constipation?

While Dostoevsky's idiot is stuck with an epileptic body, Kharms's idiot is trapped in a starving body. While the former illness is rare, incurable, and shrouded in mystery, the latter is often widespread, potentially easy to cure, and hardly mysterious. The most striking symptoms of epilepsy are seizures, loss of consciousness, and partial amnesia. In Dostoevsky's novel, epileptic spells hit Prince Myshkin at crucial moments, and always in public: however modest the sufferer, his illness is a spectacle. Hunger, however, is invisible. It does not strike. Instead, it creeps in slowly, from within, and isolates the starving subject from the mass of well-fed citizens. The first signs of hunger are psychic: the relatively normal focus on food turns into an obsession, followed by emotional instability characterized by sharp swings from depression to elation. Instead of attacking the body, malnutrition erodes it. The muscles and internal organs shrink and deteriorate. The starving man suffers from insomnia, dizziness, and chronic diarrhea. The body swells from fluid under the skin and loses hair. Eventually, anemia, immune deficiency, and various avitaminoses lead to death.[39] Before he experienced it himself, Kharms was introduced to the pathology of starvation through the hero of Knut Hamsun's novel *Hunger,* who goes through most of the above-mentioned stages of starvation and lives to tell about it.[40] In many respects, this hero resembles Prince Myshkin: like Myshkin, he is not entirely at home in the city in which he lives; like Myshkin, he gives everything he has, and he would give even more if he could; and, like the idiot-prince, he constantly stumbles over his body. But in certain other respects, he resembles Myshkin, only "the other way around." Unlike Myshkin, he is not stricken with a sickness, nor did he undergo a clinical treatment abroad. While crowds perpetually surround Prince Myshkin (children while he was sick, and all kinds of fools upon his return to Russia), Hamsun's nameless, statusless writer is desperately isolated. Whereas two women compete over Myshkin, the one girl whom the starving man meets runs away from him upon hearing about his financial predicament. But what separates them more than anything else are their professions and afflictions: while the first is a well-off free agent without a specific profession, the second is a starving writer. This idiot is caught in a vicious circle: he cannot write because he is starving, and he is prevented from getting food because he cannot write. In this incessant torture, swooning comes as a relief. The hunger locks the thought into the "dumb impassiveness" of the body:

> I felt a sort of shimmering heat inside my head, and the beating in my temples was strange. The water I had drunk did not agree with me, and I walked on, throwing up a little here, a little there, in the gutter. Finally I made it to the Cemetery of Christ. I sat down with my elbows on my knees, my head in my hands: bent over like that, it was better, and I didn't feel the small gnawing in my chest any longer. (Hamsun 1967, 56)

The empty stomach takes command of the body: it dictates movements, gestures, and bodily positions. The thought merely follows.

The discourse on stupidity produces opposites: the most obvious—intelligence versus stupidity and mind versus body; the more sophisticated stupid subject versus idiot controversy; and the seemingly irrational coupling of the glutton and the idiot. Ronell distinguishes yet another pair that emerges from the Romanticist idea of the doubling of the self into linguistic and experiential components. The first self is a "transcendental self": an infinitely mobile and agile component, "it is seen to stand above any of its experiences" (2002, 134). The other self, which has "nothing to do . . . with a consciousness" and about which "nothing can be said," Ronell dubs a "crash test dummy." This part of the self, "hitting against the phenomenal walls of experience, probes the boundaries of its own transcendence—of its self-transcendence and destruction into the other type of the self" (135). The "other way around" from the sacred idiot is the starving idiot; the ban on thinking issued by the body is the other way around from pure joy, pure lightness of thought. The other way around from the idiot who collapses, gives excessively, and even manages to issue a couple of memorable aphorisms is the bemused and starving writer. This idiot's idiot is crashing his mind against the limits of his physical endurance, and his body against the ethical limits of his mind. He chews on the pieces of cloth, bites his own finger, sucks on a dry bone, vomits, argues with God, and then sucks again.

Kharms's diary for the fall of 1937 represents a similar chronicle of starvation. The epigraph of this chapter comes from that section of his diary. The note on nonsense is preceded by the outcry: "God, now I have one single favor to ask of You: destroy me, break me up definitively, throw me into Hades; don't leave me midway, but deprive me of all hope and quickly destroy me for all times to come" (1992, 501). While starving, Kharms was still working on his collection. This is an entry from the album "The Blue Notebook":

> 27. This is how hunger begins:
> In the morning you wake lively,
> Then weakness,
> Then boredom,
> Then comes the loss
> Of quick reason's strength,—
> Then comes calm,
> And then horror.
> October 4, 1937 (Ostashevsky 2006, 135)

This entry can be called "Blue Notebook No. 27." Whereas in "Blue Notebook No. 10" writing progresses into its own disappearance, here language crashes against the body. This short text can be seen as a poetic statement, a diaristic gesture, and a piece of evidence. The event is neither in the suffering of the starving body nor in the linguistic content that documents it, but in their forceful encounter. The crash-test ends in silence, in the realm deprived of language. When it comes after birth, this realm is marked as *infans.* But what do we call the silence before death? Disaster, the silent death. The silence of the emaciated body joins the silence of history. The last record in Kharms's NKVD (KGB) file is dated December 7, 1941. It is a note saying that he was sent to the mental hospital for "compulsory treatment" (1998, 603). Some two months later, on February 2, 1942, Daniil Kharms starved to death.[41] It was an event without a witness.

It is difficult for a camel to pass through the eye of a needle, and it is equally hard for the reason, mind, to pass into that which is un-reason, mindlessness, non-sense, i.e., to make reasonable, sensical, and knowable that which does not have those attributes.

—Kazimir Malevich, "Suprematism as Pure Cognition" (1922)

5. Event and Performances

He Hiccuped

Kharms gave his last public performance at the memorial service for Kazimir Malevich, who died on May 15, 1935. The entire service was meticulously planned by Malevich himself, and executed by his family members, students, and associates.

The funeral procession that went through the streets of Leningrad was headed by a catafalque adorned with a black square, and the event was preceded by a memorial service held in Malevich's apartment. Later, the whole affair was often lauded as the last public manifestation of the Leningrad avant-garde. Kharms was very well-acquainted with Malevich's apartment. He mentions "Malevich's room" in a notebook entry from the spring of 1933, in which he briefly discusses the notion of clarity (2002a, 445). In the same notebook, we find Kharms's sketch of a detail from one of Malevich's paintings and another mention of his apartment. There is little or no mention of Malevich in Kharms's notebooks between 1928, the year of OBERIU's brief association with GINKhUK, and 1933, when the great painter was diagnosed with cancer. During his protracted illness (from 1933 to 1935), Malevich's bedroom became an avant-garde salon of sorts where his friends and former students gathered, talked about art, and presented their works to their mortally ill teacher. It seems that these conversations had a soothing effect on the dying painter. Lidia Ginzburg recorded that, during Malevich's last months, a doctor visited him on a daily basis. The visits continued long after it was certain that there was no viable medical treatment. The therapy, so to speak, turned around the other way: the doctor became interested in "left art" and Malevich lectured him on the subject (Ginzburg 1982, 416). Malevich was certain of his impending death and left precise instructions for the design of his deathbed, coffin, and monument. All stages of Malevich's "auto-thanatography" were dominated by suprematist images, most notably by the black square.[1]

The photographs of Malevich's deathbed show the face of the deceased painter, bearded and worn out by the prolonged suffering, protruding from under snow-white sheets. Two rich bouquets of white flowers are directly above the deceased man's head and on the right side of the bed. A closer inspection of the photographs reveals that the paintings and objects that surrounded the deathbed were rearranged between photo shoots. Three elements, however, remain unaltered in all surviving photographs of Malevich lying in state. *Black Square* was hung on the wall above the deceased's pillow.[2] Next to it, to the left, was the artist's "Renaissance-style" self-portrait from 1933. Underneath this painting was a coffin propped vertically against the wall:[3] a plain white trunk, its lid adorned with basic suprematist forms. The black square was painted at the topmost section of the lid, corresponding to the deceased's head, and the black circle at the bottom. The middle section was left conspicuously blank. Ginzburg explains that, according to Malevich's instructions, this section was intended for a black cross, which had to be removed because of its religious symbolism, "even though it was called," in the language of suprematism, "the intersection of two planes" (1982, 416). The arrangement of the basic suprematist forms on the lid was made to match the arrangement of the basic suprematist colors in the coffin. It seems that in the script for his thanatography, Malevich did not forget his last costume. According to some eyewitness accounts, the painter's body was clad in a white shirt, black trousers, and red shoes (Karasik 1991, 194). In *Suprematism: 34 Drawings,* Malevich wrote of the black square as "the fifth measure in art," white as "pure action," and red as "the signal for revolution" (Malevich 1968, 127). Black and white are separated from red, which is associated with the ground, the movement of walking, and the revolutionary leap. A propensity for trinitarian groupings, characteristic of Malevich, is echoed in the elegy that Kharms recited by his deathbed.

Kharms's wife Marina Malich (later Durnovo), who was present at the memorial service, recalls that the room was overcrowded with mourners. She reports that Kharms stood at the bed's head as he recited his poem "On Kazimir Malevich's Death." The poem's manuscript is dated May 5, 1935, ten days prior to Malevich's death. Most likely, the idea for the poetic eulogy came at the last moment: Nikolai Khardzhiev reported that he was present when Kharms adapted the poem "Epistle to Nikolai Oleinikov" to his poem dedicated to Malevich.[4] The poem was addressed to a living friend, and this tone remained prominent in the final version. This was a memorable recitation: several decades later, Malich remembered that Kharms delivered his verses with an extraordinary "force and pressure" that made many people in the room weep (in Glotser 2000, 70). The poem is a moan, a candid and painful call directed at the ear beyond the reach of the poet's voice: "Hey, Kazimir! Where is your friend?"

Kharms's poem is not only a homage to Malevich, but also a response to his 1919 article "On Poetry." In it, Malevich demands that poetry should not be an art of polished metaphors: "I consider the highest moment in the poet's service of the spirit to be that of his wordless dialect, when demented words rush from his mouth, mad words accessible neither to the mind, nor to reason" (1968, 81). Kharms answers:

> Pe—is the inkpot of your words.
> Trr—is your desire.
> Agalthon—is your skinny memory.
> Hey, Kazimir! Where's your desk?
> Looks as if it's not here, and your desire is—Trr.
> Hey, Kazimir, where is your friend?
> She is also gone, and your memory's inkpot is—Pe.
> Eight years have crackled away in those ears of yours.
> Fifty minutes have beat away in that heart of yours.
> Ten times has the river flowed before you.
> The inkpot of your desire Trr and Pe has ended.
> "Imagine that!" you say and your memory is—Agalthon.
> (2007, 121)

Trr. Pe. Agalthon. Unfortunately, there are no surviving reports that describe Kharms's performance of these neologisms. We have to examine the meanings and try to hear the sounds. Let's start from the end, Agalthon. In it, Yampolsky recognizes the Greek word *agaton,* used in philosophy, meaning a "higher principle of being." He also notes that Kharms's Agalthon could be related to Agathon, a young man from Plato's *Symposium,* suggesting that "it is the matter of substitution of the elderly amnesia . . . with youthful desire, which is also susceptible to forgetfulness" (Iampol'skii 1997, 223). This silenced memory is also related to the numbers in the poem:

eight, fifty, ten. The numbers refer to the innumerable flow of time ("eight years"),[5] blood ("fifty minutes have beat away in that heart of yours"), and water ("ten times has the river flowed before you"). Counting provides a silent background to the violent explosions of "mad words": Trr, Pe, Agalthon. Kharms relates Pe, Khlebnikov's *zaum* word for song and singing, to the "inkpot of [Malevich's] words." Now, in Kharms, the inkpot is a rich motif in its own right. It is, of course, related to writing, but in a completely unconventional way. On the one hand, in an untitled poem from 1930, he writes "and the bird sheds bitter tears / into its inkpot / fir fir mur mur / fir fir mur mur" (1997a, 187).[6] This shedding of tears can be related to the albatross from *Lapa* and its symbolism of bloodletting. So, if the body is the original holder of liquids used for writing, then writing itself turns from a means of representation into pure immanence. On the other hand, in Kharms's narratives from the 1930s, the inkpot is related to forgetfulness and the cessation of writing. Many of his narratives, such as "The Knights" and "Artist and His Watch," end abruptly with the writer's announcement that he has lost or misplaced his inkpot. In this context, we should also add the mention of the inkpot in "A Tract (More or Less) According to Emersen," which is essentially a meditation on the idea of renunciation and disruption of the ties between man and the objects that surround him.[7] So, the complex figure of the inkpot turns writing from a mnemonic aid into a mechanism of forgetting. Finally, the nonsense triplet begins with Trr, the word divested of the least shred of meaning. It seems to be an attempt to record in letters the pure noise produced by the tongue hitting the ceiling of the oral cavity. The powerful stream of air makes the lungs tremble. The entire body shakes: Trrrrrrrr. Malevich spoke of a dancelike language of the poets who "serve the body as it directs, make those gestures which it indicates, and speak whatever it will"; also "the poet's dialect, rhythm, and tempo divide the mass of sound and make clear the detailed gestures of the body itself" (1968, 80, 81). Malevich not only asked for the force of "demented words" but also knew how to respond to his own demand in his own "wordless dialect": he prefaced his essay "On New Systems in Art" with the cheerful *zaum* exclamation, "I follow / u-el-el-ul-el-te-ka / my new path" (1968, 83).

In his essay "He Stuttered," Deleuze talks about stuttering as the performance in language that is quite different from that which J. L. Austin described as performative speech acts. For Deleuze, stuttering is the internal outside of language through which the writer reaches "regions without memories" and becomes "something other than a writer" (Deleuze 1997,

112–13). Not quitting writing in order to become a painter, or a mathematician, or a composer, but painting, calculating, and singing in writing. Stuttering is a matter of the de-figuration of language, and of making it unintelligible. It is a matter of somatization of language. Deleuze concludes the essay with a somewhat surprising evocation of the poets Bely, Mandelstam, and Khlebnikov: "a Russian trinity thrice the stutterer and thrice crucified" (114). As in the Great Dionysia, the tragic trilogy is followed by the farce.

Kharms did not stutter. That would have been too serious a style. In the documentation of his second, fatal arrest in 1941, held in the KGB archives, there is a strange indication under the rubric of "personal peculiarities and habits": hiccups.[8] Vsevolod Nikolaevich Petrov, the art historian and artistic consultant at the Russian Museum, wrote in his memoirs about his friendship with Kharms in the late 1930s. He described his first visit to Kharms's apartment:

> With great courtesy and attentiveness Kharms helped us take off our coats. While doing that, it seemed to me that he not so much hiccuped or grunted, but inhaled through the nose in a peculiar way: nih, nih. I was alarmed a bit. It passed like that, and later I learned that grunting is Kharms's permanent manner, one of his nervous tics, some of which were involuntary, and some specially cultivated. (Petrov 1993, 191)

Kharms mentions some of his tics in his notebooks. On August 31, 1934, he meticulously notes that his eyes squint and his head shakes (2002b, 96). There are some speculations among those who knew him that he cultivated tics in order to feign a mental disorder so that he could avoid military service. This speculation could be supported by the pronounced interest in mental illness that is evident in his notebooks from 1939 to 1940. He mentions a number of books on the subject, such as Pavel Karpov's *Tvorchestvo dushevnobol'nykh* (*The Artistry of the Mentally Ill*), J. Kanbach's *What Is Mental Illness?* and O. Bumke's *Common Misconceptions about the Mentally Ill.* He made notes about the symptomatology and etiology of mental illnesses (2002b, 144–45). Still, all we can say is that it was an interest, no more. That leaves hiccups somewhat outside of the sphere of the cat-and-mouse game with the authorities.

If we accept Deleuze's suggestion that in stuttering "*language in its entirety reaches the limit* that marks its outside and makes it confront silence," then hiccuping comes across as a second rate, nonserious stutter (1997, 113, italics in the original). A bodily sound that is outside of language, indeed. It is a voice that an irritated diaphragm issues, not the powerful lungs. It is an unwanted (st)utterance that makes a staccato speech. It pierces language and shows through it, but not in it. Whenever introduced into the work of art, especially theater, it amounts to desperately trivial comedy. The third scene of *Elizabeth Bam,* entitled "absurdly comic-naïve," resounds with ceremonial hiccups:

> Petr Nikolaevich: I have placed a guard on the door, and at the slightest push Ivan Ivanovich will hiccup an aside.
> Elizabeth Bam: A demonstration, please, a demonstration.
> Petr Nikolaevich: Just look, then. I suggest you avert your eyes. (Petr Nikolaevich comes to the proscenium, Ivan Ivanovich follows him.) One, two, three. (Touches the pedestal, Ivan Ivanovich hiccups loudly. Petr Nikolaevich turns the pedestal over.)
> Elizabeth Bam: And again, please. (They repeat it. Petr Nikolaevich again touches the pedestal and Ivan Ivanovich again hiccups.) (1993, 160)

Every now and then, strong hiccups seize Kharms's writing. These tremors mark sudden turns toward nonwriting. He then becomes something other than a writer: a painter, an actor, a musician. And then, the evental leaves the writing and invades his performances.

Diagram

Kharms's earliest surviving works are drawings that precede his first poems by some three years.[9] A thin notebook without covers contains seven drawings in ink, accompanied by commentaries written in German. At the top of the first drawing, entitled *Day,* there is an inscription that designates the time and place of origin: "Drawn in the year 1919. Detskoe Selo."[10] *Day* is followed by six drawings: *Dream, Astronomer, Rest, Miracle, Cigarette,* and *Auntie.* Four out of the seven drawings include human figures and portraits, two are still lives, and one is abstract. They are surprisingly mature for a fourteen year old: as Gleb Ershov points out, regardless of style, technique, or topic, all drawings are prominently marked by the allegorical arrangement of figures (1995, 27); stylistically they all carry strong elements of cubism. The most significant difference between the Detskoe Selo series and Kharms's later drawings is the expulsion of allegory. Also, save for the caricatures and self portraits,[11] the human figure becomes less prominent in the schemas, symbols, hieroglyphs, and instances of *mise en page* of his later years. Narrativity and figuration give way to diagrammatic drawing, which is hardly noticeable in his early visual works.[12] The diagrammatic line became the most prominent feature of Kharms's visual works.

Unlike a phonetic text, which is inseparable from linearity and duration, a diagram offers the possibility of simultaneous and instantaneous reading. It differs from a pictorial representation because it does not present a likeness of an object but visualizes a movement, a process, or a relation. In this presentation of movement, the individual features disappear and are replaced by directions and tendencies. However, that does not mean that a diagram generalizes. A diagrammatic line is stripped of details, ornaments, particularities, and everything that could obscure the charting of directions, tendencies, and forces—their shifts and interactions. These lines of force are vectors, not generalizations. Diagrammatic "demonstration" is not a representation or a depiction; a diagram is not an illustration, but an enactment. The line becomes properly diagrammatic only when it departs from mimetic likeness and starts asserting its own reality. That is why Deleuze and Guattari include diagrams among those "regimes of signs" that are less than language in the sense that they are not grammatical, and at the same time more than language in the sense that they do not represent, but instead create, reality: "the diagrammatic or abstract machine does not function to represent, even something real, but rather constructs real that is yet to come, a new type of reality" (1987, 142). The most important distinction that Deleuze and Guattari make between language and diagrams concerns the unique relation between abstraction and reality that is established in the latter. Unlike language, the diagram does not involve translation of reality into a regime of signs. Instead, the diagram is "the height of abstraction, but also the moment at which abstraction becomes real; everything operates through abstract-real machines . . ." (1987, 146). According to this view, the abstract machine and language are mutually exclusive.

Taken literally, this would make the diagrammatization of text impossible. Still, in his book *Demon i labirint: diagrammy, deformatsii, mimesis* (*Daemon and Labyrinth: Diagrams, Deformations, Mimesis*), Mikhail Yampolsky shows that the diagram is not completely excluded from writing. Far from it: it is instrumental in integrating the "convulsive body" into a text. According to Yampolsky, the convulsive body is a body-machine, a body that is unconscious and automatized. The convulsive body forms a double to the reflexive body that produces meanings. The former is opposed to the classical and perspectival spatiality of the latter. The classical and perspectival body is stable: it is a grammatical body, a lawful body. Conversely, "the convulsive body behaves like a machine of transformations in which the regime of signs is changing" (Iampol'skii 1996, 81). The nonclassical and nonperspectival space of the diagram is flat. Movement on a flat surface produces a labyrinth, a map. In this labyrinthine map, text exists on the nonsemantic level. While Kharms's work on hieroglyphics and cryptography involves the translation of the purely visual into the semantic, the visualization of text entails the opposite process.[13] Here, my main concern is not with the "translation" of a visual line into a discursive text, or with the process that runs in the opposite direction. Instead, I am interested in the coexistence of a diagram and discursive language, in the relation between the convulsive and the reflexive body, between abstract machines and regimes of signs. Can a text co-opt a diagram? Is there such a thing as a diagrammatic text? And, conversely, a textual diagram?

The difference between Kharms's Detskoe Selo sketchbook and his later drawings was caused, at least in part, by his encounter with Malevich's abstract machine of suprematism. There is a curious relation between suprematism and the diagram. On the one hand, virtually all of Malevich's suprematist works can be seen as profoundly diagrammatic. On the other hand, in suprematism, the relation between abstract machines and the order of signs is inverted. Of particular interest here is the relation between the visual and theoretical aspects of suprematism. Namely, in the process that Deleuze and Guattari describe, the abstract signs are extracted from language. Malevich reverses that order: historically, his attempt to formulate a new philosophical language followed his "discovery" of nonobjectivity. Here, the image comes first.

During the civil war years, which he spent in Vitebsk, Malevich produced his boldest arguments for nonobjectivity, *Suprematism as Pure Cognition* (1922) and *Suprematism as Non-Objectivity* (1922). In these texts, the notions of "nonobjectivity" and "objectivity" are not limited to their proper meaning of abstract versus figurative painting. Instead, Malevich applies them to broad regions of human activity. According to this view, industry, religion, and science belong to the "objective mind," while art belongs to the nonobjective mindlessness (*bezumie*) (Malevich 2000a, 176). Malevich was fond of wordplay, and in this instance it translates well into English: "objective" here means not only figurative, but also utilitarian in the sense of having a practical and useful object or goal. Malevich's suprematism can be seen as, among other things, one of the most original statements of post–World War I antimilitarism. He argues that scientific thought destroys the

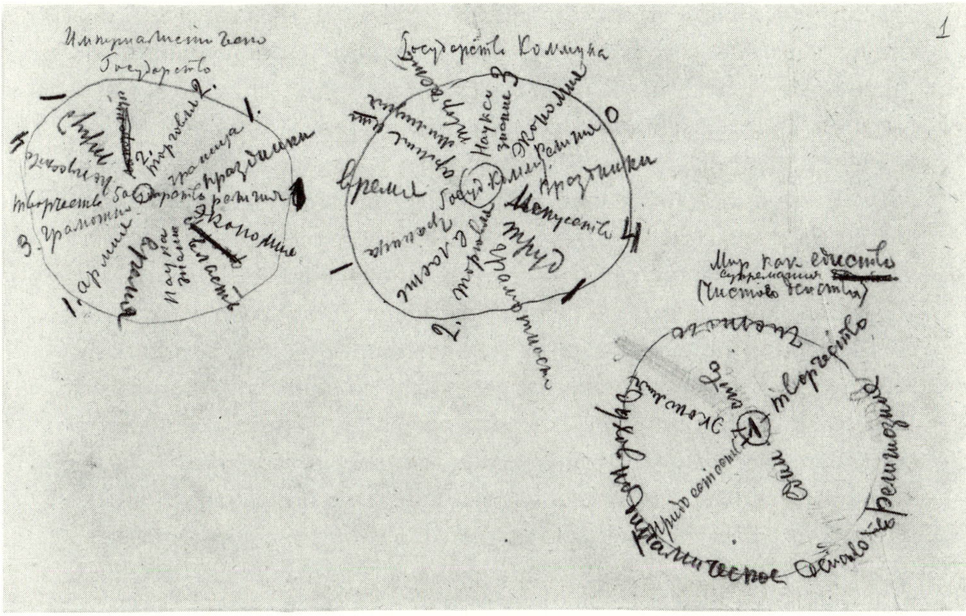

Figure 15.

Kazimir Malevich's "World as Unity: Suprematism."
Courtesy of the Stedelijk Museum, Amsterdam.

wholeness of nature. This destructiveness reaches its most violent form in wars. Consequently, according to Malevich, all human activities essentially participate in the ongoing war. Art is the only activity that is by its very nature excluded from this destructive procedure. Why? Precisely because it does not produce anything. So, it is not only art that is nonobjective but an entire system of thought that is based on it; and, conversely, everything that is outside of art is objective. In this way, art provides Malevich with the ground for a critique of the capitalist as well as the socialist order. In his Vitebsk texts, he laid out his theories in an extensive and detailed way. Then he tried to sum them up in concise diagrams. Therefore, we can say that Malevich's suprematism starts from the image (*Black Square*) and then goes to the text (*Suprematism as Pure Cognition, Suprematism as Non-Objectivity*), only to return to diagrams that often comprise both text and image, or to visual writing (figure 15).[14]

These three diagrams in the form of wheels have words as spokes that connect their rims with their centers. The first diagram on the left is entitled "Imperialist State:" here the wheel's spokes are work, trade, borders, power, time, army, literacy, holidays/religion/economy, art, and creation.

The central circle is labeled "order." The diagram at the center is "Commune State" and its spokes are similar to the previous one: economy, religion, holidays, work, art, literacy, trade, power, borders, time, army, police, creation, and science/knowledge; the center is labeled "communist order." Finally, the last diagram is "World as Unity: Suprematism," and it stands in clear opposition to the previous two diagrams. This outline of a suprematist stateless state has the fewest spikes: creativity, economy, and nature.[15] The spokes that are missing, in comparison to the other two, are just as important as those that are there: this diagram doesn't have work, trade, borders, army, time, police, power, science/knowledge, art, creation. The last two elements are an essential part of the circumferential text that is otherwise missing from the other two diagrams: "religious, pure, spiritual, dynamic. . . ."[16] The center of the last diagram is marked with the word "unity" that, so to speak, wraps around the central circle. Inside the circle is inscribed the number one. There is a strong resemblance between Kharms's drawing marked "Real" (figure 9) and Malevich's diagrams. Among Kharms's manuscripts there is a leaf with drawings that establish a direct link between the diagram "Real" and Malevich's *Black Square* (figure 16).

The connection is so obvious that one can be easily tempted to proclaim "Real" a variation of *Black Square*. However, we should acknowledge some significant differences between Malevich's and Kharms's diagrams. Due to their comparative purpose, the number of spikes in Malevich's diagrams varies. In Kharms's "Real" it is, of course, fixed at six.[17] Whereas at the circumference of Malevich's diagrams there is only one circle, in Kharms's diagram there are two, and the six-pointed star is inscribed between them. Both of these diagrammatic conceptualizations of reality have a circle, or a zero, at the center. For Kharms, this circle designates nil, or pure nothing, and as we have seen, his idea of nothingness can be related to Malevich's suprematist writings. It is interesting that, in this case, Malevich inscribes number one in the central circle. Again, this is perfectly in accordance with Kharms's ideas from the text "The Saber," where he talks about the number one as a symbol of unity rather than the first numeral. What Malevich's diagrams make us realize about Kharms's "Real" is that it refers to unity, totality, or wholeness. This unity is opposed to the fragmentariness that forms the basic condition of Kharmsian text. In that sense, "Real" complements "Amenhotep," which stands as the diagram of that very fragmentation (figure 12). Here we have a convulsive body caught in the moment of radical disintegration. This disintegration takes place on several levels:

Figure 16.

This page from Kharms's manuscripts contains shapes that resemble both Malevich's "Black Square" and Kharms's own "Real."

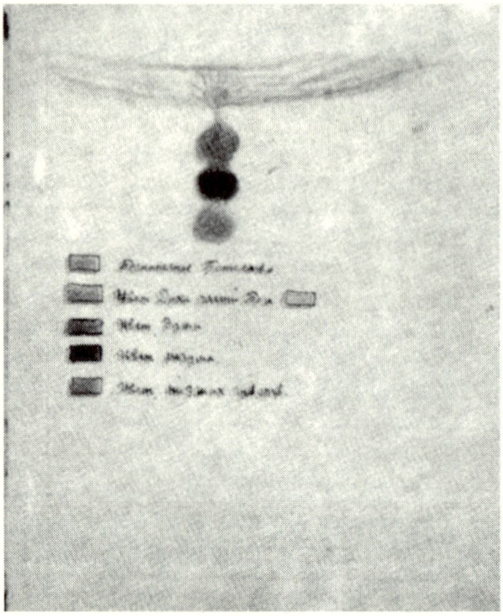

Figure 17.

The first image from the notebook "To the Philosopher: Letter No. 3"

first, it is a dead body; second, this body is decapitated; and third, on the level of representation, the image splits into the sign (letter) and the image (map). The circle, or nil, is at the core of both "Amenhotep" and "Real." However, whereas in the former, it is placed in the leg and therefore off-centered, in the latter, it is placed squarely at the center of the structure. Kharms's interest in perfection of the circular shape remains the focus of his diagrammatic drawings.

The case in point is Kharms's "To the Philosopher: Letter No. 3." This "letter" is actually a slim notebook that contains a series of diagrams tinted with ordinary colored pencils. The first page features a schema in the form of three differently colored spheres arranged vertically, with the topmost sphere touching a broad area of bright yellow (figure 17). Underneath the diagram is a key with Kharms's version of the symbolic meanings of the colors: bright yellow—infinite Divinity; orange—the color of spirit; yellow—God's particle; green—the color of soul; blue—the color of reason; red—the color of the lower feelings.

The key is followed by four sets of diagrams. The first set represents the two basic movements: "The Process of Ascension" (eleven numbered diagrams) and "The Process of Falling, or Annihilation" (eight diagrams). It is followed by three applications of these two processes: first, the schematic self-portrait "Case No. 1: I Approach This"[18] (a single diagram); then, "Case

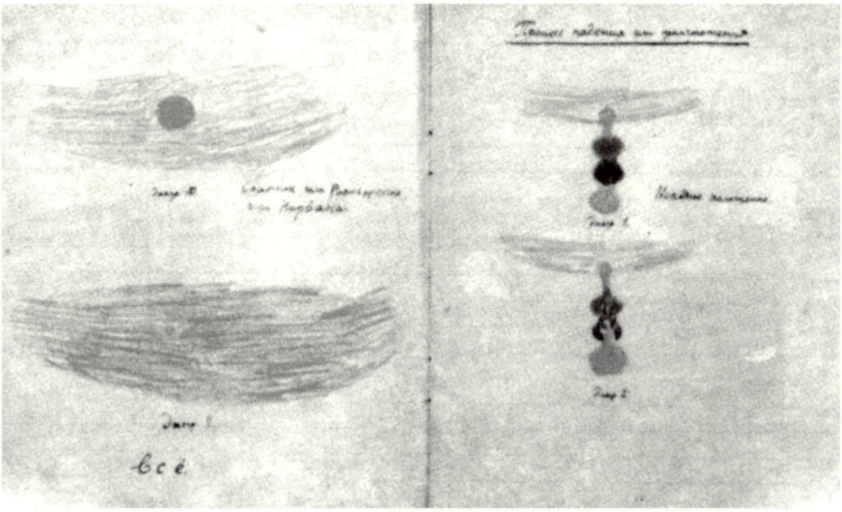

Figure 18.
Left: the final image in "The Process of Ascension" with the legend "Confluence, or Dissolution, or Nirvana"; right: the initial image in "The Process of Falling, or Annihilation"

No. 2: Lipavsky Approaches This" (seven diagrams); and finally, "Case No. 3: The Saint" (two diagrams).[19]

We are looking at the left side of the spread in Kharms's notebook (figure 18). It is the last stage in "The Process of Ascension," which begins with the bright yellow color that leaks from the yellow firmament and penetrates the core of the green, blue, and orange spheres. The source of this penetrating color is the yellow radiant form that is inscribed within the yellow "firmament." This "yellow on yellow" is hardly visible in the color image. However, the radiant shape becomes clearly visible with the change of colors into gray scale. The power of the radiant source is obvious: the yellow color that penetrates the spheres transforms them into a single spherical unit, which very gradually moves upward. The rising of the sphere is accompanied by a change of colors: close to the end of the process, we see a bright orange sphere half immersed in the yellow area with only thin traces of blue and green at its bottom. In the next step, the colors of reason and spirit completely disappear. All that remains is the bright orange sphere completely surrounded by the sea of yellow. This diagram is accompanied by the text that reads "Confluence, or Dissolution, or Nirvana." Like so many of Kharms's stories, plays, poems, and tracts, this picture story concludes with the brief, laconic announcement "that's all."

Comprehension of this series of diagrams is made possible, on the one hand, by the explanation of the symbolic meaning of colors provided in the key, and on the other hand, by the vertical movement. The key establishes a regime of signs akin to language, in which colors are semiotized. The diagrammatic images are organized into a series that simulates movement. "To the Philosopher: Letter No. 3" resembles a flipbook featuring diagrams instead of cartoons. As the series progresses, the textual explanation decreases. In the end, there are only pure diagrams, wordless and silent.

The entire series depicts two complex movements: rounding or spherization and flight versus disfiguration of the sphere and the fall. The process of ascension is at the same time the process of the sphere's gradual perfection. The vectors of elevation and perfection are accompanied by a third vector: purification of color. So, this triple movement results in the monochromatic full circle that dominates the penultimate tableau in the series The Process of Ascension (figure 18). The same image reappears at the very end of "Case No. 2: Lipavsky Approaches This," which is essentially an attempt to combine the two paradigmatic processes into a single series. It begins with a diagram dominated by the blue sphere that symbolizes reason; then, it absorbs other spheres, obliterates other colors, loses its round shape, and adopts an irregular, ellipsoid form, until it turns into a heavy lump of reason that plummets unstoppably. As it departs from the bright yellow firmament, it approaches the broad blue mass below. In the next image, Kharms replaces the blue surface with a black hole surrounded by brown and green areas. The big blue drop enters the hole. At the bottom part of the final image, only its tail protrudes from the black abyss; it is juxtaposed with the full orange sphere (Confluence . . .) positioned in the middle of the yellow zone at the top (figure 19).

This is the only diagram in which both the top and bottom sections are clearly visible. Furthermore, this is the single instance in which an already-established image (Confluence, or Dissolution) is used in juxtaposition with another image. The power of this juxtaposition comes not only from its vertical arrangement but also from the symbolism of falling and elevation attached to it. In the Lipavsky case, the progressive abstraction characteristic of the upward movement is contrasted by an equally progressive figuration that emerges from the downward movement. As the globe falls down, the colors lose their symbolic meaning and assume a purely mimetic function. The misshapen blue ball comes to resemble a big blob of water. In the final stages of the series, the diagram acquires aggressively cartoonish qualities.[20]

The first six images of the Lipavsky case, depicting the aerial segment of

Figure 19.

The final stages in the series "Case No. 2: Lipavsky Approaches This." From "To the Philosopher: Letter No. 3"

the process, are purely diagrammatic and ordered into a logical sequence. However, once the ground comes into the picture, the logical progression of images becomes disturbed. If the shape and color of the "infinite divinity" remain constant in the six aerial diagrams, the depiction of the ground changes in each of the four final images. The homogeneous blue mass that resembles a large body of water is replaced by a vivid image of a hole surrounded by fresh earth and green grass; this picture is gradually reduced to a barren landscape. While the direction of the blob's fall remains constant, its destination is altered four times. Each tableau can be seen both as an integral part of the series and as a separate image. In the last one, the drop almost completely disappears, and only its pointed tail sticks out from the darkness of the orifice. Furthermore, the color of the drop's remnant has changed from blue to green. Observed separately from the rest of the series, this image acquires a completely different meaning: it resembles a sprout germinating from the ground nourished by rich soil and abundant light. Instead of finality, the last diagram in the series has the sense of a general reversal: in form, from abstraction to mimesis; in color, from symbolism to naturalism; in direction, from falling to rising; and in meaning, from annihilation to life.

So, the lower part belongs to the ground, earth, objects, and representations, and the upper half to diagrams or abstract machines. The upper half features a bright orange circle on the solid yellow background. Here, the sphere, or circle, holds at least three interrelated meanings. The first is perfection, which Kharms sets forth in his tract "On the Circle" (1997b, 313). The second is emptiness, and it is best exemplified by Kharms and Poret's adaptation of the seventeenth-century print "Magdenburg Experiment with Half-Spheres"; here, Kharms and his friend Alisa made their interventions in the print of the famous experiment that proved the existence and strength of the vacuum.[21] And third, if Kharms referred to Goethe's *Theory of Colors* to devise his color code, then yellow stands for infinity.[22]

In hypothesizing that in the composition of his color code Kharms was relying on Goethe's *Theory of Colors,* we should keep in mind that in the first decades of the twentieth century, Russian experimental art was particularly engaged with the question of color. From Scriabin's color notation in music, to Matiushin's experiments with the psychology of colors, to Kandinsky's language of colors, the Russian avant-garde valued color for its immediacy. While the majority of these experiments was informed by the idea of the subliminal, or prelinguistic, meaning of colors, Goethe was not interested in the semiotic potential of color, but in its energetics. Particularly pertinent to the use of colors in "To the Philosopher: Letter No. 3" are the sections of Goethe's text in which he discusses the semantics of colors. In "General Observations on the Principles of Color," Goethe makes a general distinction between "plus" and "minus" colors, and places yellow and blue at the opposite sides of this polarity. Yellow is a plus color, and as such it is associated with "light," "brightness," "power," and "warmth"; blue as a minus color invokes "shadow," "darkness," "weakness," and "cold" (Goethe 1983, 268). This polar opposition of yellow and blue is clearly identifiable in Kharms's diagrams. Here, weightlessness is associated with the "plus," or yellow, and heaviness with the "minus," or blue. The further clarification of the symbolic relations of colors in the process of ascension comes from Goethe's comments on the "sensory-moral effect of color." Here, he asserts that yellow "is the color nearest light," and that it "arises from very slight moderation of light" (1983, 279). He also pays keen attention to the materials in which each color is most prominently manifested. Therefore, he observes that "gold in its unalloyed state brings us a new and exalted idea of this color, especially when enhanced by the metal gleam" (279).[23] Different hues of yellow do not necessarily signify its obfuscation and darkening. According to Goethe, the addition of red always results in an intensification of the basic color. In the hues of yellow based on admixture with red, he recognizes the gradual strengthening of its already existing characteristics: therefore, "as red-yellow, the color increases in energy and seems to grow in power and magnificence"; and finally, "the pleasant, cheerful feeling created by red-yellow is intensified in deep yellow-red to a feeling of unbearable power" (Goethe 1988, 280). If we consider Kharms's diagrams in relation to Goethe's theory of colors, we will see that the yellow-red circle inserted in a wider yellow area does not represent a difference in the meaning of colors but a difference in their intensity. It is light within light, like Malevich's *White Square.* It is an opposition without difference, and, as such, it is extremely unstable. In the final stage of The Process of Ascension, the orange circle disperses and disappears in the sea of yellow. If falling ends in rebirth and rejuvenation, then rising is total expenditure: nothing remains after the completion of the process.

According to Kharms's mechanics of ascension and descension, both processes start in the middle. In the case of the downward movement, the sphere swells; its weight increases until it loses balance and starts falling. Conversely, the rising sphere is cleansed of its contents and becomes increasingly light and pure. After purging all of its substance, it is translucent, clear, and indistinguishable from the pure, objectless light. These diagrams pertain to Kharms's larger project, which he refers to either as "clarity of order" or simply as "clarity." As we have seen, in the early 1930s Kharms wrote, somewhat mysteriously, about the necessity of passing "through the path of cleansing (*Perseveratio, Katarsis*)" and "starting literarily with the alphabet, i.e., with letters" (2002a, 444). Now, he writes to a philosopher a letter that is cleansed of words, letters, and discursive language as such. He composes a letterless letter: a mute letter consisting of diagrams and drawings. A host of polarities is recognizable in Kharms's inaudible letter: accumulation and purgation, falling and rising, abstraction and mimesis, infinity and finitude, preservation and expenditure, virtuality and actuality. Finally, we should also add bodies and effects.

The first diagram in the series marks a false beginning: to the philosopher, letter number three. The starting position can be seen as a state of affairs: not the body itself, but that which corresponds to its actions and passions. The events are neither the bodies nor the states of affairs, but effects. There is a necessity of "going back *up* to the event" and "coming *down* to the actual state of affairs"; the latter movement amounts to actualization of the event, and the former to its counter-effectuation (Deleuze and Guattari 1994, 159, italics added). Not only is the event diagrammatic, but also the diagram is an event. Kharms's letter is not a description of something that happened, or happens, or is going to happen. It is an abstract machine, an event, a new reality extracted from the state of affairs.

What, then, happens with the body? If it is not possible to go all the way down, to the body, how is it related to the state of affairs? So, the question is not, is it happening? or what is happening? but what is the state of affairs?

The answer is surprising: there is no state of affairs. The trick is to go directly back *up* from bodies to events, and to come *down* to the bodies. At least, that is the impression that Kharms creates in his playlet "Makarov and Petersen." This story shares two important properties with his diagrammatic letter: its focus is on the spherization of the body and it is subtitled "No. 3."[24] The piece opens in medias res, as is often the case with Kharms's short stories and plays:

> Makarov: Here, in this book, it is written of our desires and about the fulfillment of our desires. Read this book and you will understand how vain our desires are. You will likewise understand how easy it is to fulfill the desires of another, and how difficult it is to fulfill a desire of your own. (Kharms 2007, 62)

Petersen instantly vanishes when Makarov pronounces the book's title—Malgil. For a while, his voice lingers behind:

> Petersen's Voice: What happened? Makarov! Where am I?
> Makarov: Where are you? I can't see you!
> Petersen's Voice: And where are you? I can't see you either! What's with these spheres?
> Makarov: What do I do? Petersen, can you hear me?
> Petersen's Voice: I can hear you! But what happened? And what are these spheres?
> Makarov: Can you move?
> Petersen's Voice: Makarov! Do you see the spheres?
> Makarov: What spheres?
> Petersen's Voice: Let go! . . . Let me go! . . . Makarov! . . .
> *Silence. Makarov stands in awe, then he grabs the book and opens it.*
> Makarov: (*reading*) ". . . Gradually man loses his shape and turns into a sphere. And, having become a sphere, he loses all his desires."
> (*Curtain*) (63, ellipses in the original).

So here is another vanishing act: first it was a factor in a mathematical formula, then a group of girls in a poetic drama. Now it is one Petersen, who seems to have accidentally come across a book that has supernatural powers. Still, this vanishing is more of an act than the previous two: the mysterious disappearance is framed by yet another mechanism of veiling and unveiling: the plain theater curtain.

Teachings from the book of Malgil are reminiscent of Kharms's writings about immortality from the late 1930s. In "On Approaching Immortality," the penultimate segment of his tract written "more or less according to Emersen," Kharms proposes that "every person has a striving for pleasure, which always takes the form of either the satisfaction of sexual desire, or gastronomical satiation, or acquisition"; however, "only that which does not lie on the path toward pleasure will lead us to immortality" (2007, 250). In his diary, there is an entry on the same subject that, like the "Emersen" tract and many of his other statements and narratives, is written in the form of short, numbered theses. Here, Kharms outlines a diagram of mortality and immortality: "there is a straight line to which belongs everything that is earthly. And only those things that are not on that line can testify about immortality" (2002b, 199).

In both of these texts Kharms talks about the renunciation of desires as a slow and painstaking process, but in "Makarov and Petersen" the transformation of the body into the perfect sphere happens abruptly. Here, the word "Malgil" appears to be the key. In his comments on Kharms's story, Yampolsky suggests that the phoneme *mal* is possibly related to "word" in modern Hebrew, while in *gil* he recognizes the ancient Hebrew *galgal,* "circle," or "sphere." He writes:

> Spherical book-wheel "MALGIL" . . . is, for one, like an endless book, with constantly increasing magical and literary "potential." But it is also a book that contains an endlessly increasing quantity of words. Essentially, this whirling endlessness simultaneously turns inwards, into a "null," and becomes absorbed into the infinitely small. (Iampol'skii 1997, 295)

In short, what the word "Malgil" eventuates is the kind of dematerialization that we have already encountered in Lipavsky's chess table. Petersen's body simply disappears while his voice stays behind, disembodied and hollow. The voice reports on what the invisible body sees. In his quotation from the book Malgil, Makarov asserts that the body turns into a sphere;

accordingly, Petersen not only sees the spheres but also becomes one. A certain limit is discernable: on the one hand, the voice that speaks and the gaze that sees; on the other, the rest of the body, which has become invisible. Then, the voice shuts up, and we can assume that the process of the body's reduction continues in the invisible and inaudible sphere, reducing it to the last ball, the eyeball. This is an eye that never blinks, that is permanently fixed open—a perfect perceptor of light.

In the story "Holiday," Kharms's game of leaping directly from bodies to events, sidestepping the states of affairs, becomes even more assertive than in "Makarov and Petersen." The story opens with two "draftsmen," who sit on the roof, eat buckwheat kasha, and amuse themselves by tying a coin into a handkerchief, then hurling it down and watching as it spirals to the sidewalk. Their attention is drawn away from this game by the janitor Ibrahim, who suddenly shows up and starts hammering a stick with a "pale flag" on it to the chimney. He explains that he is raising the flag to honor a holiday proclaimed in the city because "our favorite poet composed a new poem." Upon hearing this, the two draftsmen, "shamed by their ignorance, dissolved into the air" (Kharms 2007, 202).

Here, as in *Gvidon,* Kharms associates poetry with banner-raising. The flagpole extends high into the air. It marks the final and highest point, where the heavy structure of the building cedes to the weightless air. The poet is a flag holder (*guidone*) that "holds banners over reason" (1997a, 466). Interestingly, the protagonists of "Holiday" are not poets, but draftsmen. What are they drawing on the roof? Chimneys? Clouds above them? Or perhaps the streets below? The very streets where they throw the coin tied in a handkerchief? They could be easily drawing a map of the city. They could be cartographers, makers of maps and diagrams. So, on the one hand, they are the characters who represent a concept: they experiment with the force of gravity and draw graphs of forces and resistances. They disappear inexplicably the moment a flag goes up on the chimney, "above reason." On the other hand, there is the person who raises the flag. He is not a poet but an ordinary caretaker. For Kharms, the *dvornik,* a caretaker or janitor in Soviet-era apartment buildings, is the lowest official in the vast hierarchy of law enforcement.[25] Kobrinsky points out that this figure first appears in Kharms's poem "The Constancy of Dirt and Joy":

> And the janitor with black moustaches
> stands all night long by the rusty gate
> and with his dirty hands he scratches

under his dirty hat his itching pate.
(Kharms 2007, 183)

The caretaker, who is associated with filth, keeps merriment at bay without even being aware of it. In *Events* there is a story about a watchman who, while engrossed in his favorite pastime of torturing flies, is surprised when a young man in yellow gloves asks him for the passageway to heaven. After a short argument, the young man "lifted his yellow-gloved hand, waved it over his head and vanished," leaving just the smell of burnt feathers behind him (2007, 592). Watchmen and caretakers are the *grafins*[26] and keepers of the gate between the mundane and the miraculous. They are always anonymous, except in "Holiday." The figure of the caretaker Ibrahim provides the connection not only with the invisibility and eternity of the conceptual realm, but also with the tedium of the everyday. As it turns out, the name of the caretaker in Kharms's apartment building on Mayakovsky Street No. 11 was Ibrahim Kirzhanovich Kildeev. His signature appears on the report of Kharms's arrest on August 23, 1941.[27]

The New Anatomy

"Holiday" points back to Kharms's diary entry from May 22, 1929, which begins with a simple note about the experience of sitting on the roof of the publishing house Gosizdat[28] and quickly evolves into an elaborate program for "Gosizdat Roof Guards" (2002b, 168). From the same period comes Kharms's photograph taken on the roof of Gosizdat, in which he appears to be flying over Nevsky Prospekt.[29] According to the program, the roof watchman "can be any man of OBERIU creed," and his duties include "riding on the roof," "flirting with ladies," and "inserting words into conversations of the passers-by" (169). The aerial caretaker is the complete inversion of the *dvornik*. It could also be taken as one of many poses that Kharms devised over time. He writes:

> Create a pose for yourself, and have the strength to keep it up. Once I had the pose of an Indian, then of Sherlock Holmes, then a yogi, and now of an irritable neurasthenic. I don't want to keep the latest pose. It is necessary to come up with a new one. (2002b, 128)

This list is by no means exhaustive. It does not mention, for instance, the "pose" that Kharms seems to have assumed with great gusto, that of his own imaginary brother Ivan Ivanovich, "a former privatdozent at the University of St. Petersburg." He pops up unexpectedly in "Conversations" to settle a dispute about the "rules of the game of life" that erupts between Oleinikov and Zabolotsky. Lipavsky's remark, "then D. K. presented his made-up brother Ivan Ivanovich" is followed by Kharms's short speech:

> It happens to everyone: to lose control excessively, start boasting, and raise their voice more than necessary. When you catch yourself doing that, immediately lower your tone, interrupt the conversation. For many people, the sign of such unwarranted excitation is that their nose turns red when they speak. (Lipavskii 2005, 418)

It is not too difficult to attach the tone and content of the speech to Ivan Ivanovich's physiognomy as it appears in the only preserved photograph of Kharms in the pose of his fictional sibling: mouth corners pulled down while chin and nose are thrust upward in an expression of perennial dis-

Figure 20.

Kharms in the "pose" of his fictional brother Ivan Ivanovich

gust, the right eye wide open holding a monocle, and the left eye squinting under a slightly tilted bowler hat (figure 20).

There is something frozen and static in Ivan Ivanovich. Kharms very accurately indicates the nature of these enactments by using the word "pose" instead of "personage" or "character": it denotes an arrested movement, a process stalled in place. These enactments do not take place "in life," but instead bring life to a point of stasis. In Kharms's circle, neurasthenia was considered an obstruction of the life processes, and it is not surprising that he includes it in his inventory of poses. In "Conversations," Lipavsky describes neurasthenia as a "constant repressed anxiety, a cramp of the interior, a frozen readiness for defense." The cure for this kind of psychic convulsion is, of course, "any kind of rhythm": work is offered as an example of a cure for neurasthenia because it takes "a man from a stagnant river branch to the main current, reviving the exchange between the forces of man and nature" (Lipavskii 2005, 386). From this effort to define an illness and find its cure emerges an extremely curious definition of the idea of man: "Man is the relationship between the body and the world, as if he was propped up by two waves. The man is constituted by their reciprocal rocking" (387). The body relates to the world through actions and gestures.

In *Factory of Gestures,* Oksana Bulgakova analyzes the evolution of gestures in Soviet and Russian culture from the turn of the twentieth century until its midpoint (1898–1951), noting that "body techniques" changed significantly with each historical turn. Of course, the sea change came with the October Revolution, which did away with the traditional ritualized and ceremonial gestures that marked Russian bourgeois culture. But the transformation of gestures did not stop there. In the visual culture of the 1920s, the opposition between the bourgeoisie and proletarian revolutionaries was represented as the clash between, on the one hand, a well-organized and disciplined state machinery, and on the other, the free, unconventional, undisciplined, and, indeed, neurasthenic individual. Starting with the 1930s, the revolutionary shed his neurasthenic gestures and adopted the disciplined collective gestures exemplified by the march: "Heroes-soldiers and heroes-proletarians no longer move, walk, and stand as neurasthenic, run-down decadents, but instead as erect officers" (Bulgakova 2005, 208). In the 1930s, Kharms's poses of a neurasthenic and a has-been appeared to be dangerously out of sync with the onward march privileged by Stalinist cultural politics. However, the Kharmsian gesture is not reducible to his poses.

Kharms and his friends considered bodily movement just one facet of the much more complex notion of gesture. By now, we should be accustomed to the reverse procedure of "Conversations": the body, claims Lipavsky, is a "bodily shaped act" and not the other way around (2005, 396). Following the line of reasoning we have already encountered in Kharms's "Emersen" treatise, he proposes that the space is not only perceived but also shaped, through vision and muscular exertion, which leads him to assert that there is no difference in principle between bodily act, or gesture, and thought (406). We find this gesture of thought, thinking gesture, in Kharms's verses:

> Other thought in the head
> moved their legs
> moved their arms
> opened their book
> opened their thoughts (1997b, 225)

This is probably what Russian philosopher Valery Podoroga had in mind when, asked about the "OBERIU lifestyle" and the Oberiuty's "theatricalization of life," he diverted his answer to the notion of gesture. Attempting to define what he calls "the OBERIU gesture," Podoroga resorted to Rilke's meditation on gesture in the "Second Duino Elegy":

> Weren't you astonished
> by the discretion
> of human gesture
> on Attic grave steles?
> (Rilke 1978, 33)

Podoroga proposes that the OBERIU gesture is devoid of this discretion, and describes it as "*indiscreet,* transgressive" and as having no "inner limit":

> Being directed towards objects, bodies, and events of the world, it never returns to the one who produced it, so it is a nonreturning gesture. After its intrusion into the world, the world changes its appearance, it becomes a different world. Therefore, the OBERIU gesture is always destructive (though I can't say that it is violent). (Podoroga 1993, 149, emphasis in the original)[30]

In order to better understand the gesture as Kharms's fundamental expressive tool, I want to pursue Podoroga's reference to Rilke, and continue the reading of the second elegy:

Didn't love and parting
sit so lightly
on shoulders
that they seemed
to be made of a substance
different from ours?
Do you recall
how the hands rest
without any pressure
though there is great
strength in torsos?
Those figures spoke
a language of self-mastery:
we've come to this point
this is us
touching this way
the gods
may push us around
but that is something
for them to decide.
(Rilke 1978, 33)

The discrete gesture is feather-light in appearance. It is a gesture restrained, a graceful movement, in which the largest portion of power remains in reserve. It is a movement in repose that, as Rilke asserts, speaks of self-mastery and confidence. This is the confidence not only in one's self but, even more, in the world. Here, the true exchange between the body and the world takes place through a graceful gesticulation. This gesticulation is not one-sided: the body gestures to the world, and the world responds with gesture. The discrete gesture can be directed only toward a responsive world. The great power stored in the torso is used to limit and restrain the hand's motion to the point where it hardly moves: a Herculean power is invested in the lightness with which the hand rests. Then, Rilke makes his peaceful actors ask: If we can do that much, how much can the gods do? If our force is turned inward and kept within the carefully maintained limits, is the world going to respond with similar restraint?

Kharms's gesture is always visible, excessive, and shocking, and it inevitably leads to the question: isn't that because the world stopped gesticulating in return? And, indeed, what is the Kharmsian gesture? Does it affect his writing? In other words, what is the relation between language and gesture in Kharms's work?

In Kharms, often the entire narratives boil down to gesticulation:

> The little old man scratched himself with both hands. The places that he couldn't reach with both hands, the old man scratched with one, but quick-quick. And the whole time he quickly blinked with his eyes. (Kharms 2007, 184)

The gesticulating body constitutes a world closed upon itself. All of the old man's gestures are directed toward his own body. Scratching is, of course, a masturbatory gesture: it releases tension and provides pleasure. In this case, the only sign of pleasure is another gesture, the rapid blinking of the eyes. Yet, neither their frenzied activity nor their overt autoeroticism makes these gestures indiscrete and transgressive: they become so through their separation from the body. Kharms purifies the gesture through a simple, two-step process: first, the body is isolated from its surroundings, as if it were set against a blank backdrop; second, the gesture becomes separated from the body. Kharms's personages comply with Lipavsky's dictum: the bodies are produced by their gestures, not the other way around.

The gesture is left in isolation, without response, and therefore gesticulates only to itself. Max Kommerell observed that, in relation to lyric poetry, the gesture "is not exhausted in communication. However compelling it may be for an Other, gesture always exists only for him; indeed, only insofar as it also exists for itself can it be compelling for the Other" (Kommerell in Agamben 1999, 78). Kharms's gesture is solitary. It does not need a pretext or a motivation, nor does it provoke a response: it is a pure tic, a hand that involuntarily flies into the air, a leg that kicks, or eyes that blink swiftly. A hiccup. Placing such gestures next to one another would only emphasize their noncommunicability.

If an onward march symbolizes the immortality of the community and of the state, Kharms's noncommunicable gesture always exists in relation to death. Regarding this, there are two significant developments in his writing. The first one is the new theme of sudden death, which first appears in his poetry and prose of the early 1930s.[31] By mid-decade, these sudden deaths become the staple of his prose and poetry, and are comparable to the abrupt endings of his narratives.

> A man with a stupid face ate a steak, hiccupped, and died. Waiters took him to the hallway leading to the kitchen, sat him against the wall, and covered him with a greasy tablecloth. (Kharms 1997b, 71)

Similarly, in the poem "A Horrible Death," a man dies after stuffing himself with cutlets:

> Then, moving aside the ominous food, he started to tremble and cry;
> In his pocket the golden watch stopped ticking;
> His hair turned white instantly, and his gaze brightened;
> His ears fell off, like yellow leaves that fall from poplars in the fall;
> And he suddenly died. (1997a, 271)

The second theme is the disintegration and fragmentation of the body. Already in a unfinished and untitled poetic drama from 1930 we find a character described as "Head on Two Legs" (1997a, 168). In texts such as "The Story of Sdygr Appr," the fragmentation of the body (one Petr Pavlovich tears off the arm of one Andrei Semionovich) affects the language, which becomes jumbled and unpronounceable:

> Petr Pavlovich:
> Zdygr appr oostr oostr
> I have in hand another's arm
> Zdygr appr oostr oostr
> (Ostashevsky 2006, 65)

Finally, in the story "Death of a Little Old Man," we find a complete breakdown of the body:

> A little sphere sprang out of a little old man's nose and fell to the ground. The little old man bent over to lift up the little sphere and that's when a little stick sprung from his eye and also fell to the ground. The little old man was frightened and, not knowing what to do, moved his lips. At that moment, out of the little old man's mouth sprang a little square. The little old man grabbed his mouth, but then a little mouse sprang out of the little man's sleeve. The little old man became sick with fear and, so as not to fall, he squatted down. But then something snapped inside the little old man and, like a soft plush coat, he toppled to the ground.

> That's when a longish little reed sprang from the torn hole, and on its very end sat a thin little bird. (Kharms 2007, 220)

This body is a repository of useless things. It merely covers a stockpile of bric-a-brac. This spineless body remains in the upright position simply because it is stuffed with small objects and tiny animals. Objects not only fill out the Kharmsian body, but also expand it. In "A Horrible Death," a man eats until the watch in his pocket stops ticking; the protagonist of "How One Man Fell to Pieces" swells up until he spills into myriad balls. The objects lost in dying are mundane things, trinkets seemingly inserted into the body at some point. However, even though they are not organic, these objects are vital. For Kharms, death does not represent "parting with one's soul" but parting with one's sticks, clocks, spheres, and cubes; or, quite possibly, it represents the separation of these objects from the body, which then slithers down, spongy and formless.[32]

The Kharmsian gesture is unlike any other conceptualization of gesture that emerged in the early twentieth century. We can't even begin to compare it with that of his more famous countrymen, Vsevolod Meyerhold and Sergei Eisenstein: gestures produced by both biomechanics and expressive movement are based, among other things, on Taylorist ideas of efficiency and movement analysis that are utterly foreign to Kharms.[33] Similarly, Bertolt Brecht makes his notion of "gest" or *gestus* inseparable from the social and didactic function of his theater: he writes that the actor's "physical attitude, tone of voice and facial expression are all determined by a social gest" (Brecht 1957, 198).[34] If Brecht's *gestus* is inseparable from its social and narrative function,[35] then, on the other end of the spectrum, Antonin Artaud's notion of gesture is rooted in an internal expressivity of the body. His writings are peppered with statements about "extreme gestures," mathematics of gesture, or theater's language "between gesture and thought" (Artaud 1958, 27, 55, 89). The Kharmsian gesture lacks both Brecht's sociality and Artaud's corporeality. His gesture comes from a body that is completely different from those bodies conceived by Meyerhold and Eisenstein, Brecht and Artaud: it is an empty drum that can be filled with geometric objects, small animals, or sounds; it is porous: a fly enters through the forehead and exits out the back of the head; it crumbles, disperses, vanishes; and in short, it is impermanent and always already fragmented. At the same time, it has the stubborn persistence of inanimate matter: the old lady keeps moving after she dies, the dead cashier girl passes as a living person, Amenhotep babbles to prove that he is alive. The status of a gesticulating body is always ambiguous: it is at the same time a living person and a moving object. On the one hand, everything that comes in contact with this body may turn into a gesture: the small hammer pulled out of the throat is a gestic object. On the other hand, the body is *transparent,* insufficiently distinguished from its surroundings, and always in danger of dispersing, crumbling, or simply disappearing.

The gestural body is the body-gesture. Its physiognomy consists of gestures: the man with the stupid face, the nose that turns red during an argument, the beardless Pushkin. This body, like Kharmsian gesture itself, does not have an interiority. This is a strange body, without a center from which it could extend outward. Here, the natural processes that progress from the beginning, through the middle, and toward the end are replaced by abrupt appearances, rapid swellings, and sudden dispersals. Instead of growing organically from inside out in all directions, these bodies grow by forming linkages with objects. As we have seen, the clothes become the new epidermis. The gestural body even sprouts new, inorganic organs, thus forming a body-object, or a *bio-object.*[36]

> The New Anatomy
>
> On a small girl's nose grew two blue ribbons. An extremely rare case, because one ribbon bore the inscription "Mars," and the other "Jupiter." (1997b, 88)[37]

This new anatomy is an anatomy of the body-object. For Kharms, gesture is not an external, visible expression of an internal and invisible content. On the contrary, the body gesticulates frantically precisely because it is liberated from its internal weight. Rilke also writes about parts of the body: about the hand and the torso. However, in Rilke, these bodily parts are part of the larger whole: they are organs, and their power and grace come from the organism they evoke. Kharms's bodily parts are not organs but fragments. There is nothing to hold them together, and in their movement there is no suggestion of a larger whole. Benjamin writes that Kafka, like El Greco, "tears open the sky behind every gesture" so that "the gesture remains the decisive thing, the center of the event" (Benjamin 1999, 802). This gesture, utterly foreign to the Brechtian *gestus,* borders on the inhuman: it is "animal gesture" that "combines the utmost mysteriousness with the utmost simplicity" (802). Kharmsian gesture is that which bridges the gap between the body and the event. It is positioned between them: no longer body and not yet the event.

Drawing on Benjamin's and, especially, Kommerell's "gestic" criticism, Agamben establishes two notions of mystery in relation to gesture. The first one emerges from his idea that, by the outset of the twentieth century, a "general catastrophe in the sphere of gesture" took place among the European middle classes. This interesting thesis can be boiled down to the assertion that in the course of the nineteenth century, slowly and almost imperceptibly, the European bourgeoisie lost its gestures through a general standardization of behavior rigorously enforced by all of its social institutions.[38] He finds evidence of this loss in fields as varied as philosophy, dance, literature, and cinema. Rilke's displacement of gesture into a distant past easily fits into this series of testimonies of this silent disaster. So, the mystery emerges from the fact that life suddenly became indecipherable (Agamben 2000, 53). Agamben's second notion of mystery in relation to gesture comes from Wittgenstein's famous identification of that which is outside of language and logic as mystical: "What *can* be shown *cannot* be said," reads proposition 4.1212 of *Tractatus Logico-Philosophicus.* It is set up by the following line of conclusions in 4.121:

> That which mirrors itself in language, language cannot represent. That which expresses *itself* in language, *we* cannot express by language. The propositions *show* the logical form of reality. They exhibit it. (Wittgenstein 1992, 79, italics in the original)

Agamben finds these pronouncements about the limits of language identical with the definition of the comedic gag, because they assert that the very being of gesture is in its pure mediality. The pure gesture is a means without origin and without transcendence:

> The gesture is, in this sense, communication of a communicability. It has precisely nothing to say because what it shows is the being-in-language of human beings as pure mediality. (Agamben 2000, 59)

In Kharms, this immanence of gesture transforms writing into choreographic and mathematical notation. One of his most curious performance projects is the choreography *The Ballet of the Inseparable Trio.* This ballet has no characters and no story to speak of, and it consists entirely of abstract and silent movements. Kharms not only wrote about language machines and clarity of order (*perseveratio, catharsis*), but also filled pages of his notebooks with alphabets and numerical tablets. His choreography bor-

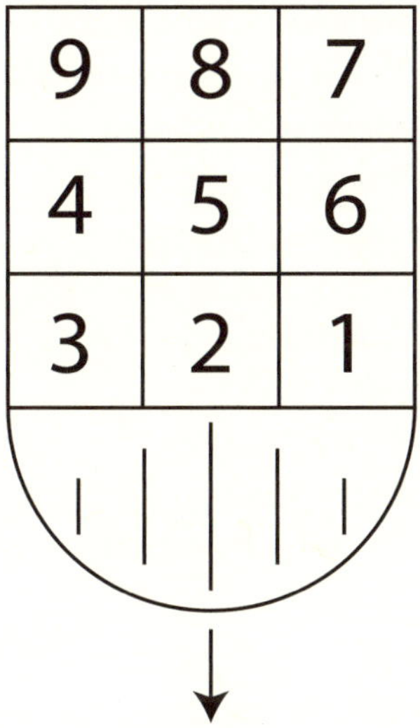

Figure 21.
Kharms's schema for his dance choreography *The Ballet of the Inseparable Trio*

ders on these elementary forms of writing.[39] It appears almost like a dance of numbers, a strange series of mathematical operations performed on an abacus consisting of nine cells arranged in three rows (figure 21).

First, the troika moves from 8 to 3 to 1, and then back to 8, thus outlining a triangle. The second section involves a series of frantic movements that outline a right angle and its axis: "straight 5-8-5-5-8," straight again on 8-9-8, then a diagonal move on 4, and then a shift to 8. During the intermezzo, the dancers are instructed to "run in place," "dance with heads," "get on all fours," stand up, and change their position into a straight line, which Kharms notates as X X X (2001a, 251).[40] The ballet ends in a flurry of complex runs that outline a forty-five-degree angle open toward the audience and a number nine.[41]

This is choreography of large and small gestures: it asks dancers to make difficult movements and readers to take a pencil and outline the movements on the grid (figure 21). Also, it presents what Kharms saw as the two poles of sociality. On the one hand is the brawl, perhaps best exemplified in entry No. 12 from "The Blue Notebook":

A certain Panteley hit Ivan with his heel.
A certain Ivan hit Natalya with a wheel.
A certain Natalya hit Semyon with a muzzle.

A certain Semyon hit Seliphan with a washbasin.
A certain Seliphan hit Nikita with an overshirt.
A certain Nikita hit Roman with a board.
A certain Roman hit Tatiana with a shovel.
A certain Tatiana hit Elena with a pitcher.
And a fight broke out.
Elena beat Tatiana with a fence.
Tatiana beat Roman with a mattress.
Roman beat Nikita with a suitcase.
Nikita beat Seliphan with a serving tray.
Seliphan beat Semyon with his bare hands.
Semyon spit into Natalya's ears.
Natalia bit Ivan's fingers.
Ivan kicked Panteley with his heel.
Ack, we thought, good people fighting each other.
(2007, 113)

This kind of gratuitous violence is not uncommon for avant-garde authors.[42] We need only think of Eisenstein's staging of the boxing match in his theater production of *The Mexican* or of the particular form of sadism that he employs in his theoretical writings. He repeatedly defines "attraction," that central unit of his montage theory and practice, in terms of aggressive moments, "emotional shocks in the spectator," or "blows to the consciousness and emotions of the audience" (Eisenstein 1988, 34, 39). The crucial difference is that whereas Eisenstein is using violence as the expressive means of the medium, Kharms is using violence within the medium. The blow is aimed at another blow, not at the audience's psyche. We will understand better this communication within the medium if we turn to the second form of sociality in Kharms: choral singing.

Kharmonius

There are numerous evidences of Kharms's fascination with the multiplication of voices. We have looked at his composite dramatic character in *Temptation* and mentioned his ambition to express in verses a large number of voices. There are a number of statements in which he explicitly speaks about his attraction to choral singing. For example, he writes in his notebook entry: "Now I understand very well: I don't like the violin.

Of solo instruments, I find closest to me piano and pipe organ. Piano is closer. But closer than anything else is—choir" (2002b, 80). Kharms's fascination with group singing is inseparable from his interest in sound, and voice in particular.

Roland Barthes talks about two kinds of "texts" in vocal music. The first one is the "pheno-song," to which belongs everything that is in the service of communication, from the rules of the genre to the specificities of the composer and the style of interpretation. The second is the "geno-song," which has nothing to do with communication and representation, and Barthes describes it as "that apex (or that depth) of production where the melody really works at the language" and as the "*diction* of the language" (Barthes 1977, 183). In performance, the former belongs to breath, associated simultaneously with the soul and with the breathing technique that produces an immaculate and powerful air stream; the latter is associated with the throat and oral cavity and their irregular sounds: the timbre of the larynx, the low resonance of nasal tones, the rolling of the tongue. The latter is what Barthes calls "the grain of voice," "the materiality of the body speaking its mother tongue" (182). Kharms often introduces this grain of voice into his writing though onomatopoeia. In his short prose piece "Power," all of the lines of the character Mishin consist of onomatopoeias: first lexical, "ho, ho," and then not: "che, che," "sho, sho, ho, ho," "siu, siu," "ml'iam, ml'iam," and finally "umn'iaf" (1997b, 151). In other instances both his lexical and nonlexical onomatopoeias approach musical notation. For instance, in "The Collision of an Oak with a Wiseman," onomatopoeia turns into notes, which then turn into language. The character named Fanfare (*Tush*) exclaims:

do
mi
sol
do be la
dobela[43]
(1997, 99)

In *Elizabeth Bam,* Kharms writes the lines of dialogue for siren and drum, "via-a bum, bum / via-a-a bum," and for the violin "pa pa pi pa / pa pa pi pa" (1999, 289). Consider the following lines written for his favorite instrument, grand piano:

Voice offstage: Nothing!
Mom: Nothing!
Pipe offstage: I—I
Ivan Ivanovich: Nothing!
Grand Piano: I—I
(1999, 282)

Kharms uses an identical system of signs in the instrumental notation of his early plays (*Elizabeth Bam, Comedy of the City of St. Petersburg*) and in his analysis of meter in poetry. In a tract that, like his many other texts, survived only in fragments, Kharms explains the two basic elements of his accent notation. First is the metric foot that opens and ends with an unstressed syllable. The notation of this meter is:

–I –I –I –I –

Kharms names it "free (*liber*)," and remarks that it is most commonly used in iambic meter (2001a, 42). While the first metric foot is based on the pair "–I," the order of accented and unaccented syllables in the second one is reversed: "I–." Kharms describes it as a "failing" (*desum*)[44] syllable and cites the trochee as the most common example of such a metric foot (43). Kharms's most elaborate experiments with rhythmic versification are collected in a notebook titled "Strophics" (*Strofika*). Instead of the conventional marking of accents above text, Kharms divides the text and notation into two parallel columns. Soon, he strips his strophes of discursive language and reduces them to pure rhythm. In the end, the poem resembles a musical composition of sounds of various lengths. Kharms named these structures "patterns."

Pattern No. 9.
- I - I - I - I a
- I - I - I - I a
- I - I - I - I - b
- I - I - I - I - b
- I - I - I - I c
- I - I - I - I c
- I [- -] I - I - I d
- I - I - I - I d
(2001a, 121)

"Strophics" is a poetry solfeggio. It is a notation that pertains not only to the rhythm of breathing but also to other bodily movements. "Pattern No. 9" directs a hand to make a gliding horizontal move, then a vertical strike, up and down, left and right. In the penultimate line, the rhythm breaks down. This is not a *desum,* a failing or descending rhythm, but the absence of rhythm altogether. For an instant, the yelping of the *staccato* falters. This is not an insignificant moment, because it appears that an entirely new structure emerges from this rubato. "Pattern No. 9" is followed by "Modus No. 10" (figure 22). Here, the square used to single out the instance of two successive unstressed accents seems to have evolved into the basic unit of an elaborate cell structure. More intriguing than this evolution of a single rectangle into a lattice is that "Strophics" concludes with this schema, which Kharms, quite unexpectedly, describes as "prose" (2001a, 122).

This schema is not only an outline of a prose structure. Even more specifically, Kharms describes it as *postroenie,* a word that has strong industrial ("construction") and military ("formation") inflections. This construction or formation orders voices: the opening segment is marked as *zapev* (commencement of a song) and not as *uvertiura* (overture), which is used in more complex musical compositions. He seems to suggest that there is a certain melodic, songlike aspect to this "prose formation." Kharms's experimentation with musical structure in prose writing is not limited to "Modus No. 10." The idea of "poetic prose" that is "music without rhythm and without rhyme" marked Baudelaire's early attempts at prose poetry and was later embraced by the symbolists.[45] In devising his symphonic texts, "The Start of a Very Nice Summer's Day: A Symphony" and "Synphony No. 2," Kharms most probably relied on the example set by the Russian symbolist poet Andrei Bely. As Kobrinsky shows, while Bely tried to transpose symphonic principles to prose, Kharms did not hesitate to devise new genres (2000, 38). One of the most prominent examples of transformation and adaptation of musical principles to prose is "Synphony No. 2," which, according to Kobrinsky, Kharms intentionally misspells in order to highlight the principle of simultaneity (*syn*) over the linear progression of the narrative (43).[46] Still, Kharms is not ready to sacrifice the intelligibility of the text to its delinearization. Even though the title suggests simultaneity, the narrative of "Synphony No. 2" consists of three successive episodes.[47]

Also, it seems that Kharms was interested in musical forms not only because of their formal structure. For one, he was interested in musical

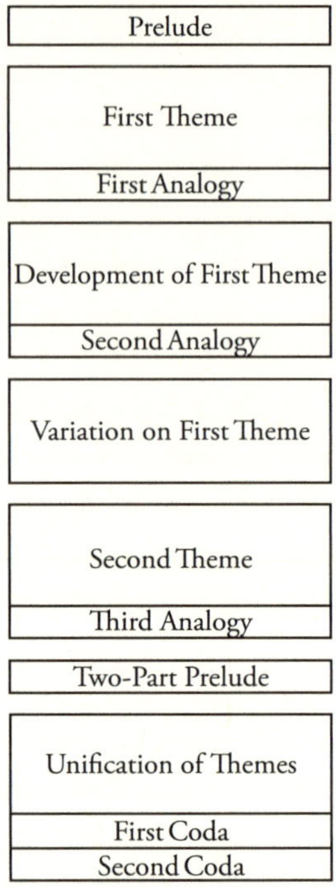

Figure 22.

"Modus No. 10." Kharms describes this schema as "prose formation."

performance. He highly valued Mozart's creativity, but was also fond of musical curiosities such as Haydn's Symphony No. 45, in which in the course of the final adagio, musicians, one by one, pack their instruments and leave as they finish their parts until the orchestra is completely deserted (Lipavskii 2005, 371). Second, he was himself an amateur musician; he played piano, harmonium, and flute. Finally, Kharms and his friends were attracted by the immediacy and movement of music. In "Conversations," Lipavsky asserts that what other art forms accomplish through representations, music does through direct presentation. Vvedensky then responds that people often sing when they row a boat or sit on a riverbank, "as if the music were the voice of nature itself."

> L.L. Yet, it can't be found in nature . . . Music seems to cleanse the man from irregularities, from accumulated poisons. She is like water to the dying plant. She resembles liquid the most, its flowing. (385, ellipses in the original)

Not surprisingly, music is directly related to water. According to Lipavsky, water's cathartic effect comes from its wave structure. Flowing water has the rhythms and vibrations that also permeate musical instruments (384). As he explains in "Water Tractatus," rhythm and vibration are properties of differentiated movement: water shares its wave structure with time. So, the truth of the stereotype of music as a temporal art does not reside only in its lack of spatiality and objectness, but from its differentiated structure. For Lipavsky, time is not a concept or a thought, but a sense "based on the relationship of our body to the world," which comes from the sense of individuality or separation. "To be means simply to be different" (373). Water is, then, directly related to temporality as a system of differences. Kharms relates water to the wheel, the figure that is clearly recognizable in the "REAL" diagram (figure 9). In an intriguing text from 1937, the year of hunger, he writes:

> (1) Do not wave the wheel around, do not whittle away the wheel, do not look at the water, do not intimidate others with the rock. (2) Do not strike with the wheel, do not turn the wheel, do not lie down in the water, do not break rock. (3) Do not befriend the wheel, do not tease the wheel, lower it into the water, tie the rock to the wheel. (4). (2007, 240)

This series of don'ts suggests that water is as sinister as it is attractive. Kharms notes that much in the diary entry on water from 1931. Here, he writes that he was always interested in water as the principle of the earth, its density and temperature. He notes that water is always horizontal and that it mirrors what is above. However: "In its depths, water is always quiet and mysterious to man, and fish swim calmly, and water vegetation swings quietly. I suggest to the curious man to look there with caution" (2001a, 407). This entry concludes with the story of the deluge in the city, from which young women are saved. As we are going to see, both of these themes (deluge, drowning girls) reemerge in his musical scores.

Therefore, water is the place of existence and of nonexistence. Kharms recognizes the nil in water circles:

> Throw, kids, rocks in the water
> For the rock makes a circle,
> And the circle, on its part, gives birth to thought,
> And thought, caused by the circle,
> Now from darkness summons the nil.
> (1997a, 242)

Further, water can be both stagnant and flowing. As we have seen, Lipavsky identifies the catalepsy of time with Dead Water, "dense water that closes over your head like a rock . . . This water is hard as a rock" (Ostashevsky 2006, 206). Curiously, Vvedensky writes in his *Grey Notebook,* "Things are like music, they stand still" (Vvedenskii 2002, 6).[48] Arrested music is, of course, architecture—that is to say, construction or formation. Kharms's modular musical notation points back to his attraction to architectural notation (floor plans of apartments, windows). Unlike Lipavsky, who associates stagnant water with the eradication of difference and the collapse of the life-giving wave structure (and consequently with neurasthenia), Kharms still finds curative powers in water: consider his phantasmagoric text [Black Water] (2007, 186). Stagnant water is never still. It evaporates and moves up or oozes down. Even when stagnant, it releases concentric circles, nils, from its dark abyss. As it turns out, the lattice structure, partially developed in "Modus No. 10," provides a perfect spatial counterpart to the complex symbolism of water: movement and stasis, succession and simultaneity, surface and depth, heights and depths, and, ultimately, life and death. He used this structure for the musical notation in his play *Circus Shardam* (see figure 23):[49]

This piece of music accompanies the central event of the play: the glass wall of a huge aquarium breaks and water flows over the stage. Kharms indicates that his music should be played during the scene of the deluge: "The stage is flooded. Water in aquarium recedes, and rises onstage. The scene 'Flooding of Circus.' *Verbal score.* The noise of water. The music plays. Voices offstage. Silence. The stage is underwater" (Kharms 1997c, 212, italics added). The illusion of the transformation of the atmosphere into a hydrosphere is accomplished by means of the "verbal score," which actually contains very few words other than onomatopoeias, most of them nonlexical. As the aquarium wall goes down, the "verbal score," *slovesnaia partitura,* goes up. The Russian word *partitura* comes from the same Latin root as the French *particion.* Kharms's *particion* is a system of windows to be looked through, and not to be looked at. The squares, or windows, are filled with noises that are grouped together. Clearly, the sense of immediacy and flow is facilitated by sound, or, more accurately, by voices unburdened by intelligible words. This pairing of music and onomatopoeia is not surprising. Both of them are seen as ways of overcoming the mediation characteristic of language, and especially of writing.[50] In Kharms's "pure music," onomatopoeia appears as precisely that part of language which is the least literary and the most subjective—in other words, for Kharms language becomes an instrument for the production of sounds. Like music, onomatopoeia "involves an unusually *direct* or *unmediated* link between language and referent" (Attridge 1984, 1121, italics in the original). Even though safely limited by theatrical conventions, the deluge still brings about the eradication of language. This time, it does not leave behind silence, but music.

The question remains, however: why did Kharms find it necessary to invent his own musical notation? If it was just a matter of surpassing the mediation of language, could he not compose his music using conventional notation? If we consider his original compositions of "verbal music," it becomes clear that the aim of his musical adventure is not merely to get rid of language in pursuit of the utopia of immediacy.

The basic properties of the "verbal score," such as grid structure and voice tonalities, are imported to *Circus Shardam* from a project Kharms devised a year earlier. "Salvation: Cantata for Four Voices" is his most extensive work on new musical notation, and on music in general (see fig-

<table>
<tr><td colspan="4">I Soprano
II Alto
III Tenor
IV Bass oi, oi, oi, oi</td><td colspan="4">My Pinhen, my Pinhen</td><td colspan="4">oi, oi, oi, oi
Shark, to the rescue!</td></tr>
<tr><td colspan="4">I (female) My dear Pinhen!
II
III (male)
IV</td><td colspan="4">ah, ah, ah, ah
A, E, I, O</td><td colspan="4">iiiiiiiiiii
what is that? what is that?
what is that? what is that?</td></tr>
<tr><td colspan="4">I i - i - i - i -
II a - a -a - a -
III tyau tyau tyau tyau
IV</td><td colspan="4">syau syau syau syau
o - o - o - o</td><td colspan="4">kyau, kyau, kyau, kyau
e - e - e - e - e - e</td></tr>
<tr><td colspan="4">I myau myau myau myau
II
III
IV o - o - o - o</td><td colspan="4">nno...tprr...noo, tprr...</td><td colspan="4">(without music)
I categorically don't understand anything!</td></tr>
<tr><td colspan="3">I tyau tyau tyau tyau
II tyau tyau tyau tyau
III tyau tyau tyau tyau
IV tyau tyau tyau tyau</td><td colspan="3">syau syau syau syau
syau syau syau syau
syau syau syau syau
syau syau syau syau</td><td colspan="3">kyau kyau kyau kyau
kyau kyau kyau kyau
kyau kyau kyau kyau
kyau kyau kyau kyau</td><td colspan="3">myau myau myau myau
myau myau myau myau
myau myau myau myau
myau myau myau myau</td></tr>
<tr><td colspan="12">Pure music</td></tr>
</table>

Figure 23.

Kharms devised his own musical notation, which he described as "verbal score" in his play *Circus Shardam*.

ure 24).[51] It consists of preparatory notes, a short, four-page draft dated October 31–November 4, 1934, and the final six-page version, dated October 31–November 8 and signed Daniil Dandan.[52] Kharms does not comment on this work in his diary or in his theoretical tracts. The very structure of the new notation system might have seemed so simple and self-explanatory that it did not require additional elaboration. First of all, this is a notation for vocal music: it is a cantata for a group of two female (soprano and alto) and two male voices (bass and tenor). The distribution of voices within the cell follows the conventional spatial representation of sound: "low" voices are positioned on the bottom, and "high" at the top.

Whereas the score from *Circus Shardam* has onomatopoeia, there is very little use for it in "Salvation." In that respect, "Salvation" is neither purely a poem nor a musical composition. Also, it is not simply poetry set to music. The most significant difference between this score and vocal music scored in the conventional way is that here the words are not accompanied by musical notation, or vice versa. Instead, here language performs the double role of semantic signification and musical notation. Like *Circus Shardam,* "Salvation" can be said to be a piece of water music. Its narrative is straightforward: two girls go swimming and are caught up in the waves made by a steamship that passes nearby; they start sinking and are saved by the ship's captain, who falls in love with one of the girls. The score is divided into three sections, or movements, of uneven length. The longest is the first movement, which is divided into two parts (the second part is reproduced in figure 24), each containing seven rows of cells. In the second movement, the bass and female voices disappear, so that it effectively becomes a brief solo for tenor, written in six single-lined rows of cells. Finally, the full scale of voices is restored in the third part, and the lattice structure of rows and columns explodes in its full complexity. The overall musical composition is in accord with the dramatic structure of the piece: an elaborate overture, a condensed crisis, and a celebratory finale.

That is the cantata's macrostructure. The crucial element of its micro-, or internal, structure is the grid. Each cell contains both musical notation and discursive writing. This structure spatializes and harmonizes the text. In contrast to linear writing, each word is related not only to that which is behind or ahead but also to the words that are above and below. The horizontal rows promote a succession of words and their meanings; the vertical columns promote the sonic aspect of words, facilitate simultaneity, and break the semantic units into meaningless phonemes. The rows contain language, and the columns, music. The former are carriers of narration, and the latter of notation.

Soprano I Counter-alto II Tenor III Bass IV	Water glows	Water glows	Water glows and the two of us Water glows and the two of us	Are entering the water Are entering the water		
	Are entering the water Are entering the water	Swimming toward a large steamship Swimming toward a large steamship	Steamship is rocking the waves Steamship is rocking the waves, waves			
	steamship is rocking the waves are rocked by the steamship	steamship is rocking the waves are rocked by the steamship, waves waves are rocked by the	steamship is rocking the waves are rocked by the steamship, waves steamship, waves are rocked by the waves			
	steamship is rocking the waves are rocked by the steamship steamship, the waves are rocked are rocked by the steamship	the steamship is rocking the steamship is rocking the steamship is rocking the steamship is rocking	the steamship is rocking the steamship is rocking the steamship is rocking waves, waves	the steamship is rocking the steamship is rocking waves, waves waves, waves		
	the steamship is rocking waves, waves waves, waves waves, waves	waves, waves waves, waves waves, waves waves, waves	the steamship is rocking the steamship is rocking the steamship is rocking the steamship is rocking	O-O-O	A-A-A O - O	A ----------- AH! stop
	stop the waves wave rocking	rocking stop	wave rocking wave rocking	let's find out who is swimming let's find out who is swimming		
	A - AH!	stop	rocking of the waves stop the waves	stop rocking	rocking of the waves rocking of the waves	let's swim to the steamship let's swim to the steamship

Figure 24.

Verbal score from Kharms's cantata "Salvation"

In "Salvation," the use of the lattice or modular structure is infinitely more complex than in *The Ballet of the Inseparable Trio* (figure 21) or in "Modus No. 10" (figure 22), more complex even than in the similar "verbal score" in *Circus Shardam* (figure 23). In "Salvation," the movement is simultaneously dictated by three different sources: the fictional narrative, the sound symbolism, and the visual structure of the grid. So, on the narrative level, the two axial vectors are symbolized by the horizontal gliding of the steamship across the water surface and by the vertical sinking of the two drowning girls. On the musical level, Kharms follows the logic of conventional notation: the low and heavy sounds of bass and tenor are placed at the bottom of the cells, and the high and light voices of alto and soprano are assigned to the top. Rhythms and lengths are suggested by repetition of words, tonality by their spatial position, and harmony by their vertical arrangement. What is missing from this score is a melody. According to this notation, each of the four voices sings one flat note. Kharms's notation is a system of four even tones stacked one on top of another to produce a simple polyphony.

The grid does not perfectly synchronize notation and narration. In

"Salvation," language and sound, story and music, horizontal and vertical forces, do not just support one another but also create paradoxical points that threaten to collapse the entire structure. One such point of irruption takes place in the second part of the first movement of "Salvation" (figure 24): as the two girls sink, their voices are still hovering at the top of the cell, and appear to float on the surface; they are pulled up and "saved" by the low voices that never depart from the bottom. Spatially, the logic of narration is opposed to the logic of notation. The place and the word translate into sound, and sound into a story. At points of irruption, this order collapses. This irruption resembles something like a syncope of meaning. The paradox is that this syncope is at the same time facilitated by and opposed to the schema (grid). It is music that is not limited only to sound, and, likewise, language that exceeds meaning. There is a language machine at the heart of the cantata "Salvation."

Both the language machine and the musical notation are inseparable from a certain sense of actuality that is specific to performance. To put music into notes, or to score a piece of music, is to direct its future performance. To notate is to prescribe action. This, however, does not mean that writing and musical notation are the same. Commenting on Adorno's axiomatic proposition that "to interpret language means: to understand language" and "to interpret music: to make music," Susan Bernstein warns that the performance of a musical score "is similar to, but only similar to, the repetition of linguistic performance. What is added is not only an addendum but a completion that is also actualization" (Bernstein 1998, 57). Interpretation, or execution, of a musical score does not produce a meaning. The writing of music always entails the materiality of performance. As Lacoue-Labarthe suggests, this is contrary to traditional beliefs about music's purity, immediacy, and nonmateriality:

> Musical signification—that which, in music, goes beyond signification (the "fiction") and, to this extent, for those who wish to translate it, can only be brought out by *écriture,* not by effusion or a review—this signification refers less to the soul in excess than to the body in excess, that is to say to the flesh, which, however, in no way lacks soul. (Lacoue-Labarthe 1994, 34)

In comparison to conventional musical notation, Kharms's "verbal score" is insufficiently precise. Its melodic indeterminacy requires a larger creative investment from the performer. Performance not only actualizes the music notated in the "verbal score," but also completes it. This kind of musical notation seems designed to enhance the performer's involvement in the final shape of the piece.

Kharms's most extensive and detailed text about musical performance is about a concert of the pianist Emil Gilels, held at the Writers' Club in Leningrad on February 19, 1939. Gilels was one of the most prized Soviet pianists of the day. During the 1930s, his career advanced steadily and peaked in 1938, a year before the concert Kharms attended, with the first prize in the Concours Eugene Ysaye in Brussels, Belgium, which brought him international recognition. Kharms begins his text by saying that "the program of his concert was bad, tasteless, and poorly put together. In our opinion Gillels[53] performed the majority of the pieces incorrectly"; and he ends with a note about the audience: "In the concert hall people talked about Gillels, shrugging their shoulders and making helpless gestures with their hands: 'That's . . . that's . . . that's not an artist, but art itself.' We have nothing to say about Gillels's concert—nothing at all" (2001a, 44, 48).[54] In order to illustrate his point, Kharms presents his own detailed reading of Chopin's thirteenth Mazurka, opus 17, No. 4. He distinguishes three phases in Chopin's composition and describes them as Accumulation, Severance, and Free Breathing (45). Then, he closely follows the pianist's hands as they strike and caress the keyboard; and further, he fixes his gaze on each awkwardly positioned finger, the key that it presses, and the tone that is thus produced:

> The first accumulation begins with the 5th bar. The left hand remains in its upper position, playing various descending triads, except the tonic (A-minor). On the 13th bar the left hand hits the low A, descending and touching the tonic for the first time. The accumulation is not over yet, as this time the right hand works through a rather complicated fast figure of triplets, in which the tonic A flies among the eights. Right away, in the 14th bar, the accumulation continues; the left hand again compresses in its upper limits and suddenly, in the 19th bar, a quick preparation for the resolution takes place: the right hand makes the maximum upward stretch (high C), while the left drops maximally down (low E), and in the 20th bar comes the complete resolution (the right hand holds the tonic for the whole ¾ while the left plays the low A and the tonic triad) and the first accumulation comes to an end. But in bar 21 the new accumulation begins, almost equal to the first; the difference is hardly noticeable. And it is this very insignificant divergence (compare bar 7

> with 23, 13 with 30, and 15 with 32), ingeniously placed, that creates the priceless "slight error." (2001a, 45)

The most significant part of the score is not written, and there is not a correct way of performing it. It is out of the grasp of even the most skilled hand. The pure music is to be found in the mismatch between bars, which is hardly perceptible. The "small error" is the point at which the composition departs from the composer, the performance from the performer. It is also the point at which the performance comes to the performer, and to itself. It is not performed: it happens. A concert is being performed tonight. It is the event. Vibrations of sound disperse, periodic movements go through space with their harmonics or submultiples. The sounds have inner qualities of height, intensity, and timbre. The sources of the sounds, instrumental or vocal, are not content only to send the sounds out: each one perceives its own, and perceives the others while perceiving its own. Kharms's notation allows this radial perception, prehension really, to take place within the work. Only then can it become an event.

Toward the end of hungry 1937, he maintained the notebook "Harmonius." It contains works left at various stages of completion, from bare structural outlines akin to "Modus No. 10" to gestic writings such as "Five Unfinished Narratives" and "Filthy Person." It contains one musical text. It deserves to be cited in full:

> Passacaglia 1
>
> The quiet water swayed at my feet. I stared into the dark water and saw the sky.
>
> Here, at this very spot, Ligudim will tell me the formula for the construction of nonexistent objects.
>
> I will wait until five o'clock and, if Ligudim does not appear among those trees by then, I will leave. The wait has started to feel insulting. I've been standing here two-and-a-half hours already and the quiet water sways at my feet.
>
> I stuck a stick in the water. Suddenly someone under the water grabbed my stick and jerked on it. I let it out of my hands. The wooden stick disappeared into the water so fast that it even whistled.
>
> I stood by the water and felt frightened and perplexed.
>
> ---
>
> Ligudim arrived exactly at five. It was exactly at five because just then

a train sped by across the river: every day exactly at five it flies by that little house.

Ligudim asked me why I looked pale. I told him. Four minutes passed, which Ligudim spent staring into the dark water. Then he said, "This has no formula. You can frighten children with such things but to us it is of no interest. We are not collectors of the fantastic. Only meaningless actions please our hearts. We detest folk art and Hoffmann. A palisade stands between us and mysterious events like these."

Ligudim turned his head in all directions and backed out of my field of vision.

November 10, 1937 (2007, 241)

The passacaglia from the title is the baroque musical form. Many of its distinguishing features are close to Kharms: a descending triple beat, an emphasis on bass tones, a cyclical structure. Early passacaglias are often described as having a gentle rocking feeling. As in Kharms's verbal scores, water is prominent in "Passacaglia 1." Passacaglia is also a dance form. In accordance with the music that accompanies it, the "passacalle" is a triple time dance characterized by calm and sustained movements.[55] The word "passacaglia" comes from Spanish *passar,* to walk, and *calle,* street. Both the music and dance forms of passacaglia are marked by a measured rhythmical progression. In Kharms's "passacaglia," there are no steps. The train rushes, the stick whistles, Ligudim somehow glides in and out of the picture. Here, only language has rhythm and measure.

"Passacaglia 1" is a dance of couples. There are two personages in the narrative, and two elongated objects (the wooden stick and the train in the distance) that whistle through the picture. The entire landscape is doubled in the reflection on the dark water's surface. This division along the horizontal axis echoes the physical layout of the text. A single horizontal line, the last remnant of the grid from the verbal scores, divides the narrative into the first phase, which describes the waiting for the formula that makes nonexistent objects and its mirror reversal in the second phase. We hear what nonexistent objects are and are not: nonsensical and real, not inexplicable and unreal.

We hear that from Ligudim. In this name, Yampolsky recognizes two meanings. The first meaning, "To Hebrews," points to St. Paul's Epistle. The second meaning comes from *lgdm,* or *lahadam,* which is an abbreviation of *lo hayou devarim meolam,* which, literally translated, reads "not existing objects never before" (Iampol'skii, 1997, 31). In his Epistle to the Hebrews, St. Paul underscores the succession of the old by the new religion, epitomized in the replacement of the old sanctuary by the new one, a "greater and more perfect tabernacle not made with hands, that is not of this creation" (Hebrews 9:11). Kharms transposes this difference between made and non-made, between *mimesis* and *achiropoiesis,* to the difference between mystery and nonsense, between music that is performed and music that happens.

> Messengers know the language of rocks. They achieve the equilibrium with small error. They speak of this and that.
>
> —Yakov Druskin, "Messengers and Their Conversations" (1933)

Conclusion: It Happens . . .

Reading Marina Malich's letters from the fall of 1941 is a heartbreaking experience. Her pleas for help are punctuated by reports of the plight of her husband and his friends: a week after his arrest, she wrote in an eerie code language: "on August 23 Danya went to Nikolai Makarovich" (Glotser 1991, 205). Nikolai Makarovich is Nikolai Oleinikov, a poet close to the OBERIU, a member of the "Club of Ignorant Scientists," and an author and editor of children's literature about whom nothing was heard after his arrest in 1937. Then, on September 30: "Leonid Savelevich [Lipavsky] disappeared without trace" and "Aleksandr Ivanovich [Vvedensky] met Danya's fate" (206). Lipavsky was drafted and sent to the front. Vvedensky was arrested on September 27 in Kharkov. Neither one of them was ever heard from again. Zabolotsky was already in the Siberian labor camps. In "Conversations," they talked about writing for oneself and for an audience of two or three (Lipavskii 2005, 375). Now there was no one to read and no one to write. What in the early 1930s began as the "pogrom of the OBERIU" ten years later turned into its extermination.

"Horror reigns at Auschwitz, senselessness in the Gulag," writes Blanchot (1995, 82). During the siege, Leningrad was the easternmost site of mass killing organized by the Nazis and the westernmost island in the Gulag archipelago. Kharms and his friends found themselves caught in the nodal point of these two disasters. Their annihilation marked the very end of the demise of the avant-garde in the Soviet Union. This process was happening across Europe: in some places, such as Germany and Spain, with similar brutality, and in others almost imperceptibly. This was the moment of folding of the avant-garde, both in the sense of cessation and of *complicatio.* If European modernity was marked by radical historization, and therefore by formalization and aestheticization of the event, we can say that the so-called historical avant-garde began the reintroduction of the event into the formalized and aestheticized action known as theater. Folding marks the avant-garde's permeation by the event. From that moment until now, it has often been misrecognized as the death of the avant-garde.

Daniil Kharms makes this process of the eventalization of the work of art strikingly visible. It would be wrong to think that this makes him an example of a larger, or universal, phenomenon. For eventalization is radical singularization, which is different from originality or uniqueness. Kharms tried to form associations and connections, to publish, to perform, and, in short, to create an audience. Overtaken by the event, he remained an avant-garde to the avant-garde—the institutional avant-garde, the avant-garde in silk uniforms, the avant-garde of museums, galleries, and textbooks. All attempts at systematizing this avant-garde have been in vain. This misfits' club is made of minor clerks, schoolteachers, mistresses, soldiers, prisoners, insomniacs, scholars, madmen, and the chronically depressed. Marginalized, subjugated, ignored, dispossessed, and diagnosed, they had access to intuitions and decisions that their culture could not see, and which it ever increasingly refuses to see. We find in their posthumous writings statements such as this one: "For those few like me who live without knowing how to have life, what's left but renunciation as our way and contemplation as our destiny?"[1]

Like many of the members of the misfits' club, Kharms often takes random points of departure. When it comes to his narratives, they open with the characteristic phrase of children's fables, *zhil byl,* "There once was a man. . . ." In "Theory of Words," Lipavsky discovers a strong resonance between this phrase and the idea of "beginning" associated with nonindividual life forms, such as plants and animals. In his own works he replaces the phrase with a three-dimensional diagram: in "Water Tractatus," it is an apple pierced with a steel wire, and in "Investigation of Dread," again an apple penetrated by a long needle. Both times, these strange assemblages are regarded as nameless worlds. These models resemble a simplified schema of a Reimannian singularity. Regardless of their form and genre, Kharms's works set the stage for theaters of singularity. A theater of singularity is characterized by its openness toward the event. It is distinguished from representational theater by its ascetic nonrelationality. This kind of theater does not take part in the process of exchange of information, in theatrical give-and-take, projection and identification, concealing and revealing. Each theater of singularity is a becoming. It can exist only in minoritarian form, as a divergence from the norm. Often, it is hardly perceptible. It forms not histories, but genealogies. Each singularity forms its own theater, whereas all of Western theater is concerned with one thing. Therefore, the proper way of addressing this theater should be in the plural: theaters of singularity. They appear in the most unexpected places: from paradoxes, destinies, and mathematical or scientific problems, to literary works, musical compositions, performances, mundane occurrences. For one last time, I will invoke one such instance in Kharms.

On August 22, 1937, Kharms exchanged letters with Yakov Druskin, who lived only a few blocks away. In all likelihood, it was Druskin who initiated the brief correspondence. He writes: "Dear Daniil Ivanovich, the messengers have abandoned me. I still can't even tell you how it happened. I was sitting at night by the open window and the messengers were still with me, and then they weren't" (Ostashevsky 2006, 236). If to sit by an open window means to have messengers by your side, then to be abandoned by them means shutting it. Druskin continues his message with the confession that, since the messengers left him, he has been unable to write.

"There was a knocking noise in the clock and the messengers came to me," wrote Kharms in his response (2006, 141). Messengers are elusive beings that were most likely conceived by Lipavsky. In his tract "Messengers and Their Conversations," Druskin writes that messengers know no time. Because of that they are motionless, have no memory, and can't experience tedium and monotony:

> Messengers live like trees. They don't have laws and order. They understand chance. Another advantage of trees and messengers is that for them nothing repeats and there are no periods. (Druskin 1998, 774)

These are messengers without a message: they don't remember or anticipate; they have no point of origin or destination; for them, there is no beginning and no end. Kharms experiences their visitation as a disturbance of time. When he hears a clunk in the timepiece, he first thinks that it has broken down, but upon closer inspection concludes that "the clock continued ticking and, in all probability, showed the right time" (Ostashevsky 2006, 141). At the same time, he notices that there is a draft in the room. Suddenly, it turns into a strong wind that flips the pages of the calendar that is hanging under the clock. The clock shows fifteen minutes before four o'clock, and when he looks at it again at the end of the messengers' visit, it is still quarter to four. Time at once freezes and accelerates.

The distortion of time is accompanied by an intense sensation of physicality. Kharms reports that his heart was beating strongly, he was afraid that he was losing his mind, and that he felt insatiable thirst. Also, this confusion of time creates a general uncertainty and the loss of differentiation. At first, Kharms is afraid that he might not be able to distinguish a messenger from a glass of water, and decides not to drink. After convincing himself that messengers are not "liquid," he continues his search for water, and shoves into his mouth a belt and a calendar. The two objects mistaken for water are related to time. Once, Kharms decided to name each day, so that "they don't get confused in the journal." So, he made up his own calendar: the days in September and October are distinguished by the suffix "at," Ikhvulat, Votvulat, Memtvulat . . . , and in October and November by the suffix "iθl," Msedliθl, Umaahgiθl, Dudurhgiθl.[2] Now, he cannot distinguish a calendar from a water pitcher. It is as if his thirst is not the craving for water, but for time. This overwhelming desire to absorb time, to let it enter into him so that he can enter it, suggests that he has been pulled out of the stream of time. The messengers' visit is experienced by becoming a messenger.[3] It is there, outside of time, in the realm of the messengers, that all distinctions disappear:

> I forgot about the water and began looking for the messengers. But how is one to find them? What do they look like? I recalled that I could not distinguish them from water, so that meant they must look like water. But what does water look like? I stood and thought.
>
> I don't know how long I stood there and thought, but suddenly I quivered.
>
> "Here's the water!" I said to myself. But it wasn't water, it was only my ear itching." (2006, 142)

Objects and sensations, inside and outside, are blurred. Kharms's search yields nothing but perfect gifts: in the dust under the cupboard he finds a ball chewed up by the dog, and some broken glass under the bed. He stumbles upon a half-eaten meatball under the chair. As soon as he eats it, the wind stops and time resumes its regular progression. The messengers are gone. Kharms also departs from his room, for, he says, he has an appointment. After being visited, he visits.

Like angels, the messengers are infinitely similar and dissimilar to human beings. They think, feel, and talk, but are also incorporeal, light, and almost imperceptible. Like angels, they bear witness to a different world, and unlike them, they are mute. In opposition to angels, they have no precisely defined purpose. Messengers are impassive, and have no memory. In short, they are conceptual beings. Their defining characteristic is the absence of time. Only in relation to time are they motionless and without memory. They can't experience beginning, ending, or repetition. They are on the other side of chance: Kharms intuits powerfully, like Mallarmé before him, that chance is abolished only through the cessation of time. The messengers' time is the zero hour. They appear in no time and bring along the pure exteriority of chance. Ligudim and the messengers are not the only conceptual persons in Kharms's work. Actually, such persons proliferate throughout his plays, poetry, and prose pieces, and they mix freely with traditional literary characters. In the *Comedy of the City of St. Petersburg,* Czar Peter, the living statue closely related to atemporal personae, interacts with other characters and even with audience members; the conceptual person Petr Nikolaevich comes to haunt Elizabeth Bam. And what about the red-haired man? Even Kharms's pseudonymic personae are gathered around concepts: the poet of spheres Daniil Shardam, the granular thinker Daniil Protoplast, or Daniil Dandan, triple dan, the composer of "verbal scores" that have the repetition of sounds as one of their main principles.

Messengers do not simply enter from the timeless into the temporal: their visit is the invasion of time by non-time. This invasion results in an exhaustion of the present. "How the Messengers Visited Me" can be rightfully subtitled "In Search of the Lost Present." Having no materiality, the messengers invade a host who is always a step ahead or a step behind but never on the dot in the now, present. It is therefore not surprising that Kharms captures the messengers' visitation in terms of lack: they are here, and something is missing. With their arrival comes an urgent need for time, water, and food. One would even be tempted to characterize the encounter with messengers as a hallucination before death. However, it does not belong to the order of sensory delusions, but to the order of events. To borrow Deleuzian terminology, the messengers are conceptual personae that take effect within the plane of immanence and produce concepts and events. In that sense, the visitation of the messengers is not a hallucination, but an eventuation. It does not belong to the order of the lived, but it nevertheless happens. One is never prepared for an event, or, to put it differently, there is no such thing as a predictable event. There is no knowledge that can counter an event: when it happens, all knowledge and memory are exhausted. An itch becomes an object, and the object flows. An event is a laying of one's palm—or foot—on the surface of the unforeseeable, a throw of the dice.

What are the main properties of the Kharmsian event? First of all, intensity: it is a pure ordinal. The "stem," a one-dimensional straight line, or an ordinal, moves infinitely at an infinite speed. The "fields of postulation" through which it passes are positioned along the ordinal itself, thus predicating a vertical movement. Here, verticality should not be confused with direction. The stem is rising from one field of postulation to another and at the same time falling toward zero. The speed of the falling/rising stem approaches zero.

Immanence as the second property is suggested already by the name Kharms coined for the order of numbers smaller than zero: cisfinity. As in the second determination of Cantor's set theory of transfinite numbers, in Cisfinitum, each set of subsets is larger than the original set. However, it can be said that, in his poetic rendering of Cantor's theory of sets, Kharms's number is not defined by power but by a lack thereof, or by its impotence. In Cantor's set theory, the event springs from the creation of the new system of purely conceptual, trans-finite, numbers; Kharms's numeric field is also purely conceptual, but it shatters the internal limit of the number on this side of the finite—cis-finite.

Third, conceived in this way, the event is the transcendental within the plane of immanence. This transcendence is infinitely approached through reduction. That is why Kharms holds that an empty set, a zero, is represented by an infinitely shrinking point. This idea is expressed differently in the notion of the fifth meaning: here, the unknown is not negative but affirmative. Through the fifth meaning, an object or a word escapes the conceptual grasp of the subject. For one thing, the unknown makes disappearance a staple Kharmsian event: it is not a dematerialization, a transformation, or an escape but rather, a sudden change of the plane of immanence. For another, the unknown undermines the subject-object relation.

Situated within the plane of immanence, the lines of intensity develop tremendous velocities. We can say that thought is the speed limit of an event. The head flies from the handle of a hammer, hits a number of objects while making a zigzagging circle, and returns to the handle, all in time to fit on the handle for the next slam on the anvil. At this velocity, the diagrammatic line of flight reaches the point of exhaustion. The circle is so stretched that it threatens to break open: at this point, the speed approaches zero, and levitation threatens to replace flight. It is precisely at that point that Kharms reestablishes the plane of immanence by inserting the conceptual persona Karl Ivanovich Shusterling into the iron's path. The plane of immanence is the plane of contiguity, of conceptual proximities and connections. In the final analysis, this field of conceptualization includes the reader. All of this is not to say that the Kharmsian event is contained within a narrative, or that it is expressed or actualized in any way. Kharms is searching for ways to eventuate language, not to narrate events. Insofar as it is an effect of language, *mise en abyme* approaches eventuation. However, we should note that it is not included in Kharms's list of language machines. While *mise en abyme* is a narrative strategy, the decisive aspect of the proper language machine is not its form, but its production of energy that is able to affect the body. Simply put, "machinic" is language that produces effects. However, it should be noted that, while not a linguistic trace, a language machine is not a linguistic act either. Also, it is not contained by a song, or by a gesticulating body. In other words, the event is not harmony between words and things, but precisely that which is unharmonizable. The event itself does not depend on the physicality of the body.

The Kharmsian event is singular because it is not a logical attribute of the body: Kharms singles out as eventual precisely that which resists logic and its concomitants, such as cause and effect, functions, and paradigms. The event is independent not only of narration but of any kind of actualization. A text, or a theatrical piece, or a musical composition is not a representation of an event. Instead, every representation is affected by an event. This is the cornerstone of the doctrine of the poetic critique of reason. For example, the poem "To Ring—To Fly" is not a demonstration of the idea of cisfinity, but an integral part of the concept. It partakes of the concept of cisfinity. Liberated from syntactic connections, the words are allowed to form disjunctive series. Kharmsian nonsense is neither existential (absurd) nor linguistic (Lewis Carroll), but evental. It begins as a disruption of linearity, and quickly turns into a general abolition of logical order and an affirmation of chance, error, and ignorance.

Kharms's work invites a consideration of the relations between performance and the event. Like the event, performance is usually defined in terms of its evanescence. Performance is always concerned with the body: its physicality, its qualities and actions, its appearance, or its efficiency. In any case, performance is inseparable from presence. The present tense of performance is an interruption of the history to which it belongs. Performance's ephemerality, its incessant disappearance, would be impossible without its original assertion of presence. In performance, the continuous present disappears in its instrumentality. If performance is physical, the event is incorporeal. Further, if performance is figural, the event is conceptual—and not only that, it is ahistorical. It occupies a time that is completely different from that of performance. It does not proceed ever onward on a wave of successive presents, but steps away from the present, into the past and future. The event has no present. The present of performance and the past-future of event are not mutually exclusive. As we have seen, Kharms understands that the concept-person is capable of splitting time into its three components: the regular onward movement of time indicated by the clock, its complete suspension, and the maddening rush into the future. What is the duration of the messengers' visit?

Under rigorous examination, the phrase "performative event" falls apart. The event is not a "concept" of a performance, just as performance is not the actualization of an event. A performance may not spark an event. If and when it happens, it becomes completely independent from it. In that sense, there is no chain of events, only a chain of performances or actions. Performance always involves a relation to the subject. It does not even need a performer: all it needs is an observer who perceives and experiences. The audience's perceptions and experiences are inseparable from performance. Even at the point of ultimate reduction, performance retains its structure. It is comprised of internal elements, and it establishes relations with external situations. Compared to performance, the event is pure and futile. Performance always involves bodies, or at least one body, that are individual and communicative. The event is preindividual and noncommunicative. (Who owns chance? What does it express?) The event is a dead end of communication: in it, there is no information or knowledge to be exchanged. The sense of efficiency that is always implied in performance (this comes in, that goes out) is completely foreign to the event. As an effect, something that just happened or is just about to happen, the event always establishes a disjunction. Events do not add to one another.

Performance's future is constructed through the alignment of successive presents. In that sense, the future becomes an extension of the present. This ordering of presents can be said to constitute performance's minimum. Even when it does not involve a physical repetition or rehearsal, that cautious colonization of the future, it still contains a certain amount of planning, forecasting, and calculation of probabilities. All of this is aimed at the removal of accidents. Still, performance remains open to chance, that is, to the event. Strictly speaking, the event is unperformable; at the same time, it is the most distinctive aspect of performance. It is a gift: that which is given to performance, and the only thing that performance truly has to offer; or, in Kharms's terms, it is a perfect gift: without purpose, a pure break or opening, a crack, an interlude in the rigorous arrangement of causality. It is a pure contingency, an incident, a hap. It brings together everything that is hap: happening, happiness, haphazard, but also happenstance. Ha!—a surprise; and ha!—laughter. Harms.

Notes

Introduction

Unless otherwise noted, translations are by the author. The epigraph derives from an undated scrap of paper, the first item in folder No. 338 of the Druskin Fond (F1232), Manuscript Division of the Public Library Saltikov-Schedrin, St. Petersburg, Russia. Many of Kharms's unconnected textual fragments are collected in this archive.

Druskin Fond. F1232, No. 338, p.1. St. Petersburg: Manuscript Division, Public Library Saltikov-Schedrin.

1. I am quoting from Matvei Yankelevich's English translation of Kharms's collection *Sluchai* published in the book *Today I Wrote Nothing* (Kharms 2007). This collection of short prose and scenes was first translated into English by George Gibian as *Incidents* (Kharms 1971) and then by Neil Cornwell as *Incidences* (Kharms 1993). Yankelevich bases his translation not on the semantic valence of the Russian word *sluchai* (which could mean "incident," "occurrence," "case," or "event") but on the sense it acquires in Kharms's writing (Kharms 2007, 31). I consider this English translation of *Sluchai* (*Events*) definitive and will rely on it throughout this book.

2. "The OBERIU Manifesto" (Kharms 1971, 195). *Zaum* (*za* – beyond, *um* – reason, mind) is the neologism Russian Futurists, principally Velimir Khlebnikov and Alexei Kruchenykh, used to describe their poetic activity. Kharms and Vvedensky were introduced to the poetic circles of Leningrad by the one-time associate of Khlebnikov and Kruchenykh, Alexander Tufanov. For more on the interaction between Kharms and Tufanov, see Jaccard (1991, 15–71).

3. For a detailed account of Radix, see Jaccard 1991, 234–36.

4. Announcement for "Three Left Hours,"reproduced in *Vvedenskii* 1993, 2:149.

5. N. Aseev, "Otrivok iz stati 'Segodishnii den sovetskoi poezii'" in *Vvedenskii* 1993, 2:155.

6. Nakhimovsky 1982, 17. Many of the scenic devices used in "Three Left Hours," including the film projection and "Entr'acte-Cataract," are reminiscent of the last big manifestation of the Parisian Dada, Picabia's "*Relache.*" Interestingly, the first public note on the OBERIU, in the November 1, 1927, issue of the journal *Zhizn iskusstva* ("The Life of Art") appeared under the title "Dadaists in Leningrad." The author D. Tolmachev reproaches the Oberiuty for their nonsensical art and for their absence of originality (Vvedenskii 1993, 144). Even though there are no references to Dada in extant writings by any of the OBERIU members, there are attempts in critical literature to establish connections between the two groups

and their poetics. See John E. Bowlt, "The Cow and the Violin: Toward a History of Russian Dada" (1998) and Anica Vlašić-Anić, *Harms i dadaizam* (1997).

7. Lidia Lesnaia, "Ytuerebo," in *Vvedenskii* 1993, 2:150.

8. See Evreinoff 1927 and Spoerri 1995.

9. Laurence Sterne, from whom Kharms learned a great deal about pen and paper, wrote: "When a man gives himself up to the government of a ruling passion,—or, in other words, when his Hobby-Horse grows headstrong—farewell cool reason and fair discretion!" and "A man's Hobby-Horse is as tender a part as he has about him" (1967, 113).

10. See Poret 1980, 345–66.

11. See Petrov 1993, 196.

12. Nadezhdinska Street was later renamed Mayakovsky Street.

13. This volume was a part of documentation produced during the first arrest of Daniil Kharms and his friends in December 1931. In the legal vocabulary, the word *delo* means case, while in everyday use it holds the meaning work, both in the sense of business and in the sense of artistic output. The first volume of this case-work contains the arrested writers' statements. I am grateful to Matvei Yankelevich for sharing with me his findings from the KGB archives.

14. Kharms's proposal, which reached the Moscow-based Writers' Publishing House, includes a poetry section (Zabolotsky, Vvedensky, Kharms, Khlebnikov, Tikhonov), the play *Elizabeth Bam,* and a prose section that, judging from the names of the contributors, was supposed to include both fictional and critical writings (Kaverin, Vvedensky, Dobichin, Kharms, Tynianov, Shklovsky, and Olesha).

15. Under the excellent editorship of two (then) young scholars, Mikhail Meilakh and Vladimir Erl.

16. Valerii Sazhin edited Kharms's collected works, as well as many other OBERIU-related anthologies.

17. In her essay "The Meaning of Art: Symbolist Theories," Irina Paperno writes that to the symbolists, "'life creation' in daily life means much more than organizing life aesthetically, as if it were a literary text. By projecting principles used to construct verbal texts into life, Symbolists realized the metaphor 'the incarnation of the Word'" (1994, 23). For more on the idea of "life-making" in nineteenth- and twentieth-century Russian culture, see Boym 1991, Ginsburg 1991, Nakhimovsky and Nakhimovsky 1985.

18. In the 1990s, the author of the book, Vladimir Glotser, tracked down Marina Durnovo in Venezuela. She managed to escape from Leningrad, and eventually from the Soviet Union. After spending some time in Paris, she ended up in Caracas, Venezuela.

19. Eleven, according to the library catalogue.

20. Tamara Meier-Lipavskaya remains the only unpublished member of Kharms's circle. Even though in his essay on Vvedensky Druskin gives her due credit, her structural interventions remain buried under his analytical writing. Her

"Dictionary" also remains buried in the manuscript archive because it is simply unpublishable, at least in conventional book form. See Kharms n. d. F1232, No. 415, Druskin Fond.

21. Sazhin 1998, 592. Druskin characterizes Vvedensky's nonsense as semantic, and Kharms's as situational (565).

22. In the English-speaking world, Kharms criticism is dominated by absurdist interpretation. The first collection of Kharms's and Vvedensky's works in English, edited by George Gibian, was entitled *Russia's Lost Literature of the Absurd: A Literary Discovery* (Kharms 1971). There followed critical works published in journals that specialize in Slavic studies: Alice Stone Nakhimovsky's "Laughter in the Void: An Introduction to the Writing of Daniil Kharms and Alexander Vvedenskii" (1982) and Neil Carrick's *Daniil Kharms: Theologician of the Absurd* (1998). To this corpus of absurdist interpretations also belongs the volume edited by Neil Cornwell, *Daniil Kharms and the Poetics of the Absurd: Essays and Materials* (1991). That leaves Graham Roberts's *The Last Soviet Avant-Garde: OBERIU—Fact, Fiction, Metafiction* (1997) as the only long work in English about OBERIU that is outside of the absurdist canon.

23. The perception of Kharms as a "case" is reflected in the title of the film *The Kharms Case* (1988). This film by the Serbian director Slobodan Pesic is based on the stories from the anthology *Events* (Kharms 2007), and it tries to situate them in the historical context of post-Revolutionary Russia. Another film based on *Events* is *Charms's Incidents* (1995) by Austrian director Michael Kreihsl. Here, Kharms's narratives are used as the basis for a series of episodes from the life of a fictional writer named Jurjavec. Finally, the Russian film *Staru-Kha-rmsa* (1991) by Vadim Gems combines documentary with a fictional approach to Kharms's prose.

24. See Bennett 1996, 137–53.

25. Ian Hacking (1980) offers a fascinating account of the transformations in the understanding of chance that have taken place over the past two hundred years.

26. See Lezra 1997, 8.

Chapter 1

The chapter epigraph is from Daniil Kharms. Valerii Sazhin, ed., *Polnoe sobranie sochinenii: Neizdanny Kharms: Traktaty i statii; Pisma,* supplement to vols. 1–3 (St. Petersburg: Akademicheskii Proekt, 2001), 15.

1. See Marcel Mauss, *The Gift: The Form and Reason for Exchange in Archaic Societies* (1950, 60).

2. For a discussion of some formal similarities between Dada and OBERIU, especially in the spheres of "negation, violence, and performance," see John E. Bowlt's essay "The Cow and the Violin: A History of Russian Dada" (1998, 137–63). See also Anica Vlašić-Anić, *Harms i Dadaizam* (1997).

3. See Kharms 1971, Jaccard 1991, Cornwell 1991, and Roberts 1997.

4. Precisely this absence of logical plotline is often taken as one of the crucial similarities between Kharms and the "absurdist" playwrights, such as Beckett and Ionesco.

5. Similarly, in the short narrative "Sonnet" from *Events,* the narrator, who has forgotten which comes first, the number 7 or the number 8, goes to a nearby shop and asks the cashier about the correct order of numbers: "Smiling a sad smile, the cashier extracted a small hammer from her mouth, and twitched her nose lightly. She said: 'In my opinion seven comes after eight, but only when eight comes after seven'" (Kharms 2007, 44).

6. See Kharms's letter to Claudia Vasilevna from October 16, 1933 (Kharms 2001a, 79).

7. Kharms's story "The Old Woman" contains a passage which, to my knowledge, describes most accurately the difference between prosthesis as an anatomical, "living" object and corpse as a potential OBERIU object. At the moment of the old woman's death, the narrator notes that "the dentures that had fallen out of her mouth bit into her nostril with one tooth." The narrator leaps to the corpse and kicks it on the chin. "Her dentures flew off into the corner" (Kharms 2007, 90). Later, when the corpse starts moving, the narrator notes that it does not collect its lost dentures.

8. The two paragraphs on bodily limits are literally at the center of the essay: they are preceded by three opening paragraphs and followed by three concluding paragraphs.

9. For an informed discussion of the water principle in Russian avant-garde poetry and in Kharms's work, see Jaccard 1991, 40–47.

10. The difference in the name of the "smoke theorist" and the vodka drinker is minimal: while the first character is named Nikolai Ivanovich *Stupin,* the second is called Nikolai Ivanovich *Serpuhov.* Consistency of names is parallel to the consistency of argument in the two parts of the tract.

11. Significantly, this radical orientation was purely aesthetic: Katsman explains that while Radix absorbed some of the aesthetic principles of the contemporaneous progressive theater such as Eisenstein's montage of attractions and the theater group FEKS's eccentricism, it insisted on distancing itself from the political radicalism that marked the experimental theater in the early post-Revolutionary era.

12. Jaccard claims that the proposal was written in Kharms's hand. For a more detailed account on Radix, see Jaccard (1991, chap. 2).

13. The text of this play was lost.

14. Kharms was interested in the near impossibility of expressing a multiplicity of voices in a single written verse. *Temptation* is the earliest extant example of his attempts to engage this question. He returned to it in 1933, when he wrote in his notebook: "How to present in verses large and small a number of voices" (2002b, 581). He tried to solve this problem though musical notation. See the discussion of *Salvation* in chapter 5.

15. *Suprematizm. Mir kak bespredmetnost', ili vechny pokoi,* in Malevich 2000a.

16. It was published in 1916 as a brochure in Moscow.

17. This situation is varied in Kharms's story "Makarov and Petersen," written seven years after *Temptation* and included in the cycle *Events* (Kharms 2007). I will return to it in chapter 5.

18. In that sense, Malevich's ideas are pronouncedly Neoplatonistic. Regarding the Platonic unity of One and All in Neoplatonism, J. Patrick Atherton writes that "the recognition of the predicateless unity of pure self-identity of the arche lay at the root of the entire Neoplatonic tradition" (1976, 173).

19. The book is another powerful symbol of perfection that Malevich uses repeatedly: in this infinite book "neither first nor last page exists, and similarly neither the first nor the last figures are known" (1968, 195).

20. Kharms carefully dated most of his writings.

21. For more on Malevich's charts for these lectures, see Linda S. Boersma's 1989 essay "On Art, Art Analysis and Art Education: The Theoretical Charts of Kazimir Malevich" in *Kazimir Malevich: Leningrad, Moscow, Amsterdam; 1878–1935*. This catalog also features the color reproductions of all twenty-two charts.

22. It seems that the offerings did not stream in one direction only, and that from the very beginning Malevich and Kharms engaged in a dialogue. For instance, Aleksandra Shatskikh locates interesting borrowings of a Kharmsian wordplay in the verses that Malevich included in his letter to one of the founders of Russian Futurism, David Burliuk, who at that time lived in New York. See Shatskikh's introduction to Malevich's *Poezia* (Malevich 2000b, 35–36).

23. Hence the question "What is Daniil Kharms?" See the introduction.

24. "The man observing a group of objects lacking all four of their working meanings stops being an observer and is transformed into an object of his own creation. He ascribes to himself the fifth meaning of his own existence" (Kharms 1997b, 306).

25. In his insightful essay on Malevich's project in relation to philosophy from Nietzsche to Heidegger, Boris Groys states that *Black Square* is "unlike all other suprematist forms primarily because it is representative and not 'abstract,' and it represents no more and no less than the painting as such" (1982, 363).

26. He writes in "Suprematism as Pure Cognition": "In the sphere of word, Art entered into '*zaum*' and in the sphere of painting, into the nonobjectivity of Suprematism" (Malevich 2000a, 140).

27. In his detailed study of the influence of futurism on the OBERIU members, Kobrinsky argues that *zaum* is not the most significant aspect of Khlebnikov's legacy that was taken over and pursued by the OBERIU poets (Kobrinskii 2000, 100). The arguments against the mechanistic approach to the influence of Russian futurists on the OBERIU members came after it was given a somewhat overrated significance by Jaccard in his 1991 work *Daniil Harms et la fin de l'avant-garde russe.*

28. Translation by Matvei Yankelevich. It seems that Kharms was unsure whether he wanted to keep this monologue in the play. Following Kharms, the editor of Kharms's *Complete Collected Works* (*Polnoe sobranie sochinenii*), Valerii Sazhin, decided to omit this monologue and to provide it in the textual notes (Kharms 1997b). The downside of this choice is that the dialogue about the letter *yat'* is also omitted. Mikhail Meilakh and Vladimir Erl, the editors of *Collected Works* (*Sobranie proizvedenii*), returned the excised parts into the main body of the play, which makes for easier connection between Kharms's comments in his notebooks and the play itself. See Kharms 1978b, 117–18.

29. According to legend, the cross on which Christ was crucified was made of cedar.

30. Nikolai Rimsky-Korsakov based his opera *The Tale of Tsar Saltan* on Pushkin's poem. I am grateful to Eugene Ostashevsky for suggesting this poem to me.

31. Upon completing the play, Kharms sent a clean copy to Ester, together with the letter in which he makes one of his rare pronouncements about the reception of his works: "Dear Ester, I am sending you the piece 'Gvidon.' Don't search in it for any particular meanings and allusions. There is nothing like that in there. Anyone is free to understand the piece as they see fit. That is the right of the Reader. I am sending you this piece because it is dedicated to you. I would like you to have it. If you don't want it, you can send it back. Daniil Khorms, December 22, 1930" (2001a, 87). "Khorms" was one of the variants of "Kharms" that Daniil Ivanovich used occasionally.

32. There is a riddle within a riddle in this story. Namely, if we take the first and last letters of Arthur Conan Doyle's names and rearrange them, they form the word "dancer."

33. "Theory of Words" is one of Lipavsky's longest essays. It was written in 1935, and it is not improbable that some of Lipavsky's ideas were developed in conversations with his friends ("Conversations" was recorded over a two-year period, 1933 to 1934). Not unlike Kharms in his entry on "language machines," in "Conversations" Lipavsky expresses his concern about the acceptance of his theory because it goes directly against the established Soviet linguistic methods and doctrines of that time, which were dominated by Nikolai Marr's theory of Japhetism. Lipavsky compares Japhetism to alchemy: it is an elaborate theory based on completely wrong premises (Lipavskii 2005, 273). For the doctrines and history of Japhetism see Alpatov 1991.

34. According to Lipavsky, rotation is the basic principle of the formation of words. See Lipavskii 2005, 217.

35. Lipavsky uses the word *stikhia,* which does not mean "element" as component. The word "element" here has the meaning of a primordial force, as in "elements of nature."

36. Bachelard also points out that "organically, human language has a *liquid*

quality, a flow in its overall effect, water in its consonants" (1983, 15, original emphasis).

37. See "Theory of Words" and "Conversations" (Lipavskii 2005).

38. This consideration of flight and the force of gravity is especially useful for the analysis of Kharms's play *Lapa.* See chapter 2.

39. In his brilliant essay on the metaphor of metaphor as literary figure, Richard Klein talks about the hollowness of metaphor: "[M]etaphor of metaphor is not, finally, a special sub-category but . . . all metaphor, if sufficiently extended, tends constantly to displace its center and to lose itself in the self-generating play of its spinning periphery" (Klein 1970, 68).

Chapter 2

The chapter epigraph is from Eugene Ostashevsky, ed. *OBERIU: An Anthology of Russian Absurdism* (Evanston, Ill.: Northwestern University Press, 2006), 28–51.

1. Klaudia Vasilievna Pugacheva was an actress in Leningrad's Theater of the Youth. In 1933, she moved to Moscow, where she worked in the Maiakovsky Theater and Moscow Theater of Satire. Kharms maintained regular correspondence with Pugacheva during the first months of her stay in Moscow. Eleven of his letters from this period still exist. Samuil Marshak was the editor of the children's literature journal *Ezh* (1928–35), to which Kharms contributed regularly. Writing for children's journals was his main source of income.

2. I retained Kharms's erroneous spelling of Emerson's last name from the original title of the tract. There are five paragraphs in this text, each individually subtitled. The first three are cleanly penned in this otherwise empty notebook, indicating they were copied from previous drafts, but the fourth and fifth paragraphs are not clean copies, which suggests that they were newly written and worked on in this version. See Kharms n. d. F1232, No. 376, Druskin Fond.

3. "Five Unfinished Narratives" is addressed to Yakov Druskin.

4. See "Eleven Statements by Daniil Ivanovich Kharms" in Sazhin 1998.

5. Yakov Druskin's text "Five Investigations" shadows Kharms's tract: this undated text also consists of five enumerated parts, and also begins with a section "On Gifts" and concludes with a section "On Immortality." Interestingly, in the second section Druskin also talks about the fountain pen and the inkwell. In the second section, "On Proofs," he takes the fountain pen as the object of his investigation of the difference between the notions of conviction and proof (in Sazhin 1998, 732). The references to these particular pieces of writing equipment are, of course, not purely coincidental.

6. This is a complete inversion of Emerson's approach to the question of gifting as coming to presence, presenting. In "Gifts," a short essay from the second series of his published meditations, Emerson talks about the true gift as an address of

the self to the other, an unequivocal extension of the giver to the recipient: "Rings and other jewels are not gifts, but apologies for gifts. The only gift is a portion of thyself. Thou must bleed for me" (Emerson 1950, 403).

7. Deleuze and Guattari also include in their discussion the case of runic writing as a unique form of writing located halfway between phonetic writing and pure ornamentation.

8. For the aborted versions of the fourth part of Kharms's tract, see Kharms n. d. F1232, No. 376, Druskin Fond, 5.

9. I am using Matvei Yankelevich's translation of Kharms's text, but am retaining my own translation of the title. Yankelevich somewhat simplifies the title, which in the original reads "Traktat (bole ili menee) po konspektu Emersena," by translating it as "A Treatise More or Less According to Emerson." Already in the title, Kharms veers away from the author he is using as his starting model. He misspells Emerson's name and writes it as "Emersen." An additional suggestion of this departure from the model is the phrase "more or less," which appears four times in Kharms's tract. Three out of four repetitions of the phrase occur in the third and fourth sections of the tract, entitled, respectively, "The Correct Negation of Surrounding Objects" and "On Approaching Immortality." In the title itself, "more or less" is added under the words "tract according" and surrounded by a comic-book-like balloon pointing toward the space between these two words, suggesting that these words were added later, presumably in the process of writing of the text. This addition to the original title can be read as an indication of the struggle with writing that becomes obvious in the fourth section of the tract, in which he completely departs from Emerson's ideas about gift giving.

10. John T. Irwin asserts in *American Hieroglyphics* that "an Emersonian essay is simply the decipherment of a hieroglyph" (1980, 15).

11. Lipavsky's tracts often have the narrative form of a dialogue usually occurring in a public place, this time in a restaurant. The four characters who participate in this conversation are "champion," "captain," "the small Greek," and "the fourth character." These same four characters are also engaged in dialogue in "Tract on Water."

12. The ideas of advanced mathematics had a great currency in Kharms and Lipavsky's circle. We find, for instance, in "Conversations," a well-informed consideration of non-Euclidean geometry: "The space of muscular actions is a variation of that which is generally attainable; that is why the laws of geometry contain a far larger significance than geometrical, in the drawing. And that is why **contemporary** geometers are trying not to rely on drawings, maintaining that points, lines, planes and volumes are words, with which you can designate anything" (Lipavskii 2005, 402).

13. This book figures prominently in the story "Makarov and Petersen," which will be discussed in chapter 5.

14. The cards contain symbols that also appear in some of Kharms's other drawings: Egyptian cross (or ankh), tree, flower, and window. See Kharms n. d. F1232,

No. 408, Druskin Fond. For Kharms's interest in esoterica see Iampol'skii 1997, chapters 8–11.

15. I italicized the sections that correspond to the portions of the original text written in red ink.

16. This poem contains openly erotic references that are absent from poems dedicated to Marina Malich and from the *mise en page*. See Kharms 2001a, 202.

17. The three crosses, which also are mentioned in Kharms's poem "Andor," can be seen as a reference to the three crosses of Golgotha (Christ's and those of the two robbers).

18. For cards, see Kharms n. d. F1232, No. 408, Druskin Fond. The column was reproduced in Kharms's *Polnoe sobranie sochinenii, Tom 2* (1997b), *Polet v nebesa* (1988a), and *Dnei katibr* (1999). It is also in *Risunki Kharmsa* (Ershov 2006).

19. Some of the italicized words are Kharms's neologisms. In Russian, this line reads "Ia O, ia sir, ia is," and it involves a complex word play. *Sir* in Russian means a poor and meager man, a speck of dust; hence the name Osiris brings together the highest and the lowest.

20. For illuminating readings of this page, see Nikitaev and Gerasimova 1991 and Iampol'skii 1997, chapter 11.

21. Using the parallel phonetic text "Ia O, ia sir, ia is," Nikitaev transcribes the cryptogram as "Osiris" (Nikitaev 1989, 99).

22. Interestingly, in this instance Kharms disturbs the symmetry by adding a splotch on the right arm of the cross. This could be an example of his and Druskin's notion of "insignificant error," which is discussed in chapter 3.

23. The wheel is in itself a poetic symbol that figures prominently in Kharms's poetry. See, for example Kharms's poem "Wheel, the wife of joy . . ." (Kharms 1997a, 249).

24. Kharms makes at least two irregular uses of the window sign: first, in the dedication to his 1930 play *Lapa* (discussed in the next paragraph), and in the interventions he made with Alisa Poret in the print of *Magenburg Experiment with Half-Spheres.* Here, as Gleb Ershov suggests, the window appears in the form of the mousetrap (Ershov 2006, 274).

25. Barbara Johnson's translation.

26. Kharms's nickname.

27. Kharms n. d. F1232, No. 413, Druskin Fond.

28. For example, the palace on Moshkov Pereulok. See Kharms n. d. F1232, No. 413, Druskin Fond, page 4.

29. Translated by Matvei Yankelevich.

30. Kharms wrote the word "REAL" underneath the emblem in English. Neither this drawing nor the schema of the universe (figure 8) are dated, and it is not clear which one was created first. There are a number of sketches of the "REAL" symbol preserved in Kharms's archive. See F1232, No. 408, Druskin Fond, page 14.

31. The line *s uma soshestvie* could be rendered also as "going out of one's mind."

32. Translated by Matvei Yankelevich.

Chapter 3

The chapter epigraph is from Leonid Lipavsky. V. Sazhin, ed. *Issledovanie uzhasa* (Moscow: Ad Marginem, 2005), 359.

1. Kharms's birth narratives will be discussed in the next chapter.

2. The volume, *Issledovanie uzhasa* (the title is taken from his original text from the mid-1930s, translated as "Investigation of Horror"), was finally published in 2005 under the editorship of Valery Sazhin (Lipavskii 2005). Eugene Ostashevsky's English translation of "Water Tractatus" was published in *OBERIU: An Anthology of Russian Absurdism* (Ostashevsky 2006).

3. In Ostashevsky's translation, "The Diminutive Greek's Tale."

4. We have already encountered the image of the corpse in possession of a non-human life in Kharms's story "The Old Woman."

5. Bataille's considerations of time are tied to his later interest in Nietzsche, and he talks about fear in relation to the sacred and to sexuality. And even years after the *Documents* period, his thinking about fear is strikingly similar to Lipavsky's: "What is sacred undoubtedly corresponds to the object of horror. . . , a fetid, sticky object without boundaries, which teems with life and yet is the sign of death" (Bataille 1993, 95).

6. See Lebel and Waldberg 1995, 10–11.

7. "Tropical melancholy" brings to mind another uncanny similarity, this time with Claude Levi-Strauss's *Tristes Tropiques* (1973).

8. For a discussion of the sublime in Kharms's works, see Jaccard 1995, 8–19.

9. See Fink, *Bergson and Russian Modernism* (1999).

10. See Dlugach 1994, 186–210.

11. Translated by Matvei Yankelevich.

12. *Lapa* in Russian means "paw." I am leaving it untranslated, following the choice of the play's translator Matvei Yankelevich, who correctly assessed that, in this case, the aural quality of the word is more important than its literal meaning.

13. See also the chapter 2 discussion on Khlebnikov's influence on Kharms and Lipavsky's understanding of language.

14. For an excellent discussion of Kharms and Khlebnikov, see Kobrinskii 2000, 97–137.

15. *Zemliak* in Russian.

16. Kharms was born on the day which, according to the Russian Orthodox Church's calendar, is dedicated to the Prophet Daniel. This prompted his father, Ivan Pavlovich Yuvachev, to give him the name Daniil (Daniel), since in Russia it was a common practice to name children after the saint celebrated on the day

of their birth. Kharms's father was strongly inclined toward mysticism. His belief in the power of prophecies and predictions was recorded in his 1915 book *Voina i vera: ocherki vsemirnoi voini 1914–1915* (*War and Faith: Essays on the World War 1914–1915*).

17. All of the images that Kharms uses in this fragment come from the inventory of what Bachelard calls the aerial signs: while the color blue and stealth are traditionally related to skies, the long and narrow cat's tail is a not-so-obvious, but nevertheless powerful, aerial symbol. Bachelard writes that "an *elongated form* is a *formal élan.* In the *formal élan,* dynamic imagination would regain its role as a creator of forms. It is to be noted that any *elongated form* reaches out toward the heights, toward light. The *elongated form* is a *formal élan* that unfolds in pure, luminous air. We could not conceive of an elongated form going downward, suggesting a fall. That would be—in the realm of imagination—aerodynamically absurd" (1988, 76, italics in the original). It would be interesting to investigate these claims in relation to the first part of Kharms's "On Phenomena and Existences I," in which the artist Michael Angelo, whose wife is "extremely long, two rooms in length," observes "a huge spoon" outlined in the sky (1993, 93).

18. See Bachelard (1988, 163–64).

19. Matvei Yankelevich suggested to me this reading of the word *Bukak.* Kharms similarly fashions a proper name for Landman. In the original, it is *Zemliak,* which comes from *zemlia* (land) and the suffix *ak.*

20. See the discussion of the play *Gvidon* in the first chapter.

21. It is worth remembering that the symmetry of the cross in the column of hieroglyphs (figure 6) is disturbed by a splotch.

22. Apart from the simple addition, Sterne plus Gogol, the cross here might designate the intersection, or combination, or mixture of the two writers. Also, the cross inscribed next to the name of Sterne unmistakably brings to mind Sterne's use of *mise en page* in *The Life & Opinions of Tristram Shandy,* where the cross designates the gesture of crossing, as in the episode of Dr. Slop's fall from the horse: "What could Dr. Slop do?—He crossed himself +" (Sterne 1967, 125).

23. This terminology is shared with Yakov Druskin, who also wrote on "this" and "that." See Druskin in Sazhin 1998, 811.

24. Deleuze writes: "Being is also non-being, *but non-being is not the being of the negative;* rather, it is the being of the problematic, the being of problem and question. Difference is not the negative; on the contrary, non-being is Difference: *heteron,* not *enantion*" (1994, 64, italics in the original).

25. Deleuze also finds significant the relation between the pure difference and the eternal return.

26. See, for example, "Tumbling Old Women" (Kharms 2007, 43).

27. Kharms spelled the last name of the English mathematician George Boole as "Bool," while Charles Sanders Peirce's last name he transcribed into Russian Cyrillic letters.

28. Ian Hacking argued that the defeat of determinism in philosophy was paralleled by the gradual rise of probability and statistics from the late-eighteenth century to the late-nineteenth. This progressive establishment of chance in philosophy, science, and social life culminated, according to Hacking, with Peirce's work on formal logic. See *The Taming of Chance* (Hacking 1990).

29. Romanian mathematician Solomon Marcus conceives of mathematical poetics as a branch of structural analysis that is primarily concerned with mathematical analysis of poetry, and to a much lesser degree to a poetic approach to mathematics. See his *Poetica Matematica* (1970). I had access to a Serbian translation of this work, *Matematička poetika* (1974). For his work in English on a similar subject, see *Algebraic Linguistics: Analytical Models* (1967).

30. Another instance of Kharms's interest in visual properties of numbers can be found in his poem "Robert Mabr," in which he compares number three with a heart cut in half (1997a, 316). Yampolsky comments extensively on this motif. See Iampol'skii 1997, chapter 8.

31. Translation by Matvei Yankelevich.

32. We can add, in passing, that the same principle of analogy appears in literature as the principle of metaphoricity. Matila Ghyka asserts that "metaphor is the elliptical condensation of analogy" (1987, 36). Indeed, this insight about the nature of the metaphor informs Paul de Man's view that Baudelaire's poem "Correspondences" is "structured like the distinction between calculus and arithmetic, with tropes of infinitude reduced to the literal, disfigured status of sheer finite numbers" (de Man 1984, 266). Kharms attempts to overcome precisely this limit of analogy.

33. As in the words *cis*atlantic or *cis*alpine.

34. Cantor's theory of transfinite numbers was well known in Russia. For example, the Russian theologian and scientist Pavel Florensky commented on Cantor's theory in his book *Stolp i utverzhdenie istini* (Florenskii 1914). For a translation of Cantor's work on transfinite numbers, see Cantor 1955.

35. It is conceivable that the symbol "t" might signify something else: time, for example.

36. The last parenthetical sentence of Cantor's definition comes from Philip E. B. Jourdain's English translation of Cantor's *Contributions to the Founding of the Theory of Transfinite Numbers* (Cantor 1955, 86).

37. Badiou takes Cantor's theory as an instance of the event in that it indicates an "absolute beginning" (2000, 91), or "that which is on the edge of the void" (85). In other words, he radically historicizes Cantor's mathematical theory in order to turn it into an example that, ultimately, supports an ideological argument. He turns Cantor's Transfinity into one of a series of examples, alongside Samuel Beckett, the French Revolution, St. Paul, and Fernando Pessoa. The question, then, is not only what all of these examples prove but what this labor of proving does to the examples themselves. And, further, what it does to the event. In Badiou's

philosophical rendering, the event acquires properties of action. On this point, see Žižek 1999, 182–83, 200. Here, my approach to the event is absolutely incompatible with Badiou's.

38. We can go so far as to say that Badiou's use of Cantor's set theory in his project of the mathematization of being is the final defeat of Cantor's project.

39. In *Difference and Repetition,* Deleuze writes: "When chance is sufficiently affirmed the player can no longer lose, since every combination and every throw which produces it is by nature adequate to the place and the mobile command of the aleatory point" (1994, 198). In writing, Deleuze identifies this aleatory point in which all of the series converge with Blanchot's notion of the "blind spot." This is the blindness of the Landman. I will return to it in chapter 4.

40. The symbol α appears in transcriptions by Meilakh and Erl. See Kharms 1978b, 52–53. Other editors of Kharms's manuscripts decided to ignore this symbol.

41. "Ity" appears in Kharms's drawings and notebook entries on at least two other occasions. See Kharms 2002b, 27, 146.

42. Transcriptions of Kharms's notes on *The Golem* were first published in Gerasimova and Nikitaev 1991.

43. See, for instance, "The Young Man Who Astonished a Watchman," "Holiday," and "The Fate of a Professor's Wife" in Kharms 1993.

44. Kharms does not mention this Gnostic sect in any of his writings. For Kharms's relation to Gnosticism, see Iampol'skii 1997, chapter 8.

45. C. S. Peirce and Joseph Jastrow coauthored the paper "On Small Differences of Sensation," published in 1885 in *Memoirs of the National Academy of Sciences 1884.* It is uncertain if Kharms and Druskin had access to information about this aspect of Peirce's work.

46. Roger Caillois, a one-time member of Georges Bataille's group Acephale, comes to similar conclusions in his study *La dissymetrie.* He says that "1) Any homogeneous and isotropic environment can be defined *equally* as an absence of a complete symmetry or as a virtual infinite symmetry, without any privileged axis, center, or plan. Such a state constitutes, to speak rightly, an asymmetry" and "3) In any established symmetry a *partial* and *non-accidental* rupture can erupt, which tends to complicate the established equilibrium. The effect of the rupture is to enrich the structure or the organism in which it occurs, i.e., to give it a new property or to take it to a superior level of organization" (Caillois 1973, 77–78, English translation by Jasminka Jakovljevic). It is not difficult to recognize resonances between Caillois, a former Surrealist who joined Bataille's circle, and Lipavsky (his writing on formlessness in "The Water Tractatus," for instance).

47. Kharms mentions this "Order" in the letter to his friend Nikolai Khardzhiev, who was a poet, literary critic, and one of the first historians of the Soviet avant-garde. See Zolotonosov 1995, 39.

48. The NKVD later became the KGB.

Chapter 4

The chapter epigraph is from Daniil Kharms. Valeri Sazhin, ed., *Zapisnye knizhki: Dnevnik,* vol. 2 (St. Petersburg: Akademicheskii Proekt, 2002), 195.

1. For an informative discussion on Kharms as children's writer, see Sokol 1984.

2. See F1232, No. 77, Druskin Fond. Besides Carroll's verses, Kharms's private anthology of children's literature contains works by Kipling (also in English) and Goethe (in German), as well as works in Russian by Pushkin, Baratinsky, and others. Interestingly, the notebook is also signed bilingually: on the verso side of the cover page, it features Kharms's pseudonym in Russian and in the English rendition, Даниил Шардам—Daniel Shardam.

3. In his essay "Metaphysics and the Mise-en-scene," Artaud capitalizes the word "Danger," which is coupled with "real humor" (1958, 42). In his note on the Marx brothers, he compares their films with "certain successful surrealist poems, if there were any" (1958, 142). Artaud's notion of humor is closely related to the idea of "black humor," which Andre Breton explored in his anthology conceived at the same time Artaud wrote about the Marx brothers (from 1931 to 1932) and published a decade later. It is not surprising that Breton declares Swift's *A Modest Proposal* (1629), which is an ironic argument for the cannibalism of children, the originary work of this kind of humor.

4. In "Self-Reliance" Emerson celebrates "the nonchalance of boys," their "independence" and "irresponsibility" (1940, 147).

5. I retained the transliteration of Russian names from Gibian's translation of the play. See Kharms 1971.

6. This quasi-autobiography and its comical plots about birth can be seen as yet another of Kharms's allusions to *Tristram Shandy,* in which Sterne takes the first two volumes to bring the narrative to the point of the protagonist's birth.

7. Kharms was born on December 30th (December 17th, according to the Julian calendar, which was used in Russia until the October Revolution), on the day of the prophet Daniil, after whom he was named. Kharms's wife Marina Malich relates the family legend about Kharms's birth, according to which his father Ivan Pavlovich Yuvachev, who was an ardent follower of Lev Tolstoy, was at Tolstoy's estate Yasnaya Polyana days before his wife's due date. "He called her on the phone and shouted very loudly, because telephones were bad and he could hardly hear. He said: 'Be prepared, delivery is very soon. You will give birth on December 30. And it will be a boy. We will call him Daniil.' The wife said something, but he was adamant: 'No negotiation! He will be Daniil. I said.' " (Glotser 2000, 41). For Ivan Yuvachev's note on his son's birth, see Alexandrov's chronology of Kharms's life. The English translation was published in Cornwell 1991, 32–45.

8. "Words-in-freedom" was one of the main poetic strategies of the Italian Futurists. See Marinetti's manifesto "Destruction of Syntax—Imagination without Strings—Words-in-Freedom" 1973, 95–106.

9. For a very well-balanced discussion of Kharms's relation to *zaum* poetry, see Jaccard and Ustinov 1991, 159–228.

10. The theme of the smithy appears in a number of Kharms's works. It figures prominently in his poem "Flight into Sky" (1997a, 84), and in the opening story of "Five Unfinished Narratives" (2001a, 26). A short narrative sketch from his notebook offers a possible interpretation of this theme: "Once Andrei Vasilevich (pasted a beard) walked on the street and lost his watch. Soon thereafter he died. His father, a hunchback, an older man, sat all night with a top hat and squeezed the twisted handle of his cane. All kinds of thoughts went through his head, this one among them: (I need a little wife, I need) life is a smithy" (2002a, 387).

11. Deleuze reads Nietzsche's "philosophizing with a hammer" as an aggressive mode of critical thinking (1983, 3). Friedrich Kittler maintains that once Nietzsche started hammering out his texts on a primitive typewriter, he moved "from arguments to aphorisms, from thoughts to puns, from rhetoric to telegram style," or, in short, it turned the philosopher into "a laconic" (1999, 203). Very few of Kharms's texts were typescripted. They were nevertheless hammered.

12. As early as 1925, Kharms mentions Bergson in his notes on the books he read (2002a, 122). The French philosopher reappears in Kharms's poem from the late 1930s, "Once Petrov went into a forest" (1997a, 283). Hilary Fink suggests that the postscript "against Kant" which Kharms added to the "Blue Notebook No. 10" can be explained by Kharms's adherence to Bergsonism: "The significance of Kharms's postscript might be elucidated by recalling Bergson's main criticism of Kant, namely that Kant categorically restricts man's epistemological capability to the function of the intellect: 'The human intellect is enough': such is precisely the Kantian solution" (Fink 1999, 97). However, as we have seen in the previous chapter, Kharms's, and especially Lipavsky's, anti-Kantianism should not be taken for granted.

13. See Deleuze 1990, 70.

14. The hillock is not necessarily a topographical element of a landscape or a spatial determination in general. It also appears as a temporal unit, a period of time comparable to an uphill progression. In a couplet, Kharms writes, "The hill of the forty-day lent / why, why, getting stuffed with a grain" (2002a, 383).

15. See the discussion of Lipavsky's "Investigation of Dread" in the second chapter of the present work. Also, for a discussion of the symbolism of the cockroach in *Elizabeth Bam,* see Jaccard 1991, chapter 4.

16. In Kharms's works, the elderly either don't speak or their speech is distorted and inarticulate.

17. The letter remained unsent. Kharms suggests that Raia Ilinichna Poliakova lived in an apartment that faced his room. Jaccard says that his extensive research did not yield any positive proof that such a person lived in his neighborhood. Kharms's surviving friends and acquaintances claim they have never met or heard of this person. See Jaccard 1991, 482.

18. It is interesting to note that in the post-Revolutionary period, the Adamic theme was transformed into a story of beginning anew. In one of his lesser-known plays, also entitled *Adam and Eve* (1930), Mikhail Bulgakov parodies the Soviet interpretation of the biblical theme.

19. The play is dated September 27, 1934, and signed Daniil Dandan. The marginal comment "good" was added in Kharms's handwriting, most probably at a later date.

20. On Bakhtin's connection with Konstantin Vaginov, one of the authors associated with the OBERIU, see Graham Roberts's *The Last Soviet Avant-Garde: OBERIU—Fact, Fiction, Metafiction,* especially the section "Carnivalizing the Author?" It is interesting to note how, once placed in this context, Kharms becomes easily identifiable with the figure of *iurodivy,* the holy fool, from Russian tradition. When Stalinism is seen through the prism of medieval despotism, not only writing but everything an author does becomes an incessant discourse in Aesop's language (1997, 37–38).

21. Literary historians often use the French version of the title, *Le Jeu d'Adam,* and more rarely, the English rendition, *The Service Representing Adam.*

22. Grace Frank locates this play "midway between church drama and the laicized mysteries." For a well-informed discussion of this play in the context of medieval theater, see her book *The Medieval French Drama* 1954, 74–85; see also Frank's essay "Genesis and Staging of the *Jeu d' Adam*" 1944, 7–17.

23. It seems that Kharms was particularly interested in *didascalia* and Figura as elements of *The Fall from Grace.* They figure prominently in his notes for this play. See 2002b, 109.

24. Both Tynianov and Gérard Genette insist on the importance of the literary model (or, according to Genette, the "hypotext") in parody. However, while Tynianov asserts that "the parodic attitude is nearly impossible towards the almost forgotten works" (1977, 294), Genette holds that "parody does not actually subject the hypotext to a degrading stylistic treatment but only takes it as a model or template for the construction of a new text, which, once produced, is no longer concerned with the model" (Genette 1997, 27).

25. This play was written in the same year as *The Fall from Grace* (1934). Kharms included it in the collection *Events,* which was published in *Today I Wrote Nothing* (Kharms 2007).

26. In Bernard G. Guerney's English translation, the title has been changed to *The Romance of Leonardo da Vinci* (Merezhkovsky 1928). This novel was published as the second part of Merezhkovsky's trilogy of historical novels, *Khristos i Antikhrist: trilogiia* (*Christ and Antichrist: trilogy*). It was preceded by *Smert' Bogov: Iulian Otstupnik* (*Death of Gods: Julian the Apostate*), and followed by *Antikhrist: Petr i Aleksei* (*The Antichrist: Peter and Alexei*). Kharms mentions the first book from the trilogy in his notebook for the period from December 1934 to January 1935. See Kharms 2002b, 126.

27. "Messer Leonardo" in Guerney's translation.

28. This parallel persists in theories of language from the Middle Ages until the present. For instance, in *A Thousand Plateaus: Capitalism and Schizophrenia,* Deleuze and Guattari see this parallel in terms of the semiotization of activity in writing and the cultivation of land (1987, 401).

29. Ostroukhova and Kuvshinov list some forty pseudonyms and abbreviations with which Kharms signed his works. See "Psevdonimi D. I. Kharmsa" 2003, 230–45.

30. The etymology of the word Adam points to the Hebrew word *adama,* meaning earth, soil.

31. In this sense, Kharms's gesture of casting Leonardo in the role of mythical tempter can be seen as a masked reference to Vladimir Tatlin, who was in the early 1930s experimenting with "Letatlin," a flying machine akin to Leonardo's projects. In 1929 Tatlin did illustrations for Kharms's children's story "Firstly and Secondly." For additional information about this collaboration, see Strigalev 1991. For reproductions of Tatlin's drawings, see Zhadova 1984, illustrations on pp. 298–312.

32. Jan Kott's discussion of the word "sting" is pointedly revealing: "The 'sting' (*piqure* in French), is present in 'instinct,' 'n-stinct.' It is derived from the Latin *stingere* (to sting), whose root is *stig,* as in *instigere* (to urge, to instigate). *Stigare* means to arouse, to instigate, to bite like a snake, to sting like wasp, and to prick. A 'prick' is a spear, a phallus, a sting. Contained in *in-stigare* and *instiguere* is the 'sting,' the Indo-European *steig,* and the Greek *stigma.* The 'stigmatized' are stung and bitten. The German *stechen* means to pierce, to sting, and, colloquially, to deflower a girl. Young women still untouched are said to be *stichreif: stich*—sting, *reif*—ripe, ready. But 'to sting' etymologically is not only to pierce, but also to arouse, to prod, and to urge with animal passion: 'For thou thyself has been a libertine / As sensual as the brutish sting itself' (*As You Like It* II. vii. 65–66)" (Kott 1984, 189).

33. Kharms's interest in pedagogic dialogue might have been sparked by Khlebnikov's 1912 dialogue entitled "Teacher and Student." A student who skipped classes in order to conduct his own investigations gives a lecture to his teacher on the hidden universal laws that govern language and history. In this preview of his famous "Tables of Destiny," Khlebnikov's "student" smoothly shows to the bemused "teacher" that, for example, waves of unification spread among nations in regular intervals of 413 years; that distances between European capitals are equal to the radius of the earth divided by 2π; and that there is a definite answer as to why Russian folk songs and Russian literature provide directly opposed answers to the ever-burning question, what is to be done? (Khlebnikov 1987, 286).

34. In the "Conclusion" of *Difference and Repetition,* Deleuze points out the positive aspect of stupidity: "Recall Heidegger's statement: 'What gives us most cause for thought is the fact that we do not yet think.' Thought is the highest determination, confronting stupidity as though face to face with the indetermi-

nate which is adequate to it. Stupidity (not error) constitutes the highest weakness of thought, but also the source of its highest power in that which forces it to think" (1994, 275).

35. In his "psycho-history" of Russian modernist literature from Romanticism to the present, Igor Smirnov offers a psychological reading of stupidity in the works of Kharms and other OBERIU authors. Smirnov uses their interest in stupidity to support his general schema, according to which the first avant-garde (primarily Russian futurists) represents extroverted masochism, while the second avant-garde (OBERIU) represents the case of introverted masochism, most prominently characterized by self-depersonalization. Following this schema, Smirnov argues that "the Leningrad avant-garde of the second generation compromises the text as such." This separates the OBERIU from "the principle of traditional parody, which always compromises some specific text, or a particular family of texts." According to Smirnov, Kharms pushes to the limit the principle of "compromise of the authorial mind" in his piece "The Blue Notebook No. 10." See Smirnov 1994, 290–304.

36. It should be noted that in "Laughter, Presence" Nancy analyzes Baudelaire's prose poem "The Desire to Paint." In his essay "On the Essence of Laughter," Baudelaire himself makes a distinction between laughter and joy: "Joy exists in itself, but it has various manifestations. Sometimes it is almost invisible; at others, it expresses itself in tears. Laughter is only an expression, a symptom, a diagnostic. Symptom of what? That is the question. Joy is a unity. Laughter is the expression of a double, or contradictory, feeling; and that is why a convulsion occurs" (Baudelaire 1964, 156).

37. For the source text, see Tolstoy 1963, 7–120. Alexei Tolstoy was one of the authors whose works were borrowed by the fictive writer Kozma Prutkov. Tolstoy published *Don Juan* under his own name, and his play is a serious tragedy in the tradition of Romanticism. The list of characters in Kharms's fragment closely follows Tolstoy's tragedy until the very end, when he introduces a girl, a boy, and himself, barely hidden behind the initials "Genius D.K." (1997b, 318).

38. For more on this aspect of Kharms's play, see Vishnevsky 1986, 355–66.

39. For a detailed description of the mental and physical symptoms of hunger, see the two-volume study *The Biology of Human Starvation* (Keys et al. 1950).

40. Hamsun's *Hunger* is briefly discussed in "Conversations" (Lipavskii 2005, 413). For more on Kharms and Hamsun, see Iampol'skii (1997, chapter 4). Also, it should be noted that Hamsun was very well aware of Dostoevsky's works, including *The Idiot.* The protagonist of *Hunger* is often addressed in the same way as Prince Myshkin. Contrary to Myshkin, he protests this characterization: "If a man only had a bite to eat. Bread—one of those marvelous loaves of rye bread that a man could chew on as he walked. I walked along, deciding on exactly the kind of rye bread that would be best now. I was unbelievably hungry, longed to be dead and gone, became sentimental and cried. My road to misery would never end! All

of a sudden I stopped on the street, stamped on the cobblestones, and swore aloud. What was it he had called me? Idiot?" (Hamsun 1967, 71).

41. The date and place of Kharms's death were confirmed forty-seven years later by the head of the NKVD for the Leningrad region. Prior to this confirmation, the exact place and date of his death had been the subject of much speculation. See Aleksandrov 1990, 8, and Glotser 1991, 204–9.

Chapter 5

The chapter epigraph is from Kazimir Malevich. *Sobranie sochinenii v pyati tomakh,* vol. 3 (Moscow: Gilea, 2000).

1. This term was coined by the philosopher of pragmatism Jeremy Bentham, most renowned for his invention of the panopticon. He elaborated his ideas on a "pragmatic" death in the work *Auto-Icon; or, Farther Uses of the Dead to the Living.* It would be rather instructive to compare auto-thanatographies and views on visuality and death by the antipragmatist painter and the pragmatist philosopher. For more on Bentham's "auto-thanatography," see Bozovic 2000, 81–98.

2. John Milner makes a perceptive observation that in Malevich's work the association of the black square with death can be dated to as early as 1911, when he did the drawing *At The Cemetery.* It depicts parents burying their child, and the black square appears in the foreground as the dark abyss of the grave. For reproduction of the drawing and commentary, see Milner 1996, 28.

3. In some photographs, the large canvas *The Peasant Woman* (1928–32) is hung directly under Malevich's self-portrait, and the coffin is placed farther to the left.

4. See Mikhail Meilakh's comments on the poem in Kharms 1999, 566.

5. The friendship between Kharms and Malevich lasted eight years, from 1927 to 1935.

6. The motif of writing with blood from a bird also appears in Kharms's untitled poetic drama in which the main character is described only as "Gnostic" (1997a, 317).

7. There is yet another layer of meaning to be found in the short scene "Baroness and Inkpot," in which this object is related to love and dedication. See 1997b, 374.

8. Kharms 1941, File No. 2196, KGB Archive. This part of the file is omitted in the published version, Sazhin 1998, 592–608. I am grateful to Mavei Yankelevich for sharing this source with me.

9. F1323, No. 408, Druskin Fond. For the reproduction of the entire series of drawings, see *Kharmsizdat predstavliaet* (Ershov 1995, 21–24).

10. Kharms's aunt N. I. Koliunakina lived in Detskoe Selo near Leningrad. All his life, Kharms visited her frequently and gladly.

11. For Kharms's work on self portraits, see Mazin 1995.

12. For example, in the drawing *Astronomer,* it is possible to discern lines that

are used to depict not objects but the imaginary movement of the astronomer's gaze through the telescope and toward the object he is observing.

13. In a diary entry from the late 1930s, Kharms writes about various kinds of literary translations, ranging from "interesting" ones to those that are hard to understand. However, he notes, there are translations that "are impossible to read. There are some strange letters: some are nothing, and the others have no understandable meaning. Once I saw a translation that didn't have a single meaningful letter. Only some squiggle. I turned that translation in my hands for a long while. Really strange translation!" (Kharms 1992, 507).

14. This is a previously unpublished work. It is held at the Stedelijk Museum Archives in Amsterdam, Box 164, 21/b.

15. Partially illegible.

16. The last word is illegible. It could be "unity."

17. In his esoteric interpretation of the "Real" diagram, Andrei Rossomakhin assigns great importance not only to the number of spikes, but also to the color of the diagram and the number of letters in the word "Real." See Rossomakhin 2005.

18. Kharms uses the word *sluchai,* the same word that serves as the title of his anthology, *Events.* As I mentioned earlier, this word also translates as "case."

19. For full-color reproductions of all diagrams except "Case No. 3: The Saint," see the special OBERIU issue of the journal *Teatr* 1991.

20. Not only in the Lipavsky case does this transformation occur: the general association of downfall with transformation of an abstract form into a recognizable image is present already in the series The Process of Falling, or Annihilation, where a red drop of "lower feelings" turns into a fireball that falls into burning flames.

21. For a reproduction of this print and Ershov's useful comments, see Ershov 2006, 24, 262–83.

22. Kharms and his friends were familiar with Goethe's controversial scientific tract. In "Conversations," Lipavsky characterized *Theory of Colors* as an "ingenious book" (Lipavskii 2005, 349).

23. The symbolism of gold as pure light is one of the central issues of Pavel Florensky's ontology of icon painting. Unlike Goethe, he insists on the distinction between gold and the color yellow, emphasizing that "gold is pure 'admixtureless' light, a light impossible to put on the same plane with paint" (1996, 123); this argument about the symbolism of gold culminates in the following claim: "*the icon is executed upon light*—the sentence perfectly expressing the whole ontology of icon painting" (136). Examination of the use of gold in sacred portraiture leads Florensky to conclude that "the nearest kin to the icon is the Egyptian [death] mask," which relates the symbolism of light to immortality. He says that "the sacred formula or everlasting life inscribed for the deceased was 'I am Osiris' " (161). Kharms inscribes this very formula at the top of his scroll-drawing from 1931 (see chapter 2).

24. In both cases, Kharms does not provide an explanation of this numerical determination. "Makarov and Petersen" is the seventeenth item in *Events* (Kharms 2007).

25. A superintendent or caretaker is sometimes replaced in Kharms's writings by a watchman or militiaman as the lowest law enforcement official.

26. Kharms brings together the figures of window, sphere, and watchman in a curious narrative that begins with a look through the window, through which the observer sees an ordinary street with passing trams, and then a "pipe" (*truba*), through which he sees the earth. He then engages in a conversation with a *bolid,* "an inhabitant of space," and *grafin,* "an inhabitant of heaven" (1997b, 23). In ancient Greek, the word *bolid* designates a flaming ball or a glimmering sphere. The name of the second interlocutor is related to *griffon,* the mythical being that has a lion's body and bird's head. In the middle ages, griffons were considered the keepers of the heavenly gates. Kharms uses the Russian word *grafin,* a carafe or bottle, which trivializes the mythological figure.

27. See Sazhin 1998, 593. Keeping the pretense of legality, the secret police kept immaculate records that required a signature of at least one witness to each house arrest. This was the only official document that Kharms's wife Marina Malich brought with her into exile. See Glotser 2000, 110.

28. It overlooked Nevsky Prospekt.

29. The photograph has been published in many recent publications of Kharms's works. See, for example, Glotser 2000. Ershov compares this photograph with Yves Klein's famous 1960 photograph *Leap into the Void* (Ershov 2006, 273).

30. Matvei Yankelevich's translation of one section of the interview with Valery Podoroga was published in a special double issue of *The Emergency Gazette* (Podoroga 2000).

31. See, for example, his 1933 untitled poem "Once upon a time lived a man in the building number thirty three" (1997a, 237) or "Variations" (281).

32. The anthology *Events* closes with the story "Pakin and Rakukin" in which Kharms offers a cartoonish and laconic view of death as departure from the soul. Here, death comes as a result of an especially vigorous exchange of gestures. See Kharms 2007, 81–82.

33. To my knowledge, Kharms mentions Meyerhold only twice: in this 1935 fragment, "Pressing her palms tight together, one person said painfully: 'I don't need money, but will to live. I am looking for rapture, not for riches. I don't need a wealthy husband, but a talent, director, Meyerhold!'" (1997b, 88); and in one of his letters to the actress Klaudia Pugachova, where he says simply that "Meyerhold did nothing" (2001a, 76). For more on biomechanics and expressive movement, see Law and Gordon 1996.

34. Among his writings about gesture in Brecht's theater, Walter Benjamin states that in epic theater, the actor's "gesture demonstrates the social significance and applicability of dialectics" (Benjamin 1977b, 12).

35. For an excellent discussion of the narrative role of *gestus* in Brecht, see Pavis "On Brecht's Notion of *Gestus*" in his book *Languages of the Stage* (1982).

36. The Polish director and visual artist Tadeusz Kantor elaborated the idea of the "bio-object" during his work on Happenings and on Stanislaw Witkiewicz's plays. He talks about the bio-object in his manifesto/tract "The Impossible Theater":

> A man with a wooden board on his back
> who is on the verge of insanity
> is an unusual case of
> absurd anatomy:
> being completely focused within
> the objectlike growth
> of his body,
> he is like a martyr crucified
> on himself.
> (Kantor 1993, 102)

37. This miniature appears in one of Kharms's lists of short works that may have been one of the working drafts of *Events.* See F1232, No. 275, Druskin Fond.

38. Interestingly, Lidia Ginzburg makes virtually the same observation. See Ginzburg quoted in Bulgakova 2005, 11.

39. See, for example, 2002a, 73, and 2002b, 30.

40. In the draft of the ballet, Kharms considered using a 12-cell system. See F1232, No. 335, Druskin Fond.

41. The open angle: 3-8-1. Number nine: they go back to cell 6 and "sit on a chair," and then follow the path 6-5-8-7-1.

42. Jaccard briefly compares Henri Michaux's *Plume* narratives with Kharms. See 1991, 242–43.

43. In Russian, *dobela* means "incandescence."

44. In Latin, *desum* means literally "to fail."

45. The present citations are taken from the epigraph to the chapter on Baudelaire in Lacoue-Labarthe's *Musica Ficta* (1994, 1).

46. In the existing English translations, Kharms's spelling has been corrected. See Kharms 1971, 49, and 1993, 150.

47. See Kharms 2007, 265.

48. For the original, see Vvedenskii 1993, 78.

49. This is Kharms's only play staged after the OBERIU performance of *Elizabeth Bam.* It opened at the Leningrad Marionette Theater in October 1935. The director, L. V. Shaporina, noted that Kharms finished the play by August 8 of the same year. For more on this production, see Sazhin's note in Kharms 1997c, 308.

50. This opposition between song as natural language and writing as alienated

language is Rousseau's legacy. In *Of Grammatology,* Derrida famously deconstructs this doctrine in the chapter dedicated to Rousseau's *The Essay on the Origin of Languages* (Derrida 1974).

51. Very little has been written on Kharms and music, and virtually nothing on his "verbal scores." The only extensive discussion of the importance of music in Kharms's circle is the essay by V. V. Feschenko, "Chinari i muzyka," in *Russkaia literatura* (Feschenko 2005, 83–102).

52. See F1232, No. 350, Druskin Fond. This version was published in the fourth volume of Kharms's *Collected Works* edited by Mikhail Meilakh and Vladimir Erl (Kharms 1988b) and in *Neizdanny Kharms,* edited by Valery Sazhin (Kharms 2001a).

53. Throughout the text Kharms misspells Gilels's last name. As we are going to see, this slight error makes his writing consistent with his argument about music.

54. It should be noted that Kharms uses the very same locution that was reportedly used by Vvedensky to describe him. See, for instance, Nakhimovsky 1982, 7.

55. It was performed at the court of Louis XIV. For more on this dance, see Hilton 1981.

Conclusion

The epigraph is from Yakov Druskin, "Vestniki i ikh razgovori." In *Sborishche druzei, ostavlennykh sud'boiu,* vol. 1, Valerii Sazhin, ed. (Moscow: Ladomir, 1998), 774.

1. Pessoa 2001, 271.

2. See F1232, No. 76, Druskin Fond.

3. In his notebook he wrote "Messenger, that's me" (2002b, 58).

Works Cited

Abirached, Robert. 1978. *La Crise du personage dans le théâtre moderne.* Paris: Grasset.

Agamben, Giorgio. 1991. *Language and Death: The Place of Negativity.* Trans. Karen E. Pinkus and Michael Hardt. Minneapolis: University of Minnesota Press.

———. 1999. *Potentialities: Collected Essays in Philosophy.* Trans. Daniel Heller-Roazen. Stanford, Calif.: Stanford University Press.

———. 2000. *Means Without End: Notes on Politics.* Trans. Vincenzo Binetti and Cesare Casarino. Minneapolis: University of Minnesota Press.

Aleksandrov, Anatolii. 1990. "Mesto smerti Daniila Kharmsa?" *Literaturnaia Gazeta,* February 21, 8.

Alpatov, V. M. 1991. *Istoriia odnogo mifa: Marr i marrizm.* Moscow: Nauka.

Aristotle. 1980. *Aristotle's Categories and Propositions (De Interpretatione).* Trans. Hippocrates G. Apostle. Grinnell, Iowa: Peripatetic Press.

———. 1987. *Poetics.* Trans. Stephen Halliwell. Chapel Hill: University of North Carolina Press.

Artaud, Antonin. 1958. *The Theater and Its Double.* Trans. Mary Caroline Richards. New York: Grove Press.

Atherton, Patrick J. 1976. "The Neoplatonic 'One' and the Trinitarian 'ARXH,'" in *The Significance of Neoplatonism. Studies in Neoplatonism.* Vol. 1. Ed. R. Baine Harris. Norfolk, Va.: International Society for Neoplatonic Studies.

Attridge, Derek. 1984. "Language as Imitation: Jakobson, Joyce, and the Art of Onomatopoeia." *MLN* 99 (5), 1116–40.

Auerbach, Erich. 1953. *Mimesis: The Representation of Reality in Western Literature.* Trans. Willard R. Trask. Princeton, N.J.: Princeton University Press.

———. 1959. *Scenes from the Drama of European Literature.* New York: Meridian.

Bachelard, Gaston. 1983. *Water and Dreams: An Essay on the Imagination of Matter.* Trans. Edith R. Farrell. Dallas, Tex.: Pegasus Foundation.

———. 1988. *Air and Dreams: An Essay on the Imagination of Movement.* Trans. Edith R. Farrell. Dallas, Tex.: The Dallas Institute.

Badiou, Alain. 1999. *Manifesto for Philosophy.* Trans. Norman Madarasz. Albany: State University of New York Press.

———. 2000. *Deleuze: The Clamor of Being.* Trans. Louise Burchill. Minneapolis: University of Minnesota Press.

Bakhterev, Igor. 1984. "Kogda my byli molodymi," in *Vospominaniia o N. Zabolotskom.* Ed. E. V. Zabolotskaia, A. V. Medvedev, and N. N. Zabolotskii. 57–100. Moscow: Sovetskii Pisatel'.

Barthes, Roland. 1977. *Image-Music-Text.* Trans. Stephen Heath. New York: Noonday Press.

Bataille, Georges. 1993. *The Accursed Share: An Essay on General Economy, Vol. II.* Trans. Robert Hurley. New York: Zone Books.

Baudelaire, Charles. 1964. *The Painter of Modern Life and Other Essays.* Trans. Jonathan Mayne. London: Phaidon Press.

Beckett, Samuel. 1954. *Waiting for Godot.* New York: Grove Press.

Benjamin, Walter. 1998. *The Origin of German Tragic Drama.* Trans. John Osborne. London: Verso.

———. 1977b. *Understanding Brecht.* Trans. Anna Bostock. London: Verso.

———. 1999. *Selected Writings, Volume 2: 1927–1934.* Trans. Rodney Livingstone. Cambridge, Mass.: Harvard University Press.

Bennett, Jonathan. 1996. "What Events Are." In *Events,* ed. Roberto Casati and Achille Varzi. Aldershot, England, and Brookfield, Vt.: Dartmouth Press. 137–51.

Bergson, Henri. 1999. *Laughter: An Essay on the Meaning of the Comic.* Trans. Cloudesley Brereton and Fred Rothwell. Los Angeles: Green Integer.

Bernstein, Susan. 1998. *Virtuosity of the Nineteenth Century: Performing Music and Language in Heine, Liszt, and Baudelaire.* Stanford, Calif.: Stanford University Press.

Bevington, David, ed. 1975. *Medieval Drama.* Boston: Houghton Mifflin.

Blanchot, Maurice. 1993. *The Infinite Conversation.* Trans. Susan Hanson. Minneapolis: Minnesota University Press.

———. 1995. *The Writing of Disaster.* Trans. Ann Smock. Lincoln: University of Nebraska Press.

Boersma, Linda S. 1989. "On Art, Art Analysis and Art Education: The Theoretical Charts of Kazimir Malevich." In *Kazimir Malevich: Leningrad, Moscow, Amsterdam; 1878–1935,* ed. Y. Korolev and N. Petrova. Leningrad: State Russian Museum / Amsterdam: Stedelijk Museum, 206–23.

Bois, Yves-Alain, and Rosalind Krauss. 1997. *Formless: A User's Guide.* New York: Zone Books.

Boole, George. 1854. *An Investigation of the Laws of Thought.* London: Watton and Maberly; Cambridge: Macmillan.

Bowlt, John E. 1998. "The Cow and the Violin: Toward a History of Russian Dada." In *The Eastern European Dada Orbit: Russia, Georgia, Ukraine, Central Europe, and Japan.* Ed. Gerald Janecek. New York: G. K. Hall. 137–63.

Boym, Svetlana. 1991. *Death in Quotation Marks: Cultural Myths of the Modern Poet.* Cambridge, Mass.: Harvard University Press.

Bozovic, Miran. 2000. "The Body and 'Psycho'; or, of 'Farther Uses of the Dead to the Living.'" *Umbr(a): A Journal of the Unconscious,* no. 1, 81–98.

Brecht, Bertolt. 1957. *Brecht on Theatre: The Development of an Aesthetic.* Trans. John Willet. New York: Hill and Wang.

Breton, Andre. 1972. *Manifestos of Surrealism.* Trans. Richard Seaver and Helen R. Lane. Ann Arbor: University of Michigan Press.

———. 1987. *Mad Love.* Trans. Mary Ann Caws. Lincoln: University of Nebraska Press.

Bulgakova, Oksana. 2005. *Fabrika zhestov.* Moscow: Novoe literaturnoe obozrenie.

Burenina, Olga. 2000. ". . . Quia Absurdum." *Die Welt der Slaven* 45, 265–84.

Caillois, Roger. 1973. *La dissymetrie.* Paris: Gallimard.

Cantor, Georg. 1955. *Contributions to the Founding of the Theory of Transfinite Numbers.* Trans. Philip E. B. Jourdain. New York: Dover.

Carrick, Neil. 1998. *Daniil Kharms: Theologian of the Absurd.* Birmingham Slavonic Monographs, No. 28. Birmingham, UK: Centre for Russian and East European Studies, University of Birmingham.

Cohn, Robert Greer. 1977. "Mallarmé's Windows." *Yale French Studies* No. 54, 22–31.

Cooke, Raymond. 1986. "Chlebnikov's 'Grid' (*reshetka*): A Missing Key to *Nochnoi Obysk*?" In *Velimir Chlebnikov (1885–1922): Myth and Reality; Amsterdam Symposium on the Centenary of Velimir Chlebnikov,* ed. Willem G. Weststeijn. Amsterdam: Rodopi, 187–216.

Cornwell, Neil, ed. 1991. *Daniil Kharms and the Poetics of the Absurd: Essays and Materials.* New York: St. Martin's Press.

Dauben, Joseph Warren. 1979. *Georg Cantor, His Mathematics and Philosophy of the Infinite.* Cambridge, Mass.: Harvard University Press.

Davidson, Donald. 2001. *Essays on Actions and Events.* Oxford: Clarendon Press.

Deleuze, Gilles. 1983. *Nietzsche and Philosophy.* Trans. Hugh Tomlinson. New York: Columbia University Press.

———. 1990. *The Logic of Sense.* Trans. Mark Lester. New York: Columbia University Press.

———. 1993. *The Fold.* Trans. Tom Conley. Minneapolis: University of Minnesota Press.

———. 1994. *Difference and Repetition.* Trans. Paul Patton. New York: Columbia University Press.

———. 1997. *Essays Clinical and Critical.* Trans. Daniel W. Smith and Micael A. Greco. Minneapolis: University of Minnesota Press.

Deleuze, Gilles, and Felix Guattari. 1987. *A Thousand Plateaus: Capitalism and Schizophrenia.* Trans. Brian Massumi. Minneapolis: University of Minnesota Press.

———. 1994. *What Is Philosophy?* Trans. Hugh Tomlinson and Graham Burchell. New York: Columbia University Press.

Derrida, Jacques. 1973. *Speech and Phenomena and Other Essays on Husserl's Theory of Signs.* Trans. David B. Allison. Evanston, Ill.: Northwestern University Press.

———.1976. *Of Grammatology.* Trans. Gayatri Chakravorty Spivak. Baltimore: Johns Hopkins University Press.

———. 1978. *Writing and Difference.* Trans. Alan Bass. Chicago: University of Chicago Press.

Dlugach, B. T. 1994. "Problema vremeni v filosofii I. Kanta i P. Florenskogo." In *Kant i filosofia v Rossii,* ed. Z. A. Kamenskii and V. A. Zhuchkov. Moscow: Nauka, 186–211.

Doyle, Arthur Conan. 1994. *Sherlock Holmes: The Major Stories with Contemporary Essays.* New York: St. Martin's Press.

Druskin, Iakov. 1988. *Vblizi vestnikov.* Ed. Orlov, G. Washington, D.C.: Frager.

———. 1998. "Zvezda bessmyslitsy" in *Sborische druzei, ostavlennikh sudboi, Tom 1,* ed. Valerii Sazhin. 549–642. Moscow: Ladomir.

———. 1999–2001. *Dnevniki.* 2 vols. St. Petersburg: Akademicheskii proekt.

Eisenstein, Sergei. 1988. *Writings 1992–1934.* Trans. Richard Taylor. London: BFI.

Emerson, Ralph Waldo. 1940. *The Complete Essays and Other Writings.* New York: Random House.

Ershov, Gleb. 1995. "Sem dnei tvorenia Daniila Iuvacheva," in *Kharmsizdat Predstavliaet: issledovania, esse, vospominania, katalog vystavki, bibliografia,* ed. Mikhail Karasik and Valerii Sazhin. 20–34. St. Petersburg: Kharmsizdat.

Ershov, Gleb, ed. 2006. *Risunki Kharmsa.* St. Petersburg: Izdatel'stvo Ivana Lambakha.

Esslin, Martin. 1961. *The Theater of the Absurd.* New York: Anchor Books.

Evreinoff, Nikolai. 1927. *The Theatre in Life.* New York: Brentano's Publishers.

Feschenko, V. V. 2005. "Chinari i muzyka." *Russkaia literatura: istoriko-literaturny zhurnal.* No. 4, 83–102.

Fink, Hilary L. 1999. *Bergson and Russian Modernism, 1900–1930.* Evanston, Ill.: Northwestern University Press.

Florenskii, Pavel. 1914. *Stolp i utverzhdenie istini.* Moscow: Tovarishchestvo tipograpii A. I. Mamontova.

———. 1996. *Iconostasis.* Trans. Donald Sheehan and Olga Andrejev. New York: St. Vladimir's Seminary Press.

Foucault, Michel. 1970. *The Order of Things: An Archaeology of Human Sciences.* New York: Random House.

———. 1972. *The Archaeology of Knowledge and the Discourse on Language.* New York: Barnes and Noble Books.

———. 1990. "Maurice Blanchot: The Thought from the Outside." In *Foucault/Blanchot,* trans. Brian Massumi, 7–60. New York: Zone Books.

Frank, Grace. 1944. "Genesis and Staging of the *Jeu d'Adam.*" *PMLA,* lix, 7–17.

———. 1954. *The Medieval French Drama.* Oxford: Clarendon Press.

Frege, Gotlob. 1968. *The Foundations of Arithmetic: A Logico-Mathematical Enquiry into the Concept of Number.* Trans. J. L. Austin. Evanston, Ill.: Northwestern University Press.

Genette, Gérard. 1997. *Palimpsests: Literature in the Second Degree.* Trans. Channa Newman and Claude Doubinsky. Lincoln: University of Nebraska Press.

Ghyka, Matila. 1952. *Philosophie et mystique du nombre.* Paris: Edition Payot.

Ginsburg, Lydia. 1991. *On Psychological Prose.* Trans. Judson Rosengrant. Princeton, N.J.: Princeton University Press.

Ginzburg, Lidia. 1982. *O starom i novom. Stat'i i ocherki.* Leningrad: Sovetskii Pisatel'.

Glotser, Vladimir. 1989. "Alisa Poret rasskazyvaet i risuet." *Panorama isskustv,* No. 12, 392–409.

———. 1991. "K istorii poslednego aresta i gibeli Daniila Kharmsa." *Russkaia literatura,* No. 1, 204–9.

———. 2000. *Marina Durnovo. Moi muzh Daniil Kharms.* Moscow: B.S.G. Press.

Goethe, Johann Wolfgang von. 1983. *Scientific Studies.* Trans. Douglas Miller. New York: Suhrkamp Publishers.

Groïs, Boris. 1982. "Malevich i Haidegger." *Wiener Slawisticher Almanach* 9, 355–66.

Guenon, Rene. 1996. *Symbolism of the Cross.* Trans. Angus Macnab. Ghent, Belgium: Sophia Perrenis et Universalis.

Hacking, Ian. 1990. *The Taming of Chance.* Cambridge: Cambridge University Press.

Hamsun, Knut. 1967. *Hunger.* Trans. Robert Bly. New York: Farrar, Straus, and Giroux.

Heidegger, Martin. 1971. *Poetry, Language, Thought.* Trans. Albert Hofstadter. New York: Harper and Row.

———. 1977. *The Question Concerning Technology and Other Essays.* Trans. William Lovitt. New York: Random House.

Heinonen, Jussi. 2003. *Eto i to v povesti* Starukha *Daniila Kharmsa.* Helsinki: Helsinki University Press.

Hilton, Wendy. 1981. *Dance of Court and Theater: The French Noble Style 1690–1725.* Princeton, N.J.: Princeton Book Company.

Iampol'skii, Mikhail. 1996. *Demon i labirint: diagrammy, deformatsii, mimesis.* Moscow: Novoe literaturnoe obozrenie.

———. 1997. *Bespamiatstvo kak istok: Chitaya Kharmsa.* Moscow: Novoe literaturnoe obozrenie.

Ichin, Kornelia, ed. 2006. *Kharms – Avangard.* Belgrade, Serbia: School of Filology, Belgrade University.

Ichin, Kornelia, and Sergei Kudriavtsev, eds. 2006. *Poet Aleksandr Vvedenskii: sbornik materialov.* Moscow: Gilea.

Irwin, John T. 1980. *American Hieroglyphics: The Symbol of the Egyptian Hieroglyphics in the American Renaissance.* New Haven, Conn.: Yale University Press.

Iuvachev, Ivan Pavlovich. 1909. *The Russian Bastille, or The Schlusselburg Fortress.* Trans. A. S. Rappaport. London: Chatto and Windus.

———. 1915. *Voina i vera: ocherki vsemirnoi voiny 1914–1915.* St. Petersburg: Tip. Pervoi petrogradskoi trudovoi arteli.

Jaccard, Jean-Phillipe. 1991. *Daniil Harms et le fin de l'avant-garde russe.* Bern: Peter Lang.

———. 1995. "Vozvyshenie v tvorchestve Daniila Kharmsa." In *Kharmsizdat Predstavliaet: issledovania, esse, vospominania, katalog vystavki, bibliografia.* Ed. Mikhail Karasik and Valerii Sazhin. 8–19. St. Petersburg: Kharmsizdat.

Jaccard, Jean-Phillipe, and Andrei Ustinov. 1991. "Zaumnik Daniil Kharms: Nachalo puti," *Wiener Slawisticher Almanach* 27, 159–228.

Jakobson, Roman, and Morris Halle. 1956. *The Fundamentals of Language.* The Hague: Mouton.

Janecek, Gerald. 1984. *The Look of Russian Literature: Avant-Garde Visual Experiments, 1900–1930.* Princeton, N.J.: Princeton University Press.

Kant, Immanuel. 2000. *Critique of the Power of Judgement.* Trans. Paul Guyer and Eric Matthews. Cambridge: Cambridge University Press.

———. 1998. *Critique of Pure Reason.* Transl. Paul Guyer and Allen W. Wood. Cambridge: Cambridge University Press.

Kantor, Tadeusz. 1993. *A Journey Through Other Spaces: Essays and Manifestos, 1944–1990.* Trans. Michal Kobialka. Berkeley: University of California Press.

Karasik, Irina. 1991. "Malevich as His Contemporaries Saw Him." In *Malevich: Artist and Theoretician.* Ed. Evgeniya Petrova. 92–198. Moscow: Avant-Garde.

Karasik, Mikhail, ed. 2003. *Kharmsizdat predstavliaet: Russkii dada, OBERIU Box, listkonstruktivizm, leningradskii literaturny andergraund.* St. Petersburg: The State Russian Museum.

Karasik, Mikhail, and Valerii Sazhin, eds. 1997. *Kharmsizdat predstavliaet: Sovetskii eros 20–30 godov.* St. Petersburg: Kharmsizdat.

Karasik, Mikhail, and Valerii Sazhin, eds. 1998. *Kharmsizdat predstavliaet: Avangardnoe povedenie.* St. Petersburg: Kharmsizdat.

Katsis, L. F. 1994. "Prolegomeny k teologii OBERIU," *Literaturnoe obozrenie.* Vol. 3/4, 94–101.

Keys, Ancel, and Ernst Simonson. 1950. *The Biology of Human Starvation.* Minneapolis: University of Minnesota Press.

Kharms, Daniil. 1971. *Russia's Lost Literature of the Absurd: A Literary Discovery; Selected Works of Daniill Kharms and Alexander Vvedensky.* Ed. and trans. George Gibian. Ithaca, N.Y.: Cornell University Press.

———. 1978a. *Sobranie proizvedenii: 1926–1929.* Ed. Mikail Meilakh and Vladimir Erl'. Vol. 1. Bremen, Germany: K-Presse.

———. 1978b. *Sobranie proizvedenii: 1929–1930.* Ed. Mikail Meilakh and Vladimir Erl'. Vol. 2. Bremen, Germany: K-Presse.

———. 1980. *Sobranie proizvedenii: 1931–1933.* Ed. Mikail Meilakh and Vladimir Erl'. Vol. 3. Bremen, Germany: K-Presse.

———. 1988a. *Polet b nebesa: stikhi, proza, dramy, pis'ma,* Ed. Anatolii Aleksandrov. Leningrad: Sovetskii Pisatel'.

———. 1988b. *Sobranie proizvedenii: 1933–1939*. Ed. Mikail Meilakh and Vladimir Erl'. Vol. 4. Bremen, Germany: K-Presse.

———. 1992. *Minuvshe*, No. 11 (1992). "Dnevniki, Zapisnie knizhki, marginalia." Edited by A. Ustinov and V. Kobrinsky.

———. 1993. *Incidences*. Trans. Neil Cornwell. London: Serpent's Tail.

———. 1997a. *Polnoe sobranie sochinenii: Stikhotvorenia*. Ed. Valerii Sazhin. Vol. 1. St. Petersburg: Akademicheskii Proekt.

———. 1997b. *Polnoe sobranie sochinenii: Proza i stsenki dramaticheskikh proizvedenia*. Ed. Valerii Sazhin. Vol. 2. St. Petersburg: Akademicheskii Proekt.

———. 1997c. *Polnoe sobranie sochinenii: Proizvedenia dlia detei*. Ed. Valerii Sazhin. Vol. 3. St. Petersburg: Akademicheskii Proekt.

———. 1999. *Dnei Katibr: izbrannye stikhotvorenia, poemi, dramaticheskie proizvedenia*, Ed. Mikhail Meilakh. Moscow: Gilea.

———. 2001a. *Polnoe sobranie sochinenii: Neizdanny Kharms: Traktaty i statii; Pisma*. Ed. Valerii Sazhin. Supplement to vols. 1–3. St. Petersburg: Akademicheskii Proekt.

———. 2001b. *Lapa*. Trans. Matvei Yankelevich. *PAJ: A Journal of Performance and Art* 23, no. 2 (May), 89–101.

———. 2002a. *Zapisnye knizhki: Dnevnik*. Vol. 1. Sazhin, Valerii, and Jean-Phillipe Jaccard, eds. St. Petersburg: Akademicheskii Proekt.

———. 2002b. *Zapisnye knizhki: Dnevnik*. Vol. 2. Sazhin, Valerii, and Jean-Phillipe Jaccard, eds. St. Petersburg: Akademicheskii Proekt.

———. 2007. *Today I Wrote Nothing: The Selected Writings of Daniil Kharms*. Trans. Matvei Yankelevich. Woodstock, N.Y.: Overlook Press.

———. n.d. Druskin Fond. F1232. St. Petersburg: Manuscript Division, Public Library Saltikov-Schedrin.

———. n.d. Box 164. Amsterdam: Stedelijk Museum Archives.

———. File no. 4246-31. 1931–32. Moscow: KGB Archive. Published in Sazhin, Valerii, ed. 1998. *Sborishche druzei, ostavlennykh sud'boiu*. Vol. 2. Moscow: Ladomir.

———. File No. 2196-41. 1941–42. Moscow: KGB Archive. Sazhin, Valerii, ed. 1998. *Sborishche druzei, ostavlennykh sud'boiu*. Vol. 2. Moscow: Ladomir.

Kharms, Daniil, Vvedenskii, Alexander, Tufanov, Aleksander, Kalashnikov, Peter, Bakhterev, Igor. 1931–32. P 81210, vols. 1–2. [The Collection of Kharms, Daniil.] Moscow: KGB Archive.

Khlebnikov, Velimir. 1968. *Sobranie proizvedenia Velimira Khlebnikova*. Ed. Y. Tynianov and N. Stepanov. 4 vols. Munich: Wilhelm Fink Werlag.

———. 1987. *Collected Works*. Vol. 1, *Letters and Theoretical Writings*. Trans. Paul Schmidt. Cambridge, Mass.: Harvard University Press.

———. 1989. *Collected Works*. Vol. 2, *Prose, Plays, and Supersagas*. Trans. Paul Schmidt. Cambridge, Mass.: Harvard University Press.

———. 1997. *Collected Works.* Vol. 3, *Selected Poems.* Trans. Paul Schmidt. Cambridge, Mass.: Harvard University Press.

Kierkegaard, Soren. 1957. *The Concept of Dread.* Trans. Walter Lowrie. Princeton, N.J.: Princeton University Press.

Kittler, Friedrich. 1999. *Gramophone, Film, Typewriter.* Trans. Geoffrey Winthrop-Young and Michael Wutz. Stanford, Calif.: Stanford University Press.

Klein, Richard. 1970. "Straight Lines and Arabesques: Metaphors of Metaphor," *Yale French Studies,* no. 45, 64–86.

Kobrinskii, Alexandr A. 2000. *Poetika "OBERIU" v kontekste russkogo literaturnogo avangarda.* 2 vols. Moscow: Culturological Lyceum.

———, ed. 2004. *Aleksandr Vvedenskii i russkii avangard.* St. Petersburg: RGPU, A. I. Gertsena.

———. 2005. *Mortira i svecha: k stoletiu so dnia rozhdenia Daniila Kharmsa.* St. Petersburg: RGPU, A. I. Gertsena.

Lacan, Jacques. 1987. "Television." *October* 40 (Spring), 6–50.

Lacoue-Labarthe, Philippe. 1994. *Musica Ficta (Figures of Wagner).* Trans. Felicia Mccarren. Stanford, Calif.: Stanford University Press.

Lacoue-Labarthe, Philippe, and Jean-Luc Nancy. 1988. *The Literary Absolute: The Theory of Literature in German Romanticism.* Trans. Philip Barnard and Cheryl Lester. Albany: State University of New York Press.

Law, Alma, and Mel Gordon. 1996. *Meyerhold, Eisenstein and Biomechanics: Actor Training in Revolutionary Russia.* Jefferson, N.C.: McFarland.

Lebel, Robert, and Isabelle Waldberg, eds. 1995. *Encyclopaedia Acephalica.* London: Atlas Press.

Leroi-Gourhan, Andre. 1993. *Gesture and Speech.* Trans. Anna Bostock Berger. Cambridge, Mass.: MIT Press.

Lévi-Strauss, Claude. 1973. *Tristes Tropiques.* Trans. John and Doreen Weightman. New York: Penguin Books.

Lezra, Jacques. 1997. *Unspeakable Subjects: The Genealogy of the Event in Early Modern Europe.* Stanford, Calif.: Stanford University Press.

Lipavskaia, Tamara. 1984. "Vstrechi s Nikolaem Alekseevichem i ego druziami." In *Vospominaniya o N. Zabolotskom.* Ed. E. V. Zabolotskaia, A. V. Medved'ev, and N. N. Zabolotskii. 47–56. Moscow: Sovetskii Pisatel'.

Lipavskii, Leonid. 2005. *Issledovanie uzhasa.* Ed. Valerii Sazhin. Moscow: Ad Marginem.

Lyotard, Jean-François. 1992. "Mainmise." *Philosophy Today* 36, no. 4/4 (Winter), 419–27.

———. 1994. *Lessons in the Analytic of the Sublime.* Trans. Elizabeth Rottenberg. Stanford, Calif.: Stanford University Press.

Malevich, Kasimir. 1959. *The Non-Objective World.* Chicago: Paul Theobald.

———. 1968. *Essays on Art: Volume 1, 1915–1928.* Trans. Xenia Glowacki-Prus. Copenhagen: Borgen.

———. 2000a. *Sobranie sochinenii v pyati tomakh.* Vol. 3. Moscow: Gilea.

———. 2000b. *Poeziya.* Ed. Alexandra Shatskikh. Moscow: Epifania.

Mallarmé, Stephane. 1982. *Selected Poetry and Prose.* Ed. Mary Ann Caws. Trans. Barbara Johnson. New York: New Directions.

Man, Paul de. 1984. *The Rhetoric of Romanticism.* New York: Columbia University Press.

Mann, Thomas. 1964. *The Magic Mountain.* Trans. H. T. Lowe-Porter. New York: Knopf.

Marcade, Jean-Claude. 1978a. "An Approach to the Writings of Malevich." *Soviet Union/Union Sovietique* 5, part 2, 225–39.

———. 1978b. "What is Suprematism?" In *Kasimir Malewitsch zum 100 Gebustag.* Cologne: Galerie Gmurzynsk, 182–95.

Marcus, Solomon. 1967. *Algebraic Linguistics: Analytical Models.* New York: Academic Press.

———. 1970. *Poetica Matematica.* Bucharest, Romania: Editura Academiei.

———. 1974. *Matematička poetika.* Trans. of *Poetica Matematica* into Serbian by Borislav Krstic and Dragan Stojanovic. Belgrade, Serbia: Nolit.

Marinetti, F. T. 1973. "Destruction of Syntax—Imagination Without Strings—Words in Freedom." In *Futurist Manifestos.* Ed. Appolonio Umbro, 95–106. New York: Viking Press.

Markov, Vladimir. 1969. *Russian Futurism: A History.* London: MacGibbon and Kee.

Mauss, Marcel. 1950. *The Gift: The Form and Reason for Exchange in Archaic Societies.* Trans. W. D. Halls. New York: Norton.

Mazin, Viktor. 2006. "Avtoportrety Daniila Kharmsa." In *Risunki Kharmsa,* ed. Gleb Ershov. St. Petersburg: Izdatel'stvo Ivana Lambakha, 319–34.

Meilakh, Mikhail. 1987. "O 'Elizavete Bam' Daniila Kharmsa." *Stanford Slavic Studies* 1, 163–205.

Merezhkovsky, Dmitry. 1928. *The Romance of Leonardo da Vinci.* Trans. Bernard Guilbert Guerney. New York: Modern Library.

Meyrink, Gustav. 1995. *The Golem.* Trans. Mike Mitchell. Riverside, Calif.: Ariadne.

Michelson, Annette. 1982. "De Stijl, Its Other Face: Abstraction and Cacaphony, or What Was the Matter with Hegel?" *October,* no. 22 (Fall), 5–26.

Milner-Gulland, R. R. 1970. "'Left Art' in Leningrad: The OBERIU Declaration." *Oxford Slavonic Papers: New Series* 3, 65–75.

Milner, John. 1996. *Kazimir Malevich and the Art of Geometry.* New Haven, Conn.: Yale University Press.

Nakhimovsky, Alice Stone. 1982. "Laughter in the Void: An Introduction to the Writings of Daniil Kharms and Alexander Vvedenskii." *Wiener Slawistischer Almanach.* Special volume 5. Wien, Austria: 1–191.

Nakhimovsky, Alexander, and Alice Stone Nakhimovsky, eds. 1985. *The Semiotics of Russian Cultural History: Essays by Iurii M. Lotman, Lidiia Ia. Ginsburg, Boris A. Uspenskii.* Ithaca, N.Y.: Cornell University Press.

Nancy, Jean-Luc. 1993. *The Birth to Presence.* Trans. Brian Holmes. Stanford, Calif.: Stanford University Press.

———. 2000. *Being Singular Plural.* Trans. Robert D. Richardson and Anne W. O'Byrne. Stanford, Calif.: Stanford University Press.

Niederbudde, Anke. 2002. "*More geometrico demonstrare:* Psevdonauchnyii diskurs i matematika v tvorchestve D. Kharmsa." *Slavica Tergestina,* no. 10, 199–214.

Nikitaev, Alexander. 1989. "Tainopis' Daniila Kharmsa: opyt deshifrovki." *Daugava,* no. 8 (August), 95–99.

———. 1991. "Oberiuti i futuristchestaya traditsia. *Teatr,* No, 11 (1991), 4–7.

———. 1994. "Pushkin i Gogol." *Literaturnoe obozrenie: zhurnal kritiki i bibliografii* 9/10, 49–51.

Nikitaev, Alexander, and Gerasimova, Ana. 1991. "Kharms i 'Golem': Quasi Una Fantasia." *Teatr* No. 11, 36–50.

Ostashevsky, Eugene, ed. 2006. *OBERIU: An Anthology of Russian Absurdism.* Evanston, Ill.: Northwestern University Press.

Ostroukhova, E. N., and F. V. Kuvshinov. 2003. "Psevdonimi D. I. Kharmsa." In *"Strannaia" poezia i "strannaia" proza.* Ed. E. A. Iablokov and I. E. Loshchilov. Moscow: Piataya strana, 230–45.

Paperno, Irina, and Joan Delaney Grossman, eds. 1994. *Creating Life: The Aesthetic Utopia of Russian Modernism.* Stanford, Calif.: Stanford University Press.

Pavis, Patrice. 1982. *Languages of the Stage: Essays in the Semiology of the Theatre.* New York: PAJ Publications.

Peirce, Charles Sanders. 1885. "On Small Differences of Sensation." Paper published in *Memoirs of the National Academy of Sciences 1884.* Washington, D.C.: Government Printing Office.

———. 1984. *Writings of Charles S. Peirce: A Chronological Edition.* Bloomington: Indiana University Press.

Pessoa, Fernando. 2001. *The Selected Prose of Fernando Pessoa.* Trans. Richard Zenith. New York: Grove Press.

Petrov, Vsevolod. 1993. "Vospominania o Kharmse," *Ezhegodnik rukopisnogo otdela pushkinskogo doma na 1990 god.* St. Petersburg: Akademicheskii proekt, 184–201.

Plato. 1973. *The Republic and Other Works.* Trans. B. Jowett. New York: Anchor Books.

Podoroga, Valerii. 1993. "K voprosu mertsanii mira." *Logos: filosofsko-literaturny zhurnal,* no. 7, 139–50. Translation into English by Matvei Yankelevich published in *The Emergency Gazette,* special double issue no. 27–28 (December 2000), 4.

Poret, Alisa. 1980. "Vospominania o Daniile Kharmse," *Panorama iskusstv,* no. 3, 345–66.

Propp, Vladimir. 1968. *Morphology of the Folktale.* Trans. Laurence Scott and Louis A. Wagner. Austin: University of Texas Press.

Pushkin, Alexander. 1978. *The Tale of Tsar Saltan, of His Son, the Glorious and Mighty Knight Prince Gvidon Saltanovich, and of the Fair Swan-Princess.* Trans. Louis Zellikoff. Moscow: Progress Publishers.

Revzina, O. G., and I. I. Revzin. 1975. "A Semiotic Experiment on Stage: The Violation of the Postulate of Normal Communication as a Dramatic Device." *Semiotica* 14, no. 3, 245–68.

Ricoeur, Paul. 1967. *The Symbolism of Evil.* Trans. Emerson Buchanan. Boston: Beacon Press.

———. 1981. "Narrative Time." In *On Narrative.* Ed. W. J. T. Mitchell. 165–86. Chicago: University of Chicago Press.

Rilke, Rainer Maria. 1978. *Duino Elegies.* Trans. David Young. New York: Norton.

Roberts, Graham. 1997. *The Last Soviet Avant-Garde: OBERIU—Fact, Fiction, Metafiction.* Cambridge: Cambridge University Press.

Ronell, Avital. 2002. *Stupidity.* Chicago: University of Illinois Press.

Rossomakhin, Andrei. 2005. *"Real" Kharmsa: po sledam okkul`tnykh studii poeta-chinara.* St. Petersburg: Krasny matros.

Sass, Louis. 1992. *Madness and Modernism: Insanity in the Light of Modern Art, Literature, and Thought.* Cambridge, Mass.: Harvard University Press.

Saussure, Ferdinand de. 1966. *Course in General Linguistics.* Trans. Wade Baskin. New York: McGraw-Hill.

Sazhin, Valerii, ed. 1998. *Sborishche druzei, ostavlennykh sud'boiu.* Vols. 1–2. Moscow: Ladomir.

———. 2004. *A. Vvedenskii i D. Kharms v ikh perepiske.* Vols. 1–2. Paris: Russkii Institut v Parizhe.

Schlegel, Friedrich. 1971. *Lucinde and the Fragments.* Trans. Peter Firchow. Minneapolis: University of Minnesota Press.

Shishman, Svetozar. 1991. *Neskol'ko veselykh i grustnykh istorii o Daniile Kharmse i ego druziakh.* Leningrad: S. Shishman.

Smirnov, Igor. 1994. *Psichodiachronologika: Psichohistoria russkoi literatury ot romantizma do nashykh dnei.* Moscow: Novoe Literaturnoe Obozrenie.

Smithson, Robert. 1979. *The Writings of Robert Smithson: Essays with Illustrations.* New York: New York University Press.

Sokol, Elena. 1984. *Russian Poetry for Children.* Knoxville: The University of Tennessee Press.

Spoerri, Daniel. 1995. *An Anecdoted Topography of Chance.* London: Atlas Press.

Stellman, Jenny. 1992. *Aspects of Dramatic Communication: Action, Non-Action, Interaction (A. P. Chekhov, A. Blok, D. Charms).* Amsterdam: Rodopi.

Sterne, Laurence. 1967. *The Life and Opinions of Tristram Shandy.* Baltimore: Penguin.

Strigalev, Anatolii. 1991. "Pervoe—Kharms, Drugoe—Tatlin," in *Teatr: Ezhemesechnii zhurnal dramaturgii i teatra.* Special OBERIU issue, no. 11.

Tokarev, Dimitri. 2002. *Kurs na khudshee: Absurd kak kategoria teksta u Daniila Kharmsa i Samuela Bekketa.* Moscow: Novoe literaturnoe obozrenie.

Tolstoy, A. K. 1963. *Sobranie sochinenii: dramaticheskie proizvedeniya.* Vol. 2. Moscow: Khudozhestvenaia literatura.

Tschumi, Bernard. 1994. *The Manhattan Transcripts.* London: Academy Editions.

———. 1996. *Architecture and Disjunction.* Cambridge, Mass.: MIT Press.

Tynianov, Iurii. 1977. *Poetika, Istoria literatury, Kino.* Moscow: Nauka.

Venclova, Tomas. 1995. "Chekhov as a Representative of 'Real Art.'" In *Freedom and Responsibility in Russian Literature.* Ed. Elizabeth Cheresh-Allen and Gary Saul-Morson. 181–90. Evanston, Ill.: Northwestern University Press.

Vishnevsky, Anatoly. 1986. "Tradition in the Topsy-Turvy World of Parody: Analysis of Two OBERIU Plays." *Slavic and East European Journal* 30, no. 3, 355–66.

Vlašić-Anić, Anica. 1997. *Harms i Dadaizam.* Zagreb, Croatia: Hrvatsko filološko društvo.

Voloshina, T. A., and S. N. Astapov. 1996. *Yazicheskaya mifologiya Slavyan.* Rostov na Donu, Russia: Feniks.

Vvedenskii, Alexander. 1993. *Polnoe Sobranie Proizvedenii.* Vol. 1, 1926–1937. Vol. 2, 1938–1941. Ed. Mikhail Meilakh and Vladimir Erl'. Moscow: Gilea.

———. 2002. *The Grey Notebook,* trans. by Matvei Yankelevich. New York: Ugly Duckling Presse.

Weiss, Allen. 1990. "K," *Art and Text,* no. 37 (September), 56–59.

Weyl, Hermann. 1952. *Symmetry.* Princeton, N.J.: Princeton University Press.

Whitehead, Alfred North. 1967. *Science and the Modern World.* New York: The Free Press.

Wittgensten, Ludwig. 1992. *Tractatus Logico Philosophicus.* London: Routledge.

Zabolotsky, Nikolai. 1999. *Selected Poems.* Trans. Daniel Weissbort. London: Carcanet.

Zhadova, Larissa. 1984. *Tatlin.* New York: Rizzoli.

Žižek, Slavoj. 1999. *The Ticklish Subject: The Absent Centre of Political Ideology.* London: Verso.

Zolotonosov, Mikhail. 1995. "Shizogramma χv, ili teoria psikhicheskogo eksrementa." In *Kharmsizdat Predstavliaet: issledovania, esse, vospominania, katalog vystavki, bibliografia,* ed. Mikhail Karasik and Valerii Sazhin, 77–83. St. Petersburg: Kharmsizdat.

Zweerde, Evert van der. 1997. *Soviet Historiography of Philosophy.* Dordrecht, Netherlands: Kluwer Academic Publishers.

Index

About the Author

Branislav Jakovljevic is an assistant professor in the Department of Drama at Stanford University, where he specializes in modernist theater and the avant-garde. He lives in Palo Alto, California.

green press
INITIATIVE

Northwestern University Press is committed to preserving ancient forests and natural resources. We elected to print this title on 30% post consumer recycled paper, processed chlorine free. As a result, for this printing, we have saved:

4 Trees (40' tall and 6-8" diameter)
1,990 Gallons of Wastewater
1 Million BTUs of Total Energy
121 Pounds of Solid Waste
413 Pounds of Greenhouse Gases

Northwestern University Press made this paper choice because our printer, Thomson-Shore, Inc., is a member of Green Press Initiative, a nonprofit program dedicated to supporting authors, publishers, and suppliers in their efforts to reduce their use of fiber obtained from endangered forests.

For more information, visit www.greenpressinitiative.org

Environmental impact estimates were made using the Environmental Defense Paper Calculator. For more information visit: www.papercalculator.org.